GEORGE GISSING,
THE WORKING WOMAN,
AND URBAN CULTURE

In memory of my mother
Carole Liggins (1943–1999)
who first introduced me to the Victorian novel

George Gissing,
the Working Woman,
and Urban Culture

EMMA LIGGINS
Manchester Metropolitan University, UK

ASHGATE

Published by
Ashgate Publishing Limited
Gower House
Croft Road
Aldershot
Hampshire GU11 3HR
England

Ashgate Publishing Company
Suite 420
101 Cherry Street
Burlington, VT 05401-4405
USA

Ashgate website: http://www.ashgate.com

British Library Cataloguing in Publication Data
Liggins, Emma
George Gissing, the working woman and urban culture
1. Gissing, George, 1857-1903 – Criticism and interpretation 2. Women employees in literature 3. City and town life in literature 4. Literature and society – England – History – 19th century
I. Title
823.8

Library of Congress Cataloging-in-Publication Data
Liggins, Emma.
George Gissing, the working woman, and urban culture / Emma Liggins.
     p. cm.
Includes bibliographical references and index.
ISBN 0-7546-3717-4 (alk. paper)
1. Gissing, George, 1857-1903—Characters—Women employees. 2. Feminism and literature—England—History—19th century. 3. Women and literature—England—History—19th century. 4. Working class women in literature. 5. London (England)—In literature. 6. City and town life in literature. 7. Women employees in literature. 8. Women in literature. I. Title.

PR4717.L54 2006
823'.8—dc22
                                                                2005017373

ISBN-10: 0 7546 3717 4

Printed and bound in Great Britain by MPG Books Ltd, Bodmin, Cornwall

Contents

Acknowledgements

I was first attracted to George Gissing's fiction by discovering *The Odd Women* as a student. I was immediately intrigued as to how a novel written by a Victorian man could be so in tune with feminist thinking at the turn of the century. The idea for this book then developed in discussions around the author's attitudes to gender at the conference on George Gissing at the University of Amsterdam in 1999 so I am grateful to the organiser Bouwe Postmus, and the community of Gissing scholars, particularly Arlene Young, Constance Harsh, and Maria Teresa Chialant, who inspired me in my research.

I would especially like to thank those careful and incisive readers who have commented on draft chapters: Gill Davies, Simon J. James, Ann Heilmann and Andrew Maunder. I have also benefited from the advice and support of John Spiers, Lyn Pykett, Regenia Gagnier, Alistair McCulloch, Scott McCracken, Jenny Bourne Taylor, Louise Jackson, and Krista Cowman. Harriet Devine Jump, Lorna Shelley, and Margaret Forsyth have all been extremely helpful in supplying references and directing me towards resources. Discussions at conferences with Margaret Beetham, Valerie Sanders, Gail Marshall, Kate Newey and William Greenslade have further stimulated me in my research.

Unlike the overworked heroine of *New Grub Street* who always left the British Library with a headache, I spent many happy hours in the reading rooms of various research libraries poring over out of print texts. I am grateful to the staff at the British Library, Manchester Central Library, the Women's Library and the libraries at the University of Liverpool for making the research process more enjoyable by dealing efficiently with my numerous requests for periodicals and rare books. Thanks must also be extended to the staff at the Learning Resource Centre at Edge Hill for their helpfulness and patience and to Trish Molyneux for her enthusiasm and willingness to assist with printing, packaging and posting. Ann Donahue has been a careful and supportive editor throughout the writing of the book, but especially in the final stages. I would also like to thank my students at Edge Hill, particularly those on the MA Voicing Women, for enabling me to look at the *fin de siècle* in new and refreshing ways.

My friends Nuria Triana-Toribio, Angela Keane, Angelica Michelis and Emma Latham must be credited both for encouraging me with my work and making sure I took time off. And, as ever, I need to thank Antony Rowland for keeping me sane in the final stages by cooking me some very fine meals, putting up with my bad moods and being prepared to discuss Gissing conundrums at the most inopportune moments. As I was eight months pregnant whilst frantically editing the final chapter, I am also grateful to Polly Eliza Rowland for making her first appearance only a week before her due date.

The completion of this book was made possible by Research Leave granted by Edge Hill and an award from the Arts and Humanities Research Board.

An earlier version of Chapter One first appeared in *Critical Survey* 15:3 (2003). Some of the material from Chapters Two and Five first appeared in Louise Jackson & Krista Cowman (eds.), *Women and Work Culture, 1850–1950* (Ashgate, 2005) and Jenny Bourne Taylor & Martin Ryle (eds.), *George Gissing: Voices of The Unclassed* (Ashgate, 2005). I am grateful to the publishers for permission to reproduce material. Thanks are also due to the Illustrated London News Picture Library for permission to use Wal Paget's illustration for the serialized version of *Eve's Ransom* from the *Illustrated London News*, January 1895.

Introduction

In a letter to his sister Margaret in 1880, George Gissing aligned himself with the enlightened views on women which were gaining currency at the *fin de siècle*,

> it is unfortunate that in past times women's education and training has been so frivolous and absurd as to inevitably produce rather contemptible creatures in the vast majority of cases. You may be happy that you are young in an age which is becoming more enlightened as to women's true place and work in the world.[1]

At the beginning of his writing career, the novelist was already expressing progressive opinions on the topical question of women's work. By endorsing the need for education and training, he set an agenda for fiction which would interrogate the familiar Victorian theme of 'women's true place' from a fresh, alternative perspective. Rhoda Nunn's often-quoted contention in Gissing's most famous novel, *The Odd Women* (1893), that 'When one woman vanishes in matrimony, the reserve offers a substitute for the world's work' (p. 37)[2] could be taken as an apposite summary of the divergent paths taken by his various independent heroines; whilst the majority either chafe against or resign themselves to the restrictions of domesticity, a significant number capitalise on their single status to achieve the liberty guaranteed by paid employment. By the early 1890s the female desire for greater economic independence, produced by the lack of financial support available from fathers and the increasing surplus of single women, ensured that more women than ever before felt compelled to enter the labour market. According to an 1894 article on 'Women's Work: its Value and Possibilities' in the *Girl's Own Paper*, 'the woman who works ... is nowadays held more admirable than she, who ... spends her days in domesticity, or profitless self-occupation ... commercially and artistically the woman of this end of the century has the world at her feet'.[3] Carving out a new place for the working woman in urban culture, Gissing's novels 'incorporate the full scope of women's work',[4] from prostitutes, bar-maids and actresses to industrial workers such as factory-girls

---

[1] Letter to Margaret, 27 November 1880. *The Collected Letters of George Gissing, Vol 1: 1863–81*, ed. Paul F. Mattheisen, Arthur C. Young & Pierre Coustillas (Athens: Ohio University Press, 1990), p. 314.

[2] All quotations are taken from George Gissing, *The Odd Women*, ed. Margaret Walters (1893; London: Virago, 1980).

[3] F.H., 'Women's Work: its Value and Possibilities', *Girl's Own Paper*, 27 October 1891, 51–3 (p. 51). The article claimed that there were now 7, 857,000 working women.

[4] Ruth M. Adams, 'George Gissing and Clara Collet', *Nineteenth-Century Fiction* (1956), 72–7 (p. 77).

and seamstresses to those working in the new professions, including shop-girls, clerks, doctors, business women and journalists. More recently, David Kramer has attested that 'his texts are historically accurate portrayals of a developing, but still vastly unequal, labour market', addressing 'the complex reality of a changing work world for English women at the end of the nineteenth century'.[5]

This commitment to accuracy was shared by the social investigators, who addressed similar concerns in their statistical studies of women's living and working conditions in the major cities. This study sets out to compare representations of the working woman in Gissing's fiction and in investigatory discourses such as government reports, periodical articles and feminist pamphlets in order to highlight common narratives about the freedoms and dangers facing the woman worker, and the value and possibilities of her labour, in the two accounts. Barbara Harrison has charted the process by which 'women *at* work', as well as the nature of that work, became a social problem at the turn of the century: 'whether it was by choice or necessity, women's participation in the public domain of paid work, even when that work was done in the home, threatened the social and moral order'.[6] But the threatening figure of the working woman was not unique to Gissing's writing - she was widely used by naturalist and New Woman novelists to symbolise both the possibilities and the risks of the newly commercialised urban culture. This book is not then limited to readings of Gissing's narratives as it also examines general shifts in the representation of the working heroine across naturalist and New Woman fiction. Cross-referencing the dominant fictional trends and paradigms in other contemporary genres enables an identification of possible influences on the author whilst locating his work in the wider context of the *fin-de-siècle* literary marketplace. Feminist historians have alerted us to the ambiguities of the balance between work and leisure in women's lives, indicating that a consideration of female employment should also take account of after-work behaviour and the ways in which it is financed.[7] Rather than confining my analysis to an examination of femininity in the workplace, I have followed feminist historians in adopting a broader view of women's work cultures in this period by also considering the woman worker's leisure activities, accommodation and, if married or widowed, her child care arrangements. A full picture of the 'new urban female style of "being at home" in the city' highlighted by Judith Walkowitz[8] only becomes apparent through an examination of women's experiences of both labour

---

[5]   David Kramer, 'George Gissing and Women's Work: Contextualizing the Female Professional', *English Literature in Transition* 43:3 (2000), 316–30 (pp. 326–7, 316).
[6]   Barbara Harrison, *Not only the 'Dangerous Trades': Women's Work and Health in Britain, 1880–1914* (London: Taylor & Francis, 1996), p. 3.
[7]   See for example Kathy Peiss, *Cheap Amusements: Working Women and Leisure in Turn-of-the-Century New York* (Philadelphia: Temple University Press, 1986) and Claire Langhamer, *Women's Leisure in England, 1920–60* (Manchester: Manchester University Press, 2000). See Langhamer, pp. 16–18, for a useful discussion of feminist theories of leisure, particularly that 'a conceptualisation of leisure as separate and opposite to paid work *distorts* the experiences of women' (p. 16).
[8]   Judith R. Walkowitz, *City of Dreadful Delight: Narratives of Sexual Danger in late-Victorian London* (London: Virago, 1992), p. 46.

and leisure in relation to class differences. At a time when both gendered identities and the parameters of women's work were still very much 'matters for negotiation', Gissing's systematic and wide-ranging dramatisation of 'the ambiguities, tensions and contradictions that the woman worker embodied'[9] made an important contribution to late-Victorian debates about new female lifestyles and women's 'restricted access to the public life of the city compared to men'.[10]

Feminist Social Investigation

Gissing's intervention in debates about women's work came at a 'timely moment', when 'the public mind had become agitated on the subject of women's labour'.[11] From the 1880s onwards a new generation of female social investigators, including Clara Collet, Eliza Orme and Clementina Black, dedicated themselves to exploring the working conditions of women across the range of occupations and campaigning for their improvement, not only in well-established workplaces such as factories and mills but in the new shops and offices and in industries carried out in the home. Collet, who was to become one of Gissing's closest friends, served her apprenticeship as a researcher for Charles Booth for 'The Trades of East London' in *The Life and Labour of the People of London* (1889) and as an Assistant Commissioner for the Royal Commission on Labour in 1892, before beginning employment as Labour Correspondent for the Civil Service at the Board of Trade in 1893, a highly unusual and well-paid job for a Victorian woman.[12] Like the aspiring urban novelist, the social investigators sought to observe and classify the occupations, lifestyles, health and morality of the urban poor, their middle-class viewpoints inevitably colouring their judgements to varying degrees. Their research and its ramifications raised a series of key questions about social status and gendered behaviour in the public sphere: what factors affected women workers' entry into the labour market and choice of occupation? Where did they live and what forms of entertainment did they spend their wages on? Was it possible or desirable to combine work with marriage and child care? Moreover, their observations did not remain limited to working-class conditions, as increasingly by the 1890s both novelists and investigators turned their attention to the lifestyles of self-supporting middle-class women, those 'poor ladies' forced into the labour market for the first time with minimal education or training. In an 1888 article on 'Woman in the Labour Market', Christina Bremner validated woman's right to labour whatever her social position, but tempered the potentially

---

[9] Carol E. Morgan, *Women Workers and Gendered Identities, 1835–1913: The Cotton and Metal Industries in England* (London & New York: Routledge, 2001), p. 170.
[10] Deborah L. Parsons, *Streetwalking the Metropolis: Women, the City and Modernity* (Oxford: Oxford University Press, 2000), p. 5.
[11] A. Amy Bulley, 'The Employment of Women: The Lady Assistant Commissioners' Report', *Fortnightly Review* 61 (1894), 39–48 (p. 39).
[12] Deborah McDonald, *Clara Collet 1860–1948: An Educated Working Woman* (London: Woburn Press, 2004), pp. 67–111. See also Adams, pp. 73–4.

radical claim that it was in everyone's interests 'that women shall work where necessary or desirable, and receive the full value of their labour' with the disclaimer that equally 'women shall remain in the home where necessary or desirable', inadvertently reinforcing the domestic ideal.[13]   The desirability and necessity of paid work for educated ladies, at a premium around the turn of the century, partly testified to their revolt against the domestic space and the role it enforced, at a time when all women faced charges of 'unsexing' by choosing to earn a living in the male-dominated public sphere.   The growth of feminist campaigning and trade unionism in this period, combined with the publication of reports, pamphlets and women's periodicals, in which 'no section is more really important than that which deals with women's employment, giving descriptions, suggestions, advice',[14] were instrumental in mapping the evolution of the modern working woman.

The uncertain social status of the woman worker identified by the investigators was the product of large-scale shifts in women's education, vocational training and employment associated with the rise of the New Woman.   Definitions of the working woman were broadening in relation to changes in female employment patterns; the working lady was no longer a contradiction in terms but a new social phenomenon, emblematic of rapid developments in late-nineteenth-century urban culture.   Similarly, those employed in industry and semi-skilled occupations were staking a claim to new liberties on the streets and in urban spaces, setting an example to be adopted by professional middle-class women.   As Clementina Black argued in 1889, 'the need of earning money has compelled them to become free, and has compelled the world to recognise their freedom ... the fact that some women, because they have to work, have to live alone and to go about alone at all hours, has made it possible for all women to do so'.   More thorough training has enabled them to become 'better fitted to control their own lives'.[15]   The freedom to 'go about' in the city guaranteed by economic independence was therefore made available to those from different class backgrounds, an argument for the revision of critical views of the New Woman as exclusively middle-class.   But class difference was often also elided in women's struggles for autonomy in the labour market.   As Philippa Levine has claimed in her discussion of feminist campaigns around female labour, 'the problems facing working-class women in industrial England were, in some ways, not as far removed from the needs of their middle-class sisters

---

[13]   Christina Bremner, 'Woman in the Labour Market', *National Review* 11 (1888), 458–70 (pp. 460, 464).

[14]   Evelyn March-Phillips, 'Women's Newspapers', *Fortnightly Review* 62 (1894), 661–70 (p. 666). This lists the number of women's newspapers begun since the 1860s, including *Women's World* (1888), *Woman* (1890) and *The Young Woman* (1893). See also Philippa Levine, "The Humanising Influence of 5 o'Clock Tea: Victorian Feminist Periodicals', *Victorian Studies* 33 (1990), 293–306. She claims that the readership of the feminist press was 'composed largely of women who did not work for a living' (p. 303).

[15]   Clementina Black, 'The Organization of Working Women', *Fortnightly Review* 52 (1889), 695–704 (p. 696).

as we tend to imagine'.[16] The old divisions between the working-class woman and the middle-class woman, reliant on the lady's exclusion from the world of work, had to be rejected as increasingly out of date. Deborah Epstein Nord has noted the tendency of female social investigators such as Collet to bring both lower-middle-class and working-class women, 'working women of a variety of nuanced class differences' into the same discussion, as 'shifts in middle-class women's lives at the end of the century made possible this perception of an unbroken continuum of women's work and experience'.[17] Whereas factory girls certainly had different priorities to office workers or aspiring female doctors, they clearly shared a set of concerns about unequal pay, potential discrimination or harassment, and their restricted access to the public sphere. These shifts in class boundaries appealed to an author with an enduring interest in the 'unclassed', who, like fellow novelist Thomas Hardy, repeatedly chose to focus on characters stranded between social groups because of changes in status, education or lifestyle. Arlene Young has suggested that the author empathised with such characters because he used them to dramatise his own lower-middle-class discontents and marginality, as he too struggled to assert his place in the new commercial culture.[18]

A focus on Gissing's interest in social investigation and its conclusions also demands an examination of his close friendship with Clara Collet and the relevance of their exchange of materials to an understanding of their divergent accounts of female labour. As an early admirer of Gissing's work, Collet had praised his 'accurate and deep knowledge of working class life' in the 1880s fiction in a lecture to the Ethical Society in 1891,[19] and then set out to engineer a meeting with a man whose interests and situation clearly overlapped with her own investigatory concerns. The dynamic of 'pecuniary struggle' which energised Gissing's writing according to Collet[20] was especially resonant for the underpaid women she interviewed, who, like his self-supporting heroines, were confined by their limited spending power in a culture organised around men. Similarly, the author evidently envied the independence of the investigator, pronouncing her 'the sole and single person of my acquaintance who is living a healthy, active life, of large intercourse with men and women'.[21] Their mutual fascination with the lifestyles of such figures as the educated working woman and the street-wise East End work-girl testifies to a shared awareness of the new class identities produced by the changing

---

[16] Philippa Levine, *Victorian Feminism, 1850–1900* (London: Hutchinson, 1987), p. 105.

[17] Deborah Epstein Nord, *Walking the Victorian Streets*: *Women, Representation and the City* (Ithaca: Cornell University Press, 1995), pp. 218, 219.

[18] Arlene Young, *Culture, Class and Gender in the Victorian Novel: Gentlemen, Gents and Working Women* (Houndmills: Macmillan, 1999), pp. 151, 156.

[19] This was then published in the journal of the Charity Organisation Society with which Collet was involved. See Clara Collet, 'George Gissing's Novels: A First Impression', *Charity Organisation Review* 7 (1891), 375–80, (p. 375).

[20] This was one of the aspects of her lecture to the Ethical Society which he felt to be particularly apt; he agreed, 'I find it a great effort to understand the daily life of people free from money cares'. Letter to Clara Collet, 28 November 1895. *Collected Letters, Vol 6, 1895–97* (1995), p. 60.

[21] Letter to Clara Collet, 17 June 1894. *Collected Letters, Vol 5, 1892–95* (1994), p. 211.

labour market, and the significant number of female philanthropists committed to helping their working-class sisters in Gissing's writing can be traced back to his appreciation of the female investigator's mission. Collet's biographer dwells on her unconventional 'determin[ation] to make an impact on the author'; she sent him a parcel of her publications and issued several invitations to meet before the usually shy writer eventually agreed to visit her at her home.[22] After their initial meeting in 1893, she acted as his informal consultant on issues such as women's earnings and frequently sent him reports and lectures that she had written, ensuring that he was always well-informed on the latest research into the economic conditions of women.[23]   Ruth M. Adams notes, 'their friendship assured the precision of his reporting of … the work of women with all its implications and ramifications'.[24] However, whilst it is clearly valuable and interesting to trace the possible connections between these reports and the details about female labour included in Gissing's novels, perhaps it is too easy to attribute his accuracy to this correspondence and his acquaintance with other important investigators such as Black and Orme from the early 1890s onwards. The fact that he did not become aware of Collet's work until 1892, after the completion of *The Odd Women* which comes closest to addressing concerns about educated working women she examined, suggests that her writing was less a direct influence than an alternative form of engagement in a very similar research project. Whilst urban novelists were clearly capable of the same sympathies with the underprivileged expressed in investigatory texts,[25] my argument that urban novelists borrowed from and drew on models of the working woman produced by investigators, and vice versa, is framed by a recognition of their divergent agendas and the fact that they wrote for very different audiences. Whereas reports and pamphlets usually had specific political objectives, often related to feminist campaigns for a minimum wage or changes in the workplace demanded by the new trades unions, urban novels were geared towards a predominantly female, middle-class readership, perhaps more inclined to appreciate radical debates about marriage than to embrace feminist ideals about employment. In an interesting argument about 'labour's inherent resistance to narratability, its essential dullness' for Victorian readers, Simon J. James has claimed that Gissing tends to show the physical effects, rather than the process of, hard work, only valuing labour 'where it is the best of a limited number of

---

[22]   McDonald, p. 122.

[23]   For example, he records in his diary that on 3 July 1895 she sent him a Board of Trade report she had written. See Pierre Coustillas (ed.), *London and the Life of Literature in Late-Victorian England: The Diary of George Gissing, Novelist* (Sussex: Harvester Press, 1978), p. 378. He also consulted her over the existence of establishments to train girls for journalism and commercial occupation when he was reconsidering Mary Barfoot's training school in *The Odd Women*. See also letter to Algernon, 1 March 1894 in *Collected Letters, Vol. 5*, p. 188.

[24]   Adams, p. 77. This friendship is then linked to 'his accuracy as a recorder of facts about working women'.

[25]   See Ellen Ross, *Love and Toil: Motherhood in Outcast London, 1870–1918* (Oxford: Oxford University Press, 1993), pp. 18–20 for a useful discussion of the female investigator's attitudes towards the poor women she interviewed.

possibilities'.[26]   But this not only overlooks the different forms of gendered investment in work reflected in the attitudes of male and female characters, but also the rhetoric of fulfilment through a new-found economic independence associated with the emancipated heroine and the growing interest in women's work cultures which may have made reading about labour a more attractive prospect in this period. Rather than speculating about Gissing's debt to developments within investigative research and writing, it is more important to acknowledge that in their focus on women's work both urban novelists and investigators were intent on mapping the same terrain but deploying their research findings to different purposes.

The recent work of feminist cultural historians such as Judith Walkowitz, Lucy Bland and Erika Diane Rappaport has demonstrated the advantages of an interdisciplinary approach to *fin-de-siècle* culture, in which fiction can be illuminated by cross-reference to contemporary periodicals and newspapers, parliamentary reports and feminist pamphlets and vice versa. In her discussion of 'the narrative challenges raised by the new agenda of cultural history', Walkowitz has highlighted the importance of departing from traditional narratives about 1880s London in order to 'convey the dynamics of metropolitan life as a series of multiple and simultaneous cultural contests and exchanges across a wide social spectrum'.[27] These cultural contests and exchanges took place between textual boundaries in the late nineteenth century, becoming particularly apparent in relation to the dominant figure of the New or modern woman, a creation of the new journalism who was immediately popularised in both popular and high-brow fiction. My reading of the working woman at the *fin-de-siècle* seeks to juxtapose literary and non-literary texts not only in order to show the contradictions and differences of opinion about the vexed subject of the female wage-earner and her modernity, but also to demonstrate that urban novelists were self-consciously engaging with the ideas and objectives of feminist campaigners, journalists and investigators and borrowing their narratives. It is no coincidence that such texts quickly became mutually informative, that the investigator Charles Booth would recommend readers to consult Gissing's *Demos* (1886) for an alternative depiction of the private lives of the working classes he was exploring for his monumental study *Life and Labour of the People of London* (1889),[28] or that in her 1907 study *Sweated Industry and the Minimum Wage* Clementina Black would make the comparison between the results of her research into the conditions of shop-girls

---

[26] Simon J. James, *Unsettled Accounts: Money and Narrative in the Novels of George Gissing* (London: Anthem Press, 2004), p. 84. This argument may be more appropriate to male characters, as James' examples suggest; women clearly had a different form of investment in the idea of paid labour than men.

[27] Walkowitz, p. 10.

[28] Letter to Nelly, 8 December 1890. *Collected Letters, Vol 4, 1889–91* (1993), p. 249. Gissing was pleased to discover Booth's recommendation whilst reading his work in the British Museum. See Charles Booth (ed.), *Life and Labour of the People of London* (London: Macmillan, 1892–7).

and the representation of their exploitation in naturalist fiction.[29] The new 'career fiction' popularised in the late 1880s, which made 'the idea of earning one's own bread ... increasingly attractive to girls of all social classes', fulfilled a similar function to the new employment manuals aimed at women first appearing around the same time.[30] As the diary and letters indicate, Gissing made regular use of such manuals whilst researching his fiction. A comparison between the accounts of women's work in the fiction and the warnings and provisos issued in magazines and manuals reveals that novelists had the capacity to be more forward-looking in their agendas, less resistant to new formations of gender identity, than has been previously imagined, as they were able to explore and comment on radical issues that lay beyond the remit of the investigatory research commissioned by the government or feminist organisations. However, they could not entirely depart from the constraints of generic convention which dictated the rules prevailing in the literary marketplace.

Social investigatory discourse thus provided a set of narratives about the potential unfemininity and uncertain social status of the working woman which urban novelists sought both to reinforce and to subvert. Jenny Ryan has argued that 'the urban narrative ... sought to account for, and thus could be used to regulate, the presence of women in the city', but this is to over-simplify 'the siting of women within this narrative' at a time when the age, class and marital status of working women generated a range of responses amongst middle-class commentators.[31] The dominant narrative reinforced the view that single women took up employment as a stop-gap before marriage, often opting for domesticity rather than continuing to suffer from exploitation, ill-health and inadequate wages. But the female 'longing for defined work' identified by Bremner could not be separated from the decline in marriage when the rise in single women meant that it was no longer possible to assume that women's work was only something to fill the time whilst 'awaiting matrimony'.[32] As Carol Dyhouse has pointed out, by the 1910s research into women's work had revealed that 'young women who had learned to value their often hard-earned economic independence might be understandably ambivalent about marriage'.[33]   A study of women's work

---

[29]   Clementina Black, *Sweated Industry and the Minimum Wage* (London: Duckworth & Co, 1907), pp. 72–3.

[30]   Sally Mitchell, *The New Girl: Girls' Culture in England, 1880–1915* (New York: Columbia University Press, 1995), p. 27. The culture of girlhood prevented such texts from becoming overtly radical, despite the independent values they promoted. Mitchell remarks of middle-class fiction that, 'Many girls' novels voice at least a rhetorical heroism in the girl-woman's independence ...[but] the fear that a massive realignment of gender roles lurked in the offing was muted ... by insisting on the youthfulness of girls' (pp. 40, 42).

[31]   Jenny Ryan, 'Women, Modernity and the City', *Theory, Culture and Society* 11 (1994), 35–63 (p. 52).

[32]   Bremner, p. 460.

[33]   Carol Dyhouse, *Feminism and the Family, 1880–1939* (Oxford: Blackwell, 1989), p. 34. She is referring particularly here to the work of B. L. Hutchins, who was involved with the FWG and the Women's Industrial Council. See *Conflicting Ideals of Women's Work* (London, 1914).

commissioned by the newly formed Fabian Women's Group in 1908 related 'the revolt of the modern woman against parasitism and dependence' to the importance of her choice of a 'life-work', and harnessed women's need for economic independence to their struggle for political emancipation.[34] An alternative subtext to investigative writing, more apparent in later studies, was that working women increasingly refused to give up the struggle to legitimise their presence in the city environment, defending their right to labour and steadfastly pursuing the ideal of economic independence in a variety of new careers. As Collet argued in her reflection on the economic progress of women between 1850 and 1900,

> more and more it is being recognised by parents that girls should be fitted to be self-supporting; and the tendency among the girls themselves is to concentrate their energies on the profession they take up, and to regard marriage as a possibility which may some day call them away from the path they are pursuing, but which should not be allowed to interfere with their plans in the meantime.[35]

With women increasingly 'fitting' themselves for professional work rather than marriage, their 'plans' for the future were potentially radically altered, which opened up the alternative 'urban female lifestyles' described by Walkowitz. Both the warnings about the dangers of urban space and the advocacy of women's new freedoms were seized on and appropriated by male and female urban novelists, who also looked to the future beyond 1900 by refusing to let the possibility of marriage interfere with their heroines' economic progress.

In order to argue the case for Gissing as a progressive writer, it has therefore been necessary to contextualise his work in relation to such debates, some of which were only just becoming public around the time of his death in 1903. Evolutionary thinking had precipitated a focus on the woman of the future from the 1880s onwards and this figure, like the New Woman, still haunted early-twentieth-century debates about femininity. Many important investigatory texts and feminist studies of women's work, drawing on research conducted in the early years of the twentieth century, did not appear until the 1910s, as feminists involved in such organisations as the Fabian Women's Group and the Women's Industrial Council assessed the ramifications of expansions in female employment and set out new agendas for future change. Yet they can supply a crucial under-explored framework for late-Victorian urban fiction. Therefore, rather than preserving an artificial break between the Victorian period and the Edwardian period and its aftermath, this study follows trends within cultural history and histories of feminism in adopting a broader view of the *fin de siècle*, taking the outbreak of the First World War as a convenient cut-off point. I have thus drawn freely on texts

---

[34] Edith Morley (ed.), *Women Workers in Seven Professions: A Survey of their Economic Conditions and Prospects* (London: Routledge, 1914), pp. xi, xiv, xv.
[35] Clara E. Collet, 'Through 50 Years: The Economic Progress of Women' (1900) in *Educated Working Women: Essays on the Economic Position of Women Workers in the Middle Classes* (London: P.S. King & Son, 1902), p. 138. This article first appeared in the *Frances Mary Buss Schools' Jubilee Magazine*.

published between 1900 and 1914, whilst trying to give a sense of the shifts in thinking in the last two decades of the nineteenth century which more directly informed Gissing's development as an author. Assessments of women's entry into the new professions tended to appear from the mid-1890s onwards, after the completion of the major novels. David Grylls's over-generalised claim that due to the 'traditionally "feminine" jobs' allocated to his female characters, 'Gissing's conception of female employment was largely conservative', can then be challenged.[36] An alternative interpretation is that his heroines' dilemmas, particularly in relation to contentious issues such as same-sex partnerships, celibacy and married women's employment explored in the later fiction, anticipate feminist debates about the working woman which were only fully developed in the early twentieth century.

Gender and Genre: Naturalism, New Woman fiction and the Male Novelist

In 1978 John Goode characterised Gissing as 'the first novelist of the modern city'.[37] Certainly, living in the capital was essential to the aesthetic development of an author who readily admitted his uneasy fascination with the tumult and energy of the metropolis: one of his early dilemmas, revealed in a letter to Thomas Hardy in 1887, was 'how to get into a lifetime the work suggested by this myriad-voiced London'.[38] Explorations of the author's representation of urban life have been instrumental in his re-evaluation as a major writer of the *fin-de-siècle*; the Centenary conference on 'Gissing and the City' demonstrated the range of interdisciplinary scholarship currently taking place in this field.[39] However, there has been a noted tendency in Marxist studies to see his representation of London both as a homage to and rewriting of the mid-Victorian fiction of the social problem novelists, in particular Charles Dickens, a writer Gissing greatly admired.[40] Like Dickens, Gissing was a self-confessed urban rambler who gained material by close observation of street life, and used his fiction to address social problems like prostitution, slum housing and destitution. But grouping both writers together as nineteenth-century urban novelists has often meant that Gissing's place within the late-Victorian literary marketplace has been overlooked or neglected. Our understanding of his position as a novelist of the modern city

---

[36] David Grylls, *The Paradox of Gissing* (London: Allen & Unwin, 1986), p. 159. Grylls does modify this position to concede that 'on all the central feminist issues, [Gissing] offers a characteristic mix of the reactionary and the progressive' (p. 162), but sticks to his thesis that the author became more conservative later in his career, as the novels increasingly reflected his growing antipathy to women.

[37] John Goode, *George Gissing: Ideology and Fiction* (London: Vision Press, 1978), p. 90.

[38] Letter to Thomas Hardy, 25 July 1887. *Collected Letters, Vol 3*, p. 139.

[39] This was held at the University of London in July 2003.

[40] See for example Goode, pp. 15–34 and James, pp. 32–62. James develops the comparison between Gissing and Dickens as part of his argument about Victorian realist narrative, showing how the *fin-de-siècle* author revises Dickens's plots and refuses the consolations of his happy endings in the interests of sincerity.

can be advanced by an assessment of his use of the generic conventions of his era, in particular locating his writing in the naturalist tradition, and further exploring his contribution to the developing genre of New Woman fiction, which enjoyed its heyday in the mid-1890s. Both genres, in which Gissing was widely read, overlapped in their concerns with the new class and gender subjectivities produced by modernity and commercial culture, and can be grouped together under the umbrella of urban fiction. An analysis of the author's reading habits suggests a marked preference for New Woman texts, particularly the work of Ménie Muriel Dowie, George Egerton and Olive Schreiner, though his often scathing criticisms of naturalist writing never prompted him to abandon his regular consumption of examples of a brand of fiction he evidently enjoyed. But they also had their shortcomings in terms of the outcomes their conventions allowed them to achieve. As Sally Ledger has pointed out, 'literary naturalism, steeped in Social Darwinism and theories of heredity, has a distinct tendency – quintessentially in certain of Zola's novels – to render the lowest sections of the working class ultimately passive and helpless', a convention she sees as 'politically disenabling'.[41] Gissing was also of his time in expressing his frustration with generic constraints, seeking to find a middle ground between the sexual explicitness of French fiction and the feminist polemic of contemporary female authors.

The sociological dimensions of naturalist writing, a genre hovering 'on the borders between art and industry', have been well documented: Rachel Bowlby, amongst others, has noted the author's function as eye-witness, an 'investigative reporter or sociologist, supplying "insider" information at once factual and sensational'.[42] Its blurring of the boundaries between author and investigator and ostensibly 'factual' subject matter clearly exercised a strong appeal to the London-based author. In a retrospective of 1897, the *National Review* celebrated Gissing's 'extraordinary knowledge of the social and moral condition of our great cities – more particularly of London', underlining his naturalist credentials by adding that 'there cannot be a corner of the metropolis which, with observant eye and quick ear, he has not explored, nor a phase of its varied existence that he has not studied'.[43] This study attempts to map Gissing's use of naturalist conventions against those deployed by contemporary French and American novelists such as Émile Zola, Guy de Maupassant, and Henry James, in order to highlight the dilemma he faced in embracing the genre's endorsement of working women's freedoms on the streets whilst shying away from its concomitant acceptance of immorality, passivity and degeneration. In an attack on naturalism in 1882, Andrew Lang complained that 'Zola spares us nothing ... he takes us into the festering garrets of unclean workpeople ... and steadily and gradually degrades his

---

[41] Sally Ledger, *The New Woman: Fiction and Feminism at the Fin de Siècle* (Manchester: Manchester University Press, 1997), p. 49.
[42] Rachel Bowlby, *Just Looking: Women and Commercial Culture in Dreiser, Gissing and Zola* (London: Methuen, 1985), pp. 10, 14.
[43] Fred Dolman, *National Review* 30 (1897), 258–66. Quoted in Pierre Coustillas & Colin Partridge (eds.), *Gissing: The Critical Heritage* (London: Routledge & Kegan Paul, 1972), p. 311.

characters to unspeakable and undreamed of depths of corruption'.[44]   Despite similar reservations, Gissing was particularly drawn to the work of the French novelist, with whom he was most often compared in reviews, sharing his fascination with commercial culture, in particular advertising, publicity, the temptations of consumption, and their relation to urban femininity. He found the significantly titled *L'Argent* [*Money*](1893) about the Parisian Bourse 'in some respects ... wonderful' but also 'lacking vitality'.[45]   *Au Bonheur des Dames* [*The Ladies' Paradise*](1883), dismissed by the *Athenaeum* as 'a mere vehicle for endless descriptions of the great shops of Paris',[46] he read whilst completing *The Whirlpool,* possibly prompting the latter's harsher vision of commercialism. In Zola's novel the arresting image of the department store 'burning like a beacon ... the light and life of the city' (p. 28) indicates its importance in the process of 'revolutionizing the market ... transforming Paris' (p. 75), from which the staggering profits of Octave Mouret, 'a man of his own time' (p. 67) are a reward for those who take the greatest commercial risks.[47]   The frenzied lady shoppers, 'helpless against advertisements' (p. 235) and unable to resist a bargain remain under the masterful control of Mouret and his 'machine for devouring women' (p. 77). As Rita Felski has argued, 'this feminization of modernity ... is largely synonymous with its demonization ... the idea of the modern becomes aligned with a pessimistic vision of an unpredictable yet curiously passive femininity seduced by the glittering phantasmagoria of an emerging consumer culture'.[48] Gissing's debt to Zola is evident in his use of similar paradigms about gender, capitalism and the city, the fact that such French novels regularly featured on his reading list offering further evidence of a direct influence.

However, as Constance Harsh has cogently argued in an article on the limits of naturalism in Gissing's *The Unclassed*, 'the naturalist impulse proves impossible to reconcile with English fictional exigencies',[49] leaving the author unable to provide a plot resolution which would offer the consolations of legitimate moral authority demanded by Victorian readers and publishers. By 1900, Gissing wrote to his friend Eduard Bertz that he had 'grown to abhor Zola's

---

[44]   Andrew Lang, 'Émile Zola', *Fortnightly Review* N.S. 31 (1882), 438–52 (p. 451). Lang was clearly disturbed by the overlaps between history, science and literature, fearing the direction 'modern literature' might take under Zola's tutelage.

[45]   Letter to Bertz, 24 August 1893. *Collected Letters, Vol 5*, p. 133.

[46]   Review of *Au Bonheur des Dames*, *Athenaeum*, 10 March 1883, p. 310.

[47]   All quotations are taken from Émile Zola, *The Ladies' Paradise,* trans. and ed. Brian Nelson (1883; Oxford: Oxford University Press, 1995).

[48]   Rita Felski, *The Gender of Modernity* (Cambridge, Mass.: Harvard University Press, 1995), p. 62.

[49]   Constance Harsh, 'Gissing's *The Unclassed* and the Perils of Naturalism', *English Literary History* 59 (1992), 911–938 (p. 933). Her argument is that the English novel remained conservative, never fully embracing 'the literature that then seemed to pose the most radical challenge to standards of acceptability', partly because the rejection of conventional hierarchies of society and thought demanded by the genre left English writers without a 'coherent narrative' based on the reassertion of moral authority (pp. 911, 912).

grossness'.[50] Simon J. James has traced his evolution as a writer to 'choos[ing] not to be Dickens',[51] but not being Zola, an alternative fictional model, also affected the ways in which he was able to carve out a distinctive space within his chosen oeuvre. In Gissing's less celebratory vision of London, commercialisation is increasingly annexed to vulgarity and the majority of his female characters do not possess the time nor the money to go beyond window-shopping, closing down the possibilities for a detailed analysis of consumption as a female urban pastime. Bowlby's broad claim that Gissing and Zola are 'against and neutral with regard to contemporary developments in commerce and culture and their relations' relies on an over-simplified version of the appeal of commerce to the lady shopper, but she does make the valid point that the 'cultural histories of each country' operate as a key factor in this distinction.[52] Though the prostitutes and shop-girls, who feature in a number of Gissing's novels, are toned-down versions of the scandalous figures already popularised as symbols of sexual freedom in French fiction, he has still been accused of perpetuating gender stereotypes through his allegiances to the naturalist camp. In her study of women's writing on the city between 1880 and 1940, Deborah L. Parsons attacks male naturalist writers for pathologising the female presence in the city, and therefore shoring up 'the convention of the woman in public as a possessable object' troped in turn-of-the-century literary and theoretical discourse.[53] But it is problematic to explain the representation of femininity so readily in terms of the gender of the author. Although Gissing's heroines are shown to be susceptible on a number of levels to 'the particular temptation of London today'[54] identified as a crucial element of urban fiction, they are liable to be demonised less as consumers in the style of Zola than in their uses of liberty and willingness to take sexual risks. It is also productive to bracket Gissing with the East End novelists such as Walter Besant, Margaret Harkness and Arthur Morrison, who narrowly avoided Zola's grossness in their shocking accounts of the urban squalor experienced in the slums of the more deprived areas of London. Comparisons with the work of Harkness also reveal that the struggle to combine motherhood and sweated labour was not just an issue for women writers, and that cautionary tales about unplanned pregnancies, female commodification and the risks of the city were not exclusively perpetrated by men. This study seeks to illuminate the common concerns about heterosocial space, sexual danger and urban freedom shared by both male and female novelists in order to question the view that it was only women writers who granted their working heroines the right to negotiate urban culture on their own terms.

---

[50] Quoted in Grylls, p. 157. It is worth noting Gissing's enduring interest in the French novelist. In the spring and summer of 1896 whilst writing *The Whirlpool*, he read three of Zola's novels in quick succession.

[51] James, p. 38. This is a development of an argument first put forward by Goode, who argued that Dickens was Gissing's 'major point of reference' so that 'we might say that Gissing was Gissing precisely because he was not Dickens'. See Goode, p. 15.

[52] Bowlby, pp. 12, 11.

[53] Parsons, p. 43.

[54] Review of *The Whirlpool*, *Bookman* (1897). Quoted in Coustillas & Partridge, p. 280.

It is equally reductive to grant female novelists the sole licence to comment on the New Woman and thus to wilfully exclude nineteenth-century male novelists from any kind of feminist sympathy with the restrictions placed on women. In his discussion of the problems for modern critics of 'reproduc[ing] a "feminist Hardy"', Peter Widdowson claimed in 1989 that, 'it would be historically suspect ... to hypothesize a male author in the second half of the nineteenth century as having a conscious and coherent feminist philosophy in view'.[55] To argue the case for reproducing a 'feminist Gissing' may seem to invite similar concerns. The tendency to deny the possibilities of any kind of feminist philosophy for an apparently misogynist male author has coloured assessments of his contribution to debates about the Woman Question, resulting in condemnations for his conservatism or anti-feminism. He has been attacked for not giving the 'would-be emancipated heroine' a chance to achieve her bids for equality, and for allowing his potentially open-minded approach to be fractured by his 'essentially anti-feminist prejudices'.[56] More recently, feminist critics have pointed out that this apparently contradictory stance could be seen to enable a more complex engagement with the many-sided debates around gender: in her comparison of *The Odd Women* with female-authored New Woman fiction of the early 1890s, Constance Harsh describes his entertainment of unprogressive ideas side by side with progressive ideology as an attempt to do 'something rather different with feminist subject matter than his contemporaries'.[57] Moreover, it is short-sighted to hold the male novelist responsible for closing down women's opportunities for independence or a career, when this was already a well-established plot resolution in *fin-de-siècle* fiction. Simon J. James has linked the author's refusal of 'utopian' solutions to his commitment to realism, arguing that 'his representation of the unsatisfactory nature of the world for educated middle-class women is at least sincere, if uncomfortable to read'.[58] Despite their promise of offering alternative lifestyles for modern women, many New Woman narratives by women writers of the period still ended very conventionally with the independent heroine's marriage or untimely death. It is also worth noting the admiration Gissing inspired in New

---

[55] Peter Widdowson, *Hardy in History: A Study in Literary Sociology* (London: Routledge, 1989), p. 216. Recent feminist studies of Thomas Hardy's fiction have not been so eager to dismiss his sympathies with women on the grounds of his gender. See, for example, Shanta Dutta, *Ambivalence in Hardy: A Study of his Attitude to Women* (Basingstoke: Macmillan, 2000) and Jane Thomas, *Hardy, Femininity and Dissent: Reassessing the 'Minor' Novels* (Basingstoke: Macmillan, 1999).

[56] Katherine Bailey Linehan, '*The Odd Women*: Gissing's Imaginative Approach to Feminism', *Modern Language Quarterly* 40 (1979), 359–74 (p. 360). Grylls has described him as 'a woman-worshipping misogynist with an interest in female emancipation' (p. 141).

[57] Constance Harsh, 'Women with Ideas: *The Odd Women* and the New Woman Novel' in Bouwe Postmus (ed.), *A Garland for Gissing* (Amsterdam: Rodopi, 2001), p. 85. Barbara Rawlinson sees the author as a cunning devil's advocate, showing his support for female education and independence 'by conspicuously arguing against [them]'. See Barbara Rawlinson, 'Devil's Advocate: George Gissing's Approach to the Woman Question', *Gissing Journal* 33:2 (1997), 1–14 (p. 10).

[58] James, p. 123.

Woman writers of the time, including Ménie Muriel Dowie and Ella Hepworth Dixon. In 1895 Dowie wrote to tell him that she considered him 'one of the *three* first novelists', in the same month that he was asked by Dixon to write for her new women's magazine *The Englishwoman* (though it is perhaps revealing that he preferred to contribute to the fashionably decadent journal *The Yellow Book* with its anti-feminist slant).[59] Although he claimed not to be able to understand 'what it is in my work that attracts the female mind', the close attention paid to feminist issues certainly earned him a loyal female readership which valued and respected his sensitive treatment of the restrictions women faced.[60]

Perhaps it was his refusal to offer the easy way out to his heroines and his attempts to stretch the boundaries of New Woman fiction which made him appealing to discerning women readers. Jane Eldridge Miller has argued that it was Edwardian novelists such as E.M. Forster and John Galsworthy who first 'had to face the inadequacy of the traditional narrative forms of the nineteenth-century novel for narrating the lives of modern women',[61] but the palpable sense of frustration about other conclusions available for the emancipated heroine suggests that Gissing was already confronting this inadequacy. As Sally Mitchell has argued, the plots of career fiction confirmed that 'heterosexual relations clearly stood on a piece of contested ground that was reshaped by the impact of work on girls' culture',[62] rendering the conventional return to domesticity increasingly dissatisfying for readers. The most sophisticated of his narrative paradigms attempt to go beyond traditional forms by balancing the marriage or death of more conventional female characters against the continuing economic independence of the woman worker. The capacity of his fiction to accommodate both types of woman, noted by Barbara Rawlinson, generates the tensions about gender identity which drive the narrative, 'while the feeble, compliant females ... reveal the power of social conditioning, the new breed of strong-minded, progressive women expose and renounce its ideology, and proclaim their right to self-determination'.[63] In their embracing of the more radical lifestyles available to single women, this new breed anticipate the self-determined suffragette heroines of the 1910s, looking forward to the less restrictive frameworks of early-twentieth-century women's fiction evident in the work of Netta Syrett and Virginia Woolf. However, Gissing's focus on the cultural pressures for women to marry and the difficulties of maintaining independence within marriage also often trap his heroines within the

---

[59] He received Dixon's request on 4 February 1895 and the letter from Dowie on 23 February 1895. See *Diary*, pp. 362–3, 364. Dowie's other top-rated novelists were George Meredith and Hardy.

[60] Letter to Bertz, 23 June 1895. *Collected Letters, Vol 5: 1892–1895*, p. 351. In the same letter, the fact that he prefixed this remark with the comment, 'it is strange how many letters I get from women, asking for sympathy & advice' offers further testimony for his attractions to the female reader.

[61] Jane Eldridge Miller, *Rebel Women: Feminism, Modernism and the Edwardian Novel* (London: Virago, 1994), p. 38.

[62] Mitchell, p. 38.

[63] Rawlinson, p. 13.

ideological thinking they are meant to expose. His complex and often contradictory engagement with debates about gender equality and work needs to be read in the light of his desire to expose the limitations of the New Woman genre for accommodating the emancipated heroine.

A feminist reassessment of Gissing's work is also long overdue because criticism has been weighted towards the fiction of the mid-1890s, and overwhelmingly dominated by readings of *The Odd Women*. Sally Ledger, one of the first critics to fully incorporate the 1893 novel into a literary-historical account of *fin-de-siècle* feminism, argued that its streetwalking shop-girl is introduced in order to 'pose the question as to who the New Woman in the modern city really is',[64] precipitating a new approach to a writer previously dismissed for his misogyny. The recent surge of interest in *The Whirlpool* (1897), *In the Year of Jubilee* (1894) and to a lesser extent *Eve's Ransom* (1895) has also been informed by interdisciplinary research on female urbanism, which has ensured that texts allowing their emancipated heroines to assume the role of the woman in public have attracted renewed critical attention.[65] In her reading of the feminisation of the city in Gissing's 1890s fiction, Maria Teresa Chialant has argued that 'some of his heroines, with their tormented, divided selves, provide convincing examples of the difficult but steady emergence of new gendered subjectivities as "signs of the times"'.[66] But this trend in criticism has helped to perpetuate the myth that these new gendered subjectivities, glossed by Lynda Nead in her study of mid-Victorian London as 'a new transgressive form of metropolitan femininity',[67] were primarily apparent in the professional classes, and thus embodied by the middle-class emancipated heroine. My argument is that Gissing's endorsement of women's claim to a public life grew out of his uneasy fascination with the street-walking

---

[64] Ledger, p. 169. Some of this material first appeared in the article 'Gissing, the Shop-Girl and the New Woman', *Women: A Cultural Review* 6:3 (1995), 263–74. Important feminist studies of *The Odd Women* published earlier than this also include Deirdre David, 'Ideologies of Patriarchy, Feminism, and Fiction in *The Odd Women*', *Feminist Studies* 10 (1984), 117–39, Kathleen Blake, *Love and the Woman Question in Victorian Literature: The Art of Self-Postponement* (Sussex: Harvester Press, 1983), 79–96 and Ardis, 87–90, 122, 156.

[65] This point has also been made in Scott McCracken, 'Performance to public sphere: the production of modernist masculinities', *Textual Practice* 15: 1 (2001), 47–65 (p. 51). He goes on to focus on London eating establishments in *Demos* and *The Town Traveller*. A number of feminist scholars and cultural critics have also recently considered Gissing's representation of the woman in public in texts other than *The Odd Women*. See for example Barbara Leah Harman, 'Going Public: Female Emancipation in George Gissing's *In the Year of Jubilee*', *Texas Studies in Literature and Language* 34:3 (1992), 347–74, the discussion of *The Whirlpool* in William Greenslade, *Degeneration, Culture and the Novel, 1880–1940* (Cambridge: Cambridge University Press, 1994), pp. 134–150, and David Glover, '"This Spectacle of a World's Wonder": Commercial Culture and Urban Space in Gissing's *In the Year of Jubilee*' in Postmus, 137–51.

[66] Maria Teresa Chialant, 'The Feminization of the City in Gissing's Fiction', in Postmus, p. 65.

[67] Lynda Nead, *Victorian Babylon: People, Streets and Images in Nineteenth-Century London* (New Haven & London: Yale University Press, 2000), p. 67.

female workers of his early fiction, who in many ways display a greater confidence in their transgressive appropriation of the masculine freedoms of London's public spaces. Ambiguous accounts of urban femininity and class were also made possible in the more open-ended, elliptical short stories and one-volume novels of the 1890s, largely ignored in critical accounts, which provide some additional variations on the restrictive paradigms and conclusions imposed on Gissing as a writer of traditional three-volume novels. In a nice twist, his 1896 story 'A Free Woman', which readers would presumably have expected to focus on the New Woman, actually depicts the freedoms of a prostitute delighted at the way she is able to triumph over the system. Rather than confining the analysis to the new professionals of the major 1890s fiction, this account addresses the author's representation of prostitutes and industrial workers in the early and shorter fiction in order to question the assumption that the version of the woman in public he sought to validate was necessarily synonymous with the middle-class emancipated heroine.

For Gissing, the concept of the odd woman, who defied conventional gender boundaries, was very much applicable to women lower down the social scale, who made the most of the potentially greater urban freedoms and sexual confidence granted to their class. The 'woman of the pavement', in all her manifestations, is central to his models of femininity; as the narrator of *The Odd Women* reminds us, the prostitute would have been classed by Rhoda as 'a not unimportant type of the odd woman' (p. 299), a figure in need of investigation. The earlier working-class novels have been too readily appropriated for Marxist criticism, which has often meant that the urban lifestyle of the working-class woman and her literary prototype has been obscured. The 'not unimportant' figures of prostitutes, barmaids, actresses, and factory girls of the 1880s fiction need to be accommodated into a broader vision of metropolitan femininity no longer based on transgressing the rules of bourgeois respectability. As Jenny Ryan has argued in her revisionist account of working women and modernity, 'the narrative of sexuality and sexual difference through which the meaning of experience in both public and private was constructed' may be in doubt because 'this construction is itself too totalising to capture the very differences of that experience and the complexities of how women negotiated their spaces in the city'.[68] In one of the later novels, *Our Friend the Charlatan* (1901), the ambitious and emancipated Constance Bride, who ultimately chooses a clerical career over marriage, is in a position to proclaim, 'I am free, and have power to assert myself – the first desire, let me assure you, of modern women no less than of modern man'.[69] But a feminist re-evaluation of his work suggests that all of his women workers across

---

[68] Ryan, 'Women, Modernity and the City', p. 55. She is one of the few feminist critics to pay attention to class differences in the city, though her argument about the visibility of working-class and lower middle-class women in the city rests on the assumption that middle-class women were excluded from paid employment, which is less appropriate to a reading of late-Victorian urban culture.

[69] George Gissing, *Our Friend the Charlatan*, ed. Pierre Coustillas (1901; Sussex: Harvester Press, 1976), p. 382.

the social spectrum exercise the power to self-assertion in various ways, pursuing the desires of modern women by staking a claim to urban space. His novels can therefore be used to demonstrate the importance of the working-class woman, as well as her middle-class sister, to discussions of gender and modernity. Chialant's view that Gissing's awareness of the possibilities of 'the new spatial opportunities of consumer culture' still results in a 'refusal of "modernity" in its more radical forms'[70] can be re-assessed in the light of the working-class woman's uses of what London has to offer. His early fiction offers a number of variations on the working woman's position in urban culture, from the fun-loving factory girls energised by the tumult of the city's streets to the quiet, more refined home-workers who restrict their enjoyment in public in the interests of respectability. Despite their restricted access to the public sphere on the grounds of gender, their class positions allow them to resist limitations on freedom of movement and to challenge rules about sexual behaviour in ways which middle-class women envied. The woman in the city narrative is employed not to demonise the modern heroine but to release her into a less restrictive framework, enabling new forms of gendered subjectivity which are not bound by assumptions about class.

Female Urbanism, the *Flâneuse* and Public Space

In the last fifteen years female urbanism, or women's unprecedented occupation of the public sphere, has come to be a preoccupation of feminist cultural critics and historians concerned with nineteenth and twentieth-century gender identities. As Parsons has argued, 'women's legitimate participation in city life was an extremely significant divergence from Victorian conventional belief', as new 'images of urban women' such as the New Woman, the working girl and the female shopper challenged traditional perceptions of femininity.[71] The 'new social actors' produced by the rapidly expanding Victorian city were not exclusively female, as Walkowitz notes – considerable critical work has been done on the *flâneur*, the leisured, middle-class observer, or man of the crowd[72] – but it is the seemingly irreconcilable elements of turn-of-the-century femininity and urban culture which have interested feminist critics. This interest was mobilised by the challenge to the theoretical view that the *flâneuse* could not be invented as she 'was rendered impossible by the sexual divisions of the nineteenth century'. Conceptualising the

---

[70] Chialant, p. 65.

[71] Parsons, p. 43.

[72] The concept of the *flâneur* arguably originated in the poetry of French author Charles Baudelaire, who has been 'credited with … heralding a new sensibility of urban life' in texts such as *Les Fleurs du Mal* (1861) and *Le Spleen de Paris* (1862). It was expanded and refined by the German theorist Walter Benjamin in critical essays on Baudelaire and his major study of urban modernity in late-nineteenth-century Paris, *Das Passagen-werk* [The Arcades Project]. For an excellent discussion of the mythologies of modernity to which these writers, and others, contributed, and the masculinisation of the concept of *flânerie*, see Parsons, pp. 2–8, 17–39.

urban woman as an 'invisible' figure, a historical and conceptual impossibility,[73] resulted in an exclusion of the feminine from narratives of modernity; as Lynda Nead has pointed out, 'our descriptions of the development of modern urban life have, it seems, been derived from the male public world, and women, confined by Victorian ideology and twentieth-century historians to the home and occasional shopping trips, are not part of the effective modern world'.[74] Highlighting the limitations of a critical position which over-emphasised women's associations with domestic privacy, Elizabeth Wilson has observed that 'it is the male-female dichotomy which has so damagingly translated itself into a conception of city culture as pertaining to men'.[75] This study is in broad agreement with her argument that the marginalised female inhabitants of the modern city could function as 'disruptive elements' as well as vulnerable objects of sexual scrutiny in desperate need of protection. It acknowledges that the *flâneuse* or woman of the crowd has now been recognised as an important figure whilst exploring the ways in which novelists and cultural commentators sought to expose the problems inherent in her tenuous position in the urban landscape.

This recognition of a potentially disruptive female presence in the city has also prompted feminist historians to reassess the kinds of public space made available to women and their importance to the formation of a new heterosocial culture. For the modern woman, travelling around the city for the purposes of work and leisure, her new-found independence was reliant on her access to 'new heterosocial spaces' such as department stores, libraries, theatres, mixed clubs and tea-rooms.[76] In her useful discussion of gender and everyday space in mid-nineteenth-century America, the historian Mary Ryan argues that, 'male-female distinctions are put to a severe test in public space', which may create more sharply defined gender differences but can also lead to their corrosion, allowing women to appropriate the liberties enjoyed by men.[77] An article on 'Manly Women' in the *Saturday Review*

---

[73] Janet Wolff, 'The Invisible *Flâneuse*: Women and the Literature of Modernity', *Theory, Culture and Society* 2:3 (1985), 37–46 (pp. 45, 43). See also Griselda Pollock, *Vision and Difference: Femininity, Feminism and the Histories of Art* (London: Routledge, 1988) and Elizabeth Wilson, 'The Invisible *Flâneur*', *New Left Review* 191 (1992), 90–110 for her response to the problems of Wolff's and Pollock's over-investment in the ideology of separate spheres.

[74] Nead, p. 67. Other critics have de-emphasised the importance of a leisured lifestyle to the practice of *flânerie*, underlining the links between work and women's urban freedoms.

[75] Elizabeth Wilson, *The Sphinx in the City: Urban Life, the Control of Disorder, and Women* (London: Virago, 1991), p. 9. Her argument about women's disruptive presence in the city is based on the view that awareness of issues around safety does not prevent them from experiencing their urban environment as 'a place of liberation' (p. 7).

[76] Walkowitz, p. 45. However, as Parsons has pointed out, women's access remained restricted throughout this period. See p. 5.

[77] Mary P. Ryan, *Women in Public: Between Banners and Ballots, 1825–1880* (Baltimore & London: Johns Hopkins University Press, 1990), p. 59. She also claims that 'by its very definition … public space defies exact boundaries between male and female spheres', as women can mix with both men and other women by entering spaces 'theoretically open and accessible to all'. For an alternative account of the geographies of American urban space in

of 1889 exclaimed in surprise, 'in London now, how many ladies delight in attending what were wont to be the exclusive resorts of men!'[78] A gradual relaxation of the rules about meeting men informally, in which 'the decay of the chaperon' precipitated a greater self-reliance and self-confidence on the part of women in public,[79] was instrumental in ushering in the new sexual behaviours gradually becoming permissible in this period. Kathy Peiss's excellent study of the commercialised amusements available to working women in turn-of-the-century New York explores the ways in which dance halls, amusement parks, cinemas and street corners became 'social spaces in which gender relations were "played out", where notions of sexuality, courtship, male power, female dependency, and autonomy were expressed and legitimated'.[80] Although Gissing's fiction never unreservedly extolled the pleasures of what Peiss refers to as 'mixed-sex fun',[81] he did situate his modern heroines in many of the new heterosocial spaces, acknowledging the importance of forms of urban entertainment to shifting gender and sexual identities. The focus on leisure also served to question quite how 'legitimate' women's participation in city life actually was, given the potentially dangerous encounters with men it often entailed. Whilst his novels often appear to stand out from those of his contemporaries in their defence of women's right to leisure, they do not pretend that this is easily achievable, and the narrative tendency to punish those heroines who enjoy themselves too much in public has earned the author a bad press. But Gissing should also be credited for his realist refusal to portray these new femininities as readily acceptable, when the female appropriation of city culture still only existed in a muted form; Wilson reminds us of the ambiguities of the female urban experience in her plea that as critics we should 'hold in balance an awareness of both the pleasures and the dangers that the city offers women'.[82] This is particularly apposite to a reading of the conclusions to *fin-de-siècle* fiction, which often undermined the validation of female participation in urban life with warnings about the regrettable consequences of risking their respectability. Gissing's novels suggest that women's presence in London's new heterosocial spaces hinged on their ability to manage both their

---

a slightly later period, see Sarah Deutsch, *Women and the City: Gender, Space and Power in Boston, 1870–1940* (Oxford: Oxford University Press, 2000). Deutsch argues that 'it is important not to mistake ... public appearance for empowerment. Even in the relatively new female spaces, spaces created by as well as for women, there were limits to female autonomy ... the women's spaces themselves were contested' (p. 23).

[78] 'Manly Women', *Saturday Review*, 22 June 1889, 756–7 (p. 757).

[79] Mary Jeune, 'The Decay of the Chaperon', *Fortnightly Review* 74 (1900), 629–38 (p. 631).

[80] Peiss, p. 4. She relates this to a loosening of the ties between leisure and male culture, arguing that 'commercialized recreation fostered a youth-oriented, mixed-sex world of pleasure, where female participation was profitable and encouraged' (p. 6).

[81] Peiss, p. 6. However, she cautions against a critical over-investment in the idea of leisure as liberating for women, pointing out that 'without economic independence such freedoms were ultimately hollow ... mixed-sex fun could be a source of autonomy and pleasure as well as a cause of [women's] continuing oppression'.

[82] Wilson, *The Sphinx in the City*, p. 10.

expenditure and their sexualities, highlighting the enjoyment of leisure as a difficult challenge on women's inadequate wages.[83] Moreover, his daring discussions of women's 'manly' occupation of environments still seen as almost exclusively male, like pubs and restaurants, provides an alternative perspective on discussions about urban space, allowing for a broader analysis of the pleasures and dangers of late-Victorian heterosociality.

Urban fiction thus reflected debates about the new freedoms available to female workers in contemporary periodicals, which also revealed the ways in which the middle-class adoption of lifestyles previously associated with working-class women had widened opportunities for all female wage-earners. Like urban fiction, periodicals helped to normalise women's occupation of public space in their mixed messages about female urbanism: as Rappaport rightly points out, popular representations of the city in newspapers, magazines and guidebooks were crucial to the invention of the *flâneuse*.[84] A typically double-edged article on 'The Working Lady in London' published in the mainstream journal the *Fortnightly Review* in 1892 promoted the self-reliance gained through independence but also linked the uncontrolled Bohemian lifestyle of working women to the 'evils' of the city:

> From 17 onwards [girls] are thrown with little or no protection into the maelstrom of London life, exposed to excitements and temptations, and to all the hazards of late hours, public conveyance, chance acquaintance. A modest, well-principled woman may go anywhere in this great city, not only without danger, but without seeing or hearing anything to shock her sense of propriety. There are hundreds, bright and self-reliant, to whom 'adventures' of all kinds are a sealed book; but there are others, headstrong, imprudent, or weak and foolish … So many women who lead independent lives resent the least control or interference, take a pride in shaking off what they consider the trammels of society … There can hardly be too much freedom in one way in a woman's life; but the barriers with which custom has fenced her in are like the rail along the edge of a precipice.[85]

This extract expresses the tensions between a modern acceptance of the 'independent lives' now available to working women and conservative fears about unprotected girls risking their reputations by behaving foolishly, subject to the 'hazards' and 'temptations' of the public sphere. A recurring cultural fear is that the 'maelstrom' of London will tempt respectable women into the sexual 'adventures' enjoyed by their social inferiors. According to Mary Ryan, one of the questions posed in discourses on increased female access to public space was, 'would the big city beckon women into promiscuous enjoyment of urban

---

[83] See Peiss, pp. 6–7, 51–6, for her astute discussion of the practice of treating, which allowed women greater access to public amusements but placed them under an obligation to the men who paid for their pleasures. As she points out, 'working women's lack of financial resources posed a problem to their participation in an active social life' (p. 51).

[84] Rappaport, p. 6.

[85] Evelyn March-Phillipps, 'The Working Lady in London', *Fortnightly Review* 58 (1892), 193–203 (p. 200).

freedom?'[86] I have made extensive use of such articles in this study, not only in order to provide a wider cultural context to Gissing's ambiguous representations of modern femininity, but also to historicise the concept of the *flâneuse* and her female counterparts. Contemporary periodicals, particularly the new women's magazines which proliferated in the 1890s and 1900s, helped to define a range of variations on the working woman, including the female bachelor, the modern girl, the working lady, the poor lady and the manly woman, in articles often published alongside or drawing on the research of the social investigators. But both feminist and mainstream journals reproduced the ambiguities about the public woman characteristic of their time, even though, as Levine has claimed, the feminist press 'sought to counteract not only the distortions of the mainstream, male-dominated press but, additionally, that sector of the mass press which concentrated on more customary women's interests'.[87] A debate about the decline of the old maid initiated by Sarah Grand in the newly established girls' magazine, the *Young Woman*, in 1899 may have highlighted the great improvements such as 'a widening of liberty, a growth of opportunity' in the lives of modern women but it also advocated marriage as a more attractive option than the drudgery of paid work.[88] More work on women's urban freedoms needs to be done in order to reinvent the *flâneuse*: as Janet Wolff concedes, 'although the solitary and independent life of the *flâneur* was not open to women, women clearly *were* active and visible in other ways in the public arena'.[89]

The *fin-de-siècle* novelist's attempts to imagine the possibilities of women's visibility in urban culture also raise key questions about the class identity of the woman in public, returning us neatly to the debates about the social status of the working woman reflected in the work of the social investigators. What is sometimes missing from theoretical debates about the *flâneuse* is a detailed consideration of her class credentials, as critics have tended to work from the assumption that the urban woman, like her male counterpart, was a bourgeois figure, making the leisured shopping lady an ideal example. Recent work on West End commercial culture, such as Walkowitz's discussion of street harassment in shopping districts and Rappaport's study of female shoppers and club-goers, has served to perpetuate this misleading mythology of the metropolis.[90] But if we are to unearth the experience of the woman of the crowd, the urban rambler, surely the working-class woman, reliant on her mobility, would qualify as a prime contender?

---

[86]   Ryan, *Women in Public*, p. 64.

[87]   Levine, '"The Humanising Influence of 5 o'Clock Tea"', p. 295.

[88]   Agnes Giberne, 'At What Age should Girls Marry?', *Young Woman* 7 (1899), 207–10 (p. 210). This was one of a number of responses to the original article of the same title written by Sarah Grand which appeared earlier in the same volume, pp. 161–4.

[89]   Wolff, p. 44. She identifies the experiences of suburban women, those in domestic service, and working-class women, all women affected by 'the advent of the modern era', as in need of further research.

[90]   See Judith R. Walkowitz, 'Going Public: Shopping, Street Harassment, and Streetwalking in Late Victorian London', *Representations* 62 (1998), 1–30 and Erika Diane Rappaport, *Shopping for Pleasure: Women in the Making of London's West End* (Princeton: Princeton University Press, 2000).

Wilson has been criticised for suggesting that 'the liberating potential of the city ... is only available to working-class women', and excluding bourgeois women from her account of street-walking,[91] but her attempts to reconsider the prostitute's role as the quintessential urban woman and to argue for women's relish of the 'disorder' of the streets actually distinguish her work from the prevailing critical tendency to privilege the respectable woman's entry into the public world which underpins later studies of female urbanism. Similarly, Gissing's representation of street life, urban entertainments and women's uses of public transport involves a reassessment of the working-class woman's experiences of urban culture, which positions her at the centre rather than the margins of the narrative of modernity in his earlier fiction. A comparison of his working-class novels with his championing of the professional woman in the 1890s texts reveals that concerns about the legitimacy of the working woman's place in the city affect both factory girls and journalists, actresses and professional musicians in their claims to a public life. The occupation of the public sphere by women of all classes constitutes a challenge to the rigid divide between ideologies of working- and middle-class femininity. In her discussion of the 'larger revision of urban etiquette' in turn-of-the-century Boston, Sarah Deutsch notes that 'with women's increasing assertion of mobility and autonomy, clear markers distinguishing between respectability and wildness faded'.[92] Rather than simply reinscribing conservative perspectives and judgements on women 'on the streets', Gissing continues to emphasise the economic difficulties and sexual risks for all women attendant on their restricted access to public space. His recurring use of the practice of stalking in his narratives, which has sometimes been misinterpreted as the male author's antagonism to female freedom of movement in the city, actually functions as a way of highlighting women's rejection of the need for male protection, at a time when the out-dated system of chaperonage was dying out. Nead's premise that 'new spaces seemed to produce new femininities and no one could be sure how these women would behave'[93] is equally pertinent to women at either end of the social scale, at a time when permitted female sexual behaviours and lifestyles were being reshaped by the gradual breakdown of the gendered hierarchies of the public sphere. Gissing's vision of citizenship thus grants women of all classes the right to occupy space on their own terms, indicating that definitions of modern femininity predicated on mobility extended beyond the female professional and the New

---

[91] Nead's criticism of earlier readings which offer 'a quite extraordinary picture of the nineteenth-century metropolis, peopled, it seems, by men, working women and middle-class female shoppers' is a valid point in her argument for a focus on other categories of bourgeois woman, such as theatre-goers and educated daughters. But it seems ultimately wrongheaded in holding Wilson responsible for 'not ... redress[ing] the absence of middle-class women from feminist accounts of the modern city streets' (pp. 69–70). Wilson was one of the first feminist critics to publish a full-length study of female urbanism and later studies by Walkowitz and Nord, largely ignored by Nead, have given ample coverage to a range of bourgeois female experiences on the Victorian streets.

[92] Deutsch, pp. 83, 84. This is part of a larger argument about the gradual collapse of distinctions between the working girl and the New Woman in this period.

[93] Nead, p. 73.

Woman. By highlighting perceptions of women's freedom which straddled urban fiction and periodical debate, I hope to provide a more nuanced and historicised account of the Gissing heroine's struggles in 'the maelstrom of London life'.

Chapter 1

Prostitution and the Freedoms of Streetwalking

When Gissing first began writing novels in the late 1870s, the subjects of prostitution and working-class life were undeniably topical. Lucy Bland argues that from the 1880s onwards, 'the casual poor – "the dangerous classes" – were policed more coercively, and their behaviour subjected to greater state intervention'.[1] Within the terms of this cultural construction, poor women were perceived to be most dangerous because of their sexualities, which in their (potential) uncontrollability threatened dominant images of womanliness. As Judith Walkowitz has argued, the prostitute functioned in late-Victorian society both as 'a powerful symbol of sexual and economic exploitation under industrial capitalism',[2] and, increasingly, as 'the quintessential female figure of the urban scene … a central spectacle in a set of urban encounters and fantasies'.[3] Debates about the social problem of prostitution, linked to the freedom, anonymity and overcrowding of urban existence,[4] also encompassed wider issues around working-class women's presence on the city streets and the impact of the newly commercialised urban culture on female sexuality. After the repeal of the Contagious Diseases Acts in 1886,[5] prostitutes had greater freedom but were also kept under surveillance by philanthropists and the medical profession. Feminist accounts of the 'reclaiming' of prostitutes proliferated in this period, often reinforcing dominant images of such women as 'the social evil' and revealing an uneasiness about working-class female sexuality. In 1885 Mary Jeune argued against the possibilities of rescuing those from the 'lowest class' of fallen women, claiming that 'many of them are too degraded to accept or wish for any help; and

---

[1] Lucy Bland, *Banishing the Beast: English Feminism and Sexual Morality, 1885–1914* (Harmondsworth: Penguin, 1995), p. 97.
[2] Judith R. Walkowitz, *Prostitution and Victorian Society: Women, Class and the State* (Cambridge: Cambridge University Press, 1980), p. 4.
[3] Judith R. Walkowitz, *City of Dreadful Delight: Narratives of Sexual Danger in Late-Victorian London* (London: Virago, 1992), p. 21.
[4] Paula Bartley, *Prostitution: Prevention and Reform in England, 1860–1914* (London & New York: Routledge, 2000), p. 10.
[5] Since the 1860s the police had been granted the power under the Contagious Diseases Acts to apprehend women of doubtful virtue in the streets and insist that they be medically examined; if found to be diseased, they could then be detained in lock hospitals. See Walkowitz, *Prostitution and Victorian Society*, pp. 90–102 for details of the repeal campaign.

the difficulty of finding any work or profession for a woman who has led, while it lasted, a gay, reckless life, which, even with its darker side, had many things which made it exciting and varied, is almost insuperable'.[6] Whilst she was associated with the degradations and destitution of the city, the prostitute was then also paradoxically to be envied for the freedoms of her 'gay, reckless life', prompting a rethinking of stereotypical ways of representing working-class women and female sexuality.

Arguably, the vogue for prostitute heroines in fiction tended to flesh out the potentially restrictive images used in feminist, medical and periodical writing on the subject. The French naturalist tradition, at times bordering on the obscene, led the way with its portrayals of feisty, outspoken courtesans, culminating in Émile Zola's notorious Nana, whose provocative image was popularised in the dramatisations running in Paris throughout the 1880s. The social purity 'crusade' which gathered force after 1885 initiated a change both in ways of conceptualising prostitution and in public opinion about ways of dealing with the sexually deviant woman. Although Gissing and his British contemporaries were more likely to draw on the language of purity used by the members of the National Vigilance Association and its advocates, the alternative influence of scandalous and sexually explicit French texts, which were available in cheap translations, is undeniable; such texts were later condemned as pornographic by purity campaigners.[7] The origins of what was to be later categorised as East End fiction are apparent in Gissing's early attempts to explore working-class life in the slums of East London, particularly through the figure of the young prostitute, a symbolic marker of both the degradation and possibilities of the late-Victorian metropolis. In 1881 Margaret Harkness claimed in the mainstream journal the *Nineteenth Century* that 'necessity now forces many women out into the world, where the law of the survival of the fittest, and therefore of the strongest, holds good for all comers'.[8] Trapped within a harsh capitalist system with inadequate wages for its female labour, working-class women can often only survive through resorting to prostitution though this may, in turn, make them 'fitter' to cope with the demands of urban culture. Elizabeth Wilson's claim that 'to be a woman – an individual, not part of a family or kin group – in the city, is to become a prostitute – a public woman' can be seen to cast the streetwalker as the quintessential female urbanite, 'recur[ring] continually in the discussion of urban life'.[9] The fictional prostitute typically has the freedom, denied to her more respectable counterparts, to roam the city and to choose when to forge relationships with the men she meets there. Her lack of respectability, however, may also be signalled in drunkenness and declining health as her spatial freedoms are ultimately restricted by police intervention. Writers as diverse as the East End novelist Arthur Morrison and the New Woman

---

[6]   Mary Jeune, 'Saving the Innocents', *Fortnightly Review* 44 (1885), 345–56 (p. 346).

[7]   Walkowitz, *City of Dreadful Delight*, p. 125.

[8]   Margaret Harkness, 'Women as Civil Servants', *Nineteenth Century* 10 (1881), 369–81 (p. 369).

[9]   Elizabeth Wilson, *The Sphinx in the City: Urban Life, the Control of Disorder, and Women* (London: Virago, 1991), p. 8.

novelist Annie Holdsworth were to develop Gissing's model into the 1890s when attention shifted to the troubled relationship between the New Woman and her fallen sister in a more sanitised approach partly dictated by the ideals of purity feminism.

Images of the Prostitute and Working-Class Sexuality

Gissing's first two novels *Workers in the Dawn* (1880) and *The Unclassed* (1884), were perceived to be shocking in their portrayals of low life, and unsuitable for women readers; the latter was banned from Mudie's circulating library. However, they were also pioneering, helping to set a new trend for 'graphic' urban fiction, which dealt with 'the gravest subjects, and with the most difficult and delicate phases of modern social life'.[10] The *Evening News*, in a positive appraisal of Gissing's 'Novel for Men', remarked that the author 'has succeeded in lifting the veil from the life of a section of the world of London concerning which serious novelists have too long kept silence'.[11] More recently, Patricia Ingham has made a similar point about the 'new' elements of Gissing's social criticism, bracketing *The Unclassed* with Hardy's *Jude the Obscure* as 'radicalised by the appearance ... of the previously invisible working-class woman as a central figure, and by a rewriting of the fallen woman'.[12] Daringly writing about prostitutes in the early 1880s was bound to invite comparisons with Zola, though reviewers tended to credit Gissing with more restraint: 'the spirit of *The Unclassed* is not the spirit of Zola, as the book is not prurient', the *Academy* claimed with relief in 1884.[13] One of the first critics to make the comparison with the French naturalists, Frederic Harrison, a leading Comtean positivist, was of the opinion that Gissing's first novel demonstrated a 'better social purpose' than the 'so-called realism of Zola' whose work he professed to 'loathe'. In his reply Gissing denied knowledge of Zola's work but revealingly explained,

> rather than to any literary influence, I think I must trace the story to my own strongly excitable temperament, operated upon by my hideous experiences of low life ... I was shocked by the gap between the two classes, – not in the mere commonplace matter of material comfort, but in the power of comprehending each other's rule of life.[14]

---

[10] Reviews of *Workers in the Dawn*, *Athenaeum*, 12 June 1880, p. 758; *Manchester Examiner and Times*, 15 September 1880, p. 3.
[11] 'A Novel for Men' (Review of *The Unclassed*), *Evening News*, 25 June 1884, p. 1.
[12] Patricia Ingham, *The Language of Gender and Class: Transformation in the Victorian Novel* (London: Routledge, 1996), p. 112.
[13] Arthur R.R. Barker, Review of *The Unclassed*, *Academy*, 28 June 1884, p. 454.
[14] Letter from Frederic Harrison to Gissing, 22 July 1880; letter to Frederic Harrison, 23 July 1880. *Collected Letters, Vol 1: 1863–81* (1990), pp. 291, 293. In the hope of receiving guidance about the future direction of his writing, Gissing sent a copy of his first novel, which included characters influenced by Comtean philosophy, to Harrison in 1880. See *Gissing: The Critical Heritage*, ed. Pierre Coustillas & Colin Partridge (London & Boston: Routledge & Kegan Paul, 1972), p. 53.

Although it is reductive to read his fiction wholly in biographical terms, it is worth noting that Gissing clearly had first-hand experience of living with, and attempting to reform, a type of woman about which other authors were only speculating: his first novels were written during his troubled marriage to his first wife, Nell Harrison, a prostitute for whom he had sacrificed his degree at Owens College in Manchester. Despite the fact that his unorthodox marriage had to be kept secret from his family and friends and is therefore only obliquely referred to in the early letters, this comment is suggestive of the 'hideous experience' of a cross-class marriage, of a wife who cannot comprehend her husband's values. His shock at the gap between the classes also signals his earnest commitment to delineating 'modern social life', with his focus on the group he was to christen 'the unclassed' testifying to his interest in the often marginalised characters he observed on the London streets.

Such a commitment underpins the crudely plotted *Workers in the Dawn*, in which the respectable artisan hero Arthur Golding marries the prostitute Carrie Mitchell in the philanthropic attempt to rescue her from destitution. Their marriage deteriorates rapidly, jeopardised by Carrie's predilection for drinking and Golding's heavy-handed attempts to educate and control her. In the more assured *The Unclassed*, the erstwhile teacher Osmond Waymark attempts a similar rescue of the prostitute Ida Starr, though they do not marry; more refined than Carrie, Ida's potential degradations are instead displaced onto the figure of Harriet Casti, who makes her husband's life a misery by her drinking, refusal to observe his rules and her uncontrollable hysterical fits. Both novels typically contrast the agency and allure of the prostitute with the passivity of the two-dimensional middle-class heroine, with the hero divided between attraction and repulsion to the prostitute, a potential sexual partner only if she can be educated out of her class. Marred by too many 'impossible long speeches'[15] and the devotion of the first volume to tedious descriptions of Golding's childhood, *Workers in the Dawn* bears too many marks of the first-time novelist trying out ideas to merit extensive critical attention; published at Gissing's own expense, only a few copies were sold and according to Jacob Korg, its 'social protest was not taken seriously'.[16] However, in its delineation of marriage to a prostitute and its depiction of working-class women, it anticipates many of the 'modern' concerns Gissing was to explore more carefully in later fiction. It can then be usefully read alongside the more sustained, if idealised, examination of the prostitute in *The Unclassed,* which as a narrative both benefits and suffers from the much more extensive revisions undertaken at the request of the publisher in 1884 and for the second, 'heavily censored and abbreviated', edition of 1895.[17] The second edition, with its appealingly articulate

---

[15] *Manchester Examiner and Times*, p. 3.

[16] Jacob Korg, Introduction to *The Unclassed* (1895; Sussex: Harvester Press, 1976), p. x.

[17] Ingham, p. 140. Her analysis is based on the first edition, which she perceives as more radical in its representations of women: she provides an interesting analysis of some of the excised passages, though the textual changes between the two editions are not always clearly identified for the reader.

and morally pure heroine, attracted much more favourable reviews, and was more than once compared to Thomas Hardy's own study of a sexually experienced but 'pure' woman, *Tess of the D'Urbervilles* (1891), which was possibly influenced by his reading of *The Unclassed*, a novel he certainly admired.

Naturalist fiction of the 1880s and early 1890s, whilst honouring the tradition of representing such women as objects of horror and pity, tended to privilege the attractive over the repulsive characteristics of the prostitute, partly by an emphasis on her victimisation under capitalism. The sexually frank short stories of Zola's disciple, Guy de Maupassant, with their refreshing refusal to hide sexual urges behind a veneer of bourgeois morality, are particularly revealing in their fascination with the quasi-respectability of prostitution and women's reasons for entering the sex trade. The respectable brothel-owner in 'Madame Tellier's Establishment' 'had adopted her present profession just as she might have become a milliner or a draper', avoiding 'the stigma attached to prostitution' by keeping her establishment outside the large towns.[18] However, the stories also foreground the uncertainty of the prostitute's position and her limited choices in the labour market. In 'The Odyssey of a Prostitute', the teenage prostitute is a former domestic servant unable to find any other work after a spell in prison, lured into soliciting by hunger and desperation: she finds it 'a hard life', particularly in Paris where 'there's too many of us'.[19] The more impassioned defence of her identity as a 'harlot' by Madame Obardi in the longer story 'Yvette', underlines the economic imperatives which drive enterprising women into the trade. She tells her horrified daughter:

> If I weren't a harlot, you'd be a kitchen-maid to-day, as I was once, and you'd work for thirty sous a day, and your mistress would send you out on errands to the butcher's, d'you here and kick you out if you were idle ... When you're only a poor servant-girl with fifty francs of savings, you must get away from it somehow if you don't want to rot in the workhouse; and there's only one way for women, only one way, d'you hear, when you're a servant! We can't make fortunes on the stock exchange or at high finance. We've nothing but our bodies, nothing but our bodies.[20]

The decision to capitalise on her sexuality is here presented as the 'only way' for the lower-class girl to escape the shame of the workhouse or the poorly paid drudgery of domestic service, the primary and much despised means of employment for poor women in this period. This was of course the socialist argument to be developed by George Bernard Shaw in the hard-hitting *Mrs Warren's Profession*, which draws heavily on Maupassant's story in its staging of the confrontation between brothel-owner Kitty Warren and her pious daughter Vivie, though Shaw's sympathetic portrayal of Kitty's involvement in the white

---

[18] 'Madame Tellier's Establishment' in Guy de Maupassant, *Selected Short Stories*, trans. and ed. Roger Colet (Harmondsworth: Penguin, 1971), p. 87. See also the hypocritical treatment of the prostitute in 'Boule de Suif' in the same collection.

[19] 'The Odyssey of a Prostitute' in Guy de Maupassant, *88 Short Stories*, trans. Ernest Boyd & Storm Jameson (London: Alfred A. Knopf, 1930), p. 120.

[20] 'Yvette' in Maupassant, *88 Short Stories*, pp. 57–8.

slave trade ensured that the play was banned in 1894. Although Gissing shied away from the explicit sexual content of naturalist writing, pronouncing one story of Maupassant's 'really and truly disgusting',[21] the French author's vision of the odyssey of a prostitute from hard but menial work to an easier lifestyle is an urban narrative which would become evident in his own work.

Gissing's focus on fallen women as victims of economic circumstances both draws on and goes beyond the conventions of naturalist fiction by mounting a stronger attack on preconceptions about working-class sexual deviance. A contemporary review of *The Unclassed* promised that, 'it will give to many readers a very different notion of the "unfortunate" class',[22] though this may have been due to the fact that the middle-class readership had no official access to shocking French texts. His prostitutes walk the streets either to supplement meagre wages from exploitation in workrooms or in domestic service, or as a 'rest' from the hard labour such employment involved. This was in line with current research on the 'just fallen' by reformers, who believed that 'this class of woman, drawn chiefly from among domestic servants, dressmakers, barmaids and needlewomen, is the largest'.[23] As Paula Bartley reiterates, 'prostitution occurred because of the inadequacy of women's wages in relation to their needs'.[24] In *The Unclassed* one of the minor characters, Sally Fisher, whose 'day work' consists of sewing ulsters for seven shillings a week, proclaims, 'All us girls are the same; we have to keep on the two jobs at the same time ... I come home at night that tired out I ain't fit for nothing ... And it's hard to have to go out into the Strand, when you're like that' (p. 109).[25] She is shown to be 'getting her living as best she could' (p. 109). Ida's tale of woe, guaranteed to tug at the reader's heart-strings, describes the 'slavery' involved in working as a lady's maid, in which 'bodily weakness, want of proper food, and overwork' (p. 138) are combined with seduction and abandonment by the master of the house. Her 'choice' of prostitution is typically based on a rejection of the exhaustive conditions of other popular industries such as needlework: 'because sewing is looked upon as a woman's natural slavery, I rebelled against it' (p. 137). Research into sweated labour around the turn of the century confirmed that unskilled needlework was very poorly paid, which meant that 'an ordinary needlewoman cannot earn her living in London' unless she is a particularly swift worker.[26] In the earlier novel, Carrie is barely surviving as a mantle-hand when she falls pregnant and is thrown out of her lodgings, though

---

[21]   20 June 1888. Quoted in Pierre Coustillas (ed.), *London and the Life of Literature in Late Victorian England: The Diary of George Gissing, Novelist* (Sussex: Harvester Press, 1978), p. 33.

[22]   'A Novel for Men', p. 1.

[23]   Mary Jeune, 'Saving the Innocents', *Fortnightly Review* 44 (1885), 345–56 (p. 346).

[24]   Bartley, p. 7. She links this to the idea that women were more likely to bear the effects of poverty as 'there was virtually no female equivalent of the prosperous male artisan'.

[25]   All quotations are taken from George Gissing, *The Unclassed*, ed. Jacob Korg (1895; Sussex: Harvester Press, 1976).

[26]   F. Mabel Robinson, 'Our Working Women and their Earnings', *Fortnightly Review* 48 (1887), 50–63 (p. 53). See also Clementina Black, *Sweated Industry and the Minimum Wage* (London: Duckworth & Co, 1907), pp. 1–10.

whether she is working as a prostitute at this point in the text seems rather unclear – we are told in the third volume that 'Carrie's experience had been that of the numberless girls in a similar destitute condition whom London nightly pillows in her hard corners, the only peculiarity being that she had found a way out of her misery without having recourse either to the workhouse or the river' (Vol 3, p. 68),[27] in which either her marriage, or streetwalking, could be the 'way out' Gissing is referring to. Symbolised by the shocking scene in which Golding picks up a desperate Carrie clutching her dead baby in the freezing streets outside the Prince of Wales Theatre, the destitute position of poor women is then linked both to economic and sexual exploitation.

The links between prostitution and destitution surfaced in other feminist accounts, underlining the rescuer's belief that 'very poor women ... were generally not driven to prostitution unless they were single, homeless or without family or friends'.[28] In 1905 Mary Higgs, a social investigator who later set up a home for destitute women in Oldham, published the findings of her undercover research, 'Three Nights in Women's Lodging Houses', based on unofficial 'interviews' with a variety of lodgers. One tale of a servant who came back too late at night to risk the wrath of her mistress ends with the foregone conclusion that 'being destitute, [she] fell at once into prostitution'.[29] Dressed as a female vagrant in order to disguise her philanthropic mission, Higgs notices that 'the bold free look of a man at a destitute woman must be felt to be realised'.[30] As Deborah Epstein Nord has claimed, her work is shot through with 'the sense of personal identification with sexual and economic vulnerability',[31] informing her belief that women's descent into the 'abyss' of homelessness and degradation is involuntary. In both novels women's living arrangements are jeopardised by their potentially disreputable behaviour, as landladies frequently comment on their female lodgers staying out late or receiving unrespectable visitors, which sometimes results in eviction. In *The Unclassed*, this works in woman's favour, though this is rare: Harriet traps Julian into marriage by luring him into her bedroom where they are seen together by another lodger; Mrs Ogle's refusal to tolerate 'the suspicion of wrong-doing under her roof' (p. 106) is enough to seal his fate. Although Higgs concedes that both 'frivolity and misfortune' are the principal contributory factors to the women's choice of profession, her conviction that the provision of 'suitable and sufficient women's lodging-houses under good management' would go some way to preventing the fall into prostitution shifts the attention away from the

---

[27] All quotations are taken from George Gissing, *Workers in the Dawn,* 3 vols. (1880; New York & London, Garland Publishing, 1976).

[28] Bartley, p. 8.

[29] Mary Higgs, 'Three Nights in Women's Lodging Houses', in *Glimpses into the Abyss* (1906), reprinted in Peter Keating (ed.), *Into Unknown England, 1866–1913: Selections from the Social Explorers* (Glasgow: Fontana/Collins, 1976), p. 275.

[30] *Glimpses into the Abyss*, p. 94. Quoted in Deborah Epstein Nord, *Walking the Victorian Streets: Women, Representation and the City* (New York: Cornell University Press, 1995), p. 232.

[31] Nord, p. 233.

degradation of working-class women towards the inadequacies of the accommodation assigned to them.[32]

Gissing's accounts of the fall from virtue both reflect and interrogate the opinions of feminists and philanthropists involved in the repeal campaign at this time, which tended to draw on more entrenched views of the 'social evil'. Mary Jeune, who published a series of articles in *The Fortnightly Review* of 1885 about her experience of helping the fallen, distinguished between 'the woman who has just fallen' and can be 'easily reached by sympathy and kindness', most probably a victim of seduction, and what she referred to as 'the lowest class of fallen women' who are 'too degraded to accept or wish for any help' (p. 346). Elizabeth Blackwell, the first woman doctor and a prominent member of the NVA, referred to this group as a 'growing army of shameless women'.[33] A variety of discourses constructed the prostitute either as an innocent victim of male lust or as a 'demon' and 'contagion of evil'.[34] Judith Walkowitz has argued that such an ideological framework excluded the experience of women who drifted into this lifestyle temporarily, and provided 'a restrictive and moralistic image' of the fallen woman.[35] In *Workers in the Dawn* Golding is initially attracted by Carrie's status as innocent victim, though we are alerted to the fact that 'It did not occur to him for a moment that the girl herself might possibly be to blame' (Vol 2, p. 271) for her pregnancy. Whilst he is intent on elevating her above the painted prostitutes in Leicester Square, her drinking and disreputable companions hasten her decline; at her lowest point she is drunk and out of control in a back-street bar, her eyes with 'that bleared, indistinct appearance so common in girls of the town' (Vol 3, p. 201), tarred by association with the 'evil-minded' Polly Hemp, whose 'long years spent on the streets ... had reduced her to something far more akin to beast than man' (Vol 3, p. 209). Apparently in the 'lowest class' of fallen women, where 'she seemed to have lost all sense of shame' (Vol 3, p. 381), Carrie is never so degraded that she loses the reader's sympathy; she is victimised by Polly and a string of greedy landladies who conspire against her to steal her money and appears incapable of dealing with her alcoholism, the temptations of which Golding as a poor man is well aware. In *The Unclassed*, streetwalking is more obviously characterised as a temporary phenomenon. Sally moves on to shop work and Ida seeks to continue her work in a laundry, though she is dismissed without notice after a spiteful tip-off about her previous profession by Mrs Sprowl. This loss of her job brings a sense of shame yet she does not return to her old ways despite the threat of starvation, perhaps because she is relying on Waymark to help her to retain her new-found respectability. As a beneficiary of middle-class sympathy, she is able to escape the 'degradation' which will ensure that Carrie dies an early and squalid death, a more stereotypical resolution to the prostitute's story.

---

[32]　Nord, pp. 283–4.

[33]　Dr Elizabeth Blackwell, *Purchase of Women: The Great Economic Blunder* (London: John Kensit, n.d. [1887]), p. 35.

[34]　Blackwell, p. 36.

[35]　Walkowitz, *Prostitution and Victorian Society*, pp. 110, 146. She argues that such images obscure the 'self-perception' of the women involved.

But middle-class disgust for, and fear of, the 'shameless class' was strong, and Gissing's contradictory responses to the illicit sexual behaviour of his working-class women cannot be entirely separated from such prevalent cultural perceptions. 'Positive representations of active female sexuality' were extremely rare in debates on prostitution, an additional constraint on writers in an age of censorship.[36] Walkowitz points out that at a time when extra-marital sexuality became a 'primary area of dangerous sexual activity', medical and police supervision helped to create 'an outcast class of "sexually deviant" females'.[37] Implying that all forms of non-reproductive sexuality are deviant, Blackwell's comments on those engaging in 'free lust and indulging the impulses of a sexual caprice'[38] blur the distinctions between commercial sex and the extra-marital sexuality associated with the working classes. The narrator's comment on Ida's mother, Lotty Starr, 'by no means a vicious girl', reinforces the idea of sexual activity as a necessary characteristic of poor young women: 'A girl who says that she is occupied in a workroom is never presumed to be able to afford the luxury of strict virtue' (p. 22). Working-class women could always be attacked on the grounds of their sexual knowledge and consequent impurity, as this passage from another of Mary Jeune's articles indicates:

> The poorer girl is not necessarily impure … perhaps in some ways her completer knowledge acts as a shield. When she is obliged to leave home for service we have no right to blame her, if chaste personally, because she is not pure-minded; pure-minded in the sense in which the term is ordinarily used she cannot be … While she may be deprived of the freshness and delicacy of an ignorant woman, she does not run the same danger of falling.[39]

By arguing that working-class girls are always already fallen, given that they have a 'familiarity' with and 'completer knowledge' of sexual matters than middle-class girls, Jeune accuses them of being very close to the shameless prostitute, even if they do not sell their bodies on the street. This reflects the wider 'anxiety over the sexual precocity of working-class girls' which feminists sought to control.[40] However, by idealising prostitution and its effects on women in *The Unclassed*, Gissing is able to reconcile Ida's sexual knowledge with the purity required for the middle-class hero; after hearing her story Waymark proclaims, 'my ideal woman is the one who, knowing every darkest secret of life, keeps yet a pure mind – as you do, Ida' (p. 131). Whilst this seems to disprove the theory that working-class women can never be 'pure-minded' because of the sexual characteristics of their class, Gissing remains hesitant about the educated man's desire for sexually active women; Golding's fear that his marriage may 'degenerate into a mere vulgar connection, subsisting mainly upon sensual emotions' (Vol 3, p. 17) is shared by

---

[36] Frank Mort, *Dangerous Sexualities: Medico-Moral Politics in Britain since 1830* (London & New York: Routledge & Kegan Paul, 1987), p. 76.
[37] Walkowitz, *Prostitution and Victorian Society*, pp. 4, 5.
[38] Blackwell, p. xii.
[39] Mary Jeune, 'Helping the Fallen', *Fortnightly Review* 44 (1885), 669–82 (pp. 672–3).
[40] Walkowitz, *Prostitution and Victorian Society*, p. 249

the author, who struggled to sustain a cross-class union based merely on sexual attraction.

In his reading of Gissing's models of femininity, David Grylls has argued that 'the graceful peasant, suitably adapted, represents the idealized working girl whose image Gissing fondles in his early books'.[41] In the more formulaic *Workers in the Dawn*, the working girl is seen as less of an ideal than the middle-class heroine, the philanthropist Helen Norman, whose womanliness and virtue guarantee her attraction to men: Golding thinks of her as a 'goddess', far 'superior' (Vol 1, p. 384) to other women. However, in *The Unclassed* Gissing moves away from this angel-whore dichotomy, as the 'timid conventionality' of the angelic teacher Maud Enderby has much less appeal than the working girl's aspirations to purity; whereas Golding realises after a disastrous marriage and Helen's early death from consumption that he has made the wrong choice, Waymark is clearly relieved to be released from his engagement to Maud, suggesting a shift in conceptions of the ideal woman. Recommending Ida to Julian as a suitable companion for Harriet, he tellingly confides that 'she is by no means the ordinary London work-girl; you can't call her educated, but she speaks purely, and has a remarkably good intelligence' (pp. 165–6). As Patricia Ingham has pointed out, Ida is 'unambiguously identified as a potential heroine' because of her voice and accent and her 'appropriation of the conventional angel's domesticity', as she 'confounds the usual oppositional signs of respectable and fallen woman'.[42] Certainly she revels in the 'domestic and womanly' act of offering tea, rather than sex, to male visitors to her rooms, as Gissing self-consciously proclaims that she 'had passed from one extreme to the other' (p. 175). She also explicitly refuses the stereotypical tag of 'degraded' and criticises Waymark for 'speak[ing] contemptuously, like that' (p. 86). But perhaps the author betrays himself by 'fondling' the working girl's image too obviously; she only remains ideal because she is *not* ordinary. Her purity is effectively achieved by displacing the shamelessness of the prostitute onto the character of the discontented shop-girl Harriet, whose marriage to Julian, like that of Carrie to Golding, to Gissing and Nell, is destroyed by her drinking, jealousy and hysterical fits. In contradistinction to Ida, Harriet is 'herself quite innocent of fine feeling' (p. 105) and plagued by the illnesses, restlessness and fits of rage also exhibited by Carrie. Like the laughing prostitute, scarred by drunken brawls, whose eyes 'twinkle with a vicious light' in the opening pages of *Workers in the Dawn,* she too seems unable to escape 'the baseness of her nature' (Vol 1, p. 8). Significantly, a key phrase used here to signify prostitution, the 'vile trade', was excised from the first edition of *The Unclassed*, perhaps because Gissing wished to keep his heroine immune from such

---

[41] David Grylls, *The Paradox of Gissing* (London: Allen & Unwin, 1986), p. 142. Grylls points out that 'blurrily idealized portraits of women' appear in many of his books, mobilised by Gissing's 'fantasy of finding a working-class girl who would satisfy his heart's desire'.

[42] Ingham, pp. 142, 157, 159.

low associations.[43] As he matured as a novelist, his models of femininity clearly became less stereotypical, prompting him to tone down the prostitute's behaviour into a more acceptable version of working-class sexuality.

By questioning the shamelessness of the streetwalker and the vileness of the 'vile trade', Gissing uncovered the potential freedoms and sexual independence she could enjoy, though this was always tempered by concerns about reputation in what was to become a characteristically ambiguous vision of woman.   The symbolic scene in which Ida swims naked in the sea at Hastings, satisfying an 'irresistible desire to leave the house' (p. 144) and immerse her 'gleaming body' (p. 145) in the water seems to confirm the delight in her own sexuality to which the middle-class hero is attracted, clearly 'a celebration of her sexuality, not an atonement for it'.[44] However, Waymark is surprised and rather unnerved by Ida's 'slight' explanation of her preference for streetwalking over the 'horrible drudgery' (p. 137) of the work-girl, reluctantly accepting that 'she liked ease and luxury; above all, ease' (p. 142) rather than the more poverty-based 'excuses' he has already imagined. This categorises her as a type of prostitute recognised by the medical journal the *Lancet,* which condemned, in strikingly similar terms, those who chose the profession as 'an easy and luxurious [life], much preferable to the life of drudgery they had hitherto led'.[45] Here economic factors are given less precedence than the working woman's enjoyment of her sexual activity, condemned by feminists as 'the absence of shame' or the prostitute's 'easy' lifestyle. According to Kathy Peiss, the prostitute was sometimes envied by young New York working women for her 'fine dress, easy life, sexual expressiveness and apparent independence'; in their appropriation of aspects of the prostitute's style, 'so-called "tough girls" ... played with the subculture of prostitution'.[46] Assessing the second edition in the context of Gissing's 1890s novels, which tackled the 'woman question' more directly, one reviewer perceptively remarked that from this novel 'one obtains an inkling of the struggles of the "odd women" in London'.[47] Certainly in *The Odd Women* (1893) the sexually knowing shop-girls who 'play' with prostitution by coming in after midnight and picking up men in the street are envied for their subversive behaviour, whilst the coarse and vulgar Miss Eade, characterised as an object of pity for soliciting at Victoria Station, a 'tawdry, abandoned creature', is nevertheless labelled on the same page by the author as a 'not unimportant type of the odd woman' (p. 299).[48] The early fiction can also be seen to anticipate a strand of New Woman fiction which was to valorise women's right to enjoy their sexualities in such controversial texts as George Egerton's short

---

[43]   Korg, p. xix. In the excised speech Ida is more forthright about her desire to reform and resist degradation. For a detailed discussion of the revisions, see Korg, pp. xviii–xxii.

[44]   Ingham, p. 158.

[45]   'The "Social Evil" in London', *Lancet,* 8 December 1888, p. 1146.

[46]   Kathy Peiss, *Cheap Amusements: Working Women and Leisure in Turn-of-the-Century New York* (Philadelphia: Temple University Press, 1986), p. 65.

[47]   Review of *The Unclassed, Buffalo Courier,* as reprinted in *The Literary News,* (July 1896), p. 205.

[48]   All quotations are taken from George Gissing, *The Odd Women,* ed. Margaret Walters (1893; London: Virago, 1980).

story collection, *Keynotes* (1893); the same reviewer admired Gissing's treatment of sexuality, seeing it as more subtle than the obtrusive approach of the New Woman novelist, Sarah Grand. Fictional prostitutes function as 'odd' women in their refusal to contain their sexualities or to passively accept the drudgery of other forms of labour available to working-class women.

It is also worth considering the underlying message of his little-known short story 'A Free Woman' (1896), which celebrates, albeit rather ambiguously, the 'life of celibacy and freedom' (p. 290) of the ebullient streetwalker Charlotte Grubb, who rejects domesticity and children in the cultivation of 'a spirit of independence' (p. 293).[49] Openly despising the restrictions of domestic service, Charlotte prefers 'the freedom of evenings', and her enjoyment of music-halls and pubs, leading her to the conclusion that 'life was not half bad; London was a fine place' (p. 293). What is striking is the framing of her defence of the prostitute's lifestyle with arguments from feminist accounts of the importance of paid labour to women's citizenship, as Maupassant's justification of the harlot's progress is taken to extremes:

> A sharp young woman, she needed no academic training to become aware of the movements of the time which chiefly concerned her. It must not be supposed that female emancipation, in the larger sense, is discussed only among educated women … Charlotte Grubb could talk with the best on the glorious claim of woman to take her share in 'the work of the world' … could cry aloud that women were no longer to be 'put upon' … However dark her mind, this one ray of reflected light had touched upon it, and served for guidance. She knew that women of the higher classes were making speeches … for her own part, down here at Haggerston, she would not be wanting to the cause, however simple her service. (pp. 291–2)

Notwithstanding the ironic tone of the story, encouraging readers of the satirical journal *The Sketch* to ridicule Charlotte's triumph over the system as rather deluded and naïve, the 'untrammelled existence' of this 'sharp young woman' who takes her place in the 'work of the world' is also held up for uneasy admiration. Linked by her independence to more emancipated middle-class heroines such as Rhoda Nunn in *The Odd Women*, this sets the struggle of the prostitute to carve out her niche in London alongside that of the emerging New Woman.

Streetwalking and the Claim to Public Territory

Recent work by feminist historians on the possibilities of a *flâneuse* figure in the late-Victorian metropolis has tended to concentrate either on the new freedoms of the middle-class woman, as philanthropist, shopper and professional, or on respectable working women, such as the shop-girl. A key area of interest has been the collapse of boundaries between classes of women, so that by becoming 'streetwalkers' respectable women demonstrate their proximity to the prostitute

---

[49]   All quotations are taken from George Gissing, *Human Odds and Ends* (1898; New York & London: Garland Publishing, 1977).

and hence compromise their reputations. However, relatively little has been said about the particular urban freedoms enjoyed by the prostitute, or her potential appropriation of the role of the *flâneuse*. Due to the fact that her occupation of the streets was hardly new, the prostitute does not qualify as one of Walkowitz's 'new social actors' in 1880s London, though Walkowitz does note the overlapping categories which 'intersected at the juncture of commerce and femininity', where 'in the elegant shopping districts around Regent Street, prostitutes, dressed in "meretricious finery" could and did pass as respectable'.[50] More recently, Jenny Ryan has considered the prostitute's occupation of public territory as a means of resisting her cultural containment in the domestic sphere, claiming that it is likely that women responded 'in more ambiguous ways' to the possible loss of social reputation on the streets 'than was figured in official discourses of the problem of city morals'.[51] However, in her reading of the gendered ideology of urban space in turn-of-the-century Boston, Sarah Deutsch has cautioned against the easy equation of 'women in public' and 'women in power'. She maintains that 'streetwalkers had been "public" women without being empowered by their presence in public', highlighting their lack of control over the spaces they inhabited and the 'limits to female autonomy' affecting all working women in the metropolis.[52] Arguably, in urban narratives of the early 1880s, the prostitute's occupation of the streets is granted a certain legitimacy, with her street-wise persona giving her access to the pleasures of urban culture. Whilst her commercialised sexuality makes her vulnerable to the corruption and dangers of the modern city, as Elizabeth Wilson has argued, 'it is necessary also to emphasise the other side of city life and to insist on women's right to the carnival, intensity and even the risks of the city'.[53]

The possible defiance of the bolder prostitutes was linked to their evil nature in contemporary accounts and their stories felt to be much more dangerous because of their associations of the prostitute's lifestyle with freedom and fun, rather than unnatural vice. Mary Jeune describes the situation in which:

> In recounting the downward history of her career, the more abandoned and hardened woman would dwell on the fun, the excitement, the gaiety of its different phases, always keeping silent ... about the squalor, misery, and degradation of the other side of it. Foul, coarse language, oaths, and jests, were used, and the darkest page of the woman's life discussed with such freedom and absence of shame that the least corrupted of women would become habituated to thoughts and aspects of vice from which they would have shrunk in horror a few weeks before.[54]

---

[50] Walkowitz, *City of Dreadful Delight*, p. 50.

[51] Jenny Ryan, 'Women, Modernity and the City', *Theory, Culture and Society* 11 (1994), 35–63 (p. 51).

[52] Sarah Deutsch, *Women and the City: Gender, Space and Power in Boston, 1870–1940* (Oxford: Oxford University Press, 2000), p. 23. She is more inclined to validate the 'new female spaces' created by women in the city, such as settlement houses and lodging-houses.

[53] Wilson, p. 10.

[54] Jeune, 'Helping the Fallen', p. 671.

Philanthropists were unhappy about prostitutes' stories, that were silent about degradation because they presented a more subversive image of the prostitute, which did not accord with the desired recognition of the sinfulness of the trade. As Paula Bartley has argued, 'rescue workers stressed that prostitutes had a wild impulsive nature, a restlessness and a need for independence which drove them onto the streets'.[55] All of the prostitutes in Gissing's fiction, to a greater or lesser extent, are presented as independent, outspoken women, who gain their 'spirit' and 'passion' from their streetwalking. In *The Odd Women*, the shop-girl's freedom of movement compares unfavourably with that of the prostitute; as a girl 'to whom the pavement was a place of commerce' (p. 64), the latter is granted more control over her occupation of urban space than the confined shop-girl, a victim of the living-in system and its restrictive curfews. Looking back, Ida laments her confined situation as a lady's maid as on the rare occasions she is allowed out, she 'walked aimlessly about the streets, watching all the girls I passed, and fancying they all looked so happy, all enjoying their life so' (p. 139). Although this gestures towards a broader concept of being 'on the streets', streetwalking ultimately gives Ida with her 'rebellious disposition' (p. 137) a purpose and a (limited) sense of enjoyment, offering her a more rewarding role in urban culture.

Despite London's aspirations to be the metropolis of choice, in the second half of the nineteenth century Paris, reaching new heights of decadence before the Second Empire collapsed in the 1870s, became 'the byword for everything that was enchanting and intoxicating about the urban scene'.[56] French naturalist fiction reflected the capital's status as 'the city sexualised' in its fascination with prostitution, a more tolerated component of the promiscuous modern city. Émile Zola's controversial and hugely successful *Nana* (1880) reflects the possibilities of social mobility in the sex trade in its narrative of a poor flower-girl who graduates from the promiscuity of the theatre, described by the manager as a 'brothel', to the quasi-respectable position of the most famous courtesan in the business. Rupert Christiansen notes that when they were evacuated from the working-class areas of central Paris to make way for new apartments, offices and shops, 'streetwalking girls wandered away from their traditional purlieus in the Palais Royal up to the rich pickings of the glittering new Paris', where 'in the constant bustle and throng it became impossible to distinguish between a lady respectably on her own and a girl for hire'.[57] Appearing almost naked on stage in the dazzling first chapter, Nana embodies the dangers and attractions of illicit female sexuality, 'a disturbing woman with all the impulsive madness of her sex' with the 'deadly smile of a man-eater' (pp. 44–5).[58] Although at times she suffers from 'the white-hot fury of a woman who is conscious of being trapped' (pp. 214–15), her financial success and

---

[55]   Bartley, p. 5. She also points out that many were 'led astray' by other girls, perhaps because they emphasised the freedoms of the lifestyle in relation to other occupations.

[56]   Wilson, p. 47.

[57]   Rupert Christiansen, *Tales of the New Babylon: Paris in the Mid-Nineteenth Century* (London: Minerva, 1994), p. 83.

[58]   All quotations are taken from Émile Zola, *Nana*, trans. and ed. George Holden (1880; Harmondsworth: Penguin, 1972).

freedoms initially suggest that she has triumphed over the system, using men to pay her way. However, Zola's preliminary notes describe the plot as 'the poignant drama of a woman destroyed by her appetite for luxury and easy pleasures',[59] as if denying that Nana's excesses are really what she deserves. Her fall into destitution and a horrific death from syphilis (thinly disguised as smallpox) then symbolises the corruption of the Second Empire and repositions the prostitute within the underclass where she should belong.

What is striking about Zola's representation of the prostitute is that the 'easy pleasures' of the city which she enjoys were traditionally associated with men at this time. Contemporary French fiction often presented the city from a male perspective, showing the men in control of sexual selection. The opening chapter of Maupassant's *Bel-Ami* (1885) positions the *flâneur* Georges Duroy in the overflowing cafés, restaurants and theatres of Paris which Nana herself frequents. Significantly, we are told that Duroy is 'fond of places where whores congregated, he liked their dance-halls, their cafés and their streets'; outside the theatre he observes that 'the whores were moving round in couples through this throng of men ... looking very much at home and at their ease like fish in their element in the midst of this stream of males'.[60] But this can also be read in terms of the marginality of the male observer, illustrating what Elizabeth Wilson has called 'the disturbed glance of the *flâneur*, recording with stoicism the challenge to patriarchal thought and existence made by the presence of women in cities'.[61] Very much at ease in the 'stream of males', Nana, like Duroy, can take her pleasure where she chooses. She is shown window-shopping in the Passage des Panorama, and dining in the place to be seen, the Café Anglais, where the clientele was 'both aristocratic and *louche*',[62] which she enters 'with the air of a woman who knew the place well' (p. 216). Although women were always accompanied by men to such places, it is the men who may be compromised by being seen in public with a known courtesan. In *The Unclassed* Ida unconventionally pays for Waymark to eat in a restaurant with her, playing on her subversion of gender roles: 'surely you won't desert me when I ask your protection?' (p. 87). Nana's fall in fortunes is signalled by her eating out with fellow streetwalker, Satin, in Laure's, a cheap *table d'hôte* in Montmartre, which Nana considers a 'low dive nobody knew anything about' (p. 261), only frequented by respectable women for the novelty value of its lesbian owner. Nevertheless, women are shown to fit confidently into the urban scene whilst men may be subjected to forms of street harassment usually reserved for women, overturning Walkowitz's model of West End harassment as the sexual objectification of women on the streets.[63] Out alone at night Muffat, one of Nana's

---

[59]   Quoted in Philip Walker, *Zola* (London: Routledge & Kegan Paul, 1985), p. 142.

[60]   Guy de Maupassant, *Bel-Ami*, trans. Douglas Parmée (1885; Harmondsworth: Penguin, 1975), pp. 27, 40.

[61]   Elizabeth Wilson, 'The Invisible *Flâneur*', *New Left Review* 191 (1992), 90–110 (p. 110).

[62]   Christiansen, p. 110.

[63]   Judith R. Walkowitz, 'Going Public: Shopping, Street Harassment, and Streetwalking in late-Victorian London', *Representations* 62 (1998), 1–30 (pp. 2, 16).

married lovers, feels a 'shame and fear' when 'some women who had come out of a café jostled him and roared with laughter' (p. 231), where women's capacity to 'jostle' others on the busy pavements signifies their centrality to the bustle of city life, and the strengths of their claim to urban territory.

Gissing's more moderate vision of the prostitute's place in the urban scene, tailored to his middle-class readers and the demands of publishers, tends to replicate the traditional gender hierarchies which Zola is attacking. Rita Felski has argued that for Zola public space is associated with 'a fear of contamination and disorder arising from a levelling of class distinctions' in 'the anonymity and promiscuity of the crowd',[64] but this overlooks the levelling of gender distinctions which is also apparent. Although Zola never denies that prostitution is a squalid business, he describes soliciting as if it were a form of entertainment:

> [Nana] and Satin would go on wild forays into the Paris streets ... The two women would scurry along, visiting all the dance-halls and cafés in a quarter ... They always returned to the main boulevards, for it was there they had the best chance of finding custom ... they scoured the whole city like this ... enduring long waits and endless walks, jostlings and quarrels, and the brutal caresses of a passer-by taken to some squalid furnished room, to come swearing down the greasy stairs afterwards ... strutting along, laughing loudly, and throwing backward glances at the men who turned to look at them, they were in their element. (pp. 270, 271)

Encompassing 'the whole city' in her nocturnal strutting, the prostitute is here shown as a more important urban figure than her brutal male clients. It is the groups of streetwalkers who are 'in their element' in the Paris streets, a phrase and sentiment echoed by Maupassant. Although Gissing's prostitutes never achieve the same mobility or camaraderie of Parisian whores, in *Workers in the Dawn* Carrie is shown returning home late at night laughing with another woman and later confesses to having been at a music-hall, considered by Golding to be 'a place in which no woman who valued her reputation would care to be seen' (Vol 2, p. 348). He later refuses to take her to the theatre because 'I don't choose that you should crowd in with a lot of vulgar people; it isn't nice' (Vol 2, p. 358). Despite his belief in women's need for 'protection' on the streets, Carrie makes her own choices about what is 'nice' entertainment for women, her 'sympathies with vulgar life' (Vol 2, p. 358) which her husband so despises and the necessity of touting for trade effectively allowing her to appreciate more of the city. After sneering at her vulgarity, her husband secretly yields to the 'ghastly fascination' of the public-houses and 'the glittering doorways of the theatres' (Vol 3, pp. 101, 109), perhaps subconsciously recalling the author's mixed feelings about the music-halls and other lowly establishments he visited whilst researching the novel. Participating in drunken pub brawls and even imitating Nana's immorality by miming 'apparently naked' in a Tableau Vivant, Carrie paradoxically appears to be both invigorated

---

[64] Rita Felski, *The Gender of Modernity* (Cambridge, Mass. & London: Harvard University Press, 1995), p. 75. Felski sees Nana as 'a product of the city, her class mobility a function of changing social conditions that allow her to make use of the new erotic and aesthetic possibilities of urban culture for her own advancement'.

and corrupted by the 'tumult' of the streets.   The label 'girl of the town' used to signify Carrie's trade is later modified to a 'child of the town', as if in her appreciation of the crowded city's 'gross delights' and her 'yearn[ing] for the lights of the shops and the coarse tumult of the pavement' (Vol 3, p. 370), the prostitute, rather than the unclassed artisan, is a more modern figure.   As Felski has shown, a nineteenth-century heroine shown to recognise the possibilities of urban culture for her own advancement, as opposed to dismissing the city for its grossness and vulgarity, is constructed through modernity, rather than existing outside it like other women.[65]

The harnessing of women's city pleasures to the dangers of drink, however, jeopardises the legitimacy of their occupation of places of entertainment, associating them with disorder and lack of control.   The word *alcoolisme*, alcoholism, was first used in French medical terminology in 1865, and, according to Christiansen, seen as 'another dreadful sign of the degeneracy of the race'.[66] Certainly, alcoholism is hereditary in Zola's fiction, with Nana's 'tipsiness' merely repeating her mother Gervaise's increasing reliance on drink to assuage the crippling effects of poverty.   In entering pubs and gin-palaces, single women compromised their reputation; as Bartley points out, 'some pubs doubled as brothels', strengthening the associations between prostitution and drink.[67]   In *The Unclassed* Harriet's frequenting of Mrs Sprowl's East End pub, where she is 'thoroughly at ease in the atmosphere of beer and pipes' (p. 187), is indicative of her proximity to the streetwalker, though her desire to work as a barmaid perhaps indicates her enjoyment of the heterosocial space where married women can gossip undisturbed.   In a familiar pattern, her more refined husband refuses to take her to the theatre, and presumably to accompany her to pubs like other working-class couples, so she is obliged to stay out until after midnight seeking her own entertainment.   This is not registered in such alarmist terms as in the earlier text, where Carrie's fight with her former landlady, Mrs Pole, is observed with 'horror' by Golding – 'his wife a drunkard, engaging in a low brawl before a public-house' (Vol 3, p. 41) – allowing the author to betray his middle-class disgust for gin-palaces, where 'human creatures, mad with liquor, tore each other with their claws like wild beasts' (Vol 3, p. 65).   Bringing Carrie down to the level of the hard-drinking Polly Hemp, who 'had several times been almost killed in the fierce brawls which were her delight' (Vol 3, p. 210), she is figured in the fight with 'her hair streaming in wildest disorder, her dress torn in places' (Vol 3, p. 39).   The alcoholism of the prostitute, indicative of the 'wildest disorder' of the city, is a disturbing reminder of women's vulnerability to the hidden corruption of London, though Gissing's Zolaesque representation of 'hardened' and aggressive drunken women was to be tempered in later novels.

In 1885 fears about the corruption of London gathered pace, and the social purity crusade began in earnest after the scandalous exposé of child prostitution in *The Maiden Tribute of Modern Babylon,* published as a sensationalist piece of

---

[65]   Felski, p. 75.
[66]   Christiansen, p. 110.
[67]   Bartley, p. 6.

journalism in the *Pall Mall Gazette*, prompted the passing of the Criminal Law Amendment Act. Although primarily concerned with raising the age of consent to 16, according to Walkowitz, it was 'mainly enforced to control adult sexual behaviour'.[68] The newly formed National Vigilance Association was instrumental in a wide-scale closure of brothels and music-halls, working in close contact with the police in cities other than London to prosecute owners and the women themselves.[69]   The repressive stance of feminists, now actively involved in 'clearing the streets of prostitutes and attempting to "clean up" indecent leisure pursuits',[70] helped to intensify perceptions of the city as dangerous.   In her discussion of how to prevent prostitution, Mary Jeune stressed that girls needed to be 'controlled and supervised' on public holidays and after work, claiming that 'very much is being done in England to guard young women … from the perils of our streets at night'.[71] Although the first editions of both of Gissing's novels were published before 1885, they clearly anticipated cultural concerns about the prostitute's place on the streets and the policing of disruptive behaviour. Policemen in the novels act as a restrictive and repressive presence, often curtailing the prostitute's freedom or sense of independence.   In *Nana*, the Parisian prostitute's fear of the police, who 'arrested as many women as possible', means that she is no longer 'in her element' on the streets: 'the moment [Satin] caught a glimpse of a policeman, she took to her heels, in the midst of a panic-stricken stampede of long dresses fleeing through the crowd. This fear of the law, this dread of the police was such that some women would stand paralysed in the doorways of cafés, while the raid was sweeping down the avenue' (p. 274). Nana's carefree lifestyle, already challenged by an abusive relationship, is undermined further by the fear of being thrown into the prison Saint-Lazare and subjected to medical inspections; she only escapes the policeman who raids her lodgings by jumping out of the window. Significantly, the crowd are shown to be on the side of the police, admiring their 'brutal tactics … as they rapidly closed in' (p. 275), highlighting the fragility of the 'panic-stricken' prostitute's position.   Though statistics suggest that arrests of prostitutes in London peaked in 1880–85, cases of wrongful arrest resulting in bad publicity for the police effectively meant that more often than not they turned a blind eye; according to Bartley, they thought 'it was the safest policy to ignore prostitution', particularly as arrest was seldom justified by the behaviour of prostitutes.[72] One of the women interviewed by Higgs remarks

---

[68]   Walkowitz, *Prostitution and Victorian Society*, p. 251.   See also *City of Dreadful Delight*, pp. 81–121 for her excellent discussion of W.T. Stead's *The Maiden Tribute of Modern Babylon* and its political effects.

[69]   Frank Mort, *Dangerous Sexualities: Medico-Moral Politics in Britain since 1830* (London: Routledge & Kegan Paul, 1987), pp. 134–5.

[70]   Bland, p. 97. See Bland, pp. 95–8 for her discussion of the reactions of purity feminist Laura Ormiston Chant to the behaviour of prostitutes at the Empire Theatre of Varieties, a music-hall in Leicester Square, in 1894. She was horrified by the indecency of the theatre allowing women to openly solicit men in a public place.

[71]   Jeune, 'Saving the Innocents', p. 348.

[72]   Bartley, pp. 164, 162, 165. This was of course linked to the Criminal Law Amendment Act and the suppression of brothels. Bartley also makes the point that Sir Charles Warren,

that she is 'afraid to solicit in town', as the '"bobbies" kept a sharp look-out', though when she was apprehended for being 'on the town', they had done no more than advise her to go home to her mother.[73] In *The Unclassed*, although Ida is not officially arrested for soliciting, she is apprehended by a policeman, tried for stealing and sent to prison for six months' hard labour. Harriet's framing of her friend is part of a spiteful campaign to reveal Ida's former profession to her husband, yet the constable is happy to believe her story of a stolen brooch, perhaps reiterating that women on the streets were in the policeman's power: after being charged, Ida, like the terrified Parisian whores, is paralysed until the constable 'touched her arm impatiently', and she is obliged to 'walk along by his side' (p. 195). Her stay in prison only enhances her purity and determination never to enter the profession again, almost as if she has been successfully reclaimed in a penitentiary.

The novels also fit into Walkowitz's model of the 'fictions of sexual danger' popular in 1880s London, such as W.T. Stead's *Maiden Tribute* and the reporting of the Ripper crimes in 1888, which she argues 'helped to consolidate a new public sphere' and 'shaped the way men and women of all classes made sense of themselves and their urban environment'.[74] In a scene symbolic of women's vulnerability to the dangers of the streets, the middle-class Maud Enderby, curious to see the squalor of Litany Lane where Waymark works as rent-collector, is caught up in an East End brawl:

> A sudden desire possessed her mind; she would go out into the streets of the town and see something of that life which she knew only in imagination, the traffic of highway and byway after dark, the masque of pleasure and misery of sin of which a young girl can know nothing … Forth from the alley just before her, rushed a woman of hideous aspect, pursued by another, younger, but, if possible, yet more foul … the one in pursuit, with a yell of triumph, sprang upon her prostrate enemy, and attacked her with fearful violence … In a moment there was a thick crowd rushing round, amid which Maud was crushed and swayed without possibility of disengaging herself … But only for a moment or two could Maud understand anything; horror and physical oppression overcame her senses. Her fainting caused a diversion in the crowd, and she was dragged without much delay to the nearest doorstep. (pp. 218, 219)

Maud's reaction to the crowds and 'fearful violence' of 'the streets' typifies her lack of knowledge about her urban environment and her middle-class fear of the dangerous classes perceived as 'hideous', 'foul' and uncontrollable. Rather than relishing such riotous scenes as Harriet does, she is 'crushed' and passive in the midst of the crowd, so much so that she has to be dragged out of it and put into a cab by Waymark. Drawing on sensationalist perceptions of the city as a modern

---

the newly appointed Metropolitan Police Commissioner who was shortly to be involved in investigating the Ripper crimes, gave directions in 1887 to discontinue watching brothels as this constituted a waste of police time. See p. 161.

[73] Higgs, p. 276. The policeman is unsympathetic to the prostitute's plea that she is 'out of work', replying 'you all say that'.

[74] Walkowitz, *City of Dreadful Delight*, p. 80.

Babylon of pleasure and sin, the passage both suggests that young girls should stay inside and that their curiosity and naivete about street-life may be a disadvantage. In contrast, Helen Norman repeatedly has to travel to this 'remote neighbourhood' (p. 219) as part of her philanthropic duties, but is dismissive of her guardian's fears about her safety after dark, framed in typically patriarchal terms: 'do you consider it altogether ladylike to be travelling about London, alone, at such hours? ... young ladies do not, as a rule, permit themselves to indulge in such night excursions' (Vol 2, p. 105). However, according to Martha Vicinus, philanthropy was one of the few occupations which granted ladies 'freedom to walk and move in areas ... previously forbidden', illustrated in the heroine's ability to gradually acclimatise herself to the alien territory of the East End.[75] Although Gissing claimed that he had 'never known' a woman like the idealised Helen,[76] she appears to be modelled on such contemporary figures as the social worker Octavia Hill, and the philanthropic women who later moved into the new East End settlement houses in the 1880s.[77] Perhaps the city is only a place of danger to those who lack the opportunity of learning how to negotiate it.

The question remains as to whether prostitutes were able to negotiate themselves a recognised position on the streets, or whether the accelerating social purity campaign stripped them of their freedoms. As feminist historians have pointed out, the closing of brothels effectively put women back on the streets against their will;[78] in 1888 some of them would fall prey to the knife of the Ripper, signalling their vulnerability and the inadequacies of police protection. Heavily influenced by the language of purity, the medical press seized the opportunity to comment on the greater freedom that streetwalkers now appeared to enjoy after the repeal of the Contagious Diseases Acts in 1886.[79] The *Lancet* claimed that women were the 'aggressive parties' in initiating encounters with potential clients and that 'men should be able to walk to and from their business without having the social evil thrust upon them night after night and year after year'.[80] This clearly attributed women's aggression to their over-active sexualities and failed to recognise the designated districts such as Charing Cross, Leicester Square and Regent Street that were the haunts of prostitutes,[81] prioritising men's

---

[75]   Martha Vicinus, *Independent Women: Work and Community for Single Women, 1850–1920* (Chicago: University of Chicago Press, 1985), p. 220.

[76]   Letter to Frederic Harrison, 23 July 1880. *Collected Letters, Vol 1*, p. 294. He linked the heroine to his conceptualisation of the 'Ideal', lamenting 'Alas! I have never known a Helen Norman; she is the creation of my own mind yearning after intellectual converse with such natures as, if my opportunities extended, I might perhaps find somewhere in the world'.

[77]   See Vicinus, pp. 213–27, for a detailed account of Hill's involvement with the new settlement houses.

[78]   Bland, p. 102. Some feminists, such as Josephine Butler, publicly registered their disapproval of such measures, which, they pointed out, were hardly in women's interests.

[79]   'The Repeal of the Contagious Diseases Acts: A Suggestion', *Lancet,* 15 September 1888, p. 529.

[80]   'The "Social Evil" in London', *Lancet,* 8 December 1888, p. 1146.

[81]   Bartley, p. 3.

commuting over women's 'patches' in certain areas of the city. It also shows prostitutes being 'treated as public nuisances', failing to acknowledge the work they were involved in as socially important.[82] But naturalist fiction increasingly sought to revise this denial of urban territory to the prostitute. In *The Unclassed*, the streetwalker is very much associated with the commercial centre but has some choice about her urban abode. Lotty chooses to live away from the 'crowded centre' and 'the quarters consecrated to her business' (p. 22), whereas Ida's relish for 'the noise and the crowds' means that she prefer to reside 'in the very middle of the town' (p. 90). In the short story 'To Bow Bridge' in Arthur Morrison's collection *Tales of Mean Streets* (1896), the 'bonnetless drab' travelling on the last tram-car to Bow is differentiated from both the 'decent woman' with children and the married women eating fried fish, yet is granted a place within the urban scene. Although the mother resists her offers of money and frowns as she greedily snatches one of the children onto her knee, whom she has been eyeing like 'dolls in a toyshop window' (p. 57),[83] neither she nor any of the other passengers comments on her profession. At the end of the story, after helping one of the children off the car, the harlot is last glimpsed pursuing a drunken man heading towards Bow Bridge, as 'tightening her shawl, she went in chase!' (p. 60). The narrator's veiled admiration, suggested by that final exclamation mark, can be read as a recognition of the streetwalker's right to travel westward to 'work her patch', in fitting with the story's lack of judgement about prostitution. Whilst the social purity campaigners were by now creating a climate of surveillance and repression in order to keep working-class women and their sexualities under control, such a recognition valorises woman's right to streetwalk as some form of resistance. It is worth pointing out that the legitimacy of the prostitute's place outside the West End theatres seems to be endorsed in both of Gissing's novels, though this is also the place from which she must be rescued by the middle-class hero. However, in the early novel Carrie refuses Golding's pleas to stay in her rooms at night, because 'it was agony to him to think of her walking about the streets without his company and protection' (Vol 2, p. 340), dismissing the need for male protection. Aspiring to the same resistance to an increasing culture of surveillance, Gissing's streetwalkers have to struggle to protect their precarious freedoms in order to mount a 'challenge to the city's sexual geography'.[84]

Reclaiming the Prostitute

The question of whether degraded prostitutes could ever be purified and reclaimed into a better life underpinned fictional treatment of fallen women at this time, increasingly in the 1890s with the advent of the New Woman novel. Persuaded by his publishers to bring out a second edition of *The Unclassed* in 1895, Gissing

---

[82] Bartley, p. 158.

[83] All quotations are taken from Arthur Morrison, *Tales of Mean Streets* (London: Heinemann, 1896).

[84] Deutsch, p. 12.

seized the opportunity to sanitise his novel, editing out seemingly inappropriate scenes and bringing it up to date by downplaying the urban degradation elements. Although he announced in the Preface to the new edition that he felt that 'nowadays, the theme and its presentment will, at worst, be "matter for a flying smile"',[85] in fact the emphasis on the prostitute's 'absence of shame' in a climate of social purity was almost as contentious as it had been in 1884. Whereas images of suffering and degraded women had been used as propaganda in the repeal cause, as it was 'politically expedient' to aim for this kind of representation,[86] more risqué 1890s novels often allowed fallen women to tell their stories openly in a way that solicits the sympathies of the reader. Drawing on the New Woman novel's concern with sexual double standards, Annie Holdsworth's *Joanna Traill, Spinster* (1894) is typical of the more sympathetic portrayal of the prostitute. The narrative of the feminist Joanna Traill's largely successful attempts to reclaim Christine Dow by removing her from the streets to her own home, a situation which had contemporary analogues in the philanthropic activities of the prominent repeal activist, Josephine Butler,[87] concludes with the marriage of the prostitute into the middle classes. Holdsworth's position as co-editor of the feminist journal *The Woman's Signal* obviously informed her views on philanthropy and necessitated her involvement in topical issues. More influenced by the language of purity feminism, her novel is also at times more radical in its emphasis on the need to alter public opinion about fallen women and its blaming of men for women's ruin. However, its radical and explicit nature did not offend the *Athenaeum* reviewer and even inspired praise for its portrayal of the prostitute, a 'delightful personage', with 'the mixture of refinement with occasional vulgarity and lawlessness' lending her character 'a novel piquancy'.[88] Christine's refreshingly open attitudes to sexuality and her absence of shame may have appealed to a new generation of female readers weaned on the sexual openness of New Woman fiction, but the 'piquancy' of her character was still contradictory: she is described as 'a luxurious, ambitious, little creature, with nothing but an instinct female purity and a strong love of cleanliness to save her from the uttermost degradation' (p. 46).[89] The *Bookman* recognised this incoherence in the history of this 'difficult young woman', pointing out that Holdsworth initially showed her to be eager to return to the excitement of the streets, but then portrayed her as amenable to reclamation and happy to accept the middle-class position of philanthropist.[90] Borrowing from feminist accounts of prostitution which tended to promote the importance of philanthropy and to stress

---

[85] Preface to the New Edition, October 1895. Quoted in Korg, n.p.

[86] Walkowitz, *Prostitution and Victorian Society*, p. 110.

[87] Josephine Butler, one of the founders of the Ladies' National Association in 1869, nursed dying prostitutes in her own home as part of her campaign against the Contagious Diseases Acts. See Paul McHugh, *Prostitution and Victorian Social Reform* (London: Croom Helm, 1980), pp. 19–21 and Walkowitz, *Prostitution and Victorian Society*, pp. 90–136.

[88] Review of *Joanna Traill, Spinster*, *Athenaeum*, 25 August 1894, p. 250.

[89] All quotations are taken from Annie K. Holdsworth, *Joanna Traill, Spinster* (London: William Heinemann, 1894).

[90] Review of *Joanna Traill, Spinster*, *Bookman*, September 1894, p. 183.

woman's vital role in 'leading [the prostitute] back to a better life',[91] the novel challenged entrenched views of the fallen by commenting on what Butler referred to in one of her pamphlets as 'the sacredness of every woman even at her lowest, most degraded, and most despised estate'.[92] However, Butler's belief in the reclamation of prostitutes enabled by sisterhood and 'solidarity' between middle and working-class women was not shared by other philanthropists of the time, nor were reviewers entirely happy to endorse such positive images of 'degraded' women in fiction.

The reclamation of prostitutes is given a specific gendered resonance in the novels, as both Holdsworth's novel and *The Unclassed* examine the nature of the relationship between philanthropist and fallen woman, classified by Walkowitz as 'hierarchical, controlling, and punitive'.[93] Holdsworth satirises the 'fashion' for philanthropy, what the contemporary feminist writer Mrs Roy Devereux described as 'a morbid appetite for coquetting with sin',[94] and explicitly uses terms and images familiar from feminist accounts. We are told that Joanna Traill 'claimed sisterhood with the fallen, and yearned to reach hands of help to them' (p. 66). Her male associate, Boas, also stresses the need for sisterhood and has no qualms about commenting on Christine's 'wild', 'undisciplined' nature and the difficulties of taming her. Joanna is initially frightened by 'the girl's stormy passions' (p. 47), but proves herself adept at moulding her into a quiet and passive Victorian woman, whilst reprimanding her for her 'easy familiarity' with men. In Gissing's novel Waymark's repressed erotic interest in Ida and his belief that she is no 'common' prostitute prevent him from seeking to control her through reclamation. After giving money to a suffering prostitute outside a West End theatre, he is unable to repeat his philanthropic action with Ida because he recognises that she is of a 'different kind':

> In the case of an ordinary pretty and good-natured girl falling in his way as Ida Starr had done, he would have exerted whatever influence he might acquire over her to persuade her into better paths. Any such direct guidance was, he felt, out of the question here. The girl had independence of judgement, she would resent anything said by him on the assumption of her moral inferiority, and, for aught he knew, with justice. (p. 108)

The admission that working-class women may resent guidance and judgement of their sexual behaviour suggests a criticism of philanthropy and the hierarchies it creates, though Waymark's later attempts to educate Ida, whilst lending her money and introducing her to his friends, seem to negate his good intentions. Jeune had cautioned that philanthropy was 'essentially a woman's work; ... too fraught with

---

[91] Jeune, 'Helping the Fallen', p. 676.

[92] Josephine Butler, *The Bright Side of the Question*, reprinted from the *Occasional Paper*, 22 December 1883, n.p. Later in the pamphlet Butler writes movingly of 'this wonderful and beautiful solidarity of the women of the world before God', which will ensure 'purer morals and juster laws' in the future.

[93] Walkowitz, *Prostitution and Victorian Society*, p. 131.

[94] Mrs Roy Devereux, *The Ascent of Woman* (London: John Lane, 1896), p. 59.

risk for any man to attempt',[95] which is demonstrated in the increasingly risky nature of Waymark's encounters with Ida as his sexual desires compete with his feelings of sympathy. He questions her about her clients and has to deny himself the pleasure of 'passionate imaginings' about her sexual experiences. However, both Ida and her friend Sally appear happy to accept both financial and emotional support, without feeling that they are sacrificing their independence and identity in the way that Christine does; feminist reservations about male philanthropy are then kept at the margins of Gissing's text, though the problems of marrying sexually knowing and potentially 'vulgar' women, to be developed with a number of variations in later novels, are instead given more emphasis.

The narrative problem is that the prostitute's inferiority cannot be so easily glossed over when it comes to questions of marriage. The recurring pattern of the refined husband's thwarted desires to educate a vulgar wife, or potential sexual partner, out of her class, is clearly ripe for biographical readings. Grylls relates this pattern to Gissing's own experience, arguing that 'this helps to explain the inapposite pleas entered in defence of [Ida's] conduct', many of which were 'carefully excised' for the second edition.[96] Certainly, in *Workers in the Dawn* the difficulties which Golding encounters with Carrie, such as her lack of interest in self-education, relate to conflicts of interest over female vulgarity which Gissing had himself experienced. Carrie remains unreclaimed and unreclaimable, preferring to return to 'the old sphere of licentious gaiety' (Vol 3, p. 384) rather than toning down her 'disreputable conduct' (p. 382) as demanded by her husband, ultimately being abandoned by the author to drink herself to death in a Zolaesque indictment of the horrors of poverty. Reviewers stigmatised her as 'a woman whom it is impossible to raise', who 'has no doubt about the impropriety of her conduct, but ... allows her appetites and passions to rule'.[97] Such limited sympathy with the prostitute, an unfashionable and conservative position to adopt in the 1880s, is modified in the later novel, which offers a more detailed account of the dangers of marrying those 'unclassed' women who attempt to rise above their degradation. Typically, Gissing is interested in the difficulties of reconciling sexual desire with the need to marry, dwelling on Waymark's fears that 'the alliance between them could only be a mere caprice on her part, such as girls of her kind are very subject to' (p. 111). Waymark's knowledge of 'the characteristics of girls of this class' (p. 141) assures him that she does not have 'the capacity for love' (p. 142), nor the ability to tell the truth, making her unsuitable as a potential wife. Branding Ida as a girl of a particular kind and class, who exhibits specific 'characteristics', betrays his belief in society's image of the sexual deviance of the working classes. For the 1895 edition, Gissing toned down the sexual content of the novel, including editing out a scene in which Waymark kisses Ida in her rooms;[98] for the later edition his repression of his desires until he is convinced of

---

[95] Jeune, 'Helping the Fallen', p. 681.

[96] Grylls, p. 33.

[97] Reviews of *Workers in the Dawn, Spectator,* 25 September 1880, liii, 1226–7. Quoted in Coustillas & Partridge, p. 62. *Manchester Examiner & Times*, p. 3.

[98] Grylls, p. 157.

Ida's purity is more important. Contemporary reviewers failed to believe in his honourable intentions, the *Academy* offering the view that 'a long-continued platonic attachment between a normal young man – even of aesthetic tastes – and a London prostitute is an incident hardly within the range of probability'.[99] The prostitute's sexual knowledge makes her an object of desire but she cannot suddenly adopt the sexual characteristics of another class in order to satisfy requirements for an ideal wife; Ida's pleas that Waymark treat her as if she were 'a modest girl' are denied by the inferiority she cannot escape. In *Joanna Traill, Spinster*, the middle-class Bevan, attracted to Christine's independence as well as her capacity to fill the role of domestic angel after her reclamation, is horrified by the revelation that his intended wife has inhabited the dens and streets of London. In a conversation about reclaiming the fallen with Boas early in the novel, he voices his lack of confidence in the project of introducing reformed prostitutes into middle-class homes: 'She'd demoralise the butler, and run away with the spoons ... I don't think a woman once polluted would ever be clean, no matter where you put her' (p. 96). Holdsworth uses the New Woman plot to critique male sexuality in the style of Sarah Grand, overtly condemning Bevan for his conventional views about female sexuality. But it is behaviour learned on the streets which has enabled Christine to attract Bevan in the first place; like Waymark, he is attracted to the prostitute's sexual agency and control as both women are confident about initiating encounters with men, whether money is involved or not. Male attitudes to working-class women are then shaped by repressed desires; Waymark's need for a 'pliant and docile' wife cannot be squared with his attraction to the passionate, sexually experienced woman.

Both texts reflect the influence of the social purity movement in their final statements about prostitution, but challenge the more conservative views of philanthropists in indicating that working-class girls can retain their purity even after life on the streets. Gissing ultimately allows Ida to become Waymark's 'ideal woman', though this is achieved by first rescuing her into the middle class after a reconciliation with her rich grandfather. Whether they marry or not remains ambiguous at the end; the conservative plot resolution may also have had more to do with the demands of publishers about the third volume than Gissing's own plans, which, as Korg notes, were more likely to have resulted in an unhappy marriage to Maud.[100] The transformation of prostitute into philanthropist used by Holdsworth is also present here as in a rather sickly symbolic scene Ida wipes the dirty faces of the girls from Litany Lane at a garden-party at her new middle-class home, in the vain hope of distracting them from the 'occupations degrading to womanhood, blighting every hope' (p. 294) to which they will inevitably turn. Her reclamation is figured in a speech she imagines delivering to Waymark, in which she proclaims, 'it is no arrogance to say that I am become a pure woman; not my own merits, but love of you has made me so' (p. 292). By crediting her male rescuer with the ability to 'wipe her dirty face' and erase her degrading occupation, the prostitute's reclamation effectively endorses the value of philanthropy, a

---

[99] Review of *The Unclassed, The Academy*, 1884, p
[100] Korg, Introduction to *The Unclassed*, p. xiii.

similar narrative trajectory to that employed by Holdsworth. Contemporary reviewers were not so positive, perceiving the purification of a prostitute as problematic and unrealistic. One remarked, 'the notion that the mind of a prostitute can remain pure and unsullied in the midst of her profession is simply contrary to fact, however well it may fit in with this or that theory. On the other hand, we fail to see how any objection can be taken to the theory that love can save the streetwalker from her life of degradation, and even purify her heart from the pollution of the past'.[101]

The theory that streetwalkers could be saved by love was unobjectionable because it fitted in so well with current thinking about reclamation, which would only work with the 'just fallen', rather than the truly degraded. The formation of Ladies' Associations intended to prevent prostitution in the 1880s and 1890s was in effect a response to 'the alleged inadequacy of the reform movement in curbing prostitution', which achieved effects precisely because they targeted those working-class girls most amenable to middle-class intervention. In her study of the Ladies Associations for the Care of Friendless Girls, Bartley reminds us that 'time after time, working-class women were categorised into the deserving and the undeserving, a division consonant with the class ideology of the time'.[102] Whereas Gissing's undeserving single mother Carrie had been abandoned to her fate, Ida's reform is hinged on her status as deserving and would-be respectable, making her purification possible. And yet this is only achieved by displacing the degraded characteristics of the prostitute onto her alter ego, Harriet, who resists any attempts at middle-class control. Whereas both Ida and Sally are able to pass as respectable women when accompanied by men on their Sunday afternoon excursions to Richmond, Harriet's behaviour on the streets gives away her lower-class status in no uncertain terms, suggesting that the prostitute cannot be so easily repositioned from her accepted sphere. In this context, Harriet's tendency to hysteria, exacerbated by her restlessness, seems to confirm her position in the underclass:

> When she remained away from home till after midnight, Julian was always in fear lest some accident had happened to her, and once or twice of late she had declared (whether truly or not it was impossible to say) that she had had fits in the open street. Weather made no difference to her; she would leave home on the pretence of making necessary purchases, and would come back drenched with rain. Protest availed nothing, save to irritate her. At times her conduct was so utterly unreasonable that Julian looked at her to see if she had lost her senses. And all this he bore with a patience which few could have rivalled (pp. 176–7)

Already compromising herself by staying out late, Harriet's fits in the 'open' street, 'open' to the observation and classification of others, suggest her inability to control her behaviour and her resistance to Julian's middle-class intervention. They also constitute another biographical detail linking Harriet to prostitution; Gissing's diary details his embarrassment on occasions when he was obliged to go and collect Nell from public places where she was suffering similar attacks. Her

---

[101] 'A Novel for Men', p. 1.
[102] Bartley, p. 111.

'unreasonable' conduct and the suggestion of madness also anticipate late-Victorian research into prostitutes as feeble-minded, unable to comprehend or modify their own actions. Here the ineffectiveness of Julian's protest and patience signals the failures of philanthropy in the face of a more degraded specimen of streetwalker. Later refusing to go to a hospital to be cured of her deteriorating condition, Harriet dies by falling downstairs in a fit after a quarrel, a fitting end for an undeserving, unlikable character. But the punishment inflicted on the undeserving version of the streetwalker, who always insisted that Ida and her mother were the 'bad' women, throws into question the models of femininity on which Gissing's narrative rests and exposes the narrative manoeuvre required for a streetwalker to be saved by the love of a middle-class hero. For Constance Harsh, the dissatisfactory 'romantic clichés' of this resolution expose 'the limits of naturalist fiction in the English tradition' and the authorial admission that 'you can't ever *really* be unclassed, and to the extent that you are you're unstable or insane'.[103] It is difficult to achieve the reclaiming of the prostitute without the concomitant recognition of her status as an 'object of class guilt as well as fear',[104] undermining the narrative endorsement of her ability to elude and resist middle-class control.

Gissing's early novels then provide a typically ambiguous commentary on streetwalking, tempering the excesses of working-class sexuality as depicted in French naturalist fiction whilst seeking to go beyond the restrictive and alarmist images of the degraded prostitute promoted by late-Victorian reformers. By rewriting the 'downward histories' of the bolder prostitutes, his alternative narratives raise a series of questions about the attractions of the prostitute lifestyle to young working women worn down by the drudgery of domestic service and other menial occupations. Through a detailed examination of the working-class woman's role as a streetwalker or 'girl of the town', he is able to delineate the urban freedoms she enjoyed in spite of the restrictions imposed by both men and the police on her cherished independence. Her confident occupation of public space suggests that she has succeeded in carving out her own niche on the London streets. However, by refusing to represent streetwalking in wholly negative terms, naturalist fiction also ran the risk of idealising the profession. As Wilson has cautioned, 'no feminist should ever romanticize the prostitute's lot in the way that men have so often done', though it is equally necessary to resist the tendency to 'overemphasize the passivity and victimization of women' built on a rigid and restrictive distinction between public and private.[105] Whilst Gissing's first novel does observe generic and cultural conventions by transforming the prostitute into a victim of the degradations of drink, this is avoided, albeit narrowly, in the more mature work *The Unclassed* by the reclamation of its working-class heroine in line

---

[103] Constance Harsh, 'Gissing's *The Unclassed* and the Perils of Naturalism', *English Literary History* 59 (1992), 911–938 (pp. 912, 933). Her argument about insanity is based, however, on the figure of Maud Enderby, rather than Harriet, who has been generally ignored by critics.
[104] Walkowitz, *Prostitution and Victorian Society*, p. 4.
[105] Wilson, 'The Invisible *Flâneur*', p. 105.

with the ideals of social purity feminism. As Maria Teresa Chialant has argued in her reading of the feminisation of the city in Gissing's fiction, this is one of the first texts to indicate the author's interest in the transgressive 'public woman', 'characterized by her relationship with the city, through a sort of appropriation of the urban space that questions the traditional opposition between the "feminine" sphere of the home and the "masculine" sphere of the metropolis'.[106] It is the working-class woman's claims to the masculinised metropolis and the concomitant freedoms of public space that he was to explore in more detail in the later 1880s fiction.

---

[106] Maria Teresa Chialant, 'The Feminization of the City in Gissing's Fiction: the Streetwalker, the *Flâneuse*, the Shopgirl', in Bouwe Postmus (ed.), *A Garland for Gissing* (Amsterdam: Rodopi, 2001), p. 52.

Chapter 2

Industrious, Independent Women: Labour and Leisure for the East End work-girl

Marked by riots, growing trade-union agitation and increased interest in the ideals of Socialism, the mid to late 1880s also saw the development of social investigatory research into the working conditions and lifestyles of the urban poor. Concerns about housing, poverty and the general state of the London slums prompted politicians, socialists and feminists to target the working classes as a major social problem. Discourses about the city then increasingly singled out working women as important objects of investigation, often identifying them as sources of degradation but also commenting on their exploitation as 'cheap labour' under a harsh capitalist system. As Clementina Black, a founding member of the Women's Trade Union Association and a tireless campaigner for the rights of women in industry, claimed in 1889:

> There is perhaps no class of whom the wealthy or the educated know so little of as working women. Everybody in these days knows something of the slums, something of the crofter's cottage and the Irish cabin; but the industrious, independent woman who spends her days working at a skilled trade in a factory crosses our path but seldom, and few of us know anything of her thoughts, her aims and her struggles.[1]

By focusing on the 'thoughts, aims and struggles' of the 'industrious independent woman', a new generation of female social investigators were able to bring to the attention of the middle classes their desperate struggles to survive and their resilience in the face of difficulties, providing a new set of narratives about working-class femininity and respectability. Barbara Harrison has noted the problems inherent in 'accessing [the] voices' of unknown working women who were often 'spoken for' by feminists and government officials with their views channelled towards political objectives.[2] Whilst novelists such as Gissing had a

---

[1] Clementina Black, 'A working woman's speech', *Nineteenth Century* 25 (1889), 667–71 (p. 667).
[2] Barbara Harrison, *Not only the 'Dangerous Trades': Women's Work and Health in Britain, 1880–1914* (London: Taylor & Francis, 1996), p. 216. She argues that 'in many instances [working-class women's] views were constituted by a context in which they were given or presented, and this was nearly always for the pursuit of political objectives'.

different agenda in their determination to 'speak for' the working woman, their attempts to represent her lifestyle authentically in the interests of realism still involved the editing of her narrative to serve their own political purposes. Nevertheless, his fiction sought to question stereotypical ways of thinking about the London work-girl at a time when, according to Philippa Levine, the demoralising nature of sweated labour ensured that, 'poor pay and monotonous work would certainly not encourage women to invest energy in their identity as workers'.[3] By fleshing out the 'unknown' lives of factory workers and other women in industry, he helped to re-energise debates about Victorian working-class gender identities which had been dormant since mid-century.

As Carl Chinn has noted, the 1880s have become associated with the emergence of 'traditional' working-class life, as the activities of social investigators and popular novelists ensured 'an explosion of interest in the urban poor and the genesis of the East End into their symbolic home'.[4] The new East End novels, including work by Gissing, Margaret Harkness, Walter Besant and, in the early 1890s, Arthur Morrison, charted the largely unsuccessful attempts of philanthropists to ameliorate the conditions of poverty, often depicting the shocking behaviour of the working classes in public spaces such as pubs and the streets as in serious need of middle-class intervention. Both Morrison and the French naturalist writer, Émile Zola, were criticised for their scenes of crime, violence and alcoholism, seen as particularly disturbing when women were the perpetrators rather than the victims. Avoiding the worst excesses of life on the streets as depicted in French naturalist fiction, both Gissing and Harkness nevertheless characterise the city girl in terms of her desire to inhabit potentially disreputable urban spaces, where the monotony of her labour is generally relieved by leisure activities conducive to casual encounters with men. As Scott McCracken has pointed out, 'paid employment is an entry ticket to *fin-de-siècle* London', which offers 'multiple stages on which new identities can be rehearsed',[5] not least the new urban femininities which fascinated the East End novelists. Deborah Epstein Nord has argued that the focus of analysis for the social investigators was primarily 'the domestic plight of working-class women',[6] but their experiences of a 'work culture', whether it be as one of many in a public workplace or completing piece work in the home to an employer's deadline, and their occupation of the public sphere for purposes of entertainment, were at least as important to the writers of fiction. Whilst 1880s narratives often seek to reinforce the working woman's place in the home, this is destabilised in Gissing's work by an insistence on women's presence on the streets and in public places in a culture

[3]   Philippa Levine, *Victorian Feminism, 1850–1900* (London: Hutchinson, 1987), p. 111.

[4]   Carl Chinn, *They Worked all their Lives: Women of the Urban Poor in England, 1880–1939* (Manchester: Manchester University Press, 1988), p. 10.

[5]   Scott McCracken, 'Embodying the New Woman: Dorothy Richardson, work and the London café' in Avril Horner & Angela Keane (eds.), *Body Matters: feminism, textuality, corporeality* (Manchester: Manchester University Press, 2000), p. 63.

[6]   Deborah Epstein Nord, *Walking the Victorian Streets: Women, Representation and the City* (New York: Cornell University Press, 1995), p. 208.

seen as hostile to the idea of working-class women's leisure. Fears about the sexualities of factory girls and workers in the public sphere, such as barmaids and actresses, are off-set by the cherished respectability of home-workers such as seamstresses, though both kinds of female labour have their drawbacks. Anticipating debates in the early twentieth century about married women's work, the novels also raise a series of questions about combining labour with childcare and the consequences of making wives financially independent of their husbands. It is in this sense that Gissing can be seen to be contributing to what Ellen Ross has characterised as 'the "discovery" of the mother', as middle-class observers of East End life increasingly recognised that 'mothers were the figures around whom ... working-class culture had coalesced'.[7] His sympathetic portrayal of both the working mother, and of the pleasure-loving work-girl, indicates his recognition of alternative models of working-class femininity.

Sweated Labour and the Factory Girl

The rise of the East End novel in the 1880s reflected both changes in social policy and advances in sociological research on the part of aspiring middle-class novelists, as the fashion for 'Amateur Philanthropy' 'penetrated into every region of daily life, and especially into literature'.[8] Because of their focus on the degradations of city life, such 'Philanthropic Romances' were often compared to the work of Zola, though English realist novels were generally considered to be superior to 'the Zolaistic taint' in their depiction of urban squalor.[9] Intent on proving his credentials as a serious novelist, and perhaps unconsciously emulating the French novelists to whom he had been compared, from the mid-1880s Gissing began to research the metropolis and its inhabitants more systematically. Reviewers of his early fiction repeatedly refer to his familiarity with the urban poor, as evidenced in his 'intimate knowledge of the conditions of artisan and pauper life in the dingiest purlieus of great cities'.[10] His agenda in developing his series of studies of the urban poor, in which early experiments with narrative in *Demos* (1886) and *Thyrza* (1887) were to culminate in the more mature work *The Nether World* (1889), has been addressed by John Goode, who argues that the fiction of the mid to late 1880s 'establish[es] the London that is to be the site of Gissing's fiction by portraying the "problematic" of working-class life'.[11] In a letter to his sister Ellen in 1886, Gissing boasted of this grand project he had

---

[7] Ellen Ross, *Love and Toil: Motherhood in Outcast London, 1870–1918* (Oxford: Oxford University Press, 1993), pp. 22, 23.

[8] Edith Sichel, 'Two Philanthropic Novelists: Mr Walter Besant and Mr George Gissing', *Murrays Magazine* (1888), 506–18. Quoted in Pierre Coustillas & Colin Partridge (eds.), *Gissing: The Critical Heritage* (London & Boston: Routledge & Kegan Paul, 1973), p. 115.

[9] Review of John Law's *A City Girl*, *Athenaeum*, 30 April 1887, p. 573.

[10] F.W. Farrar, *Contemporary Review* 56 (1889), 370–80. Quoted in Coustillas & Partridge, p. 142.

[11] John Goode, *George Gissing: Ideology and Fiction* (London: Vision Press, 1978), p. 72.

conceived, 'I have a book in my head which noone else could write which will contain the very spirit of London working-class life'. In a letter to Thomas Hardy, he cast himself in the style of a social investigator, promising 'I have something in hand which I hope to turn to some vigorous purpose, a story that has grown up in recent ramblings about Clerkenwell'.[12] To authenticate character studies, he not only explored the streets in which his characters lived, but also frequented both places of work such as factories and workshops and entertainment venues such as music halls, theatres and pubs. Whilst writing the Socialist novel *Demos* he complained to Ellen, 'the plot has cost me hours of construction ... and now I am obliged to go about attending socialist meetings'.[13] As David Grylls has shown, his extensive ramblings were supplemented by careful reading of contemporary sociological discourses about work and urban life, with details about living and working conditions in *The Nether World* drawn from Arnold White's *Problems of a Great City* (1886).[14] His aspirations to convey 'the very spirit of London working-class life' he took as seriously as the social investigators took their research.

Grylls argues that it is not until *The Nether World* (1889) that his 'carefully garnered documentary material' is able to 'sharpen [the] political edge' of his fiction but in both of the earlier novels his investigative skills are clearly deployed to 'vigorous purposes' which exceed the demands of plot. The narrative of *Demos* (1886) is organised around the changing fortunes of the mechanical engineer and fervent Socialist Richard Mutimer, whose sudden inheritance of his uncle's fortune allows him to put some of his Socialist ideals into practice. Rejecting his working-class origins means that he must also reject his seamstress sweetheart Emma Vine in order to secure his position by marrying the educated, middle-class Adela Waltham. The fluctations in Mutimer's fortunes and popularity are then mirrored in his controlling relationships with the two women, as Gissing uses the narrative of Emma and her sisters to expose the hollow ideals of Socialism and the difficulties of achieving social reform. Similarly, in *Thyrza* (1887) the philanthropist Walter Egremont sets up a series of free lectures on literature for working men in Lambeth and plans to open a library to be run by his star pupil, Gilbert Grail, until their friendship is sabotaged by Egremont's attraction to Grail's factory girl fiancée, Thyrza Trent. His schemes for bringing culture to the poor are destroyed by his subsequent rejection of the besotted Thyrza, whose death is hastened by Egremont's waning passion. Generally perceived to be the weaker novel, *Thyrza* certainly has less to say about the conditions of the workers but is nevertheless revealing about the lifestyles they achieved, with the story 'little more

---

[12]   Letter to Ellen, 31 July 1886, p. 48; letter to Hardy, 25 July 1887, p. 139. Quoted in *The Collected Letters of George Gissing, Volume 3 (1886–8)*, ed. Paul F. Mattheisen, Arthur C.Young & Pierre Coustillas (Ohio: Ohio University Press, 1992), pp. 48, 139.
[13]   Letter to Ellen, 22 November 1885, in *Collected Letters, Volume 2 (1881–5)* (1991), p. 367.
[14]   David Grylls, *The Paradox of Gissing* (London: Allen & Unwin, 1986), pp. 49–50, 54.

than a pretext for the portrayal of life in Lambeth', according to Goode.[15] In a pattern that was to become familiar in Gissing's fiction, both plots serve to illustrate that the male philanthropist's plans for social reform cannot be achieved without betraying working women and reinforcing their oppression under capitalism. Nevertheless, his wide-ranging representations of both the coarser, drunken work-girls and the more refined seamstresses and factory girls determined to rise above their oppression through hard work offered an alternative perspective on the lives of industrial women workers. According to Carl Chinn, 'the standardised image of the slum woman was of a person whose appearance and habits were commensurate with the miserable, squalid districts in which she lived … she was regarded as a foul-mouthed slut'.[16] But this image was being revised by investigators who refused to believe in the inherent 'coarseness' of women in industry: as Black claimed in an 1889 article on the 'virtues' of working women, 'the good feeling, the moderation, the kindness, ay, and the good manners, of the London working woman are a perpetual source of surprise to me … All the women, for instance, of whom I have spoken as known to myself and many more whom I know as well or better, are women of true respectability, honest, industrious, sober, self-respecting citizens'.[17] Whilst the struggles of the rejected working-class heroine came to symbolise the desperate plight of the urban poor in East End fictions targeting middle-class ignorance, Gissing sought to shift attention away from the passive acceptance of squalid conditions in the home and the workplace to the work-girl's heroic determination to preserve her respectability in the face of exploitation.

Although much of the research on sweated labour was not published until the early 1900s, the long process of gathering material about the exhaustive working conditions suffered by women began in the 1880s. The first page of Black's *Sweated Industry and the Minimum Wage* (1907) defined sweating as 'almost any method of work under which workers were extremely ill-paid or extremely over-worked'.[18] Female social investigators exposed the excessively long hours associated with certain trades – laundresses, for example, were legally permitted to work 14-hour days[19] – describing the physically demanding lifestyles imposed on women by slave-driving and inflexible employers. Insanitary working conditions were an additional factor cited in the medical press, which voiced concerns about

---

[15] Goode, p. 101. Goode actually seems to prefer *Thyrza* to *Demos* and devotes more space to the former in his consideration of Gissing's 80s' fiction, but does admit that it is 'a very thin and sentimental story'. Reviews of *Thyrza* also noted this 'thinness' and the deficiencies in plot, with one remarking on the inferiority of the third volume. See *Guardian* (London), 3 August 1887, p. 1161.

[16] Chinn, p. 18.

[17] Clementina Black, 'The Organization of Working Women', *Fortnightly Review* 52 (1889), 695–704 (p. 699).

[18] Clementina Black, *Sweated Industry and the Minimum Wage* (London: Duckworth & Co, 1907), pp. 1, 2.

[19] Black, *Sweated Industry and the Minimum Wage*, pp. 30–31. She points out that even this legal limit was frequently exceeded.

the deteriorating health of workers in badly ventilated workshops.[20] The extent of the problem can be seen in census figures from 1881 which show that 47% of women workers, or nearly half of the female working population, fell into the industrial class which suffered under such harsh conditions. Unskilled workers were particularly vulnerable, especially given limited training opportunities. Despite trade-union agitation for a minimum wage, earnings remained pitifully low, with women in some trades struggling to survive on as little as 7s a week.[21] This led some investigators towards the misguided belief that industrial workers had to resign themselves to their oppression. An 1887 article on 'Our Working Women and their Earnings', emphasising the 'starvation wages' of unskilled workers such as slop-shop sewers and match-box makers, offers the conclusion that 'the London unskilled industrial has no power of resistance' against her employers or the market.[22] In the late 1880s, however, strikes by the London Bryant & May match-girls and Leeds tailoresses, amongst others, did help to register the grievances of female 'sweaters' and to facilitate the formation of trade unions in particular trades.[23] As Levine points out, the 'new unionism' precipitated by successful industrial action and the welcome establishment of new women's organisations such as the Women's Industrial Council in the early 1890s were helped by 'shifts in the political and economic climate which made the concerns and efforts of workers' organizations both more prominent and more acceptable'.[24]

Whilst Gissing's representations of the London work-girl clearly borrowed from investigative discourse in their accurate depiction of the severe economic deprivations suffered by women in industry, they also sought to reinforce the possibilities of resistance which underpinned the increases in trade union activity at this time. The author was obviously impressed by Socialist feminist campaigns for better working conditions, which had an impact on his writing. In 1888, after his attendance of a match-girls' strike meeting, at which he listened to speeches by Clementina Black and Annie Besant,[25] he realised that 'the plot of [*The Nether World*] ... would not do' and began rewriting the end of the second volume. The

---

[20] Jenny Morris, 'The Characteristics of Sweating: The Late Nineteenth-Century London and Leeds Tailoring Trade', in Angela V. John (ed.), *Unequal Opportunities: Women's Employment in England, 1800–1918* (Oxford: Blackwell, 1986), pp. 96, 114.

[21] Robinson, 'Our Working Women and their Earnings', p. 57. This is the lowest wage cited for mill-hands.

[22] F. Mabel Robinson, 'Our Working Women and their Earnings', *Fortnightly Review* 48 (1887), 50–63 (pp. 50, 62).

[23] For details of the tailoresses' strike in Leeds in 1889, see Morris, p. 114. Clementina Black and Isabella Ford were instrumental in the formation of the Leeds Tailoresses Union following the successful strike.

[24] Levine, p. 116. The Women's Industrial Council merged with the Women's Trade Union Association in 1897; its aim was to 'watch over women in trades, and all industrial matters which concern women', as well as to provide better recreational facilities for industrial workers. See *Women's Trade Union Review* 1 (1891), p. 75. Quoted in Levine, p. 115.

[25] *Diary*, 8 July 1888, p. 35.

analysis in *Demos* centres on the figure of the seamstress, technically a home-worker but one who had to leave the home on a regular basis to collect and deliver materials. Evidence from an 1897 report by the Women's Industrial Council suggested that home-workers were 'probably the most completely wretched workers in our country'.[26] Emma Vine and her widowed sister, Kate Clay, share their poky and sparse rooms with an invalid sister, Jane, and Kate's young children, restricted to the domestic space by their trade and their caring duties. Signalling the dangers of working outside the home, Jane's ill-health has been brought on by walking long distances to work because she cannot afford any other transport; 'the fifth attack of rheumatic fever was the price she paid for being permitted to earn 10 shillings a week' (p. 35).[27] The inadequacy of this wage is confirmed in Black's study of sweated labour, in which she attests, 'all of us are aware that no young woman can really live, in a large town, the life of a civilised human being upon 10 shillings a week or less'.[28] To highlight the problems of combating the poor pay and uncivilised living conditions the Vine sisters endure, Gissing uses Mutimer as a mouthpiece for conservative ways of thinking about women's work: to Emma's complaints about her tiredness and the difficulties of providing medicines for the children, he responds by advising her to give up work, 'throw all that sewing out of the windows; we'll have no more convict labour' (p. 53). When his sister Alice no longer needs to go to work, he remarks 'I'm glad of it; a girl's proper place is at home' (p. 48). However, his flippant remarks about the undervalued labour of seamstresses and dismissal of Jane as 'another case against capitalism' (p. 35), which betray his lack of interest in the lives of individual workers, should not be seen to be shared by the author, whose wider knowledge of and antagonism to the exploitation of working women prevent him from adopting the easy solution of recommending women's withdrawal from the labour market in order to safeguard their health and dependency.

Indeed, the development of the narrative, which increasingly foregrounds the struggles of Emma and Kate, suggests that the stories of working women should not be dismissed so easily. Described by one reviewer as 'strong [and] original', Gissing's female characters were often admired, with a significant number singling out Emma as 'the most touching character'.[29] Looking back to the mid-Victorian social problem novel which broke new ground by giving working-class women voices and complex identities, Gissing devotes almost as much space to the characterisation of the Vine sisters as he does to that of his middle-class heroine. This was recognised by the *Spectator*, which claimed that Emma is 'so much more real than Adela Waltham, that we could wish his drift had enabled the author to

---

[26] Cited in Black, *Sweated Industry and the Minimum Wage*, p. 2.

[27] All quotations are taken from George Gissing, *Demos: A Story of English Socialism*, ed. Pierre Coustillas (1886; Sussex: Harvester Press, 1982).

[28] Black, *Sweated Industry and the Minimum Wage*, p. 42.

[29] Reviews of *Demos*, *Guardian* (London), 14 April 1886, p. 544; Julia Wedgwood, *Contemporary Review* 50 (1886), 294–6. Quoted in Coustillas & Partridge, p. 93.

make Emma Vine, and not Adela Waltham, his heroine'.[30]   In her study of
women's work for Charles Booth's *The Trades of East London* (1893), Clara
Collet came to the conclusion that 'mental activity is not a characteristic of East
End working women',[31] but Gissing avoids such stereotyping in his
representations of the divergent attitudes and inner lives of Emma and her
widowed sister. The 'slatternly' Kate, an unskilled slop-sewer dependent on her
more respectable-looking sister to go out touting for work, realises her frustrations
in outbursts of anger against her children and, at times, against Emma for her
passivity.   She eagerly accepts financial aid from anyone who offers and
encourages her sister to demand more money after Mutimer transfers his
affections: 'If I was in your place I'd make him smart. I'd have him up and make
him pay, see if I wouldn't' (p. 223). The flip-side of Kate's anger is Emma's
resilience and desire for financial independence through hard work.   Evidence
from feminist investigators suggested that attempts to limit working hours or
illegal overtime, such as the amendments to the Factory and Workshop Acts of
1895, were often met with antagonism by women proud of their earning
capacities;[32] in the *Englishwoman's Review* Helen Blackburn claimed that
protective legislation was 'diminishing the self-dependence of the worker'.[33]
Gissing dwells on the pleasure women gain from their self-sufficiency without
losing sight of the exploitative conditions they invariably accept: like Emma, the
hardworking Lydia Trent in *Thyrza* prides herself on saving money from trimming
hats for a pound a week, castigating her 'discontented' sister because she appears
'deficient in the practical qualities which [their] life demanded' (p. 50).[34] Emma's
claim that the sickly Jane would be 'miserable if she wasn't trying to work' (122)
may not quite ring true but her own staunch belief in the contribution women as a
collective make to the world's work, – 'we've got to work, that's all, and to earn

---

[30]   Review of *Demos*, *Spectator*, 10 April 1886, 486–7. Quoted in Coustillas & Partridge,
p. 84.
[31]   Clara Collet, 'Women's Work', in Charles Booth (ed.), *Life and Labour of the People of
London, Vol IV: The Trades of East London* (London: Macmillan, 1893), p. 267. She
expresses similar attitudes elsewhere in this section, seeming particularly concerned about
the 'immorality' of some of the younger girls.
[32]   Research on the Factory Acts revealed that working women's concerns about the Acts
'limiting the hours of work for women' were shared by some feminists. Jessie Boucherett
argued that 'restrictions on women's work are not advantageous to women' but rather
served men's interests, going on to complain about the lack of consultation with working
women before changes in the law. See Jessie Boucherett, Helen Blackburn *et al.*, *The
Condition of Working Women and the Factory Acts* (London: Elliot Stock, 1896), pp. 11, 19,
24. However, according to Barbara Harrison, the Women's Trade Union League argued that
'overtime was unnecessary, inefficient and injurious to all workers'. See Harrison, pp. 31–
2.
[33]   Helen Blackburn, 'Women's Work and the Factory Acts', *Englishwoman's Review*, 15
January 1896. Reprinted in *The Condition of the Working Women and the Factory Acts*, p.
76.
[34]   All quotations are taken from George Gissing, *Thyrza*, ed. Jacob Korg (1887; Sussex:
Harvester Press, 1974).

our living like other women do' (p. 224) – underpins her powers of endurance and 'steady opposition' to the problems of working-class life. Andrew August has characterised such attitudes in terms of 'a culture of women's work' in poor neighbourhoods, 'consistent with the general expectation of women's behaviour – that they would work hard throughout their lives',[35] where women's acceptance of the long hours required to earn economic independence and respectability is a significant element of their class identities. However, Blackburn also makes the point, particularly pertinent to unregulated home-workers, that 'the chief temptation of the British workwoman is to work too long',[36] suggesting that the disinterested attitude towards work shared by Kate and Alice Mutimer may be a healthier one than Emma's, who carries on sewing on Sundays and Bank Holidays. Mutimer's glib solutions to the working woman's difficulties may then gloss over the complex realities of her relationship to her work, where even sweated labour can bolster women's 'self-dependence', even if their sense of control over their lives remains ultimately illusory.

In *The Nether World*, Gissing attempts a broader panorama of women's work, contrasting the attitudes of factory girls with those of women entering the public sphere at a slightly higher level through acting and bar work. Extending his cast of working-class characters and pushing the middle-class philanthropists to the margins allows for a more nuanced picture of the lives of working women, with greater attention paid to the leisure activities and sexualities of women less restricted to the domestic space. Whilst Michael Snowdon and, to a lesser extent, Sidney Kirkham operate as the philanthropic figures bent on social reform, the workers struggle against circumstances in a much darker and more hopeless vision of the 'city of the damned' (p. 164) than the earlier 80s novels.[37] Vignettes of dire domestic conditions, marital conflict and street violence are interspersed with descriptions of various kinds of exhaustive and mind-numbing labour, with the more developed narratives of Jane Snowdon and Clara Hewett showing how attempts to rise above life in the London slums meet with little success. A good-looking girl who has been educated above her class and shares her socially aspiring father's 'impulse of revolt' (p. 79), Clara despises factory work, seeking to better herself by using bar-work as a route to the professions. With her unfitness for 'needle-slavery', the trade of her brother's sweetheart, Pennyloaf Candy, who makes shirts for 10d a day, 'Clara was saved from the dismal destiny of the women who can do nothing but sew' (p. 70) by taking work at Mrs Tubbs' Imperial Restaurant and Luncheon Bar on Upper Street. As a barmaid another dismal destiny awaits her in the form of 'insufferably long' hours, 'scanty earnings' (p. 84) and the constant fear of dismissal, merely an alternative form of

---

[35] Andrew August, *Poor Women's Lives: Gender, Work and Poverty in Late-Victorian London* (Cranbury, London & Ontario: Associated University Presses, 1999), pp. 118, 119. This argument 'challenges the idea that working-class women accepted a notion of the female sphere that did not include paid work'.

[36] Blackburn, p. 68.

[37] All quotations are taken from George Gissing, *The Nether World*, ed. Stephen Gill (1889; Oxford: Oxford University Press, 1992).

'detestable slavery' (p. 102). Sidney Kirkham argues for bar-work on the grounds that 'the girl can't put up with the work-room any longer. It's ruining her health' (p. 24) but once in the bar, 'her nerves were ceaselessly strung almost beyond endurance' (p. 84) and the 'outworn' Clara, on her feet until midnight, feels close to physical collapse.   The noticeable over-emphasis on the degrading and debilitating nature of bar-work may reflect Gissing's distaste for this form of industry: his heroine's turning away 'contemptuously' from the reflection of her 'vulgar' dress in the bar mirror, to be 'borne with for the present, like other indignities ... inseparable from her position' (p. 79), is a reminder of the 'demoralising tendencies' which prompted reformers to campaign against its suitability as women's work.[38] A rather alarmist article in the *Girls' Own Paper* in 1896 asserted that 'of all occupations undertaken by girls for a living, there is none more difficult and dangerous than that of serving at a "bar", or waiting in restaurants', commenting particularly on the 'language, jests and oaths' of men and the temptations of drink, prostitution and even suicide which these 'weary, lonely girls' must bear.[39] Drawing on Eliza Orme's 1893 study of conditions of work for barmaids and waitresses, Harrison deduces that 'views about this work were tainted by notions of respectability',[40] not least in the forms of sexual harassment which often eclipsed the long hours as the primary occupational hazard. A 1911 study of working women linked the likelihood of dismissal to the 'contaminating atmosphere' behind the bar, where girls may not be strong enough to fight off their employer's lascivious advances.[41]   However, it was also acknowledged by investigators that self-respecting women could learn to resist unwanted male attention: Peter Bailey argues that 'there is some significant indication that the barmaid protected herself from the beeriness and leeriness of the pub's sexual culture by her own manipulation of its particular parameters of distance and intimacy'.[42] Nevertheless, the attempt to 'abandon her work-girl existence' (p. 276) is perceived to be more dangerous for Clara, when her preferred profession involves the threat of contamination through the necessary trading on her sexuality.

---

[38]   Mrs Philipps *et al.*, *A Dictionary of Employments open to Women, with details of Wages, Hours of Work and other information* (London: Women's Institute, 1898), p. 16. However, the dictionary also noted those who, despite 'realiz[ing] the objections to a barmaid's life, consider that it would be injurious to women's interests to withdraw any opportunities of gaining an honest livelihood'.

[39]   'Barmaids and Waitresses in Restaurants, their Work and Temptations', *Girls' Own Paper*, 22 February 1896, pp. 329, 330.

[40]   Harrison, p. 113. See Eliza Orme, *Conditions of Work of Barmaids, Waitresses and Bookkeepers Employed in Hotels, Restaurants, Public Houses and Places of Refreshment* (1893–4).

[41]   M. Mostyn Bird, *Woman at Work: A Study of the Different Ways of Earning a Living open to women* (London: Chapman & Hall, 1911), p. 86.

[42]   Peter Bailey, 'Parasexuality and Glamour: The Victorian Barmaid as Cultural Prototype', *Gender and History* 2:2 (1990), 148–72 (p. 164). He quotes from George Moore's novel, *Spring Days* (1888) in which the barmaid heroine sees her bar-work as role-playing which does not affect her moral character.

Revising current trends in social investigation which similarly criticised the work-girl for her immorality, Gissing's 80s fiction instead seeks to validate the predominantly female working environment of the London factory girl. Clara Collet in particular commented on the 'mischievous influence' of factory women 'brutalized' by marriage on their companions in the workplace, claiming that their 'coarseness' would have adverse effects on 'respectable girls'.[43] In *Thyrza*, the description of the Lambeth hat factory where the Trent sisters and Totty Nancarrow work privileges respectability over the coarseness often associated with factory culture; the laughing workers who belong to 'the class of needlewomen who preserve appearances' are 'becomingly dressed' and affectionate, trading stories with 'much cheerfulness' (p. 261) as they work. In his more developed account of Whitehead's, the artificial flower factory in *The Nether World*, Gissing systematically delineates the 'various types of the London crafts-girl' (p. 127) distinguished by age, health and expectations, who choose to earn their living in the work-room. Although such types include those broken by ill health and those who have 'outlived their illusions', these are balanced against the girl who is 'already tasting such scanty good as life had in store for her'. Factory work for women is increasingly valorised in the following passage:

> If regularly engaged as time-workers, they made themselves easy in the prospect of wages that allowed them to sleep under a roof and eat at certain intervals of the day; if employed on piece-work they might at any moment find themselves wageless, but this, being a familiar state of things, did not trouble them. With few exceptions, they were clad neatly; on the whole, they plied their task in wonderful contentment. The general tone of conversation among them was not high; moralists unfamiliar with the ways of the nether world would probably have applied a term other than negative to the laughing discussions which now and then enlivened this or that group; but it was very seldom indeed that a child newly arriving heard anything with which she was not already perfectly familiar. (p. 127)

Rather than emphasising the monotony of making flowers day in and day out, the passage emphasises the camaraderie and contentment of the neatly dressed workers, who still have the ability to laugh and gossip despite the uncertainty of their employment; significantly Gissing makes no comment on the low level of wages in a 'season trade' considered by Collet to be 'extremely irregular'.[44] Here the low tone of the conversation is shown to contain nothing that a working-class girl might not already know, with Gissing explicitly distancing himself from the misconceptions of those 'moralists unfamiliar with the ways of the nether world' who might suggest otherwise. Countering current views about the 'weak emotional natures' of factory girls whose unskilled labour encourages them to 'float along with the stream, losing ... their very identity, and becoming as featureless and colourless as the very streets they live in',[45] the passage suggests that the identities

---

[43] Collet, 'Women's Work', p. 313.

[44] Ibid.

[45] Albinia Hobart-Hampden, 'The Working Girl of To-Day', *Nineteenth Century* 43 (1898), 724–30 (p. 727).

of London work-girls are far more colourful than has been imagined in the moral agendas of the social investigators.

However, such generosity is only achieved by the foregrounding of more 'refined' versions of the industrial woman worker. The ray of sunlight which lights up the head of Jane Snowdon, 'the child newly arriving', whose innocence has already been established in her suffering at the hands of her cruel and 'coarse' co-worker, Clem Peckover, symbolises Jane's superiority to most types of the London work-girl; a few pages later this is made explicit in Gissing's more judgemental comment that her laughter is so 'unlike the shrill discord whereby the ordinary workgirl expresses her foolish mirth' (p. 138). In order to atone for the 'shrillness' of the voices of more ordinary women like Clem and Bessie Byass, Jane's friend who makes flowers in her home,[46] Gissing consoles himself with the ideal of those who can rise above the vulgarities of their class. With her interest in reading and music, the cultured Thyrza, according to one reviewer, appears 'so very much above the average of the East-end hat-liner', leading W. T. Stead to conclude that Gissing had uncharacteristically idealised his heroine.[47] East End novelists usually avoided describing 'the lowest of the low', as Edith Sichel notes, with both Gissing and his contemporary Walter Besant exercising their philanthropic intentions on the 'better sort of work-girl'.[48] In *Demos*, Emma Vine, whose brief period working outside the home only serves to reinforce her separateness, also falls into the category of the 'better sort', as she refuses to enter into the banter of the workroom:

> She had no companions. The girls whom she came to know in the workroom for the most part took life very easily; she could not share in their genuine merriment; she was often revolted by their way of thinking and speaking. They thought her dull, and paid no attention to her. She was glad to be relieved of the necessity of talking … It was her terrible misfortune to have feelings too refined for the position in which fate had placed her. Had she only been like those other girls in the workroom! But we are interesting in proportion to our capacity for suffering, and dignity comes of misery nobly borne. (pp. 396, 397)

Mirroring Collet's perceptions of the factory girl's immorality, this characterises the merriment of the workroom as 'revolting' with an implied rebuke to girls who take life easily rather than suffer. The authorial intrusion at the end of the passage seems to confirm Gissing's preference for the suffering work-girl, whose dignity

---

[46]   This word was also used in Collet's descriptions of factory girls. See 'Women's Work', p. 322.

[47]   Review of *Thyrza*, *Whitehall Review*, 12 May 1887, p. 20; [W.T. Stead], 'George Gissing as a Novelist', *Pall Mall Gazette*, 28 June 1887, p. 3.

[48]   Edith Sichel, 'Two Philanthropic Novelists: Mr Walter Besant and Mr George Gissing', *Murrays Magazine* (1888), 506-18. Quoted in Coustillas & Partridge, p. 116. Predictably, this review constrasts Besant's optimism to Gissing's pessimism, though ultimately Gissing's realism wins out over Besant's 'Bowdlerised Whitechapel …[his] family edition of the East End' (p. 118).

rests on her awareness of and conscious struggle against 'the position in which fate had placed her'.

This raises the larger issue of the working-class heroine, as, perhaps if Emma, Jane or Thyrza had been like 'other girls', they would not have aroused the sympathies of the middle-class reader in quite the same way. Early in *Demos* when Alice swallows a whole pickled walnut at the dinner-table, the narrator excuses her appetite on the grounds that 'she would not have been a girl of her class if she had not relished this pungent dainty' but reassures the reader that she is 'only a subordinate heroine, and happens, moreover to be a living creature' (p. 38). In his reading of this passage, McCracken notes that 'the overt sensuality of Alice's mouthful participates at once in a gaze that renders working-class women available as sexualised beings and is at the same time a provocative critique of an ideology of domesticity that would deny women an embodied sexuality at all'.[49] There appears to be a certain problem in the concept of the working-class heroine, as if she is required to be less than 'living' or at least unrealistically desexualised in order to attain the dignity that Gissing cherishes. The narrator of *Thyrza* warns us that Egremont may see the heroine 'in the light of illusion', though closer acquaintance might reveal that 'after all she was but a pretty girl of the people, attractive in a great measure owing to her very deficiencies' (p. 245). In contrast to Mutimer's ignorance of the 'nobler features in Emma's character' which 'did not enter into his demands upon woman' (p. 135), as readers of urban fiction we are persuaded into accepting the 'nobler' qualities of working-class women, rather than their deficiencies. Notwithstanding this, Emma's refusal of a walnut, and indeed her general lack of interest in consumption, may be a sign of her idealisation, signalling Gissing's preference for deprived and suffering working women over those like Alice who know how to enjoy themselves.

The author's ambiguous attitude towards the camaraderie of factory girls, and his fears of their solidarity, from which Jane and Emma remain necessarily immune, may then help to explain his attempt to avoid confronting issues of working-class female sexuality, though this is short-circuited by his rather confused handling of Clara's alternative occupation of the public sphere. His treatment of her brief spell as an actress paradoxically suggests that straying too far from factory work carries its own punishment: her promotion from bar-work to acting, facilitated by her friendship with Scawthorne, ends in disaster precisely because of the immorality of the lifestyle and sexual rivalry between actresses. Acting, which Clara feels to be 'the work for which I was meant' (p. 286), proves to be no different from other forms of labour, another 'hateful drudgery' (p. 200) in which she 'strove so hard to make my way' with 'no friends, no money' (p. 286). Although acting was related to the modern woman who wants to 'get on' in a 1914 survey of professional work by the Fabian Women's Group, an experienced actress also warned of the 'humiliating and degrading philandering, [and] mauling sensuality which is more degrading than any violent abduction' in a 'very much

---

[49] Scott McCracken, 'From performance to public sphere: the production of modernist masculinities', *Textual Practice* 15: 1 (2001), 47–65 (p. 51).

over-crowded market'.[50]   As Tracy C. Davis has shown, despite blossoming as an employment sphere for women after 1843, the theatre was 'an unattractive alternative' to other trades because '[women's] rates of pay were lower, their professional expenses were higher, and their competition for employment grew more intense in the latter decades of the century'.[51]   Both Clara and her fellow actress, Grace Rudd, are 'abandoned to a fierce egoism, which the course of their lives and the circumstances of their profession keep constantly inflamed' (p. 203), with Grace finally accusing Clara of sleeping her way to a new part, 'We know how creatures of your kind get what they want' (p. 207). Significantly, their final exchanges before Grace jealously throws vitriol in Clara's face centre on ideas of friendship and competition: Clara claims 'there's no such thing as friendship or generosity or feeling for women who have to make their way in the world' (p. 207). More importantly, this is immediately compared to the solidarity of a 'troop' of Bolton mill-hands, whom she passes on her way to the theatre 'singing in chorus, a common habit of their kind in leaving work' (p. 208). Such a scene both serves to illustrate the precariousness and loneliness of the stage, and to redeem some of the errant heroine's dignity by positioning her outside such threatening forms of female solidarity. Gissing points out that treading the boards has ensured that 'noble feeling was extinct in the girl' (p. 203), echoing comments on the decline of Clara's character whilst working in the bar. This registers his disapproval of women who have to use their sexualities to earn a living, suggesting that the nobility he admires so much can only be acquired in the more 'feminine' trades, or maintained by a careful resistance of the coarseness of factory culture. It is only when the failed actress returns to the family home and is persuaded to take up the 'dismal destiny' of sewing that some of her nobility can be restored. However, she is scarred by her experiences in more ways than one, feeling 'an outcast' among the workers and questioning whether she can 'face life as it is for women who grow old in earning bare daily bread among those terrible streets' (p. 280). Forced to take up the role of suburban wife and mother in the house at Crouch End, her dissatisfaction with her position may be associated with her giving up work, never a wise move for a Gissing heroine. Her growing sense of separateness from the 'swarming' workers, 'driven automaton-like by forces they neither understood nor could resist' (p. 280), may gesture towards her thwarted ambitions to rise above them but also means that she cannot find her place within urban society, the 'terrible streets', leaving her in limbo at the end of the novel. Gissing's tendency to idealise the 'better sort' of East End work-girl results in a slightly sanitised version of the working-class heroine who can only make her way

---

[50]   Lena Ashwell, 'Acting', in Edith J. Morley (ed.), *Women Workers in Seven Professions: A Survey of their Economic Conditions and Prospects* edited for the Studies Committee of the Fabian Women's Group (London: Routledge, 1914), pp. 307, 299. This study stressed the actress's reliance on a good appearance and the dangers of sliding into prostitution because of the 'economic pressure' (p. 308).

[51]   Tracy C. Davis, *Actresses as Working Women: Their Social Identity in Victorian Culture* (London and New York: Routledge, 1991), p. 35.

in the world by rejecting friendships in the workplace and sacrificing her sexuality to a vision of the enervating comforts of home.

Marriage, Childcare and the Woman Worker

In her consideration of the married woman worker, Barbara Harrison notes that 'it was the perception of women's role in relation to the nurture, care and responsibility for men and children within the domestic domain which ensured that women's work in the paid labour market would become a major "social problem" of the late-nineteenth and early-twentieth centuries'.[52] Despite the relatively low number of married women workers, the question of maternal employment increasingly captivated social investigators and government officials, heavily influenced by the developing maternalist ideologies of the late 1890s and beyond. As Ross has shown, 'motherhood was all-encompassing for inner-London women throughout the two generations between 1870 and 1918', the majority of whom had many more than three or four children.[53] Fears about the neglect of children of working mothers were fuelled by anxieties about high infant mortality, inadequate housekeeping and degenerative diseases in the slums, rather than related to the problems of feeding large families on pitifully low wages. As Anna Martin shrewdly pointed out in her 1911 study of *The Married Working Woman* for the National Union of Women's Suffrage Societies, 'it is easier to attack the problem of infant mortality by founding Babies' Institutes, and by endeavouring to screw up to a still higher level the self-sacrifice and devotion of the normal working-class woman, than to incur the wrath of vested interests by insisting on healthy conditions for mothers and infants alike'.[54] In the introduction to a timely report by the Women's Industrial Council on *Married Women's Work* (1915), Clementina Black similarly argued against the middle-class opinion that 'a wife and mother who ... works must be withdrawing from the care of her home and her children time and attention of which they are really in need' and pointed out that on the contrary most married workers were 'steady, industrious women who are the very prop and mainstay of their households'.[55] Although some feminists complained that married women lowered wages to the detriment of 'the self-supporting spinster' by entering the labour market,[56] most recognised the importance of paid work to the working-class woman's economic survival,

---

[52] Harrison, pp. 34, 80.

[53] Ross, pp. 92, 97.

[54] Anna Martin, *The Married Working Woman* (London: NUWSS, 1911), p. 4. This study sought to attack public misconceptions about the married working woman which blamed her for society's failures. Her study of the working hours and careful budgeting of the lives of factory workers led her to the conclusion that 'nothing is so astonishing as the prevalence of the belief that the wives are bad managers and housekeepers' (p. 12).

[55] Clementina Black, 'Introduction', *Married Women's Work*. ed. Ellen Mappen (1915; London: Virago, 1983), pp. 1, 2.

[56] Robinson, 'Our Working Women and their Earnings', p. 54.

conceding that even if 'many employers discourage the labour of married women
… work is often a grim necessity to the married woman'.[57]

Representations of the working-class family in East End fiction tended to
reinforce this view of married women's work as a 'grim necessity' by highlighting
men's inability to provide for their wives and children. Arthur Morrison's 1890s
fiction, set in the most deprived London slums where unemployment and
starvation were facts of life, linked low family wages to the husband's reluctance
to stick to steady work, or the insecurity of the labour market. In *A Child of the
Jago* (1896), it is seen as acceptable that the respectable Hannah Perrott works 'not
only when [her husband] Josh had been "in" [prison] but at other times, to add to
the family resources' (p. 133).[58] But the rewards of the 'lucrative employment' (p.
134) of matchbox making can only be gained by enlisting the help of her children,
even the two-year-old Em who is so hungry that she eats some of the paste she
sticks on the boxes. Although Morrison's naturalist intentions prevent him from
making any direct moral comment on the practice of young children assisting their
mothers in 'sweated' home industries, this is clearly not portrayed as a desirable,
nor an isolated, situation – a widow who had died over her sack-making leaving
her children wailing with hunger by the body is another symbol of the inadequate
mothering ideologically associated with paid work. The starving, heavily
pregnant, Hannah is also shown 'tramp[ing] unfed' (p. 139) to the sack-makers on
a fruitless search for work, on the same day that she goes into labour, as if to
emphasise both her lack of control over her fertility and her employment, and the
conflicting demands they make on her labouring body. However, such disturbing
scenes are not solely intended to hold the mother responsible for her children's
poor nutrition but to show the home-worker to be at the mercy of an irregular
labour market. Hannah's shocking neglect of her children, seen as 'a never-endin'
trouble' (p. 15) to be left alone or 'disregarded' whenever possible, can also be
understood as a reaction to the difficulties of raising a family in the slums. Her
passive acceptance of her 'desolate condition as misprized wife and mother' both
positions her as a victim of environmental pressures and attempts to shift the
blame towards her unemployed husband: 'being neglected herself, it was not her
mood to tend the baby' (p. 51). As Roger Henkle has argued, 'the conditions of
Morrison's East End …diminish the capacity of women to act as an ethical force
in family and neighbourhood', reducing their status and making their subjection
more evident.[59]   Morrison's 'wretched and helpless' working mother can be
assimilated into Martin's model of the 'home-makers of the mean streets' who
struggle to survive 'without the least economic security' in the absence of regular
work for their husbands, though she is noticeably lacking in the courage attributed

---

[57]   Evidence from the Lady Assistant Commissioners' Report (1893). Cited in A. Amy
Bulley, 'The Employment of Women', *Fortnightly Review* 61 (1894), 39–48 (p. 47).
[58]   All quotations are taken from Arthur Morrison, *A Child of the Jago* ed. Peter Miles
(1896; London: J.M. Dent, 1996).
[59]   Roger Henkle, 'Morrison, Gissing and the Stark Reality', *Novel* 25:3 (1992), 302–20 (p.
304).

to Martin's interviewees.[60] Chinn's alternative image of the slum mother as one who wielded power as 'the pivot of the working-class family' is used to argue for the existence of a 'hidden matriarchy' around the turn of the century.[61] However, this is more likely to be evidenced in interviews than naturalist fiction, perhaps because investigators were able to offer a broader, if selective, spectrum of women's experiences intended to emphasise maternal courage, rather than helplessness, in order to direct future social policies.

The working mother's desperate fight for economic security is also examined in *A City Girl* (1887) by Margaret Harkness, who published several novels of working-class life in this period under the pseudonym of John Law; later novels, such as *Out of Work* (1888), address problems around employment for casual labourers, barmaids and Manchester seamstresses. Classified by the *Athenaeum* reviewer as another 'little romance of the East End',[62] her first novel offers a stern corrective to the pleasure-loving 'masher', Nelly Ambrose, in the form of an illegitimate baby and her ejection from the family home. As a struggling seamstress who finishes trousers for a sweater in Whitechapel, Nelly's romance with the married hospital treasurer, Arthur Grant, is doomed to failure, dashing her dreams about the leisured lifestyles of the West End. Arthur, who is 'accustomed to East End girls' (p. 45)[63] from his philanthropic work, is not prepared to give up his cosy middle-class existence in West Kensington, preferring to keep his exploitation of vulnerable work-girls a secret. Borrowing from the discourses of social investigation, with which she was familiar from her own journalistic work, Harkness delineates the wages, long hours and occupational difficulties of sweated labour with the same precision as Gissing: Nelly, like her 'pale-faced' co-workers, is a slave to her employer's wife, 'a driving woman' who 'could walk into a "hand's" room, and demand why trousers were not finished, without a look at the hand's dying baby' (pp. 58, 59). Sally Ledger has noted that Harkness's place in a subversive tradition of *fin-de-siècle* women writers is earned by her 'focus on the lives of London's "lost" citizens, the poorest of the poor whose plight was overlooked by all but a handful of novelists';[64] in this case, the working woman becomes 'lost' through motherhood. Once she is noticeably pregnant, Nelly's loss of respectability costs her her job; her impending motherhood is seen as a further loss of independence, as she 'grew every minute more hopeless, more desperate' (p. 108) in the search for employment.

---

[60]   Martin, pp. 10, 16, 23.

[61]   Chinn, p. 20.

[62]   Review of *A City Girl*, *Athenaeum*, 30 April 1887, p. 573.

[63]   All quotations are taken from John Law [Margaret Harkness], *A City Girl* (1887; London & New York: Dover Publishing, 1987).

[64]   Sally Ledger, *The New Woman: Fiction and Feminism at the Fin de Siècle* (Manchester: Manchester University Press, 1997), p. 50. However, Ledger argues that her choice of genre militated against her potentially feminist agenda, as 'one of the reasons why Harkness has been found to fall short both as a feminist and as a socialist in her novels is that she was locked into a literary naturalism which did not offer much in the way of affirmation for either of these political movements'.

Indeed, *A City Girl*'s subversive departure from the familiar urban narrative is most apparent in its detailed delineation of the effects of casual labour and deprivation on mothers and babies. Crying on the stairs or subjected to the violence of their drunken parents, babies are a serious economic liability to the Whitechapel mother, whose attempts to work are often thwarted by the ill-health of children brought up in insanitary conditions. Although Nelly enjoys a happy period when she, like Emma, is able to mind her baby whilst working on the machine, this is perhaps seen as a fantasy version of home work; Harkness implies that the pressures of paid work may interfere with domestic duties as 'often [Nelly] was obliged to leave [the baby] whining in its cradle, instead of taking it on her knee, for the work must be done to buy its food and provide its medicine' (p. 149). As Black reiterated, 'the question of whether young children suffer in consequence of their mothers being engaged in work for money' is an important one, but its relation to issues of neglect and infant mortality remained unresolved.[65] Without the financial support of a husband or her family, it is almost impossible for a single mother to earn enough to support herself and her child, so Nelly is obliged to accept money from her former sweetheart George for her rent. In response to Harkness's request for a critical appraisal of the novel, Friedrich Engels, Marx's Socialist ally, gave the opinion that her representation of 'a passive working class was inapplicable to London in 1887', a year after the Trafalgar Square riots had brought to the public attention the resistance of the London workers.[66] To me, this remark wilfully ignores the economic limitations under which the East End mother is shown to suffer; as Ledger points out, isolated female home-workers in the 1880s were much less likely to achieve political action facilitated by union membership than the male militant workers behind the riots.[67] Reliance on men is shown to produce instability and loss of self-respect in women, as once '[Nelly] was dependent upon him, she looked as if a breath of wind would blow her over' (p. 128). She is only able to vent her anger at the West End nurses who let her baby die, rather than Mr Grant, who reappears briefly in the narrative to be confronted with the vision of his 'little dead child'; we are told 'he had not time to think about "hands" in Whitechapel' (p. 170). Like Morrison's widowed Hannah, whose loss of a husband and her eldest son in the final pages makes her dependent on Parish relief, the bereaved mother remains 'hopeless and desolate' (p. 185), forced into a reliance on the Salvation Army and marriage to George, as the conclusion to the East End narrative typically reinforces women's limited capacity for resistance.

Nevertheless, this passivity on the part of the slum mother was to be challenged in Gissing's refusal of generic expectations, and his subversive attempts to reinstate the courageous working-class heroine and her resilience in the face of

---

[65] Black, *Married Women's Work*, pp. 4–5.

[66] Letter to Margaret Harkness, 1888. Quoted in Bernadette Kirwan, 'Introduction' to Margaret Harkness, *Out of Work* (1888; London: Merlin Press, 1990), p. vii. However, he did concede that East Enders were 'less actively resistant, more passively submitting to fate' than other working people.

[67] Ledger, pp. 46–7.

dire economic hardship. Grylls qualifies his discussion of the author's belief that 'the duties of a mother would not easily combine with a job' with the disclaimer that across his fiction paid labour was primarily for odd women and 'working-class wives, compelled to eke out their husband's wage'.[68] However, this seems a rather misleading summary which ignores the significant number of husbands in Gissing's novels who effectively force their wives into the labour market by either abandoning them, failing to get employment, refusing to give them money or simply dying. In *The Nether World*, on the insistence of her lazy new husband Bob Hewett, Pennyloaf Candy continues her shirt-making after marriage but is obliged to give up work after she has children, perhaps because she cannot afford a sewing machine so she can work at home like Emma. However, childcare and sewing are not always compatible: in Black's account of married shirt-makers, she cites an example of a home-worker obliged to go into a factory because her children were too lively, though in 1909 this woman is also able to pay 3d a day for a *crèche*.[69] In a scene where Jane visits her after work, Pennyloaf is shown feeding a dirty baby on the stairs whilst the other child plays in the squalor of the landing. Lamenting Bob's continual absence from the home, she confides, 'An' I get that low sittin' 'ere, you can't think! I can't go nowhere, because o' the children. If it wasn't for them I could go to work again, an' I'd be that glad: I feel as if my 'ed would drop off sometimes!' (p. 131). Here motherhood and work are seen as mutually exclusive, with Pennyloaf thinking longingly of her 15-hour days in preference to feeling confined to the home by the children. Although the division of labour between husband and wife is in line with current trends, it also questions the usefulness of a husband's higher 'family wage' when 'housekeeping' money is withheld from the wife: on several occasions Bob refuses to give Pennyloaf money for the children's medicine or bus-fares to the hospital. The minor character of Clara, Rodman's deserted wife in *Demos*, who works as a barmaid in order to support their son, links her economic struggles to the withholding of her share of her husband's money: 'How was I to support myself and the child? What was I to do when they turned me out into the streets of New York because I couldn't pay what you owed them nor the rent of a room to sleep in? ... But I've hungered and worked for seven years, and now it's time my husband did something for me' (p. 426). Rodman's reaction, 'Who'd have thought of you turning barmaid? With your education, I should have thought you could have done something in the teaching line' (p. 426), betrays a masculine unawareness of married women's limited choices of work: teaching is clearly not an option because of childcare problems during the day, only partially solved by Clara's decision to leave her seven-year-old son alone in bed during bar-hours, leaving her open to charges of neglect. Not only did demands for a family wage 'undermine the feminist demand for equal pay', according to Carol Dyhouse, they also left women 'at the mercy of their husbands rather than the capitalist

---

[68] Grylls, p. 159. This is part of an argument about Gissing's 'conservative' conception of female employment which I do not accept, though his comments on the incompatibility of marriage and work for middle-class women in the 1890s fiction is more persuasive.

[69] Black, 'London', *Married Women's Work*, p. 80.

employer',[70] in Pennyloaf's case, a much worse fate. The 'enslaving economic control of the husband', as the Fabian Women's Group pointed out in 1911, was another catalyst for the economic revolt of working women.[71]

By drawing attention to 'the urgency of the need to find ways of guaranteeing some economic independence to women within marriage',[72] Gissing anticipated developments in investigative research around working-class motherhood in the early twentieth century. Women interviewed for the FWG's survey of Lambeth mothers, which became Maud Pember Reeves's best-selling *Round about a Pound a Week* (1913), confirmed the huge difference marriage made to their lives: 'They tell you that, though they are a bit lonely at times, and miss the companionship of the factory life and the money of their own to spend, and are rather frightened of the swift approach of motherhood, "You get accustomed to it"'.[73] Extending the parameters of naturalist fiction, Gissing uses his narratives to develop the psychological studies of these lonely mothers interviewed by Reeves and her team; whereas in the eyes of the lady visitors working women were often 'suspicious and reserved',[74] in fiction their voices, though perhaps ventriloquising the beliefs of the author, can be made more prominent and their dissatisfactions clearly articulated. Although she never marries, in many ways by taking on the responsibility for her sister's children, the heroine of *Demos*, like Pennyloaf, quickly grows accustomed to the loneliness of motherhood. However, although Mutimer, unlike Bob, is always eager to pay for medicine for her family, Emma resents this eagerness and feels ashamed to accept money which is not 'her own to spend'. As Kate writes to Adela, 'he offered us money … but Emma was too proud, and wouldn't hear of it' (p. 270). Essentially, her powerful opposition to marriage because of its interference with her domestic duties signals her fears about becoming economically dependent on a husband; she later turns down Daniel Dabbs, Mutimer's erstwhile friend for the same reason: 'she could not imagine herself consenting to marry any man … she would have deemed it far less a crime to go out and steal a loaf from the baker's shop than to marry Daniel because he offered rescue from destitution' (p. 399). As Collet warned in her writings, envisaging marriage as a form of rescue from badly paid work was a temptation to be avoided, hence the 'wretchedness of married women' in East London once they realise 'there is no prospect of release'.[75] The reference to stealing a loaf rather than

---

[70] Carol Dyhouse, *Feminism and the Family in England, 1880–1939* (Oxford & New York: Blackwell, 1989), p. 92. See also pp. 88–91 for a useful discussion of the key arguments and contemporary responses to Black's *Married Women's Work*.

[71] 'Three years' work of the Women's Group' (c.1911). Quoted in Dyhouse, p. 57.

[72] Dyhouse, p. 62.

[73] Maud Pember Reeves, *Round about a Pound a Week*, ed. Sally Alexander (1913; London: Virago, 1979), p. 151.

[74] Reeves, p. 15. Reeves detects that some of the women were offering the kinds of answers which they felt were expected of them by visitors, though 'some were grateful, some were critical' of the interventions in their lives. See p. 16.

[75] Clara Collet, 'Prospects of Marriage for Women', *Nineteenth Century* 31 (1892), 537–52 (pp. 544, 551). She reiterated this opinion about the dangers of marriage throughout her writing career.

accepting a man's money perhaps figures the strength of women's desires to fill the role of bread-winner against the expectations of government and investigators alike.

Whatever his official views on a woman's proper place, working mothers and their economic plight certainly seem to elicit Gissing's sympathies twenty years before the Fabian Women's Group first visited the homes of poor Lambeth women. Praising the portrayal of Pennyloaf, the *Guardian* reviewer noted, 'Mr Gissing is tender enough to his poor, oppressed women, and draws them with true delicate touches of infinite pity'.[76] His touching scenes play on the reader's ignorance about the economic conditions suffered by poor women, many of whom work what Harrison has called 'the double day',[77] comprising both domestic work and paid labour. Selflessly atoning for her sister's carelessness, Emma is shown minding Kate's children and 'striving her hardest to restore order in the wretched home' (p. 393) after walking about all day in search of work. Bestowing on them the 'motherly care' (p. 393) of which Kate is incapable, she 'told her stories to the humming of the machine, and when it was nearly the children's bedtime she broke off to ask them if they would like some bread and butter' (pp. 395–6), even though they may choose to eat the breakfast she needs for her extra cleaning job. Despite the fact that her labour is so exhaustive that she is 'only fit for a convalescent home' (p. 393), Emma enjoys the feeling of economic independence in which she 'never accept[s] from anyone again a penny which she had not earned' (p. 397). Rather than complaining about the hardships of desertion, the stoical Emma acquires 'a certain hardness' (p. 396) as the novel progresses. Her central position in the narrative is then used to question the working mother's helplessness and to counter what Ellen Ross has characterised as the 'invisibil[ity]' of 'the large married women's work force in London' in this period.[78] Without a husband to control her, she stands as an inspiring, if slightly idealised, example of the independent industrious woman, who manages to combine motherhood with paid work at a time before the availability of *crèches* signals the recognition of the difficulties of child care for working mothers.

Widowed workers and deserted women are also made visible within Gissing's novels, often used to expose these difficulties of bringing up children without a husband's wage but also to suggest the potential benefits of the female-headed household. The widow is an important sub-category of the married working woman, though her significance in the labour market was not recorded in census returns until 1901.[79] Chinn has noted that 'widows and deserted women made up a

---

[76] Review of *The Nether World*, *Guardian* (London), 29 May 1889, p. 845.
[77] Harrison, p. 34.
[78] Ross, p. 45.
[79] Harrison, p. 7. The fact that women were only classified as married, unmarried or widowed in the twentieth century presents a difficulty in finding data on married women's employment prior to 1901, that may affect assessment of women's work in the period 1880–1900. See p. 6. See also Ross, p. 45, for the view that married women's work was also 'often unlisted by census enumerators either because the male "household head" failed to mention it or because the census taker viewed the wife's work as insignificant'.

significantly large contingent of the 11% of Booth's Class B, the very poor'.[80] Whilst Kate Clay's status as widow partly contributes to her deterioration and taking to drink, she clearly suffers from the lack of a husband's financial support, believing that women like her sister who seek to support themselves through work are fools. We are told 'she regarded her offspring as encumbrance, and only drew attention to them when she wished to impress people with the hardships of her lot' (p. 393). However, Kate's lack of maternal qualities is rather untypical of most other deserted women in the genre, who generally become more determined to provide for their children to prove that they can survive without a man. The reservation of certain trades for widows also implied some recognition of their desperate position: in Arthur Morrison's East End short story 'Lizerunt' from the collection *Mean Streets* (1894), 'mangling is a thing given by preference to widows' who also had 'the first call in most odd jobs'.[81] Andrew August comments on the 'severe financial difficulties' of female-headed households in the late nineteenth century, a high proportion of these households being run by employed widows.[82] But the resolution to Pennyloaf's story also suggests a way in which enterprising women can avoid the worst deprivations of the female-headed household. When her husband is fatally hit by a cab, she is left with only one surviving child, which nevertheless still prevents her from going back to her slop-work. Posing a problem as 'one whom society pronounced utterly superfluous' (p. 356), she is able to remedy her potentially 'disastrous circumstance' by combining resources with another widow, who has been struggling to run a clothing stall as well as looking after four children. By living together, they share expenses and childcare, and their partnership is then socially approved when the philanthropist Miss Lant helps to set them up in a small shop. This vision of women working together and in each other's interests forms a 'consolation' (p. 387) for Jane and perhaps also for Gissing's readers, as the vision of Pennyloaf and Jane laughing and sewing together and joking with the five children partially atones for the generally bleak tone of the novel's ending. Grylls has classified Gissing's eighties novels as 'anti-reformist fictions' exposing the author's 'uncertainty about cultural missionary work',[83] but some form of philanthropic help seems to be necessary to secure women's positions. Emma's economically precarious situation as household head is also somewhat alleviated by her acceptance of advice from Adela, whose Socialist sympathies prompt her to find the seamstress an alternative 'opportunity of work' (p. 471) outside Hoxton after Mutimer's death, though she is still too proud to accept direct financial aid. Whilst some feminists were understandably wary of State intervention into the lives of working-class women, those involved with the campaign for a minimum wage, the endowment of motherhood and 'the right of wives to a fixed share of their husbands' incomes' were clearly working in the economic interests of all women. As Black concluded, 'the grave drawback of much of the work done for money by married women is not

---

[80] Chinn, p. 2.
[81] Arthur Morrison, 'Lizerunt', in *Mean Streets* (1894; London: Methuen, 1912), p. 38.
[82] August, p. 106.
[83] Grylls, p. 26.

that it is injurious in itself but that it is scandalously ill-paid'.[84] Gissing is clearly in line with such feminist thinking in his championing of the rights of 'superfluous' widows and underpaid wives working in the home, reflecting his progressive endorsement of the greater independence to be achieved through married women's work.

The Recreation of Work-Girls: Frequenting the Streets and the Public House

Investigations of the London work-girl also encompassed the crucial issue of her recreation after work, often in order to highlight the threatening nature of working-class female sexuality if left unattended. Perennial fears about the degradation of the lower classes resurfaced in the debates about working-class leisure in the late 1870s and 1880s as the violence and drunkenness of the urban population increasingly demanded middle-class management: one article pinpointed 'the mischief arising from having no other convenient resort than the public houses', and the 'value of open space in cities' for the workers to socialise.[85] Women were specifically targeted in attempts to control occupation of disreputable public places, such as pubs and music halls, with the behaviour of factory girls singled out by investigators as dangerously immoral. The new unions such as the Women's Industrial Council attempted to provide working women with more appropriate entertainments in the safe environment of clubs, encouraging 'the autonomous development of a women's culture', according to Levine.[86] In an article on the need for clubs for working girls, Maude Stanley delineated the specific dangers of unregulated recreation:

> Our work-girls ... seek their recreation where alone they can find it, by loitering about the streets after dark when work is over, with some chosen companion; often it is with girls, sometimes in rough play with boys and lads. After a time the walk round, the looking into the shop-windows, the passing by the glaring gas-lit stalls in the evening markets, ceases to have interest. Then comes, according to their means, the visit to the music hall, the cheap theatres, the gin-palaces, the dancing saloons and the wine shop; then follow other temptations, the easy sliding into greater sin, the degradation and the downfall of all womanly virtue.[87]

Identifying the streets as a heterosocial space, where 'rough play with boys and lads' signifies the courting rituals of the working classes, the passage suggests that the 'temptations' attendant on other enclosed heterosocial spaces may seduce

---

[84] Black, *Married Women's Work*, pp. 14, 11.

[85] Rev. Harry Jones, 'The Homes of the Town Poor', *Cornhill Magazine* 13/60 (1889), 452–63 (p. 454).

[86] Levine, pp. 113, 115. The WIC, imitating the pioneering work of other unions such as the Women's Protective and Provident League, formed in 1874, 'placed considerable emphasis ... on the recreational facitilities it aimed to provide'.

[87] Maude Stanley, 'Clubs for Working Girls', *Nineteenth Century* 25 (1889), 73–83 (p. 76).

work-girls into 'greater sin', either casual sex or its commodified form, prostitution. The inclusion of the wine shop and the gin-palace underlines cultural concerns about the degradations of drinking, often associated with popular forms of working-class entertainment such as music hall and theatre, and linked later in the article to other forms of 'foul behaviour' like swearing, fighting and smoking. August offers a more positive picture of women's participation in 'the vibrant cultures of leisure in poor neighbourhoods', which may be closer to the social reality but he ignores the attendant difficulties of women's 'relaxation outside their homes'.[88] The prevalent fear is that women 'loitering about the streets after dark' are effectively trespassing on male territory and, moreover, adopting male habits, which will quickly ensure 'the downfall of all womanly virtue'.

This appropriation of the leisure activities of men was felt to be the particular province of factory girls, who were often characterised by feminist investigators in terms of their after-work behaviour. By the later 1890s, when more clubs had been established for working girls in order to teach them acceptable womanly behaviour,[89] factory girls were still being vilified for their presence on the streets. These women who 'go off in shoals to a crowded thoroughfare' and are 'always on the look-out for a lark' are shown to 'fall prey to every kind of bad influence, with no better guide than a weak emotional nature, and no higher interest than the pleasure of the moment'. However, this is qualified by the acknowledgement of their exclusion from expensive public entertainments, as the low earnings of factory girls actually prevent them from frequenting 'places of amusement except on rare occasions', compelling them to remain on the streets where they are 'learning no good'.[90] As Jenny Ryan has usefully pointed out, due to their greater visibility, working-class women had certainly acquired 'a niche in the emerging urban capitalist order ... yet in terms of urban social practices they were already marginalized and stigmatised by their status as women'.[91] Despite the sympathetic tone of some of these accounts, feminists who genuinely appeared to want to help their less favoured 'sisters' seemed unable to edit out their overriding disgust with the pleasure-seeking (and by implication, sexually curious) work-girl. As Nord has perceptively argued, 'the female social investigator's connection to the woman of the streets is a harder, more unsettling link to sustain than her affiliation with her

---

[88]   August, p. 127.
[89]   See 'Girls who work with their Hands: Insight into the Life and Work of Factory-Girls Given by Themselves', *GOP*, 16 May 1896, 517–18, compiled from letters sent into the magazine, which lists reading, evening classes and church as the main sources of female leisure. One dress-maker remarks, 'Girls in work-rooms get the name of being very careless in religious matters and of spending all their leisure time in the pursuit of pleasure, and some of it of a questionable character, but I am sure it is not so with the majority of work-girls' (p. 518).
[90]   Hobart-Hampden, 'The Working Girl of To-day', pp. 726, 727.
[91]   Jenny Ryan, 'Women, Modernity and the City', *Theory Culture and Society* 11 (1994), 35–63 (p. 55). However, as she goes on to admit, this conceptualisation rests on the totalising and misleading public-private dichotomy

working-class housewife double'.[92]   Collet's description of the factory girl is typically double-edged, half admiring and half condemning:

> She can be recognised on ordinary days by the freedom of her walk, the numbers of her friends, and the shrillness of her laugh. On Saturday evenings and Sunday afternoons she will be found promenading up and down the Bow Rd, arm in arm with two or three other girls, sometimes with a young man, but not nearly so frequently as might be imagined ... She goes to penny gaffs if nothing better is offered her; she revels in the thrilling performances at the Paragon or the music halls; and only too often she can be seen drinking in the public-house with a young man with whom she may or may not have been previously acquainted.[93]

Not to be confused with the 'thousands of quiet, respectable, hard-working girls' who also work in factories, this street-wise young woman enjoys her leisure, which ranges from the relative innocence of window-shopping to the dangers of drinking. In her informative oral history of working-class women, Elizabeth Roberts has argued that promenading was an approved social practice between 1890 and 1940, though her research suggests that for the majority of women it was an alternative, rather than a supplement, to courting in a public house.[94] Going to public houses with men is, however, a sure sign of immorality and roughness for the single work-girl; Chinn claims that it was only acceptable for older, married women to frequent such spaces.[95]

In *Thyrza* more than his other fiction, Gissing seems to celebrate rather than attack the 'air of freedom and joyousness' (p. 39) attached to this ambiguous figure of the street-wise work-girl. Collet's description seems to fit the representation of the fun-loving Totty Nancarrow, who is distinguished by her laughter and her independent walk, 'that swaying of the haunches and swing of the hands with palm turned outwards ... characteristic of the London work-girl' (p. 113). Totty snatches kisses with Luke Ackroyd in the street, talks in a 'merry, careless way' and is at her ease in the mixed company of pubs and music halls. In an exuberant early scene, Thyrza accompanies her to a 'friendly lead' at the local pub, at which money is donated to a needy barber in exchange for an evening's entertainment. Peter Bailey's argument that the late-Victorian pub 'provided [a] social space within which a more democratised, heterosocial world of sex and sociability was being constituted'[96] is borne out in Gissing's descriptions of the pub as a respectable arena for mixed-sex pleasure, which admits thirsty women with babies and companies of 'neatly dressed' girls, as well as 'liquor-sodden creatures whose look was pollution' (p. 38). Like Totty, 'the girls who sat with

---

[92]   Nord, p. 233.

[93]   Collet, 'Women's Work', pp. 322–3.

[94]   Elizabeth Roberts, *A Woman's Place: An Oral History of Working-Class Women, 1890– 1940* (Oxford: Blackwell, 1984), pp. 71–2. She avers that it was predominantly the 'bolder older women' who frequented pubs, whilst promenading was more acceptable, because, like the new dance-halls, 'it was so public that ... behaviour was strictly controlled'.

[95]   Chinn, p. 120.

[96]   Bailey, p. 167.

glasses of beer before them, and carried on primitive flirtations with their neighbours, were honest wage-earners of factory and workshop, well able to make themselves respected. If they lacked refinement, natural or acquired, it was not their fault' (p. 41). Unlike Collet who reinforced the prevalent belief that 'their great enemy is drink',[97] Gissing suggests that single women *can* retain their respectability in the pub, refuting stereotypes in his portrayal of Totty, who might enjoy a glass of ginger-beer with friends but disapproves heartily of Ackroyd's increasing drunkenness. However, the scene in the pub is also designed to reinforce Thyrza's distance from her unrefined fellow workers: refusing to drink but agreeing to sing in a public place, she advertises her sexual availability, horrifying her sister who exclaims, 'If you go on and sing in a public-house, I don't know what you won't do' (p. 48). Contradicting his earlier remarks, Gissing seems to imply that entering a pub is seen to jeopardise any aspirations to refinement on the part of working-class women, whose need for recreation should be satisfied in more cultured ways. The concert at St James' Hall that Thyrza later attends is a more suitable public place for a refined heroine, with the shilling entrance fee excluding work-girls interested in the more immoral pursuits of drinking and flirtation, though her sexuality is still on display as she spends more time admiring Egremont than listening to the music.[98]

Feminist critics have tended to approach the question of women's leisure in terms of the limited accessibility of certain public places, but Deborah Parsons' point that at the *fin-de-siècle* 'women had restricted access to the public life of the city compared to men'[99] needs qualifying in relation to the underpaid working-class woman. It is also necessary to acknowledge the need for women to be both accompanied and paid for by men, what Kathy Peiss has defined as the practice of 'treating'.[100] Although men's leisure was also dependent on their fluctuating earnings, they were much more likely than women to regard expenditure on leisure as a necessity: both Bob Hewett and 'Arry Mutimer find their pleasure on the streets when they cannot afford music halls or theatres. The author's sympathies appear to be aligned with those unable to pay their way in commercial culture, as like the work-girl, the struggling writer frequently felt himself to be shut out from urban entertainments: in a letter to his sister Ellen in 1885, during a period of intensive teaching and writing, he complained, 'I no longer feel like a citizen of London. Libraries, book-shops, museums, theatres, all are strange to me'.[101] An

---

[97]   Collet, 'Women's Work', p. 325.

[98]   Another example of working people failing to benefit from the educational opportunities of middle-class forms of leisure can be seen in *The Nether World* when Clem and Bob meet in the British Museum, the sort of space frequented by Adela and her cultured friend Stella Westlake in *Demos*, though typically the unfaithful couple are intent on flirtation and frivolity rather than culture.

[99]   Deborah L. Parsons, *Streetwalking the Metropolis: Women, the City and Modernity* (Oxford: Oxford University Press, 2000), p. 5.

[100]   Kathy Peiss, *Cheap Amusements: Working Women and Leisure in Turn-of-the-Century New York* (Philadephia: Temple University Press, 1986), pp. 51–4.

[101]   Letter to Ellen, 31 January 1885. Quoted in *Collected Letters, Volume 2: 1881–5*, p. 285.

1884 article in the *Fortnightly Review* on 'Social Reforms for the London Poor' containing two articles on women and recreation identified the problem of finding 'legitimate and desirable pleasure' for young working women. Excluded from the more respectable and expensive theatres and generally denied the reading-rooms, clubs and coffee-houses which are 'as a rule inaccessible to women and children', women instead have 'plenty of inducements to vice' and the 'excitement of low theatres and dancing saloons'.[102] The second article, allegedly by 'A London Artisan', reinforced the dangers of these spaces and the frivolities of factory girls interested only in 'feathers and ribbons'.[103] In *A City Girl*, Nelly chooses a blue feather in the opening chapters before agreeing to go to the theatre with Arthur, though in the last chapter after her unplanned pregnancy she realises 'what a heavy price she had paid for a few hours' amusement ... she had no wish now for theatres and outings' (p. 185). The London work-girl's 'fondness' for the theatre is generally perceived to be dangerous, though this is usually more to do with the intentions of the required male escorts than the immoralities of modern drama. Mutimer forbids Alice to accompany her admirer Keene to the theatre and Clara in *The Nether World* loses her job and her respectability when she accepts Scawthorne's offers of entertainment; her mother tells Sidney, 'she's been goin' about to the theatre an' such places with a man as she got to know at the bar, an' Mrs Tubb says she believes it's him has tempted her away' (p. 91). As a relief from the drudgery of labour, recreation was clearly essential but the dangers of entering heterosocial spaces and the casual encounters with men they necessitated offered many kinds of temptation. An artificial flower maker interviewed for the *Fortnightly* article admitted that she sometimes accepted 'a music-hall treat' in preference to walking the streets or going back to her lodgings, but did not like the late hours or the fact that 'they make me drink'. Significantly, when Totty agrees to go to a music hall with Ackroyd, she refuses to drink and asserts, 'I pay for myself, or I don't go at all. That's my rule' (p. 194). Without such rules to protect them, women's wishes for greater access to leisure often yield undesirable consequences, as they remained vulnerable to the economic and sexual power concealed behind 'the tacit legitimacy of treating'.[104]

The connections between low pay, drinking and the immorality of working women were variously contested and endorsed in urban fiction which struggled to find alternative explanations to influential scientific theories about the hereditary nature of alcoholism and degradation accepted by Zola and the French naturalists. The first of Zola's novels to be a popular success, *L'Assommoir* [The Dram Shop] (1877), which Gissing may have read or seen on stage in the 1880s,[105] chronicles

---

[102]   Greville, 'The Need for Recreation', pp. 20, 22, 24.

[103]   A London Artisan, 'The Wives and Mothers of the Working Classes', in 'Social Reforms for the London Poor', pp. 32–3.

[104]   Peiss, p. 54.

[105]   Frederick Brown, *Zola: A Life* (New York: Farrar, Strauss & Giroux, 1995), pp. 489–90. First produced in London in 1879, it was revived in Paris in the mid-1880s shortly before Gissing began his European tour of 1888. The English version, *Drink*, was adapted by the sensation novelist Charles Reade.

the tragic downfall of the laundress Gervaise, who takes to drink while struggling to support her children after her husband is crippled and unemployed after an accident. This notorious novel was seen as disturbing for the indecency of its portrayal of working women's behaviour. Although the laundress, proud of her involvement in 'the flurry of work' (p. 143)[106] in the poorer districts of Paris, is granted a respectability through her ownership of her own shop, as English reviewer Andrew Lang complained, '[Zola] tosses out the contents of the washerwoman's buck-basket [and] makes his laundresses fight a hideous and indecent battle'.[107] Vicious women who fight in the streets also feature in Morrison's *A Child of the Jago*, a form of 'frank' realism deplored by the *Athenaeum* for its 'revolting details'.[108] Certainly, Zola links the 'smutty talk' and flirtatiousness of the laundresses, their indecent habit of taking off their bodices in the heat and the piles of dirty underwear to 'the filth of [their] trade' (p. 166) in order to reinforce the cultural perception that 'laundresses ... are not a prudish race' (p. 245). The immorality of the predominantly married women in this trade was seen as inseparable from their drinking habits: one of Black's investigators of a London slum in the 1910s linked the dirty homes, neglected children and potential prostitution of laundresses to the fact that 'they all drink more or less – many of them a great deal'.[109] Gervaise's occupation then predisposes her to drunkenness as does her enjoyment of her leisure hours, with the dram shop increasingly offering a tempting alternative to the heat and exhausting labour of the laundry. Patricia Malcolmson contends that as the traditional breadwinner the laundress exercised a rare right of entry to such a space, as 'her economic power enabled [her] to do her drinking openly rather than joining the "stair-head drinking clubs" of women excluded from the public house'.[110] Zola's novel originally highlights women's general sense of exclusion from pubs by showing his heroine enjoying coffee and 'grown up conversation' with other women in her cosy work-room, but her later belief in her 'perfect right' to enter the bar to collect her husband effectively signals her loss of respectability rather than her economic independence; her fear that 'it wasn't really the right place for a respectable woman' (p. 335) is only abated after 'she was putting it down like a fish' (p. 339). She quickly degenerates into 'a sottish mess among all the bawling men' (p. 358), her irregular behaviour reinforcing August's view that 'male drinking or other leisure [had] a protected status',[111] as restrictions on women's leisure were seen as necessary to preserve gender differences built on public/private distinctions. Zola's

---

[106] All quotations are taken from Émile Zola, *L'Assommoir*, trans. and ed. Leonard Tancock (1877; Harmondsworth: Penguin, 1970).

[107] Andrew Lang, 'Émile Zola', *Fortnightly Review* N.S. 31 (1882), 438–52 (p. 451).

[108] Review of *A Child of the Jago*, *Athenaeum*, 12 December 1896, p. 833.

[109] L.D. 'Wage-Earning Wives in a Slum', in Black, *Married Women's Work*, pp. 119, 118.

[110] Patricia E. Malcolmson, 'Laundresses and the Laundry Trade in Victorian England', *Victorian Studies* 24:4 (1981), 439–62, p. 461. This is related to her view that laundry work was predominantly married women's work, often undertaken because it could be 'dovetailed with the irregular work of men' (pp. 445, 446).

[111] August, p. 128.

telling phrase for being drunk, or out on the town, translated as 'on the loose', suggests a lack of self-control incompatible with femininity. Gervaise's swift decline into alcoholism both illustrates Zola's naturalist thesis on hereditary degeneration amongst the poor and acts as a warning about the dangers of seeking equality with men in terms of leisure.

At a time when the 'considerable barriers' against female drinking were reinforced in the lay-out of British pubs, which often relegated women to separate rooms,[112] female occupation of pubs in Gissing's fiction is similarly related to the risks to femininity but also indicates his appreciation of the more economic triggers for alcoholism. Female investigators clearly recognised the temptations of drink for women workers; Black typically blamed low pay for poor women's alcoholism, asking bitterly, 'Is it any wonder that those who live thus take to drink?' and argued for its inevitability under current economic conditions, 'a certain proportion of well-paid women *may* be drunken and vicious; a certain proportion of ill-paid ones *must*'.[113] In *Demos*, Kate's dissatisfactions with motherhood and the monotony of slop-sewing can be seen as explanations for the new vice of drinking, partly facilitated by her friendship with Daniel Dabbs, now turned inn-keeper, but also another sign of the 'process of degradation' brought on by 'extreme poverty' (p. 391). Her demise validates the fears of feminist investigators concerned about the dangers for women on the streets:

> With scanty employment, much time to kill, never a sufficiency of food, companions only too like herself in their distaste for home duties and in the misery of their existence, poor Kate got into the habit of straying aimlessly about the streets, and, the inevitable consequence, of seeking warmth and company in the public-house. Her children lived as the children as such mothers do: they played on the stairs or the pavements, had accidents, were always dirty, cried themselves to sleep in hunger and pain. (p. 393)

As the cheapest form of leisure, drinking may then seem 'inevitable' for those with irregular employment, as well as helping to stave off hunger. The annexing of female drinking to the neglect of children of 'such mothers' was also evident in investigatory accounts, as a condemnatory remark by a rent collector interviewed in Black's study illustrates: 'Many a time have I seen babies in perambulators left outside public-houses on Saturday nights until midnight'.[114] Targeting the slum mother as the primary culprit was also a naturalist convention: in Morrison's *A Child of the Jago*, Hannah's neglect of her baby for the pleasures of drink invites condemnation, as Looey dies whilst unattended during her mother's rare enjoyment of a brief moment of leisure in the local pub. Dismissed in one review as 'the drunkard',[115] 'poor Kate' nevertheless attracts Gissing's sympathies,

---

[112] Andrew Davies, *Leisure, Gender and Poverty: Working-Class Culture in Salford and Manchester, 1900–1939* (Buckingham: Open University Press, 1992), pp. 65, 63.

[113] Black, 'The Organization of Working Women', p. 699.

[114] 'Wage-Earning Wives in a Slum', p. 120.

[115] Review of *Demos*, *Spectator*, 10 April 1886, 486–7. Quoted in Coustillas & Partridge, p. 84.

though perhaps only because her neglect of the children is assuaged by her angelic sister, offering a more uplifting alternative to the squalid death suffered by Gervaise. But those who shirk their 'home duties' for 'warmth and company' in public places, or pass on a taste for the solace of alcohol by feeding their babies gin instead of milk, are shown to have strayed too far from the quiet respectability the author cherishes. This ambiguity seems to bear out Andrew Davies' assertion that 'attitudes towards drinking varied enormously among working-class women', as 'patterns of pub attendance among women were more complex than any simple contrast between male indulgence and female exclusion might suggest'.[116]

Nevertheless, his accounts of the rowdy Bank Holiday excursion, and its opportunities for excessive drinking and violence, which were to become a set-piece of East End fiction, realise what Peter Bailey has categorised as 'the bourgeois fear of the vulgarisation of leisure'.[117] Whilst his work was generally considered superior to 'that leprous naturalism' so disgusting to English readers,[118] Gissing's portrayal of drunken women and the violence of which they are capable comes closest in *The Nether World* to acknowledging the possible influence of Zola. Characterised from the opening chapters by her love of drink, Clem Peckover's 'brutality' and 'fury' and her enjoyment of violence and cruelty, including her relish at the gruesome tale of Jeck Bartley getting one of his eyes knocked out in a marital dispute, is certainly seen as 'of no common stamp' (p. 78). In the introduction to the 1890 Colonial edition of the novel, Gissing's portrayal of the 'bold, sensuous, selfish, callous and physically beautiful London factory girl' is seen to be 'a portrait as true and distinct as Zola ever drew, and entirely devoid of the needless offensiveness wherewith the French master of Realism overloads his life-delineations'.[119] What the reviewers did consider offensive was the Zolaesque account of the Bank Holiday at Crystal Palace and its 'imbecile joviality' (p. 108), intended to bring out those aspects of the workers which Gissing most despised. In a letter to his sister Margaret in May 1882 indirectly attacking the newly implemented Public Holiday Act of 1870, he spluttered, 'Never is so clearly to be seen the vulgarity of the people as at these holiday-times. There [sic] notion of a holiday is to rush in crowds to some sweltering place, such as the Crystal Palace, and there eat and drink and quarrel themselves into stupidity'.[120] There seem to be no sexual divisions of leisure here as both men and women indulge in dancing, drinking, gorging, fighting and

---

[116] Davies, pp. 65, 61.

[117] Peter Bailey, *Popular Culture and Performance in the Victorian City* (Cambridge: Cambridge University Press, 1998), p. 29. After a series of Acts in the early 1870s served to increase public holidays, press reports shared 'a common tone and imagery expressive of the repugnance of the middle-class witness to the holiday invasion of the masses' (p. 18). See also Peter Bailey, *Leisure and Class in Victorian England: Rational Recreation and the Contest for Control, 1830–1885* (London: Routledge & Kegan Paul, 1978).

[118] F. W. Farrar, Review of *The Nether World*, p. 142.

[119] Introduction to the Colonial edition of *The Nether World* (1890). Quoted in Coustillas & Partridge, p. 135.

[120] Letter to Madge, 29 May 1882. Quoted in *Collected Letters*, Vol 2, p. 87.

potential marital infidelities. Scenes of women fighting, usually over men or slurs on their respectability, were familiar from Zola but considered to be 'unnecessarily crude and painful' by English reviewers, prompting the question, 'What is the object ... of painting such scenes?'[121] Gissing might have replied by reiterating his commitment to realism and the urge to develop the British urban novel by faithfully representing scenes he witnessed every day in the back streets of London. However, the newly married work-girl Pennyloaf is singled out from the 'pert' and shrieking women who surround her by her attempts at respectable behaviour. She refuses to drink like the others, and is intent on keeping her husband out of trouble, steering him away from the crowds so they can enjoy the music together. Gissing also hints at the imbalance between work and leisure in the lives of the workers as her enjoyment is marred by her exhaustion; in his letters he characterised 'this idea of setting aside single days for great public holidays' as 'absurd', calling for 'a general shortening of working-hours all the year round'.[122] Moreover, the work-girl is shown to find it impossible to maintain her respectability in the public sphere: she struggles to free herself from the 'jovial embrace' of a man on the crowded train home and ultimately she too is provoked into violence by the malicious behaviour of her rival Clem Peckover. As the men fight over the women 'amid a press of delighted spectators' (p. 112), Clem squirts dirty water at Pennyloaf's much-prized new hat, symbolically dirtying her social aspirations and reminding her of her bestiality by 'tearing her face till the blood streamed' (p. 112). Ellen Ross has argued that patterns of sexual antagonism in working-class London resulted in 'a culture where husband-wife violence was extremely frequent, where pubs were invaded by angry wives',[123] but violence between female rivals did occur where women were particularly outraged, or aggressive; nearly as many women as men were convicted for their unlawful public-holiday behaviour in one London police-court in 1882.[124] Returning home with 'her pretty face ... all blood and dirt' (p. 113) to the sound of her mother's 'mad drunkenness' and her father's blows in the room below, the work-girl's tears testify to her frustration at being out of control of her own limited leisure experiences.

The later short story 'Lou and Liz', commissioned by the editor of the *English Illustrated Magazine* in 1893, is arguably a more complex analysis of women's enjoyment of the Bank Holiday celebration. In its foregrounding of the ways in

---

[121]   Reviews of *The Nether World*, *Guardian*, p. 845; Farrar, *Contemporary Review*, quoted in Coustillas & Partridge, p. 144.

[122]   Letter to Madge, 29 May 1882.

[123]   Ellen Ross, '"Fierce questions and taunts": Married Life in Working-Class London, 1870–1914', in David Feldman & Gareth Stedman Jones (eds.), *Metropolis London: Histories and Representations since 1800* (London & New York: Routledge, 1989), p. 221. In her discussion of community behaviour in wife-beating incidents, she notes 'the inevitability of violence between spouses, and the "right" of husbands to beat up wives' (p. 233).

[124]   Violet Greville, 'The Need for Recreation', in 'Social Reforms for the London Poor', *Fortnightly Review* N.S. 35 (1884), 21–36 (p. 23).

which childcare affects the leisure of the working-class mother, it seeks to address what Claire Langhamer has characterised as 'the ambiguities of "work" and "leisure" in women's lives', where the conceptualisation of leisure as 'a reward for paid labour' may ignore or distort the experiences of women looking after children.[125]   The work-girls, who barely earn enough to support Liz's child between them, have 'somehow managed' (p. 2)[126] to save up in order to afford a day's entertainment. Despite the constant restrictions on leisure in the form of inadequate earnings and maternal duties, they are determined to have a good time:

> They ... drank beer when they could afford it, tea when they couldn't, starved themselves occasionally to have an evening at the Canterbury or at the Surrey (the baby, drugged if he were troublesome, sleeping now on his mother's lap, now on Lou's) and on a Bank-holiday mingled with the noisiest crowd they could discover. (p. 3)

Adopting the common practice of taking children to public venues, the girls risk their femininity by drugging the baby. At Rosherville Gardens the screaming child, who does not respond well to sweet food and beer, and is a heavy burden to be carried amongst the crowds, is more 'troublesome', as child care blurs work into leisure for women. The dancing and drunken flirtations of the women are kept in check by the duties of motherhood: ''Ow can y'expect to enjoy yerself when you 'ave to tike babbies out!' (p. 12).   The day is then 'hopelessly spoilt' by Lou's fight with the husband who deserted her, shaming them into leaving early as 'people were pointing at them' (p.12).   Liz's enjoyment is also marred by the 'personal anxieties' that Lou will abandon her either for a man or for a less restrictive lifestyle, another sobering reminder of the difficulties of single motherhood and her dependence on the support of her friend.   The story significantly ends with the return to 'the week's labour'. The imbalance of work and leisure for women is also apparent in Arthur Morrison's story, 'Lizerunt' published in the collection *Tales of Mean Streets* (1894). On the Bank Holiday the factory girl's pleasure in having two men fighting over her 'in the public gaze' may make her feel as if she were Helen of Troy, but it is only a brief prelude to a life-time of domestic violence and confinement to the home with her children.[127] The Bank Holiday scene is then used to demonstrate Gissing's advocacy of the

---

[125]   Claire Langhamer, *Women's Leisure in England, 1920–1960* (Manchester: Manchester University Press, 2000), pp. 18, 134.   She argues that this notion 'actively framed both social constructions of the relationship between women and leisure, and women's own ideas concerning their personal leisure time' (p. 51).

[126] All quotations are taken from 'Lou and Liz' in George Gissing, *The Day of Silence and other Stories* ed. Pierre Coustillas (London: J.M. Dent, 1993), p. 12. The story first appeared in the *English Illustrated Magazine* in August 1893, pp. 793–801.

[127]   Arthur Morrison, 'Lizerunt', in *Tales of Mean Streets* (1894; London: Methuen, 1912), p. 24.   After the Bank Holiday Lizerunt is constantly subject to her husband's violence and ill-treatment and at the end of the story is bullied into prostitution by him to pay for their increasing debts.

desperate need for the people to 'learn to make some sensible use of [their hours of leisure]'.[128]

Safer and more appropriate spaces for women were the new cafés frequented by single women workers and ladies of leisure and shops selling food, perhaps because eating, particularly sweet things, was considered more feminine than drinking. 'Spaces of consumption', according to McCracken, 'figure as key sites for the performance of new gendered identities',[129] though conspicuous displays of consumption could be seen to signal both vulgarity and a healthy sexual appetite. Women who enjoy their food also often enjoy their men: the fun-loving Totty is first introduced buying sardines, beer, seed cake and jam in Mrs Bower's shop and later characterised, like Alice, by her taste for the 'luxuries' of the East End diet: 'marmalade and pickles she deemed the indispensables of life' (p. 383). She is also one of the many Lambeth women enjoying the 'pleasure' of picking out the most appetising (and sexually suggestive) food on market-night, which Gissing rather falsely tries to claim is 'the sole out-of-door amusement regularly at hand for London working people, the only one, in truth, for which they show any real capacity' (p. 37). With her new husband's money and carriage to protect her from the city, Alice is able to enjoy 'the delights of shopping [and] the little lunches in confectioners' shops to which [she] ... had been much addicted' (p. 357). Laughing work-girls are glimpsed ordering cakes in the pastry-shop in which Clem and Bob meet and Rodman's first wife Clara and her child order coffee and bread and butter in an eating-house near Westminster Abbey. In his sharp distinctions between his refined heroines who rarely touch their food and the sexually curious 'girls of the people' defined by what they like to eat, Gissing, whose diary testifies to his own obsession with good food, reveals his fascination with the pleasures of consumption. Before Totty is allowed to use her uncle's inheritance to open her own shop with Bunce, Gissing glorifies her work-girl lifestyle in significantly dietary terms:

> She preferred her liberty, her innocent nights at the Canterbury Music Hall, her scampering about the streets at all hours, her marmalade and pickles eaten off a table covered with a newspaper in company with half a dozen friends as harum-scarum as herself. Deliberately, she preferred these joys to anything she could imagine as entering into the life of a 'lady'. (p. 385)

The work-girl's liberty, despite her occupation of the streets and the music hall, is seen as 'innocent' and unthreatening: Totty, nervous of Ackroyd's drunken advances, remains a 'good girl' by keeping men at a distance. Her marriage to the more dependable Bunce ensures that she can continue sharing jam with his children, where her love of food will enhance her maternal, rather than her sexual, qualities.

---

[128] Letter to Margaret, 29 May 1882. *Collected Letters*, Vol 2, p. 87.

[129] McCracken, 'Embodying the New Woman', p. 63. He also establishes the connection between eating and sexuality in this chapter, pointing out that 'food and sex are rarely unrelated' (p. 60).

Whereas shopping and eating in public, usually day-time activities which did not have to involve men, were more acceptable forms of women's leisure, occupying the streets after dark for other forms of consumption was much more problematic. There is the cautionary tale in *Demos* of Alice's frustrations at her confinement to the home, where she feels herself 'perishing for lack of amusement' (p. 420) once her husband tires of taking her to town. Rodman immediately sees through her 'foolish' pretence of 'making appointments in London' (p. 422) and locks her out of the house as a punishment. At the end of the novel, driven hysterical by her husband's neglect, she is discovered 'several miles from home, lying unconscious in the streets' (p. 446), demonstrating her inability to find her own amusements without a man and her proximity to the unprotected streetwalker once she steps over her threshold alone. Concerns about space and women's mobility in the city surface in both the novels and the periodical press. According to the *GOP*, barmaids were often obliged to walk home 'after midnight through some of the worst streets in London'[130] when the trains and omnibuses had stopped running. In *The Nether World* this situation makes Sidney and Clara's father uneasy. Despite arguing for the merits of bar work, Sidney later sneers, 'I hope you'll enjoy the pleasant, ladylike work you've found! I should think it'll improve your self-respect to wait on the gentlemen of Upper Street!' (p. 32) and takes to hanging around outside her lodging house in order to see whether she comes home alone. Given cultural assumptions about bar work, Clara's succumbing to the temptations of disreputable male company acquires a certain inevitability, though her ease at walking around the streets and anger at Sidney for 'daring to act the spy' (p. 95) outside her new lodgings suggest the work-girl's resistance to being supervised. Men's awareness of the dangers of urban culture for women are shown in the recurring scenes in which fathers, brothers and (potential) husbands join policemen in patrolling the streets: both Sidney and John Hewett occupy the back alleys of Clerkenwell looking for Clara, as policemen loom out of the darkness to remind women of their vulnerabilities outside the home. In *Thryza*, Egremont and Grail are concerned about Thyrza's safety on Lambeth Bridge, and when she later returns home in a feverish state, with her clothing 'stained ... and in disorder' (p. 269), she revives her sister's faith in the need for male protectors. Moreover, the Ripper murders of the late 1880s acted as another stern reminder of the inadequacies of the police and the lack of protection for women in the badly-lit streets of the East End. August's argument that 'women were integral parts of the lively pub and street culture in [poor] neighbourhoods'[131] therefore needs qualifying, as the urban narrative persistently warns of the dangers of street life for women, perhaps because it was more comforting to position working-class women safely within the home.

Gissing's attitudes to working women's leisure then seem rather contradictory, as his narratives appear to offer a tentative endorsement of forms of legitimate recreation for women whilst punishing those who indulge too freely or labelling them as irredeemably vulgar. Both Thyrza and Alice suffer for their enjoyment of

---

[130] 'Barmaids and Waitresses in Restaurants, their Work and Temptations', p. 330.
[131] August, p. 128.

male attention in public places: Lydia's protective attitude to her sister, 'you can't go about the streets and into public-houses without hearing bad things and seeing bad people. I want to keep you away from everything that isn't homelike and quiet' (p. 52) perhaps echoes Gissing's own feelings about his more refined heroines, as 'quietness' is seen as a marker of refinement and hence a valuable asset. Feminist historians offer different views about the social realities underpinning street scenes and descriptions of public entertainment in the novels. Whereas Ross draws on the ideology of separate spheres in her argument that women tended to share certain spaces – shops, pubs, doorways, streets – with other women rather than their spouses,[132] this has been challenged by August who cites evidence of couples going to pubs and music halls together, chiming with the view dramatised in Gissing's fiction that the streets were a place where both men and women 'walked ... visited, played, shopped and fought'.[133] As a street argument between Clara and Sidney is used to verify, the lives of the urban poor are 'enacted on the peopled ways', ensuring that they 'seldom command privacy' (p. 93). Moreover, the restricted access to recreation experienced by Gissing's overworked wives supports the gender divide recently identified by historians: 'women's claims to leisure were weaker than those of their husbands', not least because 'women's access to time and money for their own leisure depended on conditions in the family economy'.[134] In *The Nether World*, Pennyloaf's 'submissiveness' when her husband uses the household money to treat his friends in the pub may be uncharacteristic of working-class wives, according to Ross,[135] but her acceptance of her husband's right to leisure is not. Married women were not the only ones for whom leisure was a luxury, as the expenses of female home-workers also made it practically impossible to set aside money for entertainment. Jessie Boucherett used the fact that working women 'care little for amusements' beyond the occasional dance or concert to justify women's preference for unlimited home-work, though this argument followed on from a discussion about the minimum wages required 'to maintain a woman in comfort'.[136] Predictably, working women celebrated for their nobler qualities are rarely shown enjoying themselves in public places: Emma refuses to participate in a proposed Bank Holiday excursion to Epping Forest and both she and Jane prefer to socialise with other women within the home, where they have to stay to mind children. Both fit the category of the respectable factory girl, who would benefit from the educative opportunities of the girls' clubs, a more 'sensible' use of leisure for those who aspired to middle-class behaviour. By

---

[132] Ross, 'Fierce Questions and Taunts', p. 222. She maintains that in late-Victorian London, working-class men and women 'lived in quite separate material worlds organized around their responsibilities in a rigid sexual division of labour'.

[133] August, pp. 127, 128.

[134] August, p. 128. He argues that men's leisure was protected, despite financial difficulties, as money for drinking and entertainment was subtracted from the 'family wage' before they made their contributions to the household economy. See also Langhamer, pp. 50–51.

[135] Ross, 'Fierce questions and taunts', pp. 225, 235.

[136] Boucherett & Blackburn, pp. 18–19, 12.

endorsing the attitudes of his more refined heroines then, Gissing effectively seeks to reinforce women's positions within the home, where home-work, child care and domestic duties could be practically combined with leisure. This is in accordance with Langhamer's theory of 'gendered notions of leisure entitlement', which goes beyond the question of 'unequal access' in order to consider conceptualisations of recreation away from the public sphere, recognising that adult women were also able to 'carve out' opportunities for leisure by alternative uses of domestic space.[137]

Intent on exposing the unknown pressures of the lives of poor women, Gissing then develops the image of the quiet, self-respecting work-girl admired by the investigators in order to validate notions of working-class female respectability. Whilst the novels highlight the exploitation of industrial women workers, struggling against poor pay and long hours, the female characters function as more than 'cases against capitalism' in their voicing of the difficulties of survival and their ability to resist degradation in their drive for self-sufficiency. As Carol E. Morgan has argued in her account of the undervaluation of industrial work for women in this period, 'languages constructing women's work as immoral and illegitimate, or at least in opposition of women's domestic duties, circulated in a larger context in which that labour was vital and accepted.'[138] By continuing to refuse offers of marriage or making the most of widowhood, the most industrious of Gissing's work-girls avoid the domestic trap and the economic dependence on men which giving up their vital labour would entail. In an attempt to imagine a way out of the constraints of poor women's lives, August suggests that married women could have abandoned their families and fled neighbourhoods, or that single women might have avoided marriage and children, though he concludes, 'aside from the emotional costs involved in these alternatives, the economic position of women made them impractical'.[139] In a more subversive move, Gissing validates the self-dependency of the female-headed household in which Jane, Emma and Pennyloaf are shown to be capable of surviving without men, free of the authority of the demanding husband and in control of their own hard-earned wages. His participation in debates about married women's work also indicates his awareness of contemporary feminist concerns about the working mother, as his vision of the industrial worker as a courageous if underpaid home-maker can be aligned with the findings of the feminist investigators of the early twentieth century.

In his discussion of East End fiction, Roger Henkle has argued that 'for all the efforts of social services to confirm the woman as the ethical centre of lower-class life, she turns out ... to be as uncontrollable as the men, at her worst, or too

---

[137] Langhamer, p. 5. For a less positive reading of married women's leisure, see Ruth Lister, *Citizenship: Feminist Perspectives* (Basingstoke: Macmillan, 1997), p. 133. She argues that 'time poverty' detracts from women's citizenship, as 'formal equality for women in the public sphere ... is undermined by the weight of their responsibilities in the private'.

[138] Carol E. Morgan, *Women Workers and Gender Identities, 1835–1913: The Cotton and Metal Industries in England* (London & New York: Routledge, 2001), p. 15.

[139] August, p. 140.

passive to resist her own victimization, at her best'.[140] Gissing may be unable to edit out his uneasy fascination with the pleasure-loving work-girl, but by granting her citizenship of London through occupation of public space, he firmly resists the generic convention of using her merely as a repository for all the worst deprivations of the urban poor. Although his discussions of female drinking and violence pay homage to the more shocking scenes of disorder in Zola's fiction, he also taps into current debates about the need for regulation of leisure activities and the desire to find alternative public spaces than the public house. Whilst his work reflects the fears of the social investigators about the dangers of female drinking and the risk to respectability of occupying the streets, the relatively controlled behaviour of his heroines suggests the author's endorsement of the working woman's right to leisure and her capacity to protect herself from unwanted male attention. In his sympathetic handling of the difficulties of balancing childcare, paid labour and recreation, he also revises the typical naturalist portrayal of the degraded working-class mother, showing her to be less a passive victim than engaged in an active struggle against the constraints of her life, a figure of 'true respectability'.

---

[140] Henkle, p. 304.

Chapter 3

Barriers to Female Professionalism: Educated Working Women and the Threat of Celibacy

Gissing's representations of working women in the early 1890s indicate a shift of interest from the London work-girl towards her middle-class counterpart, and his engagement with a different set of debates about women's work. In late 1889, at a time when he confessed that his 'preliminary study' for novels was becoming more laborious, his letters testify to his focus on 'the "female education" question', and the beginning of his queries about the earnings and lifestyles of educated women workers.[1] Increasingly, the educated woman, particularly in cities, chose to defer or reject marriage: Clara Collet claimed that the proportion of women who remained unmarried in England and Wales was around 1 in 6, or in London 1 in 5, many of whom would constitute the new professional class of women workers.[2] Collet's research on the educated working woman and the difficulties she faced in the labour market overlapped with concerns about the woman of the future, and the threat to the race if female celibacy increased. In her discussion of the economic progress of women between 1850 and 1900, she remarked, 'we are constantly congratulating ourselves that our middle-aged spinsters have nothing in common with the old maid of the past, while we assume that the next half-century will see a still greater exaltation of the maiden lady', though she warned that the incomes earned by such women were insufficient to maintain either utility or health.[3] The single middle-class woman, newly labelled as the poor lady or the glorified spinster, was seen as both a social problem and a liberated role model, and her position in late-nineteenth-century society anatomised in the press. An article on 'The Future of Single Women' in the *Westminster Review* of 1884 championing

---

[1] Letter to Bertz, 21 October 1889. Quoted in *Collected Letters of George Gissing, Vol 4, 1889–91*, ed. Paul Matthiesen, Arthur C. Young & Pierre Coustillas (Athens: Ohio University Press, 1993), p. 130. He refers to 'the woman-education question' in a letter to Algernon, 4 November 1889, p. 142.

[2] Clara Collet, 'Prospects of Marriage for Women', *Nineteenth Century* 31 (1892), 537–52 (pp. 540, 545). She was drawing on census returns for 1881.

[3] Clara E. Collet, 'Through 50 Years: The Economic Progress of Women' (1900), in *Educated Working Women: Essays on the Economic Position of Women Workers in the Middle Classes* (London: P. S. King & Son, 1902), pp. 142, 141. This essay first appeared in the *Frances Mary Buss Schools' Jubilee Magazine*.

the 'possibilities and varieties' of legitimate womanhood proclaimed, 'there has never until to-day been found an appreciable number of celibate women who have filled worthily a wide sphere of social and public usefulness'.[4]   Judith R. Walkowitz sees the 'celibate career woman' as one of two new roles in the repertoire of genteel femininity, as 'the unprecedented expansion of private female secondary schools, teacher training, and, to a lesser extent, women's education at university levels precipitated new expectations and social possibilities for women'.[5]

Fiction of the early 1890s reflects the dominant concerns of the campaign around the employment of middle-class women, which often 'centred on the questions of opportunity and of choice for the single woman'.[6]   Whilst single women in fiction of the 1850s 'were not permitted to be single and happy outside a carefully defined set of family duties',[7] the independent lifestyle of the professional woman is variously represented in later Victorian fiction as a welcome escape from such duties, a temporary taste of freedom before the restrictions of marriage, or a difficult transition period to a lonely adulthood.   Gissing's work of the early 1890s, before he began to address the woman question directly in his most well-known novels, draws on the generic conventions of New Woman fiction in its concern with the position of the educated single woman and her employment opportunities. Gissing is tentative about the effects of education and often highlights the barriers which prevent women from taking advantage of their new freedoms. Whilst he advocated women's entry into the professions, he was, like the social investigators, keenly aware of the 'difficulties, opposition, rebuffs, and prejudice' hindering the advance in status of the professional woman worker.[8] Whereas the heroines of later New Woman novels by George Paston and Ella Hepworth Dixon are brought up expecting to pursue an independent career or benefit from the advice of family and friends, or the contacts of professional networks, Gissing's educated heroines struggle to break into the professions due to isolation and prejudice.   In this chapter I will consider the problems faced by women competing with men in professions such as medicine, art and journalism, showing how New Woman novelists seized on the figure of the lady-journalist in particular in their attempts to tell the story of the modern woman. Although she is shown to take advantage of new forms of accommodation such as flats and lodging

---

[4]   [Henrietta Muller], 'The Future of Single Women', *Westminster Review* 121 (1884), 151–62 (p. 153).

[5]   Judith R. Walkowitz, *City of Dreadful Delight: Narratives of Sexual Disorder in Late-Victorian London* (London: Virago, 1992), p. 64. However, she emphasises the visibility rather than the actual numbers of such women, arguing that 'independent single women of the order of the Glorified Spinster were very much a minority [as] marriage remained the approved female destiny for all classes'.

[6]   Philippa Levine, *Victorian Feminism, 1850–1900* (London: Hutchinson, 1987), p. 87.

[7]   Martha Vicinus, *Independent Women: Work and Community for Single Women, 1850–1920* (Chicago: University of Chicago Press, 1985), p. 11.

[8]   Edith Morley (ed.), *Women Workers in Seven Professions* (London: Routledge, 1914), p. xvi. This was a collection of lectures and essays written by experienced women in various fields for a study begun in 1908 by the newly formed Fabian Women's Group.

houses for working women, the aspiring journalist, struggling on an inadequate income, is typically forced out of the labour market into marriage, or at least encouraged to take up a more feminine occupation. Whilst the independence enjoyed by such a figure made her an ideal example of the urban freedoms of the new career woman, fictional representations often also incorporated anti-feminist views of the masculine old maid, given new impetus by evolutionary fears about the woman of the future.

Work fit for Ladies: the Poor Lady and the Lady-Journalist

In an article on the employment of educated women published in *Nineteenth Century and After* in 1901, Louise Creighton highlighted women's general ignorance about 'different possibilities of employment' and argued, 'there is need for much pioneer work; both employers and workers must be persuaded and encouraged to make experiments which lead to the opening of new fields for women'.[9] She was voicing growing concerns about the barriers to female professionalism around the turn of the century, when middle-class women's limited awareness of widening employment opportunities was perceived to be hampering their entry into an already congested labour market.[10] As Philippa Levine has argued, 'the slow process of attrition whereby women dismantled the barriers to their professional ambitions was fraught with difficulties', not least because new areas of professional expertise requiring training and qualification restricted women further.[11] In 1888 Gissing read Emily Pfeiffer's recently published report on *Women and Work*, a study of the effects of higher education on women's health and fertility. Pfeiffer welcomed the fact that 'the new impulse to female education' was helping to fit girls for the 'variety of callings' gradually being opened to them and sought to disprove some of the well-known medical arguments about women's overtaxing of vital energies in the workplace. The report reached the conclusion that 'women workers ... of the higher social class, have pressed, and must continue to press, even as their humbler sisters, against barriers which must crush them if they do not to some extent yield'.[12] In her Socialist polemic *Woman and Labour* (1911), Olive Schreiner urged women to 'demand to have the doors leading to professional, political and highly skilled labour thrown open to them' or face 'the danger of enervation through non-

[9]   Louise Creighton, 'The Employment of Educated Women', *The Nineteenth Century and After* 50 (1901), 806–11 (p. 806).
[10]   Frances H. Low, 'How Poor Ladies Live', *Nineteenth Century* 41 (1897), 405–17 (p. 405).
[11]   Levine, p. 92.
[12]   Emily Pfeiffer, *Women and Work: An Essay Treating on the Relation to Health and Physical Development of the Higher Education of Girls, and the Intellectual or more Systematised effort of Women* (London: Trübner & Co, 1888), pp. 138–9.

employment'.[13] But in attempting to 'fit [themselves] for modern requirements', girls were still often disadvantaged by over-specialised training or insufficient education; the flipside to Creighton's belief that 'a well-educated capable woman, with an open mind, unhampered by dread of the loss of social position, need not look long for work', is the fear that 'if employment in her special line is scarce, [she is] quite unable to adapt herself to anything else'.[14]

Gissing's belief in the isolation of the aspiring female professional is apparent throughout his early fiction, in which educated middle-class women are frequently marginalised in the narrative, denied the opportunity to earn their own money. Often they gain fulfilment through unpaid work in the attempt to ward off the enervation Schreiner identified. Amateur philanthropy, together with literary work, was one of the few professions open to women throughout the nineteenth century, according to a study of the careers of university-educated women in 1895, though 'these diverse occupations are hardly of a kind to be called a definite career'.[15] Whilst studying in Germany, Helen Norman in *Workers in the Dawn* (1880) begins to think of herself as 'a strong-minded woman' and asks the question that was to concern Gissing throughout his fiction: 'What can a woman do in the world?' (Vol 1, p. 327). Her unpaid work in the East End, where she runs an evening class for work-girls, is her response to 'the longing for active life growing stronger within me' (Vol 1, p. 327).[16] In *Demos* (1886) Adela Mutimer's classes for the poor and visits to Hoxton to support the seamstress Emma Vine, inspired by her friend Stella Westlake's Socialist activities, are similarly borne out of frustration with the tedium of the middle-class female existence. But neither of them become one of the 'trained workers for the poor' demanded by Octavia Hill, those 'women of power developed by the better education now open to them' who would become the professional social workers of the future,[17] as they are never able to achieve full professional status. Philanthropy is seen not only as scandalous and dangerous but inappropriate to Helen's gender: 'the work that you make your play, the amusement of your leisure hours, is not for women's hands' (Vol 2, p. 179). David Kramer has argued that the novels of the early 1890s reveal the author's 'profound, almost revolutionary support for women's pursuit of new employment opportunities as they attempted at the end of the nineteenth century to break down the mainstream Victorian assumptions about divisions of labor', but the earlier fiction often refuses to address the difficulties of the struggle against

---

[13]   Olive Schreiner, *Woman and Labour*, ed. Jane Graves (1911; London: Virago, 1978), p. 123.

[14]   Creighton, 'The Employment of Educated Women', pp. 808–09.

[15]   Alice M. Gordon, 'The After-Careers of University-Educated Women', *Nineteenth Century* 37 (1895), 955–60 (p. 958).

[16]   All quotations are taken from George Gissing, *Workers in the Dawn* 3 vols (1880; New York & London: Garland Publishing, 1976).

[17]   Octavia Hill, 'Trained Workers for the Poor', *Nineteenth Century* 33 (1893), 36–43 (p. 39). Hill found it ridiculous that there was no training requirements in place for philanthropy as there were in education and nursing, and called for more scholarships in order to 'open up to women one more branch of honourable and useful remunerative work' (p. 42).

gender bias, indicating a failure to recognise educated women's work as anything other than a source of amusement.

In the late 1880s and early 1890s Gissing was clearly reformulating ideas about the position of the educated woman in society. David Grylls has noted the complications in assessing the author's generally supportive attitude to female education, highlighting a tendency in his fiction for female learning to lead to loneliness and estrangement. However, he adds, 'whether he also believed that women could profit less from [education] than men is still a question worth asking'.[18] Gissing was certainly intrigued by the unconventional lifestyles of educated women such as the Jewish intellectual Edith Sichel and the Socialist Olive Schreiner, whose rejection of the middle-class family home in order to live alone and pursue 'the intellectual kind of life' he found 'remarkable'.[19] Schreiner linked the modern woman's demands for 'labour and the training which fits us for labour' to new urban conditions, bracketing the young girl in her 'city garret' with the 'heroic figure' of the student, 'battling against gigantic odds to take her place besides man in the fields of modern intellectual toil'.[20] In 1889 Gissing wrote to his sister Nelly in admiration of the linguistic skills and knowledge of current affairs of Sichel and her friends:

> Now you remember the problem we once talked over. – Are these London women of larger brain than women in the country? ... They know everything that appears in our day, & can talk intelligently on any subject current in intellectual circles. Well, the explanation of course is that they have always lived in intellectual society. It is not remarkable brain-power that distinguishes them, but *opportunity*. Had you lived in the same way, your attainments would be no less than theirs. These people learn most of what they know in conversation. They live much in foreign countries, & so acquire languages with comparative ease. On their tables lie all the new books, - either purchased or from Mudie's. They live at the *centre* of things.[21]

In common with Schreiner, he rejects current scientific thinking about the correlations between the smaller weight of the female brain and the 'marked inferiority of intellectual power in [women]'.[22] His view of the modern middle-class woman is that she is advantaged not by a larger brain but by her environment; being in London, 'at the centre of things' enables her to profit from the 'new

---

[18] David Grylls, *The Paradox of Gissing* (London: Allen & Unwin, 1986), pp. 160, 161.

[19] Letter to Margaret, 29 September 1889. *Collected Letters, Vol 4*, p. 117.

[20] Schreiner, pp. 33, 126.

[21] Letter to Ellen, 29 September 1889. *Collected Letters, Vol 4*, pp. 115–16. Gissing met Sichel for the first time in 1889 after they corresponded about her favourable review of *The Nether World*.

[22] George J. Romanes, 'Mental Differences between Men and Women', *Nineteenth Century* 21 (1887), 654–72 (pp. 654–5). This article draws on Darwinian thinking to demonstrate women's intellectual inferiority, and dismisses the view that inequality in education may have contributed to current mental differences between men and women. See also Schreiner, p. 183.

educational opportunities' in ways which women in the provinces, like the disadvantaged Ellen, would have found difficult.

In fiction of the early 1890s Gissing explores the idea that brain-power has to be harnessed to opportunity through a cast of educated women confined to rural houses largely controlled by men. A review of this period noted his growing interest in 'the miseries of the needy professional classes', whose 'intellectual needs' fostered by the system of universal education could not be satisfied on limited incomes.[23] This clearly has repercussions in terms of gender, though his recurring comments on the larger brains of these women does not coincide with his apparent rejection of theories about brain size. The geographical barriers to 'intellectual enterprise' (Vol 1, p. 72) for women had already been outlined in the earlier novel, *Isabel Clarendon* (1886), in which the aspiring journalist Ada Warren, a 'very clever and very learned' (Vol 1, p.100) girl, suffers from her isolated position in a rural community.[24] In *New Grub Street* (1891) the rising journalist Jasper Milvain works his way up on Grub Street through vigorous networking in London after college, whilst his sisters Maud and Dora, far from reaping the benefits of the new education system, suffer from 'an intellectual training wholly incompatible with the material conditions of their life' (p. 70).[25] Although 'nature had endowed them with a larger share of brains than was common in their circle', their unfitness to struggle against 'the restrictions of poverty' (p. 70) is compounded by their confinement to the rural family home in which they feel themselves 'sacrificed' (p. 41) to their brother's career prospects. After their mother's death, they seek to benefit from having 'books within reach, and better opportunities every way' (p. 146) in the metropolis. Their story is set against that of Marian Yule, who only gains access to the labour market by acting as her journalist father's unpaid researcher. The later two-volume novel *Denzil Quarrier* (1892) less successfully addresses the plight of the 'large-brained' Mrs Wade, an agitator for women's rights and suffrage denied the opportunities for public speaking and social action granted to the rising politician Quarrier. The decision to fix one of his most obviously emancipated heroines in a rural backwater, where she is unable to 'associate with people of [her] own way of thinking' (p. 97)[26] seems rather inconsistent with the suffrage campaigner's demands for 'full citizenship' for women. Mrs Wade does finally move to London to gain access to books for her writing, as if Gissing realises that her claim that 'there's too much of that centralization' (p. 97) is unconvincing and historically inaccurate. There are hints that Mrs Wade, who reads Greek history and proclaims herself 'by nature a student' (p. 169), has attended university, not least because her use of the abbreviated word 'exam' 'smacked of an undergraduate' (p. 96) but this

---

[23] N.O.B., 'Survey of Gissing's Work', *Echo*, 16 October 1893, p. 1.

[24] All quotations are taken from George Gissing, *Isabel Clarendon* 2 vols. ed. Pierre Coustillas (1886; Brighton: Harvester Press, 1969).

[25] All quotations are taken from George Gissing, *New Grub Street*, ed. Bernard Bergonzi (1891; Harmondsworth: Penguin, 1968).

[26] All quotations are taken from George Gissing, *Denzil Quarrier*, ed. John Halperin (1892; Sussex: Harvester Press, 1979).

is never confirmed. Even if she has, she is still positioned in a friend's modest library for the duration of the narrative; we only catch a glimpse of her political activities in Quarrier's aside that she has 'taken up with ... rampant women – extremists of many kinds' (p. 333), suggesting a reluctance to describe the lifestyle a suffrage campaigner might lead in the capital. *Born in Exile* (1892), a novel exploring the barriers to higher education for lower-class men to be taken up in Thomas Hardy's more famous *Jude the Obscure* (1895), tends to ignore the barriers affecting middle-class women. The emancipated Marcella Moxey, despite possessing a powerful intellect and radical opinions superior to her brother's, is, like Mrs Wade, doomed to pursue her 'studious habits' in the home, where she feels 'fenced around with books' (p. 335).[27] She is later kicked to death by a horse in punishment of her advanced views. The narrative of the educated heroine's progress can only gain momentum once shifts in material circumstances or the deaths of parents precipitate a move to London, in order to demonstrate the urgent need for aspiring professional women to be 'at the centre of things'.

One might expect the increasing opportunities of higher education for women to enable this pursuit of new employment opportunities and for the female graduate to feature prominently in New Woman fiction. By the 1890s women could attend lectures and take examinations at a number of institutions, but London University was one of the few to actually award them degrees.[28] Educational theorists dwelt on the wider choice of lucrative careers open to female students,[29] whilst an article in the *Nineteenth Century* in 1887 by a Newnham graduate offers a typical student's view in its emphasis on both the social advantages and common pursuit of intellectual goals in a liberated environment. Although the intellectual challenges and 'corporate life'[30] associated with the new women's colleges were explored in contemporary novels such as L.T. Meade's *A Sweet Girl Graduate* (1891), the Girton girl was just as likely to be satirised as admired for her learning, as contemporary *Punch* cartoons illustrate. In an informative discussion of cultural stereotypes around women's higher education across the periodical press and commercial fiction, Chris Willis has noted these contradictory portrayals, whilst criticising the use of the popular term 'Girton girl' for 'implicitly denigrat[ing] the achievements of university women by suggesting that they were not fully adult'.[31]

[27] All quotations are taken from George Gissing, *Born in Exile*, ed. David Grylls (1892; London: J. M. Dent, 1993).

[28] Levine, p. 27. Women were still not able to acquire degrees from Oxford or Cambridge at this time, and many had to be chaperoned by men when attending lectures.

[29] J.G. Fitch, 'Women and the Universities', *Contemporary Review* 58 (1890), 240–55 (pp. 254–5).

[30] Eva Knatchbull-Hugessen, 'Newnham College from Within', *Nineteenth Century* 21 (1887), 843–56 (pp. 854, 853).

[31] Chris Willis, '"All agog to teach the higher mathematics": University Education and the New Woman', *Women: A Cultural Review* 10:1 (1999), 56–66 (p. 58). For an alternative account of the educated New Woman heroine in commercial fiction, see Chris Willis, '"Heaven defend me from political or highly-educated women!": Packaging the New Woman for Mass Consumption', in Angelique Richardson & Chris Willis (eds.), *The New*

Clever heroines were forced to accept that higher education was for their brothers and even those lucky enough to attend university rarely use their education to enter professional life. The 'freelance' attendance of Oxford lectures by the eponymous heroine of Ménie Muriel Dowie's New Woman novel *Gallia* (1895) allows her to hold her own in intellectual debate but not to profit from her learning as she devotes her time to finding a suitable mate. The rebellious Herminia Barton, the Girton-educated heroine of Grant Allen's best-seller, *The Woman who Did* (1895), who gives up her degree to teach, rejects the 'cramping' college lifestyle as offering only 'a pretence of freedom', claiming that 'the whole object of the training was to see just how far you could manage to push a woman's education without the faintest danger of her emancipation'.[32] Unmarried motherhood then prevents her from capitalising on her intelligence and shatters her ideals of an unconventional life. Although his scrapbook from this period does contain notes on Girton, Newnham and London University, Gissing decided against a detailed examination of the effects of a university education for women.[33] This may be partially explained in the links with the traditionally feminine career of teaching: despite the claims to the contrary, an 1895 statistical study of the careers of female graduates reached the conclusion that 'the development of the higher education of women has not opened any new profession for women', revealing that an expensive university training did no more than produce better qualified teachers.[34] Denying the educated heroine access either to the colleges or to the wider career choices they promised seems to have been a fairly common fictional strategy even in the era of the New Woman.

So does Gissing's denial of opportunities to the educated heroine signal a reluctance or unwillingness to allow her to benefit from her intellectual endeavours, or merely reflect dominant patterns in New Woman narrative? Drawing on advice given to his sisters about their reading, Alice Markow has argued that 'Gissing was of his age in demanding improved education for women, but ... he did not believe that women were capable of the same intellectual rigor as men.'[35] It is difficult to assess the authorial position on the sentiments espoused by

---

Woman in Fiction and in Fact: Fin-de-Siècle Feminisms (Basingstoke: Palgrave, 2001), 53–65.

[32]　Grant Allen, *The Woman who Did*, ed. Sarah Wintle (1895; Oxford: Oxford University Press, 1995), p. 27. Women's colleges are rejected as evidence of 'one-sided culture', perpetuating women's dependence on their fathers, rather than encouraging them to pursue independence for themselves.

[33]　See *Collected Letters, Vol 4*, f.n., p. 123.

[34]　Gordon, pp. 958, 960. Statistics collected from the women's colleges show that almost half of the graduates went on to a career in teaching, with only 'a very few exceptions' entering medicine or government employment. This is disputed by Anne Jemima Clough, the first principal of Newnham, in her 1890 article 'Women's Progress in Scholarship', which notes the 'variety of paths' her graduates chose. Quoted in Dale Spender (ed.), *The Education Papers: Women's Quest for Equality in Britain, 1850–1912* (New York & London: Routledge & Kegan Paul, 1987), pp. 301, 304.

[35]　Alice B. Markow, 'George Gissing: Advocate or Provocateur of the Women's Movement?', *English Literature in Transition, 1880–1920* 25 (1982), 58–73 (p. 62).

Quarrier in his speech on 'Woman: Her Place in Modern Life' in *Denzil Quarrier*, seen as lamentably 'timid' by Mrs Wade but also functioning as some kind of acknowledgement of the educated woman's anomalous position. A far cry from Schreiner's advanced views, the agenda behind Quarrier's plea for the 'judicious training of young girls' (p. 84) by their mothers is to fit them better for marriage rather than the labour market, and all eyes turn to Mrs Wade, as he jokes, 'I repeat that I don't want to see them trained for politics' (p. 85). The 'maiden ladies' listening to Quarrier's speech, 'the army of women who, by force of mere statistics, are fated to the frustration of their *raison d'etre'* (p. 85), are disappointed that his offers of solace amount to nothing more than 'a pitying shrug of the shoulders'. The lack of support and problems of unemployment facing untrained women were being addressed at this time by investigators: Frances Low's interviews with 'aged and friendless' women workers in the late 1890s present a bleak picture of 'silent heroism' in the face of acute poverty, illness and dependency 'on the charity and compassion of friends and strangers'. The experience of the older poor lady suggests that she is unable to compete with younger, better trained girls and the 'smart, sharp semi-educated women' now flooding the market.[36] In this context, the authorial criticism of *Born in Exile*'s educated heroine for failing to make the effort 'to go in search of female companions' (p. 236) seems dismissive, unfair and contradictory. The fact that Marcella is unable to profit from rare connections with 'women of a sympathetic type' is linked to the argument that 'the emancipated woman has fewer opportunities of relieving her mind than a man in corresponding position' (p. 236). However, even a fellow school-mate who has become a successful artist is unable to offer her any practical advice and she reaps no apparent benefits from gaining access to Agatha's limited intellectual circle. Gissing also revealingly draws attention to her ignorance and indolence, claiming that she 'know[s] little of life' (p. 237), as if to reinforce the view that the educated woman has 'no place in society' (p. 276).

This focus on the 'needless isolation' (p. 239) of educated women like Marcella can also be read as a coded demand for more financial support for the 'army of women' unwilling to accept their status as second-class citizens. Ironically, Marcella is only allowed to support professional activity by leaving money to the struggling hero Godwin Peak after her death; she does not know how to use the money to support herself. In *Denzil Quarrier*, Lilian, recognising that her new friend's emancipatory stance is restricted by her material circumstances, conceives of 'the hopeful project of smoothing Mrs Wade's path in life' (p. 172), in which 'she was withheld by poverty from seeking her natural sphere' (p. 171), but in reality hopeful projects were noticeably absent for educated women, who more often resembled the 'friendless ladies' interviewed by Frances Low. The newly established women's employment bureaux in major cities, intended to 'investigate and regulate the educated female labour market',[37] were only just beginning to alleviate some of the difficulties of finding positions by the late 1890s. As public

---

[36] Low, 'How Poor Ladies Live', pp. 408, 413.
[37] Ibid., p.416.

institutions these looked back to the first of the women's employment societies at Langham Place, and their emphasis on training and placing women in a wider variety of situations recalls the ground-breaking work of the Society for Promoting the Employment of Women in the 1860s and 1870s. But SPEW's activities were limited; they were only able to find positions for about 50 women a year, primarily those functioning as 'pioneers in unusual occupations', and from the mid-1870s attention had shifted to the working-class woman.[38] The employment bureaux' negotiations with employers about salaries and hours on behalf of the 'isolated woman, who … is not in a position to make conditions' reflect changing concerns about women's work and more closely parallel the activities of the newly established Women's Industrial Council.[39]   However, it could be argued that despite a valorisation of widening employment opportunities, educated women were still being discouraged from entering certain 'unwomanly' professions. In an ongoing discussion of poor ladies in the *Nineteenth Century* in 1897, the social investigator Eliza Orme criticised a fellow journalist's suggestion for a bureau, because it was hinged on the proviso that training should be focused on fields of labour 'where a real and not an artificial need for women's services exists'.[40] She perceptively points out that most men would seek to deny the 'real need' for female labour in their professions, perpetuating a system whereby employers were restricted to offering only what was deemed '*suitable* employment' to educated women.

Periodicals of the time, particularly the new women's newspapers with their job advertisements and employment columns, offered expert advice on a range of new careers from journalism and library work to music and medicine, though the slant on the difficulties of finding well-paid work varied between journalists. Orme urged women to replace the question, 'Has this work been pronounced fit for ladies?' with 'Can I do this work with a chance of earning sufficient money to live upon, and without losing my self-respect'?[41] In her introduction to a series of articles on 'ladies at work' reprinted from the girls' magazine the *Monthly Packet*, Lady Jeune's claim that 'in … [her] choice of professions a woman's field of

---

[38]   Ellen Jordan, *The Women's Movement and Women's Employment in Nineteenth-Century Britain* (London & New York: Routledge, 1999), pp. 174, 195–6. Jordan argues that 'the importance of the Society's work lay far more in the propaganda campaign which spread its ideas than in the actual efforts, important though they may have been for individuals, to find work for particular women' (p. 193). After the mid-1870s, SPEW acted primarily as a loan society to help women undertake training or establish themselves in business.

[39]   Additional functions of such bureaux were to direct applicants to other employment agencies and to advise parents. Similar organisations in existence, such as the Working Ladies' Guild, which offered a loan fund, grants and a small number of pensions, were felt to be rather ineffectual because they were on such a limited scale. Applicants also had to be introduced by an associate. See Frances Low, 'How Poor Ladies Live: A Rejoinder and a "Jubilee" Suggestion', *Nineteenth Century* 42 (1897), 161–8 (p. 164).

[40]   Low, 'How Poor Ladies Live', p. 416.

[41]   Eliza Orme, 'How Poor Ladies Live: A Reply', *Nineteenth Century* 42 (1897), 613–19 (p. 614). She attacks the suggestion that women should be content with unpaid work to preserve their gentility.

choice is hardly less limited than that of a man' is significantly attributed to 'the improvement in the education of women, the increased facilities of communication and the influence of America'.[42] *Queen* journalist Margaret Bateson was more cautious in her view that 'the centre of feminine professional activity is for [the young girl] so near and yet so far', particularly when her ignorance may lead her to take 'desperately ill-advised steps'.[43] Her interviews, offering readers the benefit of 'half an hour's talk with an experienced woman', stress the 'spirited' and often pioneering nature of the female professional but advise girls to curb high expectations about salaries; there may be 'plenty of well-paid work for capable people' but unequal and inadequate pay was more than likely. It is interesting to consider the reasoning behind Gissing's choice of profession for his educated heroines, which seems to indicate that the poor lady's struggle to gain self-respect in one of the new careers served his fictional purposes better than the representation of the benefits of well-paid work. In late 1889 he began making preliminary notes on the kind of honours degree, training and certificates required to achieve promotion in teaching for a novel to be called *The Head Mistress*. However, the information about 'the salary, privileges, social opportunities' of High School head mistresses he requested from his sister Nelly may partially explain his decision to abandon the novel in March 1890.[44] The exceptional women promoted to the position of head mistress could expect to earn at least £200 a year, but the social opportunities they enjoyed were more circumscribed; as teaching was traditionally one of the few female-dominated professions, the all-female community and evening preparation may have precluded heterosocial interaction, though one could 'take advantage of special facilities for study or for travel' in the long holidays.[45] Socialist studies emphasise the intellectual stimulus of a career in secondary-school teaching, where 'the woman with brains' and 'the tastes of the scholar' is very much in demand,[46] but as a traditionally feminine occupation it did not generate the same narrative interest as the new careers. Although jaded teachers did feature in contemporary New Woman novels such as Netta Syrett's *Nobody's Fault* (1896), teaching was generally portrayed as an isolating, dispiriting experience, a safe rather than an appealing option for educated women in search of independence.

---

[42] Lady Jeune (ed.), *Ladies at Work: Papers on Paid Employment for Ladies by Experts in the Several Branches* (London: A.D. Innes & Co, 1893), pp. 1, 3. The volume is designed to show 'how wide and far-reaching are the results of modern life, and training, on educated and intelligent women' (p. 2).

[43] Margaret Bateson, *Professional Women upon their Professions: Conversations Recorded by Margaret Bateson* (London: Horace Cox, 1895), pp. iv, vii.

[44] Letter to Ellen, 11 October 1889. *Collected Letters, Vol 4*, p. 121. See also f.n., p. 123, for details of Gissing's research. In a paragraph in his scrapbook entitled 'Course preliminary to getting a Head Mistress-ship', he noted the requisite two-year attendance at training college and two years charge of a national school, before the acquisition of 'a certificate of Teaching Capacity'.

[45] Bird, p. 159. Bird's account of teaching makes it seem much more attractive than other professions, as there are fewer comments on the health risks and long hours.

[46] 'Teaching' in Morley, p. 28.

A career in journalism for the 1890s heroine allowed for more extensive discussions of women's competition with men in the labour market around an equally realistic but more glamorous role model for the aspiring professional reader. The new genre of career novels, according to Sally Mitchell, gained in popularity as paid work grew 'increasingly attractive to girls of all social classes'. She argues that the titles of 1880s and 1890s career fiction aimed at a bourgeois readership indicate that 'middle-class girls, who would probably become typists and teachers, were fantasizing about medicine, art and journalism'.[47] In her 1911 study of women wage-earners, M. Mostyn Bird characterised journalism as the 'most favourable' of all professions for women, allowing 'more freedom and independence ... than any other' for 'the well-educated girl of shrewd intelligence'.[48] The New Woman writer George Paston, the pseudonym of Emily Morse Symonds, who published a number of lively and well-researched novels in the 1890s emphasising the attractions of a professional career, used the experiences of her spirited heroines to attack stereotypes about the ailing poor lady. In the significantly titled *The Career of Candida* (1896), the boyish heroine is advised to train for two years as a gymnastic-instructor, a profession 'not as yet overcrowded, few ladies having taken it up, while there are new openings ... every year' (p. 17).[49] The novel dwells on 'the robust health and excellent spirits which distinguished the majority of ...wage-earning women' (p. 172) and appears to validate 'the prospect of freedom and independence won by her own work' (p. 204) over the heroine's pregnancy and married life. In *A Modern Amazon* (1894), the healthy Regina Haughton is first pictured striding purposefully down Fleet Street, appearing 'blissfully unconscious of the existence of such things as nerves' (Vol 1, p. 5),[50] and seems able to meet deadlines whilst keeping her editor at arm's length. Such narratives typically pit an 'up to date lady journalist' against a 'philandering editor'; the *Athenaeum* sided with the editor, characterising Regina as 'remarkably innocent and unsuspicious ... as *farouche* in manner as the most unlovely of her type'.[51] The male editor W.T. Stead reminded readers of *The Young Woman* that 'no women need apply for journalistic work on even terms with men' if they were not prepared to accept potentially 'unladylike' aspects of the career such as late-night reporting and criticisms of their writing, though 'forward' and 'aggressive' women who ape men 'compete voluntarily at a disadvantage'.[52] Far from aping men, Regina has secured her position over 279 other applicants

---

[47] Sally Mitchell, *The New Girl: Girls' Culture in England, 1880–1915* (New York: Columbia University Press, 1995), pp. 27, 32.

[48] M. Mostyn Bird, *Woman at Work: A Study of the Different Ways of Earning a Living open to Women* (London: Chapman & Hall, 1911), pp. 222, 225.

[49] All quotations are taken from George Paston [Emily Morse Symonds], *The Career of Candida* (London: Chapman & Hall, 1896).

[50] All quotations are taken from George Paston [Emily Morse Symonds], *A Modern Amazon*, 2 vols. (London: Osgood, McIlvaine & Co, 1894).

[51] Review of *A Modern Amazon*, *Athenaeum*, 5 May 1894, p. 574.

[52] W.T. Stead, 'Young Women and Journalism', *The Young Woman* 1 (1892), 12–14. Quoted in Margaret Beetham & Kay Boardman (eds.), *Victorian Women's Magazines: An Anthology* (Manchester: Manchester University Press, 2001), p. 115.

through a photograph rather than her qualifications. Her editor, whilst admiring the 'steadiness, sobriety and industry' of women workers, has been discouraged in the past by the fact that 'the ladyhood of the lady-journalist was too often disguised, if not effaced, by her professional manner and customs' (Vol 1, p. 25). Despite such barriers, Regina's experience suggests the satisfaction of disproving her editor's belief that she is only a 'glorified amateur'; once married off, she thinks fondly of the 'journalistic world of which she had once been proud to call herself a citizen' (Vol 2, p. 114). Paston sets her heroine's professional experience against that of the 'poor ladies who have seen better days' (Vol 2, p. 231), who struggle to find work in a labour market favourable to the younger generation of women. The middle-aged Miss Wynne has been unable to find work as a governess, because she lacks the certificates and advanced language and musical skills, nor is she 'young, bright and nice-looking' (Vol 2, p. 204) as required. However, the heroine's habit of revisiting her old desk after her marriage and 'pretending to be very busy and important' (Vol 2, p. 114) ambiguously signals both the severity of her withdrawal symptoms from work and the male editor's belief in women's amateurish 'playing at journalism' (Vol 1, p. 10). The feminist potential of the novel is then typically compromised by the short-lived nature of the female career.

Although he does not foreshorten his heroines' careers to quite the same extent, Gissing's examination of the lady-journalist in *New Grub Street* also emphasises restrictions on employment through male judgements about what was deemed suitable work for educated women. The Milvain sisters are eager to progress from the typically feminine occupations of governess and teacher of music to the more exciting new profession of writing: Dora writes to Marian, 'So perhaps our literary career will be something more than a joke, after all … anything rather than a life of teaching' (p. 119). But they can only break into this career by writing typically feminine stories for religious and girls' magazines, considered by Maud to be 'an inferior kind of work' (p. 43). Employment manuals confirmed that even journalists could not afford to abandon their femininity: although she encouraged women to write articles on a variety of topics from clothes and children to history and politics, Bird warned that 'in fact, the girl journalist will find her best openings, to start with, in … dress or housekeeping', feminine subjects guaranteed to appeal to the public. The more astute Marian is 'wounded' by Jasper's suggestion that she try her hand at romantic fiction because 'love-scenes … would be very much in [her] line', and responds coldly, 'I think that is not my work' (p. 455). This anticipates an important scene between Mary Erle and her male editor in Ella Hepworth Dixon's *The Story of a Modern Woman* (1894), in which she is ordered to include more romance in her novel, as 'the public like love-scenes' (p. 183). Although Mary leaves his office angry, she fits herself to Bird's model of the successful journalist as astute 'business woman'[53] by accepting her editor's judgements of the market, 'This was what she was to write – if she wanted to make

---

[53] Bird, p. 226.

any money, to keep her head above water' (p. 183).[54]   Whilst Gissing's novel seems to approve of journalism as a ladylike occupation, the male characters are too quick to judge literary work as unfit for ladies: Jasper says of his sisters, 'they were clever girls, and with energy might before long earn a bare subsistence; but it began to be doubtful whether they would persevere in literary work' (p. 423), suggesting that Gissing's women lack the requisite 'energy and push'[55] seen as requisite to succeed in a male-dominated profession. Alfred Yule also notes Marian's lack of commitment, her 'lukewarmness towards literary enterprise' (p. 348), leading him to the conservative view that like other clever girls she has been 'overtaxing her strength' (p. 343) in her work. Ellen Jordan's study suggests that up to 1880, 'status considerations and the contemporary definition of femininity were constraints on the expansion of middle-class women's employment',[56] but the category of 'suitable' women's work certainly remained a moot point throughout the era of the New Woman.

The 1890s novel then tended to reinforce the isolation of the educated female worker and her reliance on men, rather than other women, to help her onto the career ladder. The lascivious behaviour of male editors, coupled with lack of experience and contacts, ensured that 'the immense difficulty a woman finds in getting into an office in any recognised capacity makes a journalistic beginning far harder for her than for a man'.[57] Lady-journalists often only gain access to Grub Street after their work has been edited by fathers or brothers, and struggle to survive on their own literary merits. In *The Story of a Modern Woman*, Mary Erle's venture into journalism is achieved not by the quality of her writing but by the editor's recognition of her father's publishing history, and despite her confidence on the streets, she seems out of place in the 'jostling', 'hurrying' crowds on the 'wind-swept Strand', where 'hardly any women were to be seen' (p. 184). The *Tattler*'s acceptance of Ada's first sketch in *Isabel Clarendon* is more closely related to her literary skills but these have been developed whilst lodging at a friend's house in Chelsea during an informal 'apprenticeship' with Rhoda's father, who fortuitously happens to be an editor. In *New Grub Street* this reliance on male support is explored more fully. The gifted Marian 'doesn't write independently' (p. 66) but as a collaborator and researcher for her more well-known father. Jasper makes contacts for his sisters and negotiates with editors on their behalf, and the only other practical advice they receive is found in the guidelines for writers published by the struggling journalist Whelpdale, which pay no attention to the particular difficulties of women. Although it is anticipated that female friendship will be beneficial to professional development – Marian promises Jasper to 'be a friend to the poor girls' (p. 147) who envy her earning power and status as a 'literary lad[y] in London' (p. 74) – it remains under the

---

[54]   All quotations are taken from Ella Hepworth Dixon, *The Story of a Modern Woman*, ed. Kate Flint (1894; London: Merlin Press, 1990).
[55]   Bird, p. 226.
[56]   Jordan, p. 67.
[57]   'The Experiences of a Woman Journalist', *Blackwood's Edinburgh Magazine* 153 (1893), 830–838 (p. 832).

control of men./At a time when 'the desirability of a special training for journalists has been recognised', the women have to rely on men's limited knowledge of the rapidly changing market, a far cry from the practical tuition provided by the new School of Journalism in London.[58]   There is predictably no reference to the Institute of Journalists formed in 1890, though this could only offer assistance to women engaged in professional practice for at least two years, rendering it useless to aspiring lady-journalists.   Moreover, judging from the experiences of a woman journalist writing in *Blackwoods* in 1893, the Ladies' Employment Office was no better; she left 'with a sinking heart' and a religious tract, her conclusion 'not much chance for me there evidently', borne out by a letter offering her the clearly unsuitable post of female detective.[59]   Whilst Vicinus's grand claim that 'a network of women's organizations and institutions supported each single woman entering the newly developing professions for women'[60] may be debatable, it is certainly the case in Gissing's fiction written before *The Odd Women* that educated women are unlikely to benefit from their contacts with such a network, their limited contact with other professional women, and their inadequate training often directly affecting their decisions to withdraw from the labour market and capitulate to the cultural pressures to marry.

New Living Conditions

Historical accounts of the lifestyles of the single woman have drawn attention to her occupation of the city as one of the key aspects of her new freedoms. In her study of independent women between 1850 and 1920, Martha Vicinus argues that women entering the professions for the first time also pioneered 'new living conditions and new public roles', embracing 'a whole new way of structuring their lives'.[61] Although institutionalised communities, particularly the new settlement houses and training colleges, were the main arenas for restructuring urban femininities in the 1880s and 1890s, subsidised housing aimed primarily at 'isolated' working women in cities also offered 'protection, convenience and opportunities for a fuller social life'.[62] In her discussion of the educated working woman's need for affordable, residential space in the city, Deborah Parsons has noted the wider availability of bed-sits and self-contained flats catering for better-

---

[58] Fanny L. Green, 'Journalism', in *Ladies at Work*, pp. 30, 36. Founded in 1890, the Institute of Journalists, a development of the National Association of Journalists, did admit women, but only on the proviso that they had been engaged in actual practice as professional journalists for at least two years, which restricted its capacity to help the aspiring lady-journalist.
[59] 'The Experiences of A Woman Journalist', p. 832.
[60] Vicinus, p. 31.
[61] Ibid., p. 6.
[62] Ibid., p. 295. Ladies' dwellings were often unpopular because of their 'restrictive regulations', leading to a decrease in morale, as 'women fought with the stigma of living with other "failures"' (p. 296).

paid professional women, part of the increase in 'the standard and provision of housing ... by the turn of the century'.[63] In this period the newly established Ladies' Dwellings Company set out to address 'the great want that exists of suitable and cheap dwellings for cultivated women' by providing flats for rent as an alternative to the existing lodging houses for working girls. Sloane Gardens House, completed in 1889, was promoted to readers of *The Englishwoman's Review* as 'centrally situated, easy to reach, and convenient for the residence of busy women whose position and occupations require them to be near the wealthier districts of London'.[64] The lodging house was recognised as another new urban space for women; as Sarah Deutsch has claimed in relation to women's living arrangements in Boston at the turn of the century, 'boarding or lodging was not evidence of [wage-earning women's] depravity but of a life stage, not evidence of isolation, but of networks'.[65] But contemporary periodical debate reveals a range of views on women's attitudes to the potential isolation of urban living; according to an 1895 article in the *Girl's Own Paper*, the city girl may have rejected living in a community because she 'wishes for freedom which cannot be so well obtained unless she live alone'.[66] In an article on 'The Home Life of Professional Women', Margaret Bateson sought to disprove myths about the loneliness of spinsters but advised *Queen* readers to 'take ... a flat in a central situation' to facilitate meetings with friends.[67] The new flats and women's lodging houses helped to legitimise middle-class women's position in urban culture and to facilitate female friendships and professional development.

But despite women's increasing power to 'shape' their urban environments, these new forms of accommodation do not comfortably fit Deutsch's model of 'female-controlled public and semi-public spaces'.[68] Women often could not control whom they lodged with, which affected their opportunities for socialising and their reputations. Some of the poor ladies interviewed by Low express dissatisfaction with their lodgings, one because she feels her respectability

---

[63] Deborah L. Parsons, *Streetwalking the Metropolis: Women, the City and Modernity* (Oxford: Oxford University Press, 2001), p. 111.

[64] 'The Ladies' Dwelling Company', *Englishwoman's Review* 19 (1888), 344–7 (pp. 344, 345). The rents of 5–8s. 6d. a week are practically identical to those quoted in relation to homes for working girls in existence since the late 1870s in places such as West Smithfield and Bayswater. See also 'Homes for Working Girls in London', *EWR* 11 (1880), 374–5 and 'Homes for Working Girls', *EWR* 16 (1885), 331–2.

[65] Sarah Deutsch, *Women and the City: Gender, Space and Power in Boston, 1870–1940* (Oxford: Oxford University Press, 2000), p. 95. In 1900, 28% of adult working women in Boston, excluding servants and waitresses, lived as boarders or lodgers (p. 91).

[66] Josepha Crane, 'Living in Lodgings', *Girl's Own Paper*, 8 June 1895, p. 562.

[67] Margaret Bateson, 'The Home Life of Professional Women', in *Professional Women upon their Professions*, p. 132. This article has a rather strange ironic tone which is difficult to interpret; even though Bateson is celebrating the spinster's freedom, she also says of the professional married woman that she 'admittedly has the best of both worlds' (p. 130).

[68] Deutsch, p. 6.

compromised by sharing lodgings with a policeman,[69] others because they are compelled to borrow the money to pay the rent on their meagre salaries. One account of the experience of a High School teacher in her late twenties suggests the difficulties of living outside the family home:

> The worst of my life – and, I fancy, the lives of most women teachers – is its intense isolation. Here I am in this great city, and I don't know a soul but the other teachers living in lodgings like myself, and of whom I am heartily sick after nine months of the year's daily and close intercourse. I don't know a man up here, and I long – it is most unenlightened and retrograde, isn't it? – for the society of a sensible man ... The kinds of lives we lead are utterly unnatural and unhealthy.[70]

The teacher's loneliness is here compounded by her inability to socialise with anyone apart from her colleagues, though the necessity to prepare classes in the evenings may have reduced leisure opportunities in her profession. The 'cramped, unnatural' experience of living alone is reinforced in Syrett's novel, *Nobody's Fault*, in which the teacher Bridget Ruan protests against the 'loneliness, the blankness of the social side of her life' suffered in her dingy lodgings; the 'women-only' lifestyle is clearly shown to be unrewarding.[71] Living separately from men is not a sign of liberty but a marker of the unnatural lifestyle of the spinster, who feels herself deprived of 'masculine intercourse' by choosing to live in lodgings. In a survey on women's accommodation conducted by the Women's Industrial Council in the late 1890s, participants significantly complained that 'one of the great drawbacks to the lives of women workers is the lack of men's society'.[72]

Despite its drawbacks, living away from the family home was seen as a hallmark of the New Woman's freedoms, which often coincided with her first experiences of city life. In Gissing's early novels, independent occupancy of urban residential space remains a fantasy for women. In *Isabel Clarendon*, Ada's 'great yearning' (Vol 2, p. 121) for Chelsea with its 'pleasant' air and literary associations underpins her 'ambition' to live there: 'she promised herself that, when the day of her freedom came, she would take one of the houses in Cheyne Walk' (Vol 2, p. 122). For the Paston heroine, the independence of living in lodgings is favourably contrasted with the 'narrow' existence of the wife and mother. Candida initially rejects marriage on the grounds of being 'at the beginning of a career' (p. 64) in order to lodge 'like a bachelor' with an actress in Bloomsbury. In *A Modern Amazon*, Regina initially lodges in Guildford Street

---

[69] In her response to Low's article, Edith Shaw scoffs at the poor lady who makes this complaint and cites it as an example of the way in which 'poor ladies themselves make it still harder for one another by fixing their own standard'. See 'How Poor Ladies might live: An Answer from the Workhouse', *Nineteenth Century* 41 (1897), 620–27 (p. 624).

[70] Quoted in 'How Poor Ladies Live', pp. 414–15.

[71] Netta Syrett, *Nobody's Fault* (London: John Lane, 1896), pp. 100–101, 106.

[72] Emily Robhouse, 'Women Workers: How they Live, how they wish to live', *Nineteenth Century* 47 (1900), 471–84 (pp. 481, 482). The women surveyed looked forward to mixed accommodation as 'a great step on in social evolution', arguing that 'women have everything to gain by association with men on an equal footing'.

with her elder sister, a superintendent at an orphanage before marriage eclipses her 'personal freedom'. But her attempts to reclaim this freedom when she separates from her husband are more difficult; with her sister working abroad, she only endures the loneliness and the struggle to survive in cheap rooms in Holborn, because she expects her husband to force her to return to the marital home in Kensington. This is similar to the experience of the would-be professional sisters in Ethel F. Heddle's *Three Girls in a Flat* (1896), who at first relish the refreshing Bohemianism and 'the glorious privilege of being independent' (p. 14) in their Chelsea flat, before square meals become unaffordable on a journalist's inadequate wages and all three have to be rescued into marriage to avoid serious illness.[73] Female difficulties in budgeting for accommodation, food and transport, let alone leisure activities, bear out the results of Collet's 1898 investigation of the expenditure of middle-class working women: she notes that most workers had to 'exercise rigid economy' in order to limit their spending, often skimping on food and recreation at the cost of their health.[74] In *The Odd Women*, the poverty-stricken Madden sisters have to abstain from spending money on leisure and transport, eking out their inadequate wages on rice and porridge, so that cheap romances, religion and alcohol have to act as poor substitutes for nutrition and the joys of independence. As Ann Heilmann has perceptively argued in her exploration of living and working spaces in *fin-de-siècle* feminist narratives, 'the image of a privately rented room encompasses both the experience of relative intellectual freedom and that of economic hardship. The often fragile independence the heroines of such narratives enjoy is constantly threatened by their frustrated hopes of professional success and their disillusionment with the monotonous drudgery of a working life'.[75] The often insurmountable difficulties of surviving in a 'room of one's own' whilst struggling against what Heddle calls 'the sordid, matter-of-fact worries incident on having very little money' (p. 14) tend to highlight the fragility, rather than the benefits, of the independent lifestyle for the woman worker in the genre of career fiction.

In Gissing's 1890s narratives single women tend to live in lodgings with sisters or female friends, rather than attempting to live alone. Brothers also intrude into female dwellings, questioning women's control over their own space. In a discussion of living arrangements in *Born in Exile*, it is Godwin who imagines the potential for intellectual intercourse in such abodes, 'life in London lodgings made rich promise; that indeed would be freedom, and full of all manner of high possibilities!' (p. 68). The same conversation informs us that Marcella 'lives with friends' but Gissing seems to purposefully exclude her from such 'high

---

[73]   All quotations are taken from Ethel F. Heddle, *Three Girls in a Flat* (London: Gardner, Darton & Co, 1896).
[74]   Collet, 'The Expenditure of Middle-Class Working Women', pp. 86, 78. Office workers and journalists often had to spend a high proportion of their income on clothes. In this survey clerks are shown to be guilty of 'feed[ing] themselves unwholesomely at tea-rooms or extravagantly and monotonously at restaurants'.
[75]   Ann Heilmann, 'Feminist Resistance, the Artist and "A Room of one's Own" in New Woman Fiction', *Women's Writing* 2:3 (1995), 291–308 (p. 294).

possibilities' by relocating her without explanation to a house in Notting Hill shared with her brother, Christian. Anticipating the unexpected occupancy of a London flat by the Madden sisters in *The Odd Women*, Dora and Maud are compelled to move to the city to look for work on the death of parents. Living in rented rooms overlooking Regent's Park is seen both as a 'risk' and an adventure, though the sisters are protected from some of 'the hardships they [will] have to face' (pp. 146–7) by their brother's proximity and greater urban knowledge. According to an 1888 article on 'The Glorified Spinster', such old-fashioned women who cohabited with relations fully deserved the label of Old Maid for failing to embrace the new living conditions associated with the new 'sisterhood'.[76] On Marian's first visit to the flat, the Milvain sisters are seen as poor ladies 'oddly out of place', their 'refinement ... out of harmony with these surroundings', as if to reinforce that middle-class women were not the natural habitants of 'this bare corner of lodgers' London' (p. 208). On the other hand, Marian's respectable occupation of the family home in remote Camden, where her father forbids her to receive visitors and watches over her movements, is represented as a confinement which stunts her professional and sexual development: the sisters are surprised that their new friend 'used none of the fashionable turns of speech which would have suggested the habit of intercourse with distinctly metropolitan society' (p. 51). Alfred Yule's concerns about Marian's 'new life of her own', in which socialising with the Milvains at the girls' rooms lends her the confidence to pursue her work independently from him, mask a fear of what is 'alien to, and in some respects irreconcilable with, the existence in which he desired to confirm her' (p. 309). The modern working woman is then seen to occupy an odd position, her access to the possibilities of the metropolis controlled by men imposing the 'limits to female autonomy' associated with new female living spaces.[77]

Deutsch brackets lodging houses with restaurants and workplaces as 'sites that simultaneously manifested and created community ties that enhanced [working women's] safety',[78] but the New Woman heroine is more likely to come to terms with her isolation than to benefit from the ties with other women that lodgings may encourage. In Dixon's novel the 'dingy' lodgings in Bulstrode Street occupied by Mary after her father's death compare unfavourably with her family home; throwing herself onto the 'hard sofa' in the 'bitter cold' room after her day's work, she thinks 'after all, the place would do well enough as a makeshift' (p. 87). Nevertheless, it is 'her own domain' (p. 85), shared with her brother only on his vacations from Oxford, and the recurring scenes showing the journalist writing her copy at her 'ink-stained desk' suggest an enviable capacity to carve out a quiet female workplace at the centre of the city, a place in which to 'live her own life', however 'dispiriting' (p. 87). Although the loneliness of such a position cannot be denied – we are reminded that 'living by herself in lodgings, she never saw any one' (p. 245) – it is significant that Mary chooses not to move into the flats occupied by her philanthropist friend Alison Ives, and other 'ladies ... of limited

---

[76] 'The Glorified Spinster', *Macmillan's Magazine* 58 (1888), 371–6 (p. 374).
[77] Deutsch, p. 23.
[78] Ibid., p. 114.

vocabulary', as if to reject the support of a female community. Women workers interviewed for the WIC survey on living conditions highlighted the problems of 'segregation into "hen-communities"', and pointed out that mixed accommodation would be 'a great step on in social evolution'.[79] Interaction with other lodgers in women-only accommodation often reinforces the rather desperate plight of the middle-aged poor lady, precipitating the New Woman heroine's rejection of new living spaces and the grim future of continued economic struggle they appear to offer. In *A Modern Amazon*, Regina's attempts to combat isolation by drinking tea with other 'lady lodgers' in her building are rather pitiful; her 'bond of union' with the middle-aged Miss Wynne is a stark reminder of the proximity of destitution: 'both were alone and friendless, and both were conscious that only a few pounds stood between themselves and actual want' (p. 206). The new boarding houses designed 'exclusively for working women' in cities such as New York and Boston may have bolstered the 'untiring energy and pluck' of the American career woman at this time,[80] but British authors did not tend to promote the advantages of women-only communities in the New Woman narrative.

Nevertheless, lodging houses *did* function as safe spaces not only to work but also to entertain men, theoretically allowing women eager for male company to invite friends and *fiancés* over their thresholds without fear of compromise. At a time when the out-dated system of chaperonage had yet to be entirely discontinued, however, visiting still had to be kept respectable and reputations safeguarded by the presence of a landlady, female housemate or sibling. Even in the liberated environment of the new women's colleges, such a system prevailed and was accepted; a graduate of Bryn Mawr in the late 1880s, where women are 'as free as in their own homes', had no objection to the rule that a mistress of the hall had to be present when students were receiving men in their private sitting rooms.[81] Lodgings become one of the few heterosocial arenas outside private homes in which professional women could socialise at a time when leisure activities were restricted and expensive, and the new women's clubs remained over-priced and therefore largely inaccessible.[82] Amy Levy's plea for an urban space for intellectual women to socialise in her 1888 article 'Women and Club Life', hinged on her awareness of the 'practical disadvantage[s]' and 'isolated position' of professional women, did not exclude men from the imagined space.[83] For Gissing,

---

[79] Robhouse, p. 481.

[80] Nora C. Usher, 'In a New York Boarding House', *Young Woman* 1 (1893), 349–50 (p. 349).

[81] Alys W. Pearsall Smith, 'A Women's College in the United States', *Nineteenth Century* 23 (1888), 918–26 (p. 920). The student precedes her comment on the freedoms of college life with the telling (and rather contradictory) statement that 'there are no rules'.

[82] Patricia Marks, *Bicycles, Bangs and Bloomers: the New Woman in the Popular Press* (Kentucky: University Press of Kentucky, 1990), pp. 118, 120. Marks highlights the philanthropic basis of many late-nineteenth-century women's clubs, 'allowing women sequestered in the home entrée into the public sphere in an acceptable way', but points out that in the popular press they were viewed with alarm as 'places of preparation for public life'.

[83] Amy Levy, 'Women and Club Life', *Woman's World* 1 (1888), 364–7 (p. 365).

women's occupation of rented rooms in London becomes a testing-ground for their respectability. There was an assumption that women who lived alone or in the new flats had no regard for propriety when entertaining men: we are told in *Denzil Quarrier* that Polterham society would have deemed it 'highly improper' that Quarrier had spent three hours at Mrs Wade's house, though the latter 'would have spoken her mind very distinctly to anyone who wished to circumscribe female freedom in such respects' (pp. 143–4). In the later novel, *Eve's Ransom* (1895), Maurice Hilliard is conscious of the impropriety of visiting Eve at her lodgings, aware that 'she was not likely to invite a perfect stranger into the house' (p. 40), a consciousness shared by the women who are careful not to allow male acquaintances over their thresholds. Articles on women's lodging houses often disguised fears about female sexual activity in warnings about space: in 1895 the *Girl's Own Paper* urged readers to avoid speaking to gentlemen-lodgers and 'never go to their sitting room or permit them to come to yours'.[84] The 'new privileges of woman' (p. 331) attributed to the heroine of *New Grub Street*, which permit 'friendly' relations between the sexes, compromise the safety of the lodging house, which may encourage 'the chance encounters associated with crowds'[85] and a radical promiscuity. Mixed messages about heterosociality ensured that the Glorified Spinster's supposed freedom from supervision remained difficult to put into practice.

The attention paid by men to what women felt to be the 'unnecessary rules' of respectability governing heterosocial encounters in lodgings is significantly related to the precarious position of flats on the borders between public and private space.[86] Sharon Marcus has described apartment buildings as 'fluid spaces perceived to be happily or dangerously communicating with the more overtly public terrain,' which could function as 'nodes of commercial and sexual exchange'.[87] Although he was able to conquer his 'prejudice against Flats' sufficiently to admire their cheapness, convenience and suitability to London life, Gissing later revised this view, attacking 'the wretchedness of life in lodgings',[88] which could not hope to offer the secure privacy associated with the Victorian home. In *New Grub Street*, Jasper comments to Marian, 'It's bad enough for a civilised man to have to rough it, but I hate to see women living in a sordid way' (p. 215), where the sordid side of rented accommodation included the greater possibility of mixed-sex interaction. In his discussion of the gendering of flats in Gissing's work, Richard Dennis has noted that not only do they form 'part of the threat posed by women's liberation', but they also operate as 'promiscuous

---

[84] Josepha Crane, 'Living in Lodgings', *GOP*, 8 June 1895, p. 563.

[85] Sharon Marcus, *Apartment Stories: City and Home in Nineteenth-Century Paris and London* (Berkeley: University of California Press, 1999), p. 3.

[86] Robhouse, p. 483.

[87] Marcus, p. 3.

[88] Letter to Algernon, 28 December 1884. *Collected Letters, Vol 2*, p. 279. *Diary*, 15 August 1891, pp. 253–4.

spaces', associated with intrigue, duplicity and the challenge to social propriety.[89] In *The Odd Women*, Monica's potentially adulterous visits to Bevis in his Bayswater flat inadvertently compromise her reputation in relation to Barfoot, who occupies rooms in the same apartment block, simply because her ambiguous presence on the public stairway can be linked to both men. According to Jasper, women need to be aware that 'liv[ing] without conventional protection ... necessitates ... being very careful' (p. 303). Whilst Dora is happy to spend her evenings at home, Maud suffers from the 'insuperable' difficulties of a position which 'isn't quite regular'; the poverty which restricts her entrance into society is compounded by the fact that 'she had no one to chaperon her' (p. 303). The recurrent Gissing scenario of anxious men waiting for women to return home late at night is then connected to the glorified spinster taking advantage of her new freedoms: the over-protective brother is not 'comfortable' until he witnesses Maud's safe return in a cab at midnight from a trip to the Gaiety Theatre. The circumscribing of female freedom also works in men's favour, as Jasper dictates where his sisters will live in order to facilitate his courtship of Marian. His decision to share with his sisters in larger more expensive lodgings, with two sitting-rooms so Marian can come to his room 'without any difficulty', is an attempt to satisfy 'these astonishing proprieties' (p. 367), though one senses that his pleasure in having the girls 'all under the same roof' (p. 420) is also linked to the greater ease with which he will be able to observe and control their behaviour. These shared lodgings then function as a safe environment where Whelpdale's courtship of Dora can take place under the watchful eyes of her brother, who relishes his chaperoning role.

Male protection in lodgings is used to combat Gissing's uneasiness about the irregularities associated with new living conditions for women, and his fears about the effects a Bohemian lifestyle may have on his educated heroines. In *Born in Exile* he exposes Marcella's picture of an artist's liberated lifestyle as illusory. Anticipating the freedoms of her own entry into a liberated set, 'she pictured Miss Walworth as inhabiting a delightful Bohemian world, where the rules of conventionalism had no existence, and everything was judged by the brain-standard' (p. 237). But the shocking reality is that Agatha lives 'like any other irreproachable young woman' and works in a studio in the family home in Chiswick. Perhaps his nearest approach to representing a female appropriation of Bohemia is in the later novel, *The Crown of Life* (1899), in which the artist Olga Hannaford goes to London 'for the convenience of artistic studies' (p. 103) and lodges above a shop in Great Portland Street with a female friend. A painter of advertising posters, the ebullient Miss Bonnicastle, who sings music-hall songs whilst painting and welcomes male visitors to the flat, is used to highlight the dangers and vulgarities of Bohemia. Olga's 'freer way of living' is seen as disconcerting and 'strange' to her friends and family: though she speaks of her flat with pride as 'a queer place' (p. 141), her friend Irene asks in horror, '*Why* do you

---

[89]   Richard Dennis, 'Buildings, Residences and Mansions: George Gissing's "Prejudice against Flats"', unpublished conference paper delivered at the Gissing and the City Centenary conference, (July 2003), University of London.

live in a place like this?' (p. 128). The lifestyle of a lady lodger is seen as both economically and morally uncertain: 'she lived here and there in lodgings, at times seeming to maintain herself, at others accepting help; her existence had an air of mystery far from reassuring' (p. 127).[90] Visitors to women's lodgings are often surprised to find a disregard for rules about femininity: a scene in the earlier novel in which Quarrier is repulsed by Mrs Wade's dishevelled appearance is echoed when Irene finds Olga at her drawing-board at midday, 'her careless costume and the disorder of her hair suggesting that she had only just got up' (p. 127). Despite the artist's belief in Bohemia as 'freedom [from] society nonsense' (p. 128), it is not seen to improve women's professional development. Olga later admits to herself:

> She was doing no good; all the experience to be had in a life of mild Bohemianism was already tasted, and found rather insipid. An artist she would never become; probably she would never even support herself. To imagine herself really dependent on her own efforts, was to sink into misery and fear. (p. 140)

She is forced to revert to Agatha's irreproachable position of working in a studio in the family home, where she 'chastened her expressions' and became 'a more serious person than hitherto' (p. 185). But this more respectable position is also shown to be unstable; made 'penniless' on her mother's death, she again contemplates living with Miss Bonnicastle: her flat-mate is recognised as 'the most sensible girl I know, and she did me good ... She helped me against myself' (p. 247), as if in validation of the ties between women forged in the lodging house. But Piers fears the masculinity associated with Bohemia: Miss Bonnicastle is regarded as 'an abnormality', with 'no single characteristic of her sex which appealed to him' (pp. 259, 260). It is the modern woman's occupation of urban living space, as she reaps the benefits of lucrative professional work 'that interferes with [man's] ideal of the eternal womanly', according to Schreiner, as the notion of a woman earning a salary of £150, who has 'a comfortable home of her own, and her evening free for study or pleasure, distresses him deeply'.[91] By emulating the lifestyle of the London bachelor or male university student, the spinster threatened accepted gender boundaries, though her interference with the ideal of the 'eternal womanly' had more serious implications for the future of the race.

Unwomanliness, Celibacy and the Woman of the Future

The conflict between professionalism and womanliness which permeated 1890s discourses was underpinned by evolutionary fears about the woman of the future, both in terms of her unacceptable celibacy and the physical debilities produced by working. Medical arguments current in the 1880s linking infertility to women's

---

[90] All quotations are taken from George Gissing, *The Crown of Life*, ed. Michel Ballard (1899; Sussex: Harvester Press, 1978).
[91] Schreiner, p. 204.

greater access to higher education gathered momentum from evolutionary fears
about the deficiency of reproductive power in intellectual, masculinised women, at
a time when 'the single woman was being constructed as an unwanted and
unnatural deviant'.[92] In 1889, Grant Allen's bold assertion that the 'self-supporting
spinster ... [is] an abnormality, not the woman of the future' is typically annexed
to an attack on contemporary feminists for neglecting their reproductive duties.[93]
A rather contradictory article on 'What Woman is Fitted For' celebrated the
'multitude of types of womanhood' of the future, but then lamented the fact that
the woman of today has to choose between the intellectual and the emotional sides
of her nature, creating 'two somewhat gruesome types of womanhood, the one all
mind and no heart, but the other all heart and no mind'.[94] The weak ending of
Denzil Quarrier is over loaded with such pseudo-scientific arguments about
woman's nature, as a chorus of male voices condemns strong-minded women as
'the weakest of their sex. Let their energies be submitted to any unusual strain, let
their nerves ... be overwrought, and they snap!' (p. 325). The risk to health and
the dangers of over-work cast a shadow on 'the increased scope of women's work
in the future',[95] with many articles, even those in periodicals aimed at women,
reproducing anti-feminist medical arguments that the 'ardours' of a professional
career take their toll on women's nervous energy. Such an argument often masked
a fear of women's earning capacities: as one study pointed out, the callings which
are often seen as taboo and unwomanly 'are precisely such as offer the highest
rewards in money or consideration'.[96] The threat of women competing with men
in the labour market often lay behind advice about work 'fit for ladies', for in late-
Victorian public opinion 'the unwomanly woman is a hideous thing in any
profession'.[97] An 1894 series on 'How Can I Earn a Living?' aimed at the middle-
class readers of the new periodical *The Young Woman* reminded 'girls of today'
faced with the necessity of working side by side with men 'never to forget that they
are women'.[98] Women's fitness for the labour market, ideologically harnessed to

---

[92] Lucy Bland, *Banishing the Beast: English Feminism and Sexual Morality, 1885–1914*
(Harmondsworth: Penguin, 1995), p. 172. The spinster's barrenness was linked to the rising
strength and threat of feminism, at the same time that women were being encouraged to
produce more healthy children to serve the needs of empire.

[93] Grant Allen, 'Plain Words on the Woman Question', *Fortnightly Review* N.S. 46 (1889),
448–58 (p. 455).

[94] [Henrietta Muller], 'What Woman is Fitted For', *Westminster Review* 71 (1887), 64–75
(pp. 71, 74).

[95] Jeune, p. 10.

[96] Pfeiffer, p. 8. The same point is made by Schreiner in her argument about men's
objections to women doctors, legislators and professors. See p. 204.

[97] 'Young Women and Journalism', p. 115. Despite such anti-feminist remarks, the article
is generally supportive of women's entry into the profession, from the point of view of an
editor who 'would never employ a man if I could find a woman who could do the work as
well'.

[98] Miss Billington, 'How can I earn a Living?: Journalism, Art or Photography', *Young
Woman* 2 (1894), 307–11 (p. 309). This sentiment was also expressed in her concluding
article in this series, 'Miscellaneous', (412–15), p. 415.

the spinster's unfitness for motherhood, continued to be contested throughout the period.

The link between unwomanliness and financial solvency goes some way towards explaining Gissing's lack of interest in the new career of medicine, the only example being the minor character of Janet Moxey in *Born in Exile*, who trains at the new London School of Medicine for Women founded in 1874. A discouraging account of the 'unwomanly' but well-paid medical profession in the *Monthly Packet* promised 'hardship, fatigue ... incessant self-denial' and 'almost complete isolation', evoking stereotypes about suitable women's work by concluding that 'the number of their sex fitted by nature for such endurance are in the minority'.[99] A less biased article in *The Nineteenth Century* attacking stereotypes about nervous lady doctors was forced to concede that 'it is only exceptional women who even think, in the first place, of entering the medical profession' with its five-year training and '(to her) special difficulties'.[100] The rare appearances made by lady doctors in 1890s fiction tended to reinforce women's inability to cope with the long training, rather than the successes of their campaigning in the 'strenuous battle' for equal pay.[101] Arabella Keneally's anti-feminist novel *Dr Janet of Harley Street* (1893) focuses on the young flirtatious heroine who fails to dedicate herself to the intensive study required for the medical profession rather than the older experienced doctor, a self-defined 'neuter' whose loneliness and asexuality are ambiguously held up for ridicule or pity as well as admiration.[102] The fact that owing to the expense and long training, the profession 'attracted a large proportion of working women not subject to immediate economic stress'[103] perhaps explains Gissing's cursory handling of the figure of the lady doctor; Janet may be a clear example of 'modern womanhood, refreshing, inspiriting' (p. 339) but she is not engaged in the same struggle for survival which usually drives the lady journalist. In his positive reading of the doctor as a pioneering modern figure, Kramer contends that 'by not presenting a debate about [Janet's] career, Gissing leaves room for her argument only',[104] but he omits to mention the effects on her health. Reinforcing evolutionary beliefs in women's finite energy, Janet has to take 'an enforced holiday' because she is 'overworked a little' (p. 339), and is then married off to her cousin in order to avoid her imminent breakdown, '[she] mustn't go on with professional work ... her strength isn't equal

---

[99] Caroline W. Latimer, M.D, 'The Medical Profession', in *Ladies at Work*, pp. 80, 84, 81.

[100] Mary L. Breakell, 'Women in the Medical Profession', *The Nineteenth Century and After* 54 (1903), 819–25 (pp. 823–4).

[101] 'The Medical Profession', in Morley, p. 140. The prevalence of independent women, who have the time and resources to campaign, is here seen as important in securing the satisfactory conditions across the profession.

[102] See introduction to Ann Heilmann, *Anti-Feminism in the Victorian Novel* (Thoemmes Continuum, 2003) for a closer consideration of this novel.

[103] 'The Medical Profession', in Morley, pp. 140, 148.

[104] Kramer, p. 321. I am unconvinced by the view that 'the very fact of her being a minor character might speak to how deeply Gissing sympathizes with her'. See also pp. 319–20, in which Kramer dates Janet's attendance at the London School of Medicine in 1876, the first year that the University of London could admit women.

to it' (p. 389). New Woman writers seemed reluctant to accommodate heroines able to withstand the nervous strains of a medical career, as if such exceptional women were either too threatening or pioneering to appeal to a range of women readers.[105]

1890s fiction also ambiguously reproduces anti-feminist medical arguments about the effects of journalism on women's health. Strangely, these seem to have been perpetuated by female journalists themselves, perhaps in order to preserve the idea of female professional exceptionality. An interviewer for the *Young Woman* of 1894 noted that, despite professing to be 'a sound advocate of lady journalism', the famous Emily Crawford 'seldom encourages others to engage in the work in which she has herself been so successful', bolstering the 'superwoman' image of the lady journalist as a woman of 'exceptional health and powers of physical endurance'.[106] Even the experienced feminist journalist Frances Power Cobbe warned young women about the 'deficiencies' and 'disabilities' which might prevent their 'ever ... compet[ing] on equal terms with male journalists', claiming that 'few women possess the steady health and equable brain-power ... to perform the serious mental labour' of daily original composition.[107]   On her first research trip to the British Museum, Paston's heroine Regina neglects to eat the bun she has brought for lunch and has to be rescued 'trembling from head to foot with pain and exhaustion' (Vol 1, p. 68) by her husband-to-be, a doctor horrified by her 'unnatural and unseemly' (Vol 1, p. 81) working life, who pronounces her 'not fit' to work in such an environment.   Similarly engaged, Marian does remember to eat her sandwich at midday but still returns home 'faint with weariness and hunger' (p. 115) after six hours under the harsh electric lights in the 'warm, headachy air' (p. 137) of the library.   According to Ruth Hoberman, in popular representations women's work in the British Museum reading room often brings on 'illness and eccentricity' rather than the excitement of working in the 'centre of London intellectual life', though this is specifically attributed to their lower-middle-class status.[108] However, this may be a strategy for defusing the threat of the lady-journalist's

---

[105] An exception to this rule is Graham Travers [Dr Margaret Todd], *Mona Maclean, Medical Student* (1892), about a female medical student modelled on Emily Flemming. This was reviewed favourably in the *Englishwoman's Review*, but seen as rather unrealistic. See *Englishwoman's Review* 24 (1893), p. 53.   I am indebted to Ann Heilmann for this reference.

[106] 'A Famous Lady Journalist: A Chat with Mrs. Emily Crawford', *Young Woman* 2 (1894), 183–5 (p. 183).   A regular contributor to *The Daily News* and the *Pall Mall Gazette*, the widowed Crawford disagreed with the idea that home life would interfere with journalistic duties.

[107] Frances Power Cobbe, 'Journalism as a Profession for Women', *Women's Penny Paper* 1 (1888), 5. Quoted in Beetham & Boardman, pp. 69, 70.

[108] Ruth Hoberman, 'Women in the British Museum Reading Room during the late-nineteenth and early-twentieth centuries: From Quasi- to Counter-Public', *Feminist Studies* 28:3 (2002), 489–512 (pp. 495, 497). She argues that in the popular press the over crowded room became a 'contested space' as it was depicted as 'inappropriately overwhelmed by women's bodies' (p. 496).   Many women refused to sit in the designated 'ladies' seating', preferring to make themselves 'doubly visible' as readers.

occupation of intellectual male space, distancing the heroines from notable female writers and intellectuals such as Eleanor Marx and Clementina Black, 'conspicuous presences in a room full of men, [who] delighted also in their sheer visibility at the heart of public life'.[109] Whilst Gissing's journalist does threaten gender boundaries by competing with men on male territory, she also functions as a warning of the dangers of over work, a means of exploring (or exploding) cultural concerns about female fitness for intellectual study. By the end of the novel she suffers from 'attacks of nervous disorder' (p. 542) which we are invited to attribute to her writing, potentially bearing out Milvain's initial diagnosis that she is not 'the kind of girl to make a paying business of literature ... [as it] doesn't agree with her disposition' (p. 66). Nevertheless, her father's fear that she is 'overtaxing her strength' (p. 343) taps into biological fears about women's finite energy refuted in Pfeiffer's study as 'alarmist': her research reveals a lack of evidence for the connection between work and ill-health and the view that money anxieties rather than over work were a more likely cause of stress.[110] Whilst others might 'imagine her contentedly busy, absorbed in the affairs of literature', Marian considers herself 'not a woman, but a mere machine for reading and writing' (p. 137). Despite its connections with unwomanliness, the mechanistic image of the grind of library research also aligns Marian with the struggling Gissing, who significantly described himself as 'only a machine for producing volumes' in a letter shortly before beginning *New Grub Street*.[111] In fact, in Gissing's Darwinian scheme the risks to health associated with earning a living through writing bear more heavily on men, as the suicide of the struggling novelist Edwin Reardon signals his inability to compete on a professional level with the dynamic Milvain. Women's failure 'to make a paying business of literature' in the novel perhaps says more about their lack of support, rather than their unfitness to survive, in a male-dominated competitive marketplace.

This unwomanly penetration of the male working environment, from which Paston heroines typically retreat, became inseparable from the self-supporting spinster's 'abnormality', seen in both her physical appearance and her (a)sexuality. Dominant images of the educated working woman in both fiction and scientific debate tended to categorise her professionalism in terms of her 'unnatural' gender and sexuality, even as feminist writers struggled to defend the modern woman's right to celibacy. In Gissing's fiction, the well-educated woman is stereotypically described as 'slight' or boyish, with masculine facial features, a new 'androgynous' type who both repels and fascinates the modern man.[112] According to John Sloan, Ada Warren in *Isabel Clarendon* 'heralds the emergence in Gissing's fiction of the image of those "hybrids" or "men-women" caricatured by

---

[109] Hoberman, pp. 491, 495.

[110] Pfeiffer, pp. 70–72, 117–19.

[111] Letter to Bertz, 22 June 1890. *Collected Letters, Vol 4*, p. 226.

[112] Markow, p. 65. She groups Mrs Wade and Ada Warren with Rhoda Nunn in *The Odd Women* and Constance Bride in the later novel *Our Friend the Charlatan* (1901), all examples of 'portrayals of radical feminists'.

journalists and ardent anti-feminists of the period'.[113] Both Ada's appearance and her learning are far from feminine: her face is 'irregular in feature and harsh in expression' (Vol 1, p. 10), even 'decidedly ugly' (Vol 1, p. 133), she can only be said to have a good figure when 'seen from behind' and her tastes in reading are 'deplorably masculine' (Vol 1, p. 144).[114] On first sight, Milvain finds Marian, who wears a hat 'of the shape originally appropriated to males ... Neither pretty nor beautiful' (p. 45), but admires her short hair and strong neck. He denies the 'old-fashioned' view that 'the modern literary girl' is a 'fright' and notes her 'nice eyes' and a 'figure not spoilt yet' (p. 46), perhaps in veiled admiration of her choice of a career over motherhood. The Socialist and eugenicist Karl Pearson voiced a common perception when he claimed that the new professional woman who typically 'abstain[s] from marriage' could not become the woman of the future because 'such women cannot transmit the asexualism which fits them for competition with men to a numerous offspring'.[115] Schreiner argued vehemently against the theory that intellectual power rendered woman 'undesirable to the male', emphasising the endurance of the sexual instinct and the increased compatibility between 'the highly evolved female' and the New Man.[116] But Gissing's appropriation of such evolutionary arguments cannot be taken at face value as they are often challenged within the narrative. Kingcote initially recoils from Ada as 'cold and hard ... intellectual ... in the way one does not desire in a woman' (Vol 1, p. 179), but paid work seems to make her 'more feminine', and by the end of the novel we are told that 'the harshness of her features was softening' (Vol 2, p. 296). Although men are puzzled by the asexuality of educated heroines, their appreciation of such women's capacity for intellectual conversation often leads them to reassess their views on their physical attractions, in order to re-evaluate 'the new type of celibate women'.[117]

---

[113] John Sloan, *George Gissing: The Cultural Challenge* (Basingstoke: Macmillan, 1989), p. 45.

[114] In *Denzil Quarrier*, the heroine is described in similar terms: Mrs Wade asks Lilian whether she finds her 'what the French call *hommasse*' [masculine] (p. 168) and appears relieved to be reassured of her womanliness.

[115] Karl Pearson, 'Woman and Labour', *Fortnightly Review* 55 (1894), 561–77 (pp. 567, 568). Pearson thus revived fears about the redundancy of single women, arguing that 'when once the professions now opening to women are fully stocked, the premium on spinsterdom will be immensely increased'. His argument, heavily influenced by pro-natalist fears about the future degeneration of the race, is that emancipated women, by neglecting their child-bearing capacities, ensure that 'the sex-impulses' remain undeveloped, putting an excessive burden of child-rearing onto others, or inviting 'a crushing out of the maternal instincts on which the stability of society essentially depends' (pp. 568–70).

[116] Schreiner, pp. 225, 237. She does however admit that if there is 'the smallest danger' of the decay of the sexual instinct and by extension, the extinction of the race, it would be better 'to lay aside new labour' (p. 227).

[117] 'The Future of Single Women', p. 153. The article challenged the view that 'an unmarried woman is undeveloped and incomplete', commenting on the health and vigour of the new single woman.

Advocating celibacy as a choice for women seems to have been a particular project of Ella Hepworth Dixon, as her heroine rejects offers of marriage and sex in order to forge ahead with her career. Vicinus notes that single women may have 'accentuated their age and asexuality to emphasize a professional identity and minimize their youthful eligibility'[118]. In her article 'Why Women are Ceasing to Marry' (1899), Dixon championed the attractions of 'the modern spinster's lot' and the 'social liberty' of remaining single:

> If young and pleasing women are permitted by public opinion to go to college, to live alone, to travel, to have a profession, to belong to a club, to give parties, to read and discuss whatsoever seems good to them, and to go to theatres without masculine escort, they have most of the privileges [of marriage] ... Indeed, the disadvantages of marriage to a woman with a profession are more obvious than to a man, and it is just this question of maternity, with all its duties and responsibilities, which is, no doubt, occasionally the cause of many women forswearing the privileges of the married state.[119]

Although her educated heroine chafes against the 'impotence, the helplessness of woman's lot' (p. 254) and only seems to endure the privations of a journalist's life because, like Regina, she expects it to be a temporary phase before marriage, her final decision to deny her sexual attraction to the philandering Vincent Hemming is represented as an active choice of the spinster's 'social liberties' and an acceptance, rather than a fear of her 'certain vagueness about the future' (p. 165). Contemporary reviewers criticised Dixon for promising readers a 'self-assertive', 'sexless' modern woman, when instead there was 'little modernity' in Mary's resigned acceptance of 'her role as a failure in life',[120] but this is a short-sighted view of a heroine who does assert her right to choose an alternative role for women. In her reading of the novel, Erin Williams has emphasised the problematic sacrifice of sexuality underpinning 'the choice of celibacy', arguing that this results in a loss of citizenship, which 'precludes the spinsters' full incorporation into the urban public space they claim'.[121] However, this does not seem to be borne out in a narrative which values work over sexual desire. Disregarding her doctor's diagnosis of an over-strained nervous system because she 'live[s] too much in London' (p. 175) and adopts an 'unnatural' lifestyle 'not fit for girls' (p. 176), Mary's attempt to literally grasp the possibilities London offers her in the conclusion seems to confirm her place within the city. Despite echoing negative representations of the spinster as 'lonely, tired, discouraged ... cling[ing] to the thought of ...marriage' (p. 92), Dixon's bravely realistic portrayal

---

[118] Vicinus, p. 40.

[119] Ella Hepworth Dixon, 'Why Women are Ceasing to Marry', *Humanitarian* 14 (1899), 391–6 (p. 394).

[120] Review of *A Story of a Modern Woman*, *Athenaeum*, 16 June 1894, p. 770.

[121] Erin Williams, 'Female Celibacy in the fiction of Gissing and Dixon: the Silent Strike of the Suburbanites', *English Literature in Transition, 1880–1920* 45:3 (2002), 259–80 (p. 278). The article makes some useful comparisons between Dixon's novel and *The Odd Women*, though Rhoda's rejection of Everard is viewed in the same light, her 'repudiation of marriage ... a frustrating compromise' (p. 270).

of her modern woman's story emphasises the benefits, as well as the difficulties, of paid work for women. Her assertion that 'all we modern women are going to help each other' (pp. 213–14) gestures towards the future possibilities of the professional woman's London lifestyle, and the networks of women needed to combat inequality in the workplace. She stands as an example of the new type of celibate woman, who 'having weighed the advantages and disadvantages of married and single life, deliberately choose[s] the latter'.[122]

Nonetheless, the atavistic type of the old maid also haunts the New Woman narrative, casting doubt on the temporary freedoms of the professional lifestyle and offering a sobering reminder of the destiny which may await the celibate career woman. Frances Low categorised some of her interviews with poor ladies as 'histories of want and distress and destitution', not least for those 'elderly cultured women' reduced to starvation due to dependency on 'their own precarious earnings and the intermittent aid of strangers'.[123] Even though the term 'old maid' was 'dying out' by the end of the century,[124] the concept, despite its new labels, was still very much in existence, and the New Woman heroine is often shown to think of herself in these terms, whatever her claims to modernity. Typically, the celibacy Paston seems to advocate for her heroines is seen as problematic in the long run. In *The Career of Candida*, the heroine's attempts to resume her old profession after separation from her husband, and to maintain platonic friendships with men have to be proved unsuccessful to prevent a too radical validation of a career over marriage. Fears about the uncertain status of single women are explicitly addressed in Candida's father's concern about her 'anomalous position' (p. 234). Despite the fact that her energetic working life is explicitly privileged over the idle existence of her sisters-in-law, whose ill-health she attributes to their 'lack of occupation', in the predictable resolution she is returned to a more 'fitting' career, the 'grave responsibility' (p. 289) of caring for her estranged husband. The capacity of her earlier Amazonian heroine to 'talk, eat and walk like a man' (Vol 1, p. 185) ensures that she is ominously 'not adapted to make a satisfactory wife and mother' (Vol 1, p. 197). The unnaturalness of Regina's preference for intellectual discussion with men over sexual intimacy is explicitly signalled in the derogatory labels given to women who abstain from marriage: her feminist acquaintance Agatha Staunton, who lectures on women's rights, is classed as 'a freak of nature' (Vol 1, p. 193), whilst her husband-to-be considers the old maid, 'a crime against

---

[122] 'The Future of Single Women', p. 155.

[123] Low, 'How Poor Ladies Live', pp. 415, 408. Low goes on to point out 'but I do not conceive any useful purpose can be gained by detailing these harrowing life-histories, my object being to compel a consideration of the entire problem rather than to excite sympathy for individual cases of suffering', though she also admits that she has concentrated on 'the most gloomy and unhopeful' side of the picture of women's work.

[124] Response to Sarah Grand, 'At What Age should Girls Marry?', *Young Woman* 7 (1899), 161–4 (p. 164). Responses by a number of important feminist writers were included at the end of Sarah Grand's article in the same edition and in the number for the following month, pp. 207–10, which also remarked on the decline of the old maid (p. 209). See also 'The Glorified Spinster', p. 372, as the journalist maps the evolution of the Old Maid, 'a woman *minus* something' into the Glorified Spinster, 'a woman *plus* something'.

nature' (Vol 1, p. 132). Paston's novels certainly dwell on the sorry plight of the older poor lady, condemned to unemployment, poverty and illness, as a warning. The poorly dressed Miss Green, who gave up work as a secretary due to ill-health and family duties, is reduced to tears when she cannot get her position back. Fear of an uncertain future prompts Regina's decision to marry to avoid becoming 'as helpless and forlorn' as those compelled into 'poverty-stricken old-maidenhood' (Vol 1, pp. 282–3). Struggling to survive alone in a rented room in Holborn suggests 'a bond of union' with Miss Green, and the unappealing prospect of 'a life spent in loneliness, poverty and ill-paid labour' (Vol 2, p.214), making the return to marriage a more attractive option than such a 'terrible future' (Vol 2, p. 267).

Whilst Gissing's fiction sometimes follows a similarly conservative trajectory in advocating the security of marriage over the uncertainty of a career – after all, in *New Grub Street* the Milvain sisters are only able to progress beyond their original 'ambiguous' position as over-educated teachers by marrying and withdrawing from the labour market – he seems to be working towards a more enabling account of the loneliness the female professional must endure in order to achieve fulfilment through work. In *Denzil Quarrier*, the author leaves the story of his 'problematic' and 'eccentric' heroine unfinished, neutralising her potential radicalism by showing that she accepts her celibacy out of necessity rather than choice. Although 'the pleasures of independence and retirement' (p. 231) do not satisfy Mrs Wade, her radical desire to rise above being seen as 'unfit for anything but cooking and cradle-rocking!' only thinly veils her 'bitter sense of her poverty and loneliness' (p. 230). The weak melodramatic ending of the novel transforms her into a hysterical, sexually frustrated figure, consumed by jealousy, whose failure to prevent Lilian's suicide invites her condemnation as 'a source of incalculable harm to all who are on friendly terms with her – especially young and impressionable women' (p. 324–5). The final image of the celibate woman seems particularly harsh, perhaps to satisfy the readers of the popular magazine, as the 'tired, harassed' Mrs Wade now with 'the appearance of a much older woman' (p. 335), continues to flirt rather desperately with the hero. However, in the later short story 'Comrades at Arms' (1896), Gissing appears much less confused about the attractions of a celibate, working lifestyle to the modern woman, granting his successful journalist heroine the same liberties as her male colleagues, and allowing her to choose her career over marriage. The 'mannish', thirty-something Bertha Childerstone initially appears as another case-study of the effects of over-work in the 'nervous collapse' which produces a weakness that prevents her from working. Stereotypes about her unnatural existence in her untidy and 'dreary' lodgings are filtered through the perspective of her fellow journalist Wilfrid Langley, who nurses her back to health and ponders 'how a woman could live amid such surroundings. But was Miss Childerstone to be judged as a woman? ... She seemed to have been growing less feminine ... he liked her, admired her, and could imagine her, in more natural circumstances, a charming woman' (pp. 7, 8).[125] But the narrative of withdrawal from paid work is subverted in the heroine's

---

[125] All quotations are taken from 'Comrades at Arms', in George Gissing, *Human Odds and Ends* (1898; New York & London: Garland Publishing, 1977).

rejection of Wilfrid's offer of marriage, and her feminist claim to a room of one's own:

> That longing for domesticity gave me a shudder. It's admirable, but it's the part of you that must be outgrown … I don't want to marry. Look at this room, dirty and disorderly. This is all the home I care for … In poverty … I prefer the freedom of loneliness. (p. 16)

The reframing of the friendless isolation of the poor lady into 'the freedom of loneliness' destabilises current thinking about the disadvantages of the new living conditions, as Bertha's reply is used to validate women's sole occupancy of lodgings at the heart of the city, showing her spinster pad as the true 'home' of the new female professional. Significantly, it is the female who is better fitted to 'outgrow' the longing for marriage and children which hinders social progress; as one of the 'many women left outside of domesticity',[126] Gissing's self-supporting heroine exercises her right to choose an alternative and potentially more satisfying destiny.

Ann Ardis's view that *fin-de-siècle* narratives of female professionalism work to 'delegitimize women's ambitions'[127] can then be challenged by recognising that Gissing's conclusions often also offer muted support to alternative feminist visions of the 'fitness for labour' of the educated working woman. Women's difficulties in carving out a successful career in journalism in Gissing's narratives need to be seen in the broader context of 1890s fiction. The open-ended conclusion to *Isabel Clarendon* seems to validate Ada's choice of earning a living by writing over the privileges of inherited wealth. The links made between publication, the prospect of 'find[ing] some work in the world' (Vol 2, p. 196), and citizenship recall the feminist mantra of women's right to work, so that the writer's anticipation of 'earn[ing] by writing enough to live upon' (Vol 2, p. 197) looks forward to her final sense of satisfaction, full of 'the joy of her youth, and health, and freedom, in the delight of things achieved, and in glorious anticipation of effort that lay before her' (Vol 2, p. 296). Although this rosy vision of the spinster's uncertain future may be uncharacteristically optimistic and hastily conceived, it is worth noting that the mature novel, *New Grub Street* offers a more positive resolution to the professional woman's story than George Paston imagined, which again avoids the safe option of marriage. After her father dies, and the loss of her inheritance diminishes her attractiveness to Milvain, Marian has to be 'rescued' from her 'desperate' situation by one of his publishing friends, who is able to secure her a position as an assistant librarian in a provincial town for £75 a year. Librarianship, a potentially more lucrative and certainly more secure profession than journalism, did not require formal training at this stage and, given a much needed increase in schemes to assist those interested, would provide 'splendid openings for women of

---

[126] Mabel Collins, 'Journalism for Women', *Woman*, 15 February 1890, p. 2.
[127] Ann Ardis, *New Women, New Novels: Feminism and Early Modernism* (New Brunswick & London: Rutgers University Press, 1990), p. 152. The plots Ardis describes in this section by contemporary women writers such as Sara Jeanette Duncan and Mrs Andrew Dean often end with female suicide or capitulation to marriage and motherhood.

education'.[128] Miss James, the head librarian of the new People's Palace in the East End, laments the lack of 'women coming forward with quite the ability and the education that would qualify them for the most responsible posts' and argues for the need for a Library School on the American model.[129]   As Kramer notes, this pioneering work is 'unprecedented for a Victorian heroine', showing Gissing to be 'ahead of his time'.[130] Although frustratingly the lifestyle of the lady librarian is not represented in the text, the fact that the educated heroine is now being paid to occupy a public intellectual space, and more importantly on her own terms, suggests his recognition of the professional woman's capacity to profit from her intellectual powers. In her timely discussion of women's restricted participation in public life in 1887, Edith Simcox commented, 'the intellectual capacity of women … is a problem – and a very pressing one – for the future to decide'.[131] By sanctioning Marian's pioneering fitness for library work, Gissing gestures towards the professional woman's future position in intellectual culture, releasing her into a career so new it remained undocumented in the Women's Institute dictionary of employment of 1899.

The difficulties of finding a paradigm to represent the spinster in the 1890s remain only partially resolved, but in his refusal to accept the incompleteness of the spinster's life, Gissing's vision of the educated heroine seems at least as progressive as those offered by contemporary New Woman novelists. The blinkered view of the men in *Born in Exile* that the 'plain' emancipated woman is 'an incomplete woman' (p. 96) for whom '[no] future could be imagined' (p. 237) is contested in conclusions which recognise both women's fitness for a range of new careers and their right to celibate, independent lifestyles. Sloan encourages us to think beyond a simple reading of the educated heroine as 'an image of unfulfilled and incomplete womanhood' by drawing attention to Ada as an authentic representation of 'the possibility of a new type of woman – one who refuses to accept her incompleteness'.[132] Even in the spinster fiction popularised by New Woman writers in the 1910s, it is rare for women to gain fulfilment through a career or to complete professional training. F. M. Mayor's *The Third Miss Symons* (1913) is structured around the educated heroine's abortive attempts to fill her time with travel, philanthropy, art and writing, but none of them assuage her boredom. Instead, the disagreeable Henrietta Symons chafes against being left

---

[128] Albert Dawson, 'What they need in the East End: an interview with the Lady Librarian at the People's Palace', *Young Woman* 1 (1893), 411–4 (p. 414). Miss James saw librarianship as an ideal career for university-educated women.

[129] M.S.R. James, 'Librarianship', in *Professional Women Upon their Professions*, pp. 114, 115. Opportunities in this profession were seen as much better in America; Miss James was going to work there because of its better-equipped libraries and higher salaries (p. 112).

[130] Kramer, p. 319.

[131] Edith Simcox, 'The Capacity of Women', *Nineteenth Century* 22 (1887), 391–402 (p. 400).

[132] Sloan, p. 45. He argues that 'Isabel's "Poor Ada!" may denote the world's condescending, disingenuous pity for what is seen to be Ada's repulsive, jarring sexlessness, but it also expresses a fear of one who resists incorporation within the symbolic securities of gender'.

'on the shelf' and envies her sisters their maternal duties, registering her dissatisfaction with her enforced single status until she becomes an irritable old lady. In a nod to Gissing's work, Mayor draws attention to the potential suitability to clerical work of her 'odd woman' but denies her the chance to pursue this by setting the novel in the mid-Victorian period 'before the days of women's colleges' and the new careers, ensuring a more conservative view of the spinster's restricted lifestyle. The difficulties of the position of ordinary as opposed to pioneering single women are constantly reiterated: 'Even now, when there is a certain amount of choice and liberty, a woman who is thrown on her own resources at thirty-nine, with no previous training, and no obvious claims or duties, does not find it easy to know how to dispose of herself. But a generation ago the problem was far more difficult'.[133]

Whereas the plot structures of 1890s New Woman fiction often reveal professional activity to occupy only a brief period of a woman's life, as marital duties prevent women from reaping the long-term benefits of their training, Gissing both registers the inadequacies of this enduring paradigm and attempts to map out alternative destinies for the celibate career woman. The New Woman's political and artistic ambitions are typically thwarted, according to Ann Ardis, as 'the very implausibility of [*fin-de-siècle*] novels' "boomerang" plots ... brings the narratives back into alliance with ... the Victorian code of womanliness'.[134] But this could also be challenged by endorsing the unwomanliness and celibacy associated with the female professional. Williams' view of spinster heroines as 'belonging to an in-between generation that must be sacrificed' as 'the narrative forecloses upon any prospect of progress towards either felicity or independence'[135] is not always appropriate to the resolutions of Gissing's fiction of this period. Although his masculinised, emancipated heroines are sometimes used to reflect the poor lady's lonely existence, their anomalous status is not accepted, and his more positive accounts of the spinster's occupation of new living spaces in *New Grub Street* look forward to a period when women will have more 'choice and liberty' in rooms of their own. A career in journalism might offer the best option for the educated woman seeking 'work fit for ladies', but it would have been historically inaccurate to represent this as a career choice to be implemented without a struggle. The new female professional was still in desperate need of financial assistance, training opportunities and advice if she was to become the woman of the future, a situation that was to be further explored in Gissing's next major work, *The Odd Women*.

---

[133] F. M. Mayor, *The Third Miss Symons* ed. Susan Hill (1913; London: Virago, 1980), p. 72.

[134] Ardis, p. 154.

[135] Williams, p. 270.

Chapter 4

White-Collar Work and the Future Possibilities of the Odd Woman

As the 1890s developed, the professional working woman, to be championed as odd in Gissing's most direct engagement with the Woman Question, was increasingly presented as an attractive role model both in social investigatory accounts and in the new women's journals. It was now more acceptable for middle-class women to earn their own money and to choose work rather than an early marriage. One of the early editions of the new moderately feminist weekly *Woman*, established in 1890, argued that the 'woman of today' has evolved with the 'ever-changing conditions of modern life':

> With the spread of education, and the stern necessity which compels an ever-increasing army of women to provide for themselves and fight their own battles in life, we find ... women are every day more distinguishing themselves in the various callings which the necessities of the time, primarily, have compelled them to adopt ... Women are gradually getting alive to their possibilities in life, and are so surely – with many abortive efforts, maybe – evolving to a higher ideal from that of our grandmothers.[1]

As modern women are increasingly compelled to take up the role of breadwinner, their new-found independence and self-sufficiency demonstrates the enlarged possibilities for future womanhood achieved by education and training. Investigators revealed that in broad terms women's large-scale employment in the new white-collar professions such as clerical work, the retail industry and the Civil Service, granted them respectability, credibility and social status. As Lee Holcombe has argued, by 1914 'middle-class working women, a respected and self-respecting force, were an essential part of the country's labour force', rather than a self-pitying and pitied 'surplus and depressed minority'.[2] However, Clara Collet's research findings based on interviews with clerks, teachers, and journalists, typically emphasising the potentially prohibitive costs of the required training and education, indicate that the social status of the educated working woman was not guaranteed. The 'abortive efforts' of this pioneering generation suggest that their entry into public life was a slow and painful process. Middle-class women's unprecedented occupation of working environments in central

---

[1]   Harriette Raphael, 'Women of To-Day', *Woman*, 1 February 1890, p. 2.
[2]   Lee Holcombe, *Victorian Ladies at Work: Middle-Class Working Women in England and Wales, 1850–1914* (Newton Abbot: David & Charles, 1973), p. 20.

London, such as the modern City office or the new West End department stores, also fuelled concerns about the breakdown of gender roles. Elaine Showalter has related the renewal of attention to perennial concerns about the single woman to periods of gender crisis, which prompts the key question, 'What … made the odd women of the *fin de siècle* so conspicuous, troubling, and dramatic?'[3] One answer lies in the capacity of evolving gender identities to produce new and troubling sexualities, from the unacceptable celibacy of the unwomanly feminist to the glamorised promiscuity attributed to the type writer girl and the shop-girl, which were feared to be encouraged by urban existence, rather than attributed to the 'period's construction of unmarried women as a new political and sexual group'.[4]

   The appearance of the female white-collar worker in fiction of the 1890s both testifies to the increasing acceptance of her place in the labour market and to the fears and fantasies which surrounded her entry into urban culture. Arlene Young has noted the 'liberating effect' of white-collar work on women in *fin-de-siècle* narratives, showing how bachelor girls 'provide spirited and adventurous heroines for many novels of the 1890s and early 1900s', typified in Grant Allen's popular tale of female enterprise *The Type-Writer Girl* (1897).[5] Gissing's ambitious accounts of white-collar work constitute a broader, more economically grounded comparison between the working conditions and lifestyles associated with the shop and the office in the style of the social investigators. His attempt to generate sympathy for the exploited shop-girl forced into marriage to escape an unbearable work environment is also relatively new at a time when the figure of the shop-girl was more likely to appear as an object of erotic fascination in the work of male naturalist authors. In the 1880s, both Émile Zola and the American novelist Henry James used the streetwise shop-girl, with her urban knowledge and enjoyment of heterosocial culture, and the department store in which she was placed to symbolise the threatening effects of commerce on urban femininity. In this chapter I will argue that in *The Odd Women* (1893) and *Eve's Ransom* (1895) Gissing seeks to provide alternative accounts of the modernity and liberation of the shop-girl and the type writer girl, in terms of both their participation in public entertainments and, for the latter, her allegiance to the developing feminist movement. But his commitment to realism dictates that the capacity of his streetwise heroines to negotiate the city on their own terms must be circumscribed; their entry into heterosocial culture often places them in the position of prostitutes, dependent on the favours and money of men. Despite the cultivation of a 'new urban female style of being "at home" in the city' from the 1880s onwards, London, as Judith Walkowitz has pointed out, could still prove to be 'a negative environment for respectable women'.[6] It is also in this fiction that Gissing engages

---

[3]   Elaine Showalter, *Sexual Anarchy: Gender and Culture at the Fin de Siècle* (London: Virago, 1992), p. 21.

[4]   Showalter, p. 21.

[5]   Arlene Young, *Culture, Class and Gender in the Victorian Novel: Gentlemen, Gents and Working Women* (Houndmills: Macmillan, 1999), p. 128.

[6]   Judith R. Walkowitz, *City of Dreadful Delight: Narratives of Sexual Danger in Late-Victorian London* (London: Virago, 1992), p. 46.

most obviously with feminist debates about free unions, marriage and celibacy in his focus on the figure of the odd woman. *The Odd Women,* rewriting Henry James' forward-thinking but tentative account of the failure of romantic friendships between professional women in *The Bostonians* (1886), validates the oddity of the spinster explored in his earlier fiction in order to align her more obviously with the woman of the future, showing how her independence, commitment to women's emancipation and involvement with a network of professional women anticipate the figure of the suffrage worker of early-twentieth-century fiction.

Modern, Ideal Occupations? The Shop-Girl and the Lady Clerk

By the early 1890s social investigators had begun to modify definitions of women workers to encompass women from all social classes, so that rather than being a contradiction in terms, the middle-class or educated working woman could be classified as part of a distinct group. A particular focus of investigatory research on this group was the effect of marriage on female employment and earnings. In a lecture to the South Place Ethical Society in 1890 on 'The Economic Position of Educated Working Women', Collet highlighted the importance of vocational training to protect the woman worker from 'the temptation to accept marriage as a means of livelihood and escape from poverty', a view she was to reiterate throughout her writing.[7] With the benefit of education and training, women workers would be more likely to remain single and gain fulfilment from their chosen vocation. In 1892, her article 'Prospects of Marriage for Women' more forcefully linked the desire for marriage to the inadequacy of women's wages: it was the woman worker's perception of employment as 'filling up a brief interval before marriage' which underpinned her acceptance of 'badly paid drudgery' and restricted her efficiency.[8] Her research on London shop assistants as a Lady Assistant Commissioner for the Royal Commission on Labour's report on women's industrial employment of 1893 underlined her belief that shop work in particular fostered this unhealthy expectation of being rescued from unbearable working conditions by a man. In her summary of the report for the *Fortnightly*, A. Amy Bulley picked up on the 'fines, long hours, unjust dismissals, and bad domestic and sanitary arrangements' suffered by the shop assistants interviewed by

---

[7]   Clara E. Collet, 'The Economic Position of Educated Working Women' (1890) in *Educated Working Women: Essays on the Economic Position of Women Workers in the Middle Classes* (London: P.S. King & Son, 1902), p. 24. The subtext of her argument here as elsewhere is that spinsters benefit the economy by becoming more efficient workers: 'women who have been trained for a special work, and who like their work, either do not marry at all or marry comparatively late in life' (pp. 23-4).

[8]   Clara Collet, 'Prospects of Marriage for Women', *Nineteenth Century* 31 (1892), 537–52 (pp. 542, 546).

Collet, which lead them to 'look upon marriage as their one hope of release'.[9]   In contrast, office work, perhaps partly due to the operation of the recently implemented marriage bar,[10] was generally recognised by investigators to constitute an ideal female occupation. Competition for places in the Post Office and the Civil Service was extremely keen, according to Clementina Black, not least because the 'considerable squadron' of female postal workers were placed in 'comfortable offices' with good facilities, enjoying a position 'not brilliant, but ... safe and comfortable, and exceedingly respectable'.[11] As Meta Zimmeck has argued, in this period clerical work was promoted as 'the one occupation which avoided all the pitfalls of the occupations available to or proposed for middle-class women'.[12]

The shared concerns of feminist social investigation and naturalist fiction are apparent in the sociological focus on women's work underpinning naturalist narratives, a technique popularised in Émile Zola's depictions of modern Paris. Based on extensive research and interviews with those employed in the new department stores, *Au Bonheur des Dames [The Ladies' Paradise]* (1883) sets out to raise awareness about the exploitative 'daily working life' of the exhausted shop-girl: 'ill-fed and ill-treated, she suffered agonies of fatigue, in continual fear of being brutally dismissed' (p. 123).[13] However, the reader has to beware of taking seemingly factual information about the living-in system, the slack season and the occupational diseases brought on by being 'always on their feet' (p. 112) at face value, as the naturalist novelist is of course editing and selecting material to shape his own fictional agenda. Gissing's decision to focus on 'that class which he wishes to exalt, the self-supporting unmarried women'[14] in his fiction of the early 1890s suggests an awareness, albeit limited, of debates amongst the feminist investigators. Although the letters reveal that the author did not meet Collet until 1893, he was certainly aware of her 'sociological article' in the *Nineteenth Century*

---

[9]   A. Amy Bulley, 'The Employment of Women: The Lady Assistant Commissioners' Report', *Fortnightly Review* 61 (1894), 39–48 (p. 44). The other three commissioners were May Abraham, Margaret Unwin and Eliza Orme.

[10]   Jane E. Lewis has discussed this in relation to sexual difference in the office. The marriage bar operated until the First World War and 'was most effective in forestalling debate about women's promotion'. See 'Women Clerical Workers in the late nineteenth and early twentieth centuries', in Gregory Anderson (ed.), *The White-Blouse Revolution: Female Office Workers since 1870* (Manchester: Manchester University Press, 1988), pp. 33, 40.

[11]   Clementina Black, 'The Post Office for Women', in John Watson (ed.), *Our Boys and Girls and What to Do with them* (London: Ward, Lock, Bowden & Co, 1892), pp. 135, 130, 131.

[12]   Meta Zimmeck, 'Jobs for the Girls: the expansion of clerical work for women, 1850–1914', in Angela V. John (ed.), *Unequal Opportunities: Women's Employment in England, 1800–1918* (Oxford: Blackwell, 1986), p. 158.

[13]   All quotations are taken from Émile Zola, *The Ladies' Paradise*, trans. and ed. Brian Nelson (1883; Oxford: Oxford University Press, 1995).

[14]   This phrase was used in an unsigned review in the American journal *Nation*, 13 July 1893, 30–1. Quoted in Pierre Coustillas & Colin Partridge (eds.), *Gissing: The Critical Heritage* (London: Routledge & Kegan Paul, 1972), p. 221.

in 1892.[15]   Certainly, his own sociological analysis of the working conditions and lifestyles of women workers in white-collar professions can be seen to reproduce the agenda of the Royal Commission on Labour by mounting an enquiry into 'the alleged grievances of women and the effects of employment on health, morality and the home'.[16]   Full details of wages, hours, illnesses and injustices are conveyed to the reader through the speeches of exploited workers, mirroring the interview data collected by the Lady Commissioners.   In the eyes of reviewers, his 'intensely modern' theme, powerful characterisation and ability to 'keep his story very free from sociological dialectic' placed his work above the 'narrative tracts' on the Woman Question of women writers such as Sarah Grand and Mrs Humphrey Ward.[17]   The fact that Black was asked to review *The Odd Women* is also revealing; her authoritative commentary on the successful fictional treatment of 'the problem of the unmarried and untrained woman' sets it in the context of her own interpretation of statistics about surplus women.[18]   Modern critics have sometimes accused Gissing of neglecting to represent the realities of the working environment for the white-collar worker – Lise Shapiro Sanders for instance finds it surprising that there is 'little in-depth analysis of the actual labor involved in shop work' in *The Odd Women*[19] – but this is to misunderstand his modern privileging of women's urban lifestyles and their interactions with men in heterosocial culture over a more sociological analysis of actual working conditions, which, as the reviews suggest, would have been out in place in realist fiction.

The particular social phenomenon Gissing chooses to dramatise is the middle-class woman worker's struggle to remain single in the face of the temptations of marriage, rather than the fight against the injustices of her chosen field of work, though the two are of course revealed to be interdependent.   When asked to provide a plot summary for an advert in the *Athenaeum*, he wrote:

---

[15]   Letter to Nelly, 11 April 1892.   Quoted in Paul F. Mattheisen, Arthur C. Young & Pierre Coustillas (eds.), The *Collected Letters of George Gissing, Vol 5, 1892–95* (Athens: Ohio University Press, 1994), p. 41.   See also Deborah McDonald, *Clara Collet 1860–1948: An Educated Working Woman* (London: Woburn Press, 2004), pp. 121–3.

[16]   Bulley, p. 39.

[17]   Reviews of *The Odd Women*, *Athenaeum*, 27 May 1893, p. 667, *Pall Mall Gazette*, 29 May 1893, p. 4.   The adjective 'modern' recurred frequently in reviews of Gissing's work but appears to have been particularly prominent in relation to the novels of the early to mid 1890s, though this may just be a convention of reviewing New Woman fiction.

[18]   Clementina Black, Review of *The Odd Women*, *Illustrated London News*, 5 August 1893, p. 155.   Like the *PMG* reviewer, she also credits Gissing with success in 'the feat, so often attempted in the modern novel, but so seldom achieved, of giving to discussions of social problems the twofold interest attaching to them in real life', that is, of demonstrating the effects of theory on character.

[19]   Lise Shapiro Sanders, 'The Failures of the Romance: Boredom, Class and Desire in George Gissing's *The Odd Women* and W. Somerset Maugham's *Of Human Bondage*', *Modern Fiction Studies* 47:1 (2001), 190–228 (p. 200).

It deals with the lot of women, who, for statistical or other reasons, have small chance of marriage. Among the characters, militant or conventional, are some who succeed, and some who fail, in the effort to make their lives independent.[20]

Described as a novel 'written in ... praise and honour' of the old maid,[21] in effect the 1893 text sought to replace this dated term with the less pejorative label 'odd woman', connoting a more modern figure whose militancy would fit her to succeed. This quickly came into use as a more positive alternative, particularly favoured by women themselves, linked to the progressive discussion of a set of alternatives to accepted versions of the lonely single lifestyle, provided by New Woman novelists and cultural commentators.[22]   Whereas *The Odd Women* compares shop-girl Monica Madden's claustrophobic marriage with the liberation of the office workers Rhoda Nunn and Mary Barfoot, and their fiercely protected independence from men, this is reversed in *Eve's Ransom* in which the office worker Eve Madeley succumbs to the safety of the marital tie and her more spirited friend Patty Ringrose is happy to remain an unmarried shop-girl. The unlikely friendships between shop-girls and clerical workers, and their occupation of public space, then act as a means of exploring alternative perceptions of independence and professional identity. Commissioned by the editor of *The Illustrated London News* in 1894, the one-volume novel *Eve's Ransom* has attracted more critical attention in recent years in relation to debates about female urbanism. Young has pertinently noted that the author's contrasting treatment of the fictional type of the white-collar working woman in the one-volume text is 'in part a recasting of some of the un- or underexamined issues in *The Odd Women*', facilitating a more 'complex study of an important social and literary problem'.[23]   Its handling of this problem, ignored by reviewers at the time who had little to say about its female characters beyond noting the enigmatic unconventionality of its heroine,[24] links it to the more well-known novel in interesting ways. Finally published after *In The Year of Jubilee*, it was in fact a reworking of ideas, first formulated in 1893, for a 'Birmingham story' Gissing always disliked,[25] but his contempt should not be

---

[20]   Review of *The Odd Women*, *Athenaeum*, 25 March 1893, p. 379.

[21]   Review of *The Odd Women*, *Nation*, 13 July 1893, pp.30–31. Quoted in Coustillas & Partridge, p. 220.

[22]   He may have taken the term 'odd' from Amy Levy's 1888 poem, 'A Ballad of Religion and Marriage', whose anti-marriage sentiments lead her to the belief that 'in a million years or most/Folk shall be neither pairs nor odd'. I have not come across any other uses of this adjective as an alternative to 'single' before it was used in the title of the novel.

[23]   Arlene Young, 'Eve Madeley and Rhoda Nunn: Gissing's Doubled Enigma', in Bouwe Postmus (ed.), *A Garland for Gissing* (Amsterdam: Rodopi, 2001), pp. 130, 135.

[24]   Review of *Eve's Ransom*, *Bookman*, May 1895, p. 265. Cited in Coustillas & Partridge, p. 254.

[25]   Gissing recorded in his diary that he 'grew sick of my Birmingham story' on 1 August 1893. See Pierre Coustillas (ed.), *London and the Life of Literature in late-Victorian England: The Diary of George Gissing, Novelist* (Sussex: Harvester Press, 1978), p. 310. He was always very disparaging about the necessity to earn a living by producing one-volume texts after the decline in marketability of the three-volume novel. He referred to *Eve's*

shared by modern readers: the compact structure and elliptical characterisation of the single volume text here result in an ambiguous and subtle treatment of familiar Woman Question themes, such as the 'long[ing] for freedom' noted by the *Athenaeum*.[26] Whilst *The Odd Women* pushes at the boundaries of New Woman fiction by endorsing the office worker's independence and radical celibacy, the later novel turns this on its head by questioning the availability of a liberated urban lifestyle to a representative type of 'the age in which we are living', albeit ultimately less emancipated than her shop-girl companion. But rather than acting as a denial of clerical labour as a worthy pursuit of the odd woman, Gissing's preoccupation with the modernity of the shop-girl and her urban freedoms is a key element of his treatment of the literary problem of the white-collar woman worker and her place in the city.

Representations of the shop-girl as a streetwise urbanite, a knowing city character of questionable respectability, were particularly predominant in male-authored naturalist fiction of the 1880s and 1890s, often fixated on sexually attractive and outspoken women who worked in the large and fashionable West End department stores. They also manifested themselves on the late-Victorian stage in the figure of the glamorous, shop-girl heroine in theatres such as the Gaiety.[27] In Henry James's London novel *The Princess Casamassima* (1886), which Gissing read in 1892, the 'magnificent' but common Millicent Henning, who sells jackets and mantles at a great haberdasher's near Buckingham Palace, is positively portrayed as a 'very handsome' young woman, 'already perfectly acquainted with the resources of the metropolis' (p. 45).[28] By modelling the fashionable clothes which have also been 'exhibited in the window on dummies of wire' (p. 530), the shop-girl has to trade on her commodified body and her 'feminine curves' (p. 46) - 'on her person [outfits] appeared to such advantage that nothing she took up ever failed to go off' (p. 50) - in order to convince customers of their beauty and value for money. Moreover, Millicent's literal embodiment of the commercialism of the retail industry associates her with the tumult of the city:

> There was something about her indescribably fresh, successful and satisfying. She was, to her blunt, expanded fingertips, a daughter of London, of the crowded streets and hustling traffic of the great city; she had drawn her health and strength from its dingy courts and foggy thoroughfares, and peopled its parks and squares and crescents with her ambitions; she understood it by instinct and loved it with passion; she represented

---

Ransom as 'unutterable rubbish' in a letter to Collet in 1894 and as 'certainly not one of my best' in correspondence with Bertz the following year. See letter to Clara Collet, 7 July 1894 and letter to Bertz, 9 May 1895. Quoted in *Collected Letters*, Vol 5, pp. 214, 331.

[26] Review of *Eve's Ransom*, *Athenaeum*, 11 May 1895, p. 605.

[27] Erika Diane Rappaport, *Shopping for Pleasure: Women and the Making of London's West End* (Princeton: Princeton University Press, 2001), pp. 197, 198. Extremely popular musical comedies of this period such as *The Shop Girl* (1894) used the department store as a key 'site of cross-class heterosexual interaction' in the process of 'packaging anxieties about consumer culture as entertainment' (p.180).

[28] All quotations are taken from Henry James, *The Princess Casamassima* (1886; London: Macmillan, 1889).

its immense vulgarities and curiosities, its brutality and its knowingness, its good-nature
and its impudence. (p. 46)

The vulgarity of the true 'daughter of London' is then tempered by her association
with potentially more modern urban values such as impudence and knowingness,
values which render her troublingly attractive to the more refined hero Hyacinth
Robinson. Emphasising James's admiration for the success of the department
store, Deborah L. Parsons has argued that this is not simply a way of equating
women, consumption and prostitution, but a means of 'question[ing] the role of
woman as object, implying that the female body is a garment worn and paraded for
a purpose',[29] but Zola's tendency to evoke stereotypes of salesgirls as 'tarts',
'hussies as well as decent girls' (p. 311) suggests otherwise. It is significant that
the writers of employment manuals for women envisaged shop work in similar
terms to bar work, requiring prospective applicants to demonstrate 'pleasantness of
appearance' prior to employment, as the 'neat and even stylish dress of the young
lady behind the counter is an attraction' to customers.[30] Shop-girl narratives used
the department store to stage dangerous encounters between the attractive young
assistant and her male customers or employers, in order to underline the corruption
of women by commercialism. In Zola's *The Ladies' Paradise,* the newly recruited
Denise, unused to 'displaying [her] salesgirl charms' (p. 89), feels 'violated,
defenceless, naked' (p. 115) as she is 'treated like a machine' (p. 114) for
modelling clothes. By accepting a job requiring women 'to be attractive for the
sales rooms' (p. 54), she effectively consents to be attractive to both the leering
salesmen and the womanising owner of the Ladies Paradise, whose routine
seduction of salesgirls is seen as a privilege granted by his position. Although
Millicent in *The Princess Casamassima* advises Hyacinth to stay away from her
haberdasher's, 'as the visits of gentlemen, even when ostensible purchasers ...
compromised her in the eyes of her employers' (p. 589), the reader's final glimpse
of her shows her modelling a jacket for Captain Sholto, 'his eyes travelling up and
down the front of Millicent's person' (p. 590). The shop assistant's exposure to the
lascivious eyes of men inevitably puts her in a compromising position.

Sympathy for the working conditions of shop-girls was a significant feature of
investigatory discourse on working women; Clara Collet, amongst others,
commented on the poor earnings, 'hard work, long hours and close rooms' they
endured,[31] and an article on 'The Ethics of Shopping' diverged from the pleasures
of consumption to the ill-health and 'the pressure of the life led by many of these
poor women'.[32] The findings of the Lady Assistant Commissioners' Report in

---

[29] Deborah L. Parsons, *Streetwalking the Metropolis: Women, the City and Modernity*
(Oxford: Oxford University Press, 2000), p. 58.
[30] M. Mostyn Bird, *Woman at Work: A Study of the Different Ways of Earning a Living
open to Women* (London: Chapman & Hall, 1911), p. 64.
[31] 'Prospects of Marriage for Women', p. 546. Shop girls were bracketed with dressmakers in this article as suffering from some of the worst working conditions.
[32] (Lady) M. Jeune, 'The Ethics of Shopping', *Fortnightly Review* 63 (1895), 123–52 (p.
130).

1892 indicated that 'as a class, shop assistants seem more discontented than any other'.[33] In *The Odd Women* Gissing's representation of Monica's 'slavery behind the counter' (p. 62)[34] initially reproduces narratives familiar from social investigatory accounts of the shop-girl's escape from harsh and unhealthy working conditions into a speedy early marriage. The opening chapters describe in detail the various complaints of the employees who are 'worked to death' (p. 23) in a draper's establishment in Walworth Rd; the sixteen-hour Saturdays cause some girls to faint and others suffer from varicose veins from excessive standing and even a burst blood-vessel from over-work. Trade unionism was slow to develop in the retail industry, with the more effective Acts about regulation of shop hours not being passed until the 1910s; the Seats for Shop Assistants Act was not implemented until 1899.[35] Taking up the role of the feminist investigator, Rhoda interviews Monica about her routine, establishing that even the meagre twenty minutes allowed for meals may be interrupted by the demands of the store and that girls may be dismissed if their book of takings is not satisfactory to the employers. Zola had already noted that 'from their daily contact with rich customers, nearly all the salesgirls had acquired airs and graces, and had ended up by forming a vague class floating between the working and middle classes' (p. 155). Rhoda's classification of Monica as 'half a lady and half a shop-girl' (p. 107) shows Gissing to be similarly in tune with debates about status, as are her questions about whether the other girls at the draper's are to be considered ladies – only some are described as 'nice, quiet girls'. However, his descriptions of the working life of the 'showily dressed' Patty Ringrose in *Eve's Ransom* are less concerned with the shop-girl's exploitation in the workplace, perhaps because her class credentials are less obscure; she 'belong[s] to a class, which, especially in its women, has little intelligence to boast of' (p. 31). Bird pronounced the work 'desirable' to women because a shop would confer more 'social status' on them than the less attractive choice of domestic service: 'no wonder every kind of girl, drawn from every class and strata of society, is found behind the counter of the modern emporium'.[36] By living above her uncle's music shop, Patty does not suffer from the restrictions attendant on 'living in' in accommodation provided by employers, so she is not

---

[33] Bulley, 'The Employment of Women', p. 44).

[34] All quotations are taken from George Gissing, *The Odd Women*, ed. Margaret Walters (1893; London: Virago, 1980).

[35] Holcombe, pp. 120–30. Bills about shop hours were introduced from the mid-1880s onwards, but Holcombe argues that many of these were still 'inadequate' and 'ineffective' once they became law. Bills about early closing first appeared in the 1890s. In 1884 it was estimated that female shop assistants had to stand behind the counter for between 75 and 90 hours per week for wages of between £15 and £50 a year, though this excluded living-in costs (p. 109).

[36] Bird, p. 64. Shop assistants were revealingly bracketed with waitresses and barmaids in this study under the heading of 'Distribution', reiterating the view that shop work was also the province of uneducated girls with 'no special talent'. However, Holcombe notes that the upper and middle classes continued to align them with servants, whilst the working classes 'sneered at their pretensions to respectability, derisively calling them "counter-jumpers"' (p. 107).

subject to fines for staying out late, limited leisure hours or the bad influence of vulgar companions, which made the system 'the bugbear of reformers and practically at the root of all the evils shop assistants suffer', according to Bird.[37] The vision of her working life then obscures the harsher realities experienced by the majority of female shop assistants, instead emphasising her power in the labour market:

> It's easy enough for anybody like me to get a place. I've had two or three offers the last half-year, from good shops where they were losing their young ladies. We're always getting married, in our business, and places have to be filled up. (p. 59)[38]

Placing a premium on the ease of acquiring shop work, Patty may, like James's over-confident Millicent, who takes 'endless comfort' in the knowledge that shop-work ensures 'never work[ing] with her 'ands' (p. 530), be exhibiting the desirable qualities of the modern working woman, but this can only be achieved by representing her as a far from typical shop-girl. Rhoda's verdict that the hours are 'outrageous' (p. 23) and the illnesses shocking, coupled with a lack of confidence about a government which does not care whether such 'superfluous females' choose to work themselves to death, is indicative of a more realistic and committed desire to highlight the pressing need for reform in an industry driven by exploitation.

By the 1890s women's entry into the clerical profession, and the less dangerous environment of the modern office, was much more likely to offer them respectability. This was the most attractive of the new professions for middle-class women, with female employees in clerical labour increasing 400 times between 1861 and 1911.[39] In comparison to the shop-girl, the new female clerk worked shorter hours for higher wages, and whilst also being required to dress smartly, was not required to look attractive for male customers. An 1890 article in *Woman* significantly titled 'The Lady Clerk in Clover' celebrated the experience of working for the Prudential Assurance Company, one of the new large-scale companies behind the rising demand for female clerical labour from the 1870s onwards.[40] The girl interviewed appeared satisfied with her pay and prospects and felt privileged to benefit from the comfortable chairs, the 'splendid library' and lunch-time promenades on the roof-terrace, which provided 'a splendid view of central London'.[41] The company's policy that all employees had to be under 25

---

[37]   Bird, p. 64. See also Holcombe, pp. 112, 117.

[38]   All quotations are taken from George Gissing, *Eve's Ransom* (1895; New York: Dover, 1980).

[39]   Holcombe, p. 146. In comparison, male clerks increased fivefold during the same period.

[40]   Gregory Anderson, 'The White-Blouse Revolution', in Anderson, p. 4. The rise in demand was linked to the increased role of Government in provision of services and the expansion of foreign trade and financial services in the City, all of which generated masses of paperwork.

[41]   M.C.[Mabel Collins], 'The Lady Clerk in Clover', *Woman*, 26 April 1890, 2. This article was part of a regular series called 'The World of Breadwinners', featuring women in

and daughters of professional men aimed to secure a 'high-class' work-force, which in turn helped to promote the enduring image of clerical work for women as desirable and respectable. Bird's list of the attractions of the profession, including the shorter hours, good career prospects and liberal holidays, led her to the conclusion that 'undoubtedly this is a very suitable sphere for the woman worker'.[42] Certainly in the 1890s it was considered a profession fit for educated ladies, though the *Englishwoman's Review* expressed reservations about the numbers of half-educated women flooding into clerical work, whose acceptance of starvation wages does 'much harm ... to the status of the profession'.[43] In the early twentieth century there were growing concerns about the overstocked market, the exploitation of the woman clerk as 'cheap labour', limited promotion opportunities and the difficulties of finding well-paid positions in a profession in a 'chaotic condition'.[44] By 1907 Black was declaring clerks to be in the same sweated position as shop assistants.[45] Whilst office work was then generally seen as desirable and suitable for the woman in search of 'genteel employment',[46] it did not entirely exclude uncertainties about social status and professional identity.

Women's magazines of the time frequently encouraged self-supporting women to attend the new business schools offering training in shorthand, typewriting and book-keeping, skills which helped to command higher salaries and increased future career prospects. The Society for the Promotion of Employment of Women had been providing courses in book-keeping and clerical skills, and placing women in clerical posts since the 1870s; the popularity of the typewriting offices, first opened in 1884, then helped to ensure that the society's *protégées* were predominantly clerks and typists.[47] As Ellen Jordan has argued, these small-scale efforts, in combination with a more effective propaganda campaign alerting employers to the advantages of female clerical labour, ensured that by around 1880 'the androcentric view of office work [had been] broken down'.[48] In *The Odd*

---

both trades and professions which ran in the early numbers of the magazine. This is the only title I came across which had been modified to indicate the desirability of the work.

[42]   Bird, p. 127.

[43]   R.V. Gill, 'Is Type-Writing a Successful Occupation for Educated Women?', *EWR* 22 (15 April 1891), 82–8 (pp. 83, 84). See also Miss Cecil Gradwell, 'Clerkships' in Bateson, p. 108.

[44]   Elspeth Keith Robertson Scott, 'Women Clerks and Secretaries', in Edith J. Morley (ed.), *Women Workers in Seven Professions* (London: Routledge, 1914), p. 283.

[45]   Clementina Black, *Sweated Industry and the Minimum Wage*, (London: Duckworth & Co, 1907), p. 71.

[46]   Anderson, p. 10.

[47]   Mrs. H. Coleman Davidson, 'The Society for the Promotion of the Employment of Women', in *What our Daughters can do for Themselves: A Handbook of Women's Employments,* (London: Smith & Elder, 1894), pp. 259, 261. In 1891 79 girls had benefited from special technical training through the direct agency of the society, the majority of whom were now employed as book-keepers in commercial houses.

[48]   Ellen Jordan, *The Women's Movement and Women's Employment in Nineteenth-Century Britain* (Routledge: London & New York, 1999), pp. 174–9, 193. Jordan stresses that 'the importance of the Society's work lay far more in the propaganda campaign, which spread its

Women, Mary Barfoot trains ladies to use typewriters in her school on Great Portland Street, which also offers library facilities and, more unusually, a monthly lecture series to its pupils. Gissing's disclaimer that he was unaware of the existence of establishments for the training of girls in commercial occupation during composition of the novel in 1892 when he believed the training school to be 'an original idea' seems rather surprising, as does Collet's seconding of this opinion in 1894,[49] but is perhaps explained by the minimal publicity granted to such places in the early 1890s. Manuals aimed at working ladies, such as Mrs Davidson's *What our Daughters can do for themselves: a Handbook of Female Employment* (1893), which Gissing recommended to his brother in the same letter, were only just beginning to appear. Cecil Gradwell's School of Business Training for Gentlewomen in Westminster, first opened in the autumn of 1893 in response to the 'urgent' need for a system of training in typewriting and clerical skills in which young office workers were visibly deficient, was described in Margaret Bateson's *Professional Women upon their Professions* (1895), also published after the completion of Gissing's novel. Purposefully excluding applicants from 'the half-educated class', Gradwell assured *Queen* readers that her success in finding well-paid work for trainees was based on selecting 'bright, intelligent girls' as the first generation of trained clerks.[50] The Great Portland Street school also observes SPEW's system of supporting only individuals capable of acting as pioneers: Mary's emancipatory mission is typically aimed at committed and deserving middle-class women, 'girls of like mind' (p. 135) to herself. The bitter dispute over Bella Royston's suicide questions these exclusionary policies. Whereas Mary does not refuse to 'devote [her]self to poor hopeless and purposeless women' (p. 52), supporting and subsidising promising pupils who may not quite fit the category of lady, Rhoda and her *protégée* Winifred Haven are adamant that their work for the 'solidarity of women' should not extend to the lower classes. However, Monica's marked lack of interest in the gleaming Remingtons lined up in the office, only introduced into England a few years before the novel is set, suggests that 'the good deal of employment for women who learn to use a type-writer' (p. 36) is not seen to be universally appealing to middle-class women. Instead, the younger girl fears both the alternative work culture and the new femininity Rhoda stands for: 'this energetic woman had little attraction for her ... To put herself in Miss Nunn's hands might possibly result in a worse form of bondage than she suffered at the shop' (p. 36). The feminist's apparently unsympathetic 'disdain for such timidity' (p. 36) perhaps shows the difficulty of

---

ideas than in the actual efforts, important though they may have been for individuals, to find work for particular women'. The day school for clerical skills only ran until 1875, after which time SPEW acted primarily as a loan society to support women's training.

[49]   Letter to Algernon, 1 March 1894. *Collected Letters, Vol 5*, p. 210. He did add that 'probably something of the kind is going on somewhere', suggesting his knowledge of likely developments in training for middle-class women.

[50]   Cecil Gradwell, 'Clerkships', in Margaret Bateson (ed.), *Professional Women upon their Professions: Conversations recorded by Margaret Bateson* (London: Horace & Co, 1895), pp. 108, 111.

identifying worthy pioneers; although Monica appears the more suitable candidate, she finds the training tedious and quickly leaves, whereas the less respectable Bella may have actually been more deserving of sisterly support.

Across visual images and fictional representation the typist became popularised as the figure of the 'type-writer girl', an embodiment of the modern, desirable qualities associated with the woman clerk. An article on women's work in *The Young Woman* for 1894 featured an appealing illustration of the 'fair typist' in front of her machine, her 'nimble fingers' poised as if playing the piano, an analogy used in both fiction and journalism to reinforce the femininity of the skill. The journalist enthused, 'Type-writing appears to have "caught on" with young girls more quickly than any other form of modern occupation', showing how it had also caught on in modern fiction by concluding with a contemporary romantic tale of a secretary who marries her employer.[51] In his excellent discussion of the type-writer girl as a 'carefully conceived product' used to legitimise 'the identification of gentility with commerce', Christopher Keep has drawn on illustrated advertisements and naughty post cards of the period to highlight the figure's attractiveness to both aspiring working girls and male employers.[52] Olive Pratt Rayner's *The Type-Writer Girl* (1897), hailed as 'a story of to-day' by the *Athenaeum*,[53] was in fact the work of the anti-feminist journalist Grant Allen under the female pseudonym he adopted for writing in certain popular genres. Allen's feisty and 'audacious' heroine is close to being a parody of the New Woman in the style of *Punch*: Girton girl Juliet Appleton smokes, joins a group of anarchists and wears rational dress to facilitate riding her bicycle. She is the 'typical New Woman heroine of commercial fiction', according to Chris Willis, whose youth and sexual attractions are coupled with authorial comment on 'the supposed folly of her desire for independence' in order to 'defuse the threat of the New Woman'.[54] Although the jaunty tone of the first-person narrative and the comic episodic plot tend to detract from any realistic attempts to reproduce a clerk's working life, such texts did allow for progressive criticisms of women's roles. The short story the heroine publishes about clerical work, significantly about 'a *modern* girl who earns her own living in London' (p. 171, my italics),[55] is presumably intended to reinforce the accompanying glamorous lifestyle, but this is not shown to exclude sexual and financial exploitation. Working for a solicitors' firm, Juliet feels she is being assessed on her face and figure rather than her words per minute and the other clerks treat her like a 'defenceless barmaid' (p. 34). The novel also picks up

---

[51] Marion Leslie, 'Women who Work', *The Young Woman* 3 (1894), 230–34 (p. 230).

[52] Christopher Keep, 'The Cultural Work of the Type-Writer Girl', *Victorian Studies* 40: 3 (1997), 401–26 (p. 404).

[53] Review of *The Type-Writer Girl*, *Athenaeum*, 11 September 1897, p. 348.

[54] Chris Willis, '"Heaven defend me from political or highly-educated women!": Packaging the New Woman for Mass Consumption', in Angelique Richardson & Chris Willis (eds.), *The New Woman in Fiction and in Fact: Fin-de-Siècle Feminisms* (Houndmills: Palgrave, 2001), p. 53.

[55] All quotations are taken from Olive Pratt Rayner [Grant Allen], *The Type-Writer Girl* (London: C. Arthur Pearson Ltd, 1897).

on debates about pay, one employer delivering a speech on the state of the labour market, where young gentlewomen are competing with lower-middle-class girls in order to 'add to their own pin-money' (p. 123). Juliet is then located within the second category as a girl with 'nothing to live upon save what I can earn by type-writing' (p. 124), though her decision to accept a lower wage appropriate to 'a person of my presumed position in society' (p. 126) was precisely what feminists and union leaders were cautioning women against; Black considered such decisions 'wicked'.[56] However, such attempts at realism are diverted into the stereotypical romance between typist and employer, though the story comically avoids marriage in favour of extending the heroine's office adventures. It is certainly possible to accept Young's reading of the heroine's 'voluntarily remaining single and independent – and in the lower middle class' as an optimistic ending,[57] but the increasing references to office work as shameful and demeaning – by the end of Allen's novel, Juliet is significantly lamenting her restricted identity behind her machine, 'at the office, what was I but the type-writer girl?' (p. 201) – also make this a rather dissatisfactory conclusion for feminist readers.

Gissing's female office workers do not fit comfortably into the role of the type-writer girl, a concept he appears to have shied away from as unrealistic. Imitating Collet's rise to a senior position in the Civil Service, his educated heroines reject unfulfilling careers in teaching in order to work their way up to more skilled forms of clerical labour than typing: Rhoda has worked as a cashier in a shop and as a secretary before graduating to the position of instructor in the typing school and Eve is able to earn her pound a week as a book-keeper, primarily because she was 'always clever at figures' (p. 17). This topical attack on the more lucrative but womanly career of teaching, which caused Rhoda 'extreme discontent' (p. 17), Eve always found unbearable and Gissing himself particularly disliked, shows the author's recognition of what Deborah McDonald calls Collet's own 'dilemma', that is, finding the only profession considered suitable for women 'limited' but struggling to find an alternative.[58] The modern career path of his heroines is then indicative of a progressive validation of a training in business and commercial skills for women; indeed, the typing school's explicit aim is 'to draw from the overstocked profession of teaching as many capable young women as [possible] … to fit them for certain of the pursuits nowadays thrown open to their sex' (p. 54). Graduates of Mary's typing school, like their real-life counterparts, have indeed become fitted for new careers, such as the pharmaceutical industry or shop-keeping, an appealing prospect for the aspiring business woman, though we are not

---

[56] Black, 'Type-writing and Journalism for Women', in Watson, p. 45.

[57] Young, p. 146.

[58] McDonald, p. 89. Although Collet campaigned for increased career opportunities for women, she continued to regard teaching as respectable and secure employment for middle-class women which would be improved by higher wages. McDonald argues that her belief that women should not take over men's jobs was an indication of her pragmatic nature in a culture hostile to 'extreme' ideas: 'in showing that there would be no threat to the work and livelihood of men, her views were more likely to be treated as credible, resulting in an advance in her cause'.

told how many faced unemployment. Not all clever heroines could expect to reap the benefits of their business training, as the later novel overturns Black's view of the profession as a 'safe' one for all 'careful, competent and business-like' women.[59] In the later novel, whilst Eve appears grateful for an education enabling her escape from the 'drudgery' of unskilled work to the lifestyle of a professional woman – 'If I hadn't been clever at figures, what would have become of me? I should have drudged at some wretched occupation until the work and the misery of everything killed me' (p. 74) - her story of a lonely year in London in which she 'starved herself, all to save money' (p. 75) and had no money for leisure does not suggest a positive experience of book-keeping. Defined by Collet as an occupation on a par with domestic service chosen only by the 'average girl', office work was also seen as slightly demeaning work for the educated lady.[60] Unemployment is also highlighted as an occupational hazard for the clerk in the later novel. Although both women are subject to the precarious nature of the labour market, Eve is unable to find another clerical position when her employers close the business, whereas Patty is quickly reemployed when her uncle sells his music-shop; as she points out, the demand for shop assistants is always high. Contemporary articles warned of the 'pressure and competition … when the labour market for women is overstocked',[61] in order to encourage training as a safeguard against unemployment, arguing that 'the thoroughly trained woman is nearly always able to find work'.[62] However, Eve's training seems to restrict her options; although she could take up a position behind the counter like Patty, who boasts, 'there's plenty of shops where I can get an engagement' (p. 49), regressing to shop-work would put her on a level with her lower-class friend. Perceiving of herself as a professional woman, Eve's education and aspirations have then unfitted her for less skilled kinds of work and distanced her from her class; unlike her sister, Laura, who escaped from the family to work in a sweet-shop in Birmingham, she can no longer accept work which compromises her social position. These alternative accounts of the clerk's tenuous position in the labour market force the reader into an uncomfortable awareness of the harsher realities of clerical labour which type-writer girls rarely had to confront.

But this avoidance of reproducing the glamour surrounding the type-writer girl also served to privilege the process Zimmeck calls 'the feminization of clerical labour'[63] over the womanly occupations previously available to ladies. In Mary Cholmondeley's later New Woman novel, *Red Pottage* (1899), which is concerned with male opposition to women publishing their own work, typewriting is rejected as a more womanly but much less appropriate form of employment for middle-class women than journalism and fiction-writing. Despite its anti-feminist slant, *The Type-Writer Girl* also picks up on contemporary feminist concerns about the

---

[59] Black, 'The Post Office for Women', p. 131.
[60] Collet, 'Through 50 Years: The Economic Progress of Women', p. 139.
[61] Jeune, 'The Ethics of Shopping', p. 131.
[62] Evelyn March-Phillipps, 'The Working Lady in London', *Fortnightly Review* 58 (1892), 193–203 (p. 193).
[63] Zimmeck, p. 164.

labelling of Remington operators as typewriters. Allen's self-conscious references to the condescension implicit in the terms 'typist (female)' and 'type-writer *girl*' and the troubling analogy between the machine and its female operator,[64] – Juliet 'continued to click, click, click, like a machine that I was' (p. 34) - suggests a more ambiguous response to the phenomenon he is representing, though his heroine's view that as a 'lady type-writer' she forfeits her claim to gentility by working in an office is more contradictory. In Gissing's novels, such terms, though current in the early 1890s, are never used, perhaps because 'clerk', the label favoured by investigators, is both more professional and ungendered. The pivotal lecture on 'Woman as an Invader' in *The Odd Women* deconstructs the conservative view that 'in entering the commercial world, [women] ... unsex [them]selves' (p. 134) and supplant and 'out-crowd' lower-class men. Instead, this invasion of 'what had been exclusively the men's sphere' (p. 135) is seen to be a deliberate feminist strategy: Mary's drive to 'show girls the way to a career which my opponents call unwomanly' (p. 135) is part of the large-scale process encouraged by Collet in which 'the vast number of girls' forced to be self-supporting have to be fitted for the full range of posts, not just those deemed 'strictly suitable for women' (p. 135). By the 1890s the womanly occupations of governess and lady's companion chosen by Alice and Virginia Madden were seen as the last refuge of the unskilled 'poor lady', who cannot produce the 'certificates, and even degrees ... asked for on every hand' (p. 14). Woman's entry into the offices previously barred to them is then explicitly associated with both the independent New Woman and the suffragette, as Gissing radicalises clerical training in Mary's pleas for a 'new type of woman, active in every sphere of life: a new worker out in the world', a 'militant, defiant' figure who 'must push her claims to the extremity' (p. 136). Women's emancipation will only be advanced by the adoption of new forms of training, 'free from the reproach of womanliness' (p. 136) which will help to secure independence and self-reliance for the woman of the future. By harnessing a defence of female clerical labour to a broader argument about woman's right of entry to the masculine sphere, the lecture shows the type-writer girl to be a potentially more radical and unfeminine figure, whose agitation for sexual equality in the workplace heralds a shift in ways of thinking about respectable femininity.

Urban Pleasures and Chance Encounters

Feminist cultural historians and literary critics have already identified the middle-class professional woman as an important representative of women's urban

---

[64]   Black begins her 1892 account of typewriting with the forceful statement that 'the lady who works a type-writing machine ... is not a type-writer but a "typist"'. See 'Type-writing and Journalism for Women', p. 35. Keep has shown that 'the cultural "fit" between the normative values of femininity and typing' was partly produced by advertising campaigns and picture postcards, some of which played on the 'possibilities for innuendo that arose from the fact that "type-writer" could refer as much to the woman as the machine' (pp. 404, 414–15).

freedoms. Drawing on *Macmillans*' 1888 typology of the Glorified Spinster, Walkowitz highlights the confidence in the crowded metropolis of those employed in the feminised tertiary sector, whose limited incomes do not prevent them from 'satisfy[ing] a keen appetite for urban amusements'.[65] In her discussion of late-Victorian London as 'a place of opportunity for [middle-class] women', Deborah Epstein Nord has also noted that the freedoms of the independent single life have to be qualified by an awareness of women's struggles against marginality at a time when 'there was no wholly respectable context for her appearance in the city landscape'.[66] But these arguments about female urbanism rely on certain types of professional woman, such as charity workers or investigators and female novelists, to advance a particular model of middle-class femininity in 1880s London. The shop-girl and the office worker have not been fully incorporated into such a paradigm. This partly arises from an uncertainty about the basis of their respectability. The shop-girl's uncertain social status does not preclude her function as a *flâneuse*; on the contrary, she may be better placed to perform this role than workers seen as less ambivalently middle-class. She is a 'threatening', alienated figure, according to Deborah Parsons, but more importantly, she is 'often a mobile figure, capably traversing the city'.[67] The potentially threatening mobility of the clerk or typist has not been given much attention, as historical accounts have tended to focus on her experiences of the working day rather than after office hours. Nord's view of the metropolis as 'a place of opportunity for middle-class women' is shown to be particularly relevant to those in the clerical profession. To facilitate her rise up the career ladder, Rhoda could not rest until she achieved 'a move towards London' (p. 22), and Eve follows a similar trajectory, her employment in a large building in Holborn, the location of the new Prudential building extended in 1879, suggesting that she may have become one of the 'lady clerks in clover' on the roof-terrace at the centre of the City. The descriptions of the pleasures of Eve's independent London lifestyle – 'I delight in London. I had dreamt of it all my life before I came here' (p. 33) she declares – are meant to contrast favourably with the depressing leisure hours of her early working life in Birmingham, which she spends reading travel books, explaining, 'I wished to enjoy myself like other girls, but I couldn't. For one thing, I thought it wicked; and then I was so afraid of spending a penny' (p. 75). Observing her ease in public space, Hilliard marvels that 'London had done much for her' (p. 30). In her study of working women and leisure in turn-of-the-century New York, Kathy Peiss has emphasised the trend towards 'a pleasure-oriented culture', arguing that 'among working women, leisure came to be seen as a separate sphere of life to be consciously protected'.[68] The belief that cheap amusements were 'wicked' and

---

[65] Walkowitz, p. 63.

[66] Nord, p. 182.

[67] Parsons, p. 50. Parsons is here drawing on the important arguments of Sally Ledger, to be discussed in more detail later in the chapter.

[68] Kathy Peiss, *Cheap Amusements: Working Women and Leisure in Turn-of-the-Century New York* (Philadelphia: Temple University Press, 1986), p. 35.

that instead women should save their money was increasingly regarded as inappropriate to the modern woman.

The shop-girl's lifestyle, like the department store in which she worked, was particularly associated with the pleasures of the metropolis and heterosocial culture, where in some cases the smart clothes and hats she favoured were perceived to signal sexual availability. The majority of the salesgirls in Zola's Ladies Paradise, who 'talked about men all the time' (p. 131), rely on lovers waiting for them at the end of the day for entertainment; 'everyone did it in the end because in Paris a woman could not live on what she earned' (p. 185). An article in the new journal, *The Young Woman*, saw the 'many dangers' and 'hidden evils' to which shop-girls would be exposed in very similar terms to those of bar work; in such an environment, 'there is the danger of making undesirable acquaintance, and there is also the great temptation to an excessive love of dress ... a shop life may make a girl smart and bright, but it scarcely helps to fit her for the duties of a wife and mother'. It was thought that shop-girls were likely to become 'fast', learning 'to love excitement, and to crave for it', generating fears about their potential sexual immorality and consequent unfitness for domesticity.[69] Sanders has related this to the 'department store's culture of industrial display labor, in which the employee becomes one of many elements in the display of goods for sale', where the boredom of shop life 'resulted in a perceived desire on the part of the shopgirl for stimulation and excitement'.[70] Certainly, the excessively long hours and minimal leisure time suffered by shop-girls often meant that they led an existence of 'continued dullness, driving and discomfort', according to Clementina Black's 1907 study of sweated labour.[71] And yet the eagerness of bored retail workers to seize on 'any offered means of escape' in the form of public entertainments can be read in more liberating terms as the determination to cultivate the independence they have fully earned. Their endurance of sweated conditions must have heightened their enjoyment of their unchaperoned leisure activities, which were relatively unrestricted compared to those available to other women positioned away from the city centre. The limitations on the shop-girl's leisure time became another example of exploitation used by feminist campaigners to mobilise public sympathy; Jeune significantly saw the imposed limits as 'a great privation',[72] and Black considers them as a likely cause of anaemia, headaches, nervous collapse and indigestion, criticising the employers for claiming so much of the workers' time that 'many young women never, except on Sundays or holidays, go out of doors in the daylight'.[73] Whilst such limitations may have ensured that shop-girls were never criticised to quite the same extent as factory girls for their out-of-hours

---

[69] C.J. Hamilton, 'Life Behind the Counter', *Young Woman* 1 (1892), 128–30 (pp. 129, 130).

[70] Sanders, p. 191.

[71] Black, *Sweated Industry and the Minimum Wage*, p. 73.

[72] Jeune, p. 132. In line with conservative thinking about keeping women off the streets, she voiced her disapproval of a system which ensured that shop assistants were 'unable to join clubs, guilds, or enjoy many of the recreative evening amusements which abound'.

[73] Black, *Sweated Industry and the Minimum Wage*, p. 54.

behaviour, they were nevertheless similarly perceived as likely to exhibit their sexual freedoms in the public spaces of the city.

The shop-girl's 'escape' into the public sphere has been viewed both as a sign of her vulgarity and her modernity. Sanders's argument that, in turn-of-the-century British narratives, 'as a result of the degradation of self produced by the shop … the shopgirl's desires themselves become debased', part of a process by which 'the shopgirl became the focus of a set of cultural anxieties over the unsatisfied desires associated with late Victorian and Edwardian femininity',[74] certainly fits the unchecked promiscuity of some of Zola's salesgirls. Even though she typically aspires to middle-class domesticity, Monica in *The Odd Women* cannot escape the vulgarity of the public sphere, risking the downfall of the brash and 'coarse' Miss Eade, whose degeneration into prostitution acquires a certain inevitability. Like the 'nice, quiet girls' also employed at the draper's, Monica may be 'no representative shop-girl' (p. 238) but her struggle to maintain her respectability in the face of the uncertain new rules of heterosocial culture also marks her out as an emergent modern type. In her excellent reading of the New Woman in the modern city, Sally Ledger has more usefully pointed out that in *The Odd Women* Gissing's shop-girl 'inhabits the metropolis in a more self-confident and disruptive way' than both her Zolaesque counterparts and his New Woman characters, who do not pose a challenge to 'the masculine public arena'.[75] The skills learnt behind the counter, referred to derisively by Rhoda as 'shop-training', can be used to deflect the unwanted attentions of men, such as the counterman, Mr Bullivant, undeniably boosting her confidence in the metropolis. The freedom to interact with men in urban space is a prerogative the over-worked shop-girl has come to cherish: the forceful manner in which Monica articulates and exercises 'a woman's right to the same freedom as a man' (p. 216) is strong evidence of her alignment with the New Woman. Her 'free wandering about London' (p. 25) on Sundays mostly consists of time spent in tea-shops, parks, and by the river at Richmond, her choice of 'safe' heterosocial spaces frequented in the day-time by middle-class women showing her urban knowledge. The 'commercialized recreation' of the new heterosocial spaces of the city, as Kathy Peiss has contended in her study of contemporary New York, 'fostered a youth-oriented, mixed-sex world of pleasure, where female participation was profitable and encouraged'.[76] Although late-Victorian British culture might not have been so commercialised or so tolerant of new forms of female behaviour, the traditional public segregation of the sexes was clearly breaking down, as women's opportunities for meeting men informally and regularly increased. It is also interesting to note that, in *The Odd Women*, despite the 'unenviable reputation' some of the rowdier girls acquire, the shop-girl's independence is still shown to attract envy; once her escape from the draper's has been achieved, Monica still misses the liberty of her former existence. When

---

[74] Sanders, p. 192.

[75] Ledger, pp. 162, 168.

[76] Peiss, p. 6. According to Peiss, the spaces where women's presence was most noticeable were dance halls, amusement parks and movie theatres – there are detailed analyses of these three spaces in her book.

Widdowson accuses his wife of getting the idea that life should be 'as full of enjoyment as possible' from 'those people at Chelsea' (p. 163), her correction that they are more interested in work reinforces this association of freedom and leisure with the retail industry. The shop-girl's ease in male company, encouraged by her interaction with male customers, employers and fellow employees in a controlled environment, may also have allowed her to develop strategies for holding her own in heterosocial culture.

But Gissing shows that the New Woman can also pose a challenge to the masculine public arena in *Eve's Ransom*, where the clerical heroine, intent on enjoying herself, operates as a more challenging and disruptive figure than her shop-girl counterpart. Patty's ability to keep her suitor Mr Dally at arm's length, coupled with her 'frank remarks' (p. 39) to Hilliard and the ease with which she talks and jokes with men she barely knows, suggest that she has been trained in essential social skills. However, in a reversal of stereotypes, when Eve lodges above the shop with her friend, she is the one staying out late and risking being locked out so that Patty's uncle fears that 'she'll do you no good' (p. 53). Like some of the wilder girls who share Monica's dormitory, it is not unusual for Eve to make use of her latchkey, an essential accessory of a modern, city girl,[77] to return to her Gower Street lodgings around midnight. Before meeting Eve, Hilliard has 'imagined her leading a life of clockwork regularity' (p. 23), 'taking no pleasure' (p. 74) and is both 'bewildered' and 'disappointed' (p. 74) to have this image shattered when he first sees the fashionably attired woman extravagantly hailing a cab in the Euston Road:

> Her appearance struck him as quite unlike that he would have expected Eve Madeley to present. He had thought of her as very plainly, perhaps poorly clad; but this attire was ornate, and looked rather expensive; it might be in the mode of the new season ... They were going to a theatre, of course. And Eve spoke as if money were of no consequence to her. She had the look, the tones, of one bent on enjoying herself, of one who habitually pursued pleasure, and that in its most urban forms. (pp. 24, 25)

Although we later learn that it is the shop-girl who has instructed her 'how much enjoyment she could get out of an hour or two of liberty, with sixpence to spend' (p. 75), the office worker is actually in a much better position to 'take life more easily'. The 'liberty' and spending power associated with the shop-girl actually fits better with the office worker's hours and accommodation; the claim made about 'The Working Lady in London' in the *Fortnightly Review* in 1892 that 'after working hours ... if they are living in one room, they must go out in search of cheap amusements' is less appropriate to the shop-girl's lifestyle.[78] It is worth noting that the Glorified Spinster interviewed in the 1888 *Macmillans* article, who had to be 'a financial genius in extracting the greatest possible amount of pleasure out of every shilling', is evidently not a shop-girl, as she would only rarely be able

---

[77] A. T. Schofield, 'On the Perfecting of the Modern Girl', *Girl's Own Paper*, 20 July 1895, p. 663.
[78] March-Phillips, 'The Working Lady in London', p. 200.

to enjoy theatres, concerts and foreign travel if she worked six evenings a week and had to live in.[79] Both Eve and Patty are in their element after dark, mingling with the crowds in the theatre, in Parisian restaurants and at the international Health Exhibition at South Kensington. By the early 1890s the vulgar behaviour of the audiences had confirmed Gissing's suspicions that the theatre was not a refined place, though revealingly, his visit to the exhibition in 1884, which he described as 'a sort of London in little' with its impressive displays of manufactured goods,[80] does not occasion any outbursts on vulgarity. Certainly, the women's choice of entertainment seems tame in comparison with Hilliard's own arrival in the 'metropolis, alone and free' when he 'yielded to London's grossest lures', 'a succession of extravagances' (p. 20) which have to remain unspecified. Gissing's readers are encouraged to share the progressive view later championed by Collet of the 'right of a girl wage-earner' to leisure, and to recognise that Eve's embracing of urban pleasures is less an extravagance than a necessary counterbalance to her professional working life, making the female clerk 'perhaps the most representative of the middle class [sic] working women of the future'.[81]

The later text allows women greater access to a wider variety of heterosocial spaces but places more of an emphasis on the dangers of adopting male attitudes to the metropolis. The white-collar heroine's occupation of public space may be accepted as an inevitable element of her new work culture, but it becomes conventional for male and older female characters in late-Victorian narratives to act as mouthpieces for dominant cultural views by continuing to see it as a cause for concern. Maria Teresa Chialant has argued that, 'Eve can be seen as a real *flâneuse* on account of the genuine pleasure she feels in inhabiting the city, in the way she takes possession of its spaces and of the new opportunities for women',[82] but the female possession of urban space is questioned within the text. The enjoyment of public entertainments is seen to be irreconcilable with the office-worker's lifestyle, one early chapter opening with the question, 'How did Eve Madeley contrive to lead this life of leisure and amusement?' (p. 32). Hilliard's shock that a respectable book-keeper can be 'so uncertain in her comings and goings' (p. 23), in some ways reminiscent of Barfoot's surprise that Rhoda frequents the Savoy theatre, suggests that even a woman employed in business in Holborn would struggle to afford such a lifestyle in both financial and social terms. We later learn that Eve pays for her and Patty's entertainments with £20 given as a reward for finding some letters, a rare and expendable source of income equivalent to almost six months' earnings. The cheap amusements enjoyed by women are then only financed with difficulty by their own earnings from paid work, suggesting that modern women inevitably come to rely on the economic support of

---

[79] 'The Glorified Spinster', *Macmillans Magazine*, 58 (1888), 371–6 (pp. 372, 373).

[80] Letter to Margaret, 25 August 1884. *Collected Letters, Vol 2*, p. 246.

[81] Collet, 'The Expenditure of Middle Class Working Women', p. 85. In a rare moment of admiration for the female clerk, Collet applauds her enjoyment of the new sports and the pleasures of society.

[82] Maria Teresa Chialant, 'The Feminization of the City in Gissing's Fiction', in Bouwe Postmus (ed.), *A Garland for Gissing* (Amsterdam: Rodopi, 2001), p. 63.

men with all the strings attached. Significantly, the acknowledgement of the difficulties the working lady experiences in maintaining her confidence in public testifies to an awareness of the effects on respectability of women's 'free wandering' around London.

The familiar trope of stalking, often referred to as 'spying' or 'espial' in the texts, is used in Gissing's narratives not only as a means of aligning the reader's sympathy with the persecuted New Woman, but also to dismiss, through a marked authorial antagonism to the stalker and his irrational fears, the belief that respectable women require the protection of men in the city. Whilst the 1880s fiction had tended to confirm the stalker's suspicions that work-girls were at risk of corruption or had been lying about their whereabouts, stalking in the 1890s novels is represented as more of an intrusion, saying more about men's anxieties and inadequacies as (potential) sexual partners than about unacceptable kinds of female behaviour. In addition to agitatedly hanging around outside women's lodgings late at night in familiar paranoid fashion, both Widdowson and Hilliard reveal their inability to appreciate the use of public transport which white-collar women workers both relied on and took for granted. As a new acquaintance, Widdowson's disapproval of Monica's 'ready knowledge of London transit' (p. 46), and insistence on accompanying her to the station is both ridiculous and creepily obsessive, as is Hilliard's unsatisfactory explanation for 'the persistency of his observation' of Eve on the underground train to Earl's Court, that 'choice he had none – the girl drew him irresistibly to follow and watch her' (p. 27). Hilliard's checking up on Eve's movements with Patty and her frequent 'unaware[ness] of her acquaintance's proximity' which allows him to 'scrutinis[e] her appearance … at his ease' (p. 40) make him appear unnaturally controlling and voyeuristic. Their aggressive accusations that by staying out late or desiring the stimulus of company, women are sacrificing their womanliness, make the men into increasingly sinister patriarchal figures. In *The Odd Women* the shop-girl's resentment at her admirer's spying may initially be 'confused with a certain satisfaction' (p. 63) as she plans her escape from Walworth Rd, but its intensification when he intrudes on her visits to art galleries, berates her for staying ten minutes later than agreed when he collects her from Milly's rooms and demands 'ocular proof' (p. 150) of where she is going again suggests that it is his behaviour, not hers, which is inappropriate. His desperate hiring of a private detective to obtain further proof of her disobedience constitutes the most extreme example of stalking in Gissing's fiction. Ledger's argument that, 'his paranoid surveillance … transforms him into a parody of the *flâneur*'[83] is a useful way of looking at the reversal of urban gender roles the relation between observer and observed creates in these texts. But it is also necessary to acknowledge that the stalker's unshakeable belief that an unprotected woman is 'in danger' in the city cannot be entirely dismissed. Although the detective's report that Monica is having an affair with Barfoot is incorrect, her short-lived liaison with Bevis is not entirely innocent and some uncertainty surrounds the ensuing pregnancy which links her back to the potentially

---

[83]   Ledger, p. 166.

promiscuous Amy Drake. Similarly, Eve's dalliance with the unnamed married man, never fully explained in the text, results in her absence from London for a few weeks, ostensibly to escape the angry wife but certainly enough time to arrange and recover from a speedy abortion. But the fact that unsupervised meetings with men in places of public entertainment or on the streets posed a risk to women with limited access to birth control does not suggest that Gissing is siding with the stalker, rather that surveillance was not the kind of protection women might have found most useful.

Women's metropolitan freedoms are constantly read by men in terms of their sexual availability and lack of respectability; 'to enter the public domain', as Ledger has contended, 'the New Woman had to confront and avoid the label 'public woman', which at the *fin-de-siècle* was synonymous with 'streetwalker'.[84] Being approached by unknown men, or experiencing the 'chance encounters' with men she hardly knows, becomes a regular occurrence of urban life for the shop-girl in *The Odd Women*, which threatens her reputation. In order to preserve her respectability, Monica has to constantly ward off associations with the prostitute, her potential closeness to such a figure symbolised when she meets her sisters late at night outside the shop and notices 'only a few yards away, a girl, to whom the pavement was a place of commerce ... laughing with two men' (p. 64). The mobility of the woman worker and her positioning on the pavements means that she is also liable to be approached by men: on her Sunday expeditions Monica finds that 'men had followed her in the street and tried to make her acquaintance' (p. 31). Her unchaperoned meetings with Bevis on Oxford Street and in his flat, where 'it was doubtfully permissible for her to sit *tete-à-tete* with a young man, under any excuse' (p. 206), may seem to pose to her 'several distinct dangers' (p. 247), but the danger inherent in her desire to satisfy her sexual needs is compounded by the reaction of her husband to her potential adultery. The brief sexual liaison between Barfoot and the shop-girl Amy Drake, who boldly 'puts herself in his way' on a railway platform' (p. 95), is also suggestive of the new casual sexual encounters encouraged by the city. Although Barfoot defends himself by suggesting that this was 'perhaps a sign of innocent freedom in the intercourse of men and women' (p. 95), it is the man who must be seen as the seducer in this scenario and women's sexual agency paradoxically both downplayed and characterised as recklessly inappropriate; certainly, the ensuing pregnancy makes the woman appear vulnerable. Parsons has coupled Amy with Miss Eade, reading their 'sexually provocative advances in sites of modern transport', as a sign of Gissing's ambivalence about women's freedoms and his 'connection of the independent mobile woman with loose female sexuality'.[85] Such a view seems to be more appropriate to the more scandalous lifestyles permitted in Zola's Paris, such as the casual prostitution of the shop-girl Clara, explicitly described as a 'loose girl', 'always on the arm of a different man' (p. 133). However, rather than seeing sexually active unmarried or unfaithful women as 'loose' like his more conservative contemporaries, Gissing's attitude is perhaps

---

[84] Ledger, p. 154.
[85] Parsons, p. 51.

more reflective of the new sexual moralities to which women from different occupations may have subscribed. An alternative interpretation is to see these examples as evidence of Peiss's model of the 'mixed-sex fun' of heterosocial culture,[86] an important element of working women's leisure activities which allows men and women to approach each other more easily, though maintaining sexual innocence in the new heterosocial spaces was far from easy.

The city certainly allowed women to break some of the rules about social intercourse with men, which may have encouraged them to express their sexualities in new ways. In *Eve's Ransom*, waiting up for her to return to Patty's house, Hilliard links Eve more obviously to the prostitute by asking her angrily, 'Do you often walk the streets until midnight?' (p. 54). At the Health Exhibition, where she is observed talking with an unknown man, the potential slur on her reputation is confirmed in the question he puts to himself, 'Dare I approach her?' (p. 28), as if she were indeed the same type of urban woman as Miss Eade, who plies her trade at Victoria Station. Hilliard's meditations on Eve's sexual innocence, 'Is she a good-hearted girl or – ' (p. 91) are meant to be read as the typical male reaction to this bold new type but Patty too is startled to see Eve 'in conversation with a man she did not know' (p. 31).　The exhibition crowd significantly encompasses various social types, from the 'frankly rowdy' to the 'solemnly superior' (p. 30), including 'a sprinkling of unattached young women with roving eyes' (p. 30) which may or may not be a reference to prostitutes. In her study of London between 1855 and 1870, Lynda Nead has argued that it was not only the prostitute who might be seeking a casual sexual encounter. Rather than reinforcing the prevailing view that respectable women always avoided men's eyes, let alone having 'roving eyes' of their own, Nead argues for 'a repatterning of sexuality in the spaces of the city' and the 'bold new type of metropolitan femininity' this may have produced.[87] Eve's reluctant admission that she has been meeting a married man prompts Hilliard to comment on the new sexual behaviour of the urban woman:

> 'You haven't misled me; I knew from the first that – well, a girl of your age, and with your face, doesn't live alone in London without adventures. I shouldn't think of telling you all mine, and I don't ask to know yours – unless I begin to have a part in them' (p. 55)

Although this appears to suggest that urban women, like men, are entitled to their sexual 'adventures' even if married, Hilliard also continues to treat Eve like a prostitute in this passage, by slyly letting her know that he is attracted to her and making assumptions about her sexual availability. Eve's admission that she feels

---

[86]　Peiss, p. 6.

[87]　Lynda Nead, *Victorian Babylon: People, Streets and Images in Nineteenth-Century London* (New Haven and London: Yale University Press, 2000), pp. 68, 78, 131. See also pp. 66–7 for her excellent discussion of Eliza Lynn Linton's *Saturday Review* article 'Out Walking', which raises some interesting questions about the male gaze and the metropolitan woman.

'ashamed and disgusted' (p. 79) about her behaviour with the unknown man, once she learns of his wife, suggests her nervousness about such encounters. The 'ease of manner, the frank friendliness' (p. 68) with which she later accompanies Hilliard to restaurants and museums in Paris appears unsustainable, as she is also assailed by doubts that her living at his expense makes her acquiescent in his control of her movements.

Whatever their sexual inclinations, the sense that modern women are treated like prostitutes by men is undeniably borne out in the exchange of money which underpins many of these heterosocial encounters. As Rachel Bowlby has argued in her excellent study of commercial culture, in male-authored naturalist fiction, 'involvements with men deprive [women] of th[e] self-sufficiency identified with the possession of money'.[88] This idea is explored in detail in *Eve's Ransom*, where the exchange of money for female company or pleasure casts doubt on the innocence of both women, who then find themselves in debt to the men with whom they are involved. This has to be seen in the light of the scarcity of women's earnings and the 'widely accepted practice' of 'treating' which, according to Peiss, grew out of developments in leisure activities. In the 1890s, men usually earned at least twice as much as women in the same jobs,[89] and, as already discussed, working women were advised to save from their meagre wages rather than 'wasting' money on leisure. Eve also finds herself trapped by her flirtations as her difficulties with the married man prompt her to borrow money from Hilliard, who bargains that he will only lend it to her if she agrees to meet him in Paris on an expenses-paid holiday. Whereas Patty has fewer qualms about a free holiday, even accepting payment from Hilliard for persuading her friend to agree, Eve is much more reluctant, at first refusing to take the condition seriously and then responding, 'How can I live at your expense?' and 'The shame of it – to be supported by you' (p. 57). Despite being recommended on health grounds, foreign travel would have been out of the reach of the majority of poorly paid working girls at this time, which suggests that we should read Eve's consent to a public kiss on the banks of the Seine as a form of repayment she cannot refuse, rather than a sign of attraction. However, later in the novel, dwindling finances dictate that the glamour of Paris be swapped for the misery of rainy afternoons spent in museums in Birmingham, where Hilliard bemoans the conducting of their courtship in public places, because 'I can't talk – can't say half the things I wish to' (p. 83). Her increasing reluctance to accept money when she visits Hilliard's rooms in Birmingham, as she becomes 'frightened' of 'ow[ing] too much gratitude' (p. 90) to him, is a further indication that the financial dependency on men occasioned by treating was an unacceptable condition to some women.[90] His response 'Pay me back with your lips!' (p. 90),

---

[88] Rachel Bowlby, *Just Looking: Consumer Culture in Dreiser, Gissing and Zola* (New York and London: Methuen, 1985), p. 49.

[89] Peiss, p. 54.

[90] Peiss, p. 140. Another potentially unacceptable condition was the 'rebellious assertions to parents', which might take the form of continued deception.

as Bowlby notes,[91] underlines her position as a kept woman, who only accepts the conditions of dependency because of the poverty she faces through unemployment. Patty reveals that 'she says that – even if she wished – she could never break off with [Hilliard]' (p. 99). In contrast to the clerk's struggle against the sacrifice of her respectability, the less restrained shop-girl is shown to be unable, or perhaps unwilling, to think beyond the offers of money to the obligations and dependency on men to which she is consenting. Indeed, Patty's reputation does not seem to be as important to her, as she is content to travel alone with Hilliard, visit his rooms without her friend and even 'asked leave to hold by her companion's arm' (p. 100) in the crowds at Dudley railway station, leading Narramore to the conclusion that they are a couple. This serves to sharpen the contrast between the shop-girl and the professional woman, not in order to emphasise the shop-girl's potential 'looseness' but to show that the latter's concern about protecting her reputation and avoiding financial dependence on men is perhaps a more sensible and realistic manifestation of the new metropolitan femininities.

The conclusions to these narratives of urban freedom increasingly came to reinforce the fantasy, associated with the dullness of shop work by investigators, of rescue into marriage by richer men, as the desire for money and security overrides the advantages of a certain amount of sexual licence. Clementina Black's investigations of shop work for the Women's Industrial Council inclined her to the view that amongst shop-girl narratives Zola's vision of the seductive employer was 'certainly the exception', as for the majority of shop-girls, 'the temptations of shop life take the form not of illicit lovemaking within the shop' but of the fantasised escape from dullness.[92] In Katherine Mansfield's later short story 'The Tiredness of Rosabel' (1908), the shop-girl comes to recognise 'the slight tinge of insolence, of familiarity' of her male customer and protects herself by 'not pay[ing] the slightest attention' to forward remarks about her 'damned pretty little figure'. More importantly, she then enjoys an extended (and surprisingly sexual) fantasy about the romantic escape he could offer her from her tiredness, though this is framed by the harsher routine of her bus journey home and her early waking in a cold flat; even when she imagines the fine food and public entertainments she could enjoy as an engaged woman, the reality of her tiredness cannot be escaped as if 'the real Rosabel' recognises that 'chang[ing] places' with the lady shopper must remain a fantasy.[93] One of the shop-girls interviewed by Collet claimed that she would 'marry anybody to get out of the drapery business',[94] a sentiment apparently

---

[91]   Bowlby, p. 43. She argues that, 'the objective capacity of the money to purchase whatever may be considered necessary or desirable is inextricably linked to structures of gratitude, guilt and the sense of obligation'.

[92]   Black, *Sweated Industry and the Minimum Wage*, pp. 72–3. The realities of shop work, in her opinion, were most faithfully expressed in Mr Maxwell's *Vivien* (1905), H.G. Wells's *Kipps* (1902) and Gissing's *The Odd Women*.

[93]   Katherine Mansfield, 'The Tiredness of Rosabel' (1908), in Angelique Richardson (ed.), *Women who Did: Stories by Men and Women, 1890–1914* (Harmondsworth: Penguin, 2002), pp. 337, 339.

[94]   Bulley, 'The Employment of Women', p. 44.

shared by Monica, whose hasty marriage to the older, patriarchal figure of Edmund Widdowson, and confinement to the suburban home it entails, she almost instantly regrets. Displaying the effects of exploitation identified by Black, 'that collapse of health and nerves ... so frequent among women shop assistants',[95] the shop-girl in Rhoda's diagnosis later becomes 'fit for nothing else [but marriage]' (p. 107). Gissing's narrative trajectory then dramatises the investigator's fears about accepting the conditions attached to male support rather than the continued struggle to become self-supporting. In the later novel this paradigm is subverted in order to relate this struggle to the office worker's experience. Patty's resistance of offers of marriage from her persistent suitor, Mr Dally, probably attributable to the favourable (and unrepresentative) working conditions in another family-run shop, may function as a denial of current trends but she appears to be left in limbo, rather than celebrated for her ability to supply all her own needs from meagre wages. Instead, it is Eve, weakening under the pressures of depression, who comes to see marriage to the enterprising and wealthy business man Narramore as providing the 'safety' which her profession cannot offer, though it remains uncertain whether her depression is caused by her unemployment or her discontent with her choice of occupation, neither of which are reconcilable with her modern view that 'work is the best thing for me' (p. 91). A retreat to the suburbs is, of course, no guarantee of the end of her struggle against illness or dullness; like Monica, whose mobility in the city is gradually curtailed by the pregnancy that kills her, she has been forced into confinement, which poses its own dangers. Significantly, the doctor's response to Monica's first suburban ailment, 'Had she wholesome variety of occupation?' (p. 158) highlights what may be missing from marriage to over-protective men. As a textual strategy, relocating the *flâneuse* away from the opportunities of the city, rather than conservatively denying her right to agency and autonomy, serves to reinforce the temporary and conditional nature of the freedoms working women held dear.

'Living Single': the Struggle to Maintain Independence

In these New Woman texts Gissing is at his most radical in granting middle-class women the right to live either alone or with friends, independent of family ties or male control and supervision. The best way to avoid the stultifying effects of suburban marriage is to cultivate the lifestyle of the glorified spinster, whose urban freedoms and fulfilling work can only be achieved by an embracing of new living conditions for single women. In her reading of girls' culture at the *fin-de-siècle*, Sally Mitchell has argued that the new girl can be seen to occupy 'a quasi-public space' between the family home and the marital home, where, 'for however many years that space might last – the new girl has a degree of independence'.[96] It was

---

[95]   Black, *Sweated Industry and the Minimum Wage*, p. 55.
[96]   Sally Mitchell, *The New Girl: Girls' Culture in England, 1880–1915* (New York: Columbia University Press, 1995), p. 9. Her argument is that the new girl 'occupied a provisional free space' as girls' culture sanctioned 'new ways of being, new modes of

this space that preoccupies the author in these novels where women's resistance to entering the marital home is at its strongest; indeed, for some, resistance will take the radical form of a definite refusal to sacrifice independence. The evolution of the Old Maid, 'a woman *minus* something' into the 'Glorified Spinster, a woman *plus* something', classifies the older type as those who still expect marriage as their destiny or 'lack strength and spontaneity to make a full and satisfactory life for themselves'.[97] By ensuring that the age range of his heroines encompasses both girls and more mature women, Gissing aims for a complex analysis of the factors which might grant self-supporting women the strength to persevere with the struggle for independence, whilst avoiding the temptation to lapse into the ways of the Old Maid. The comparison between the safe but out-dated co-habiting of sisters, and the modern sharing of lodgings with female friends results in an idealising of the latter arrangement, a more effective means of securing lasting independence for the odd woman than other available alternatives to marriage, such as a free union with an enlightened male partner. In its challenging examination of the lifestyle of the cheerfully single type writer girl whose preference for the companionship of women may or may not indicate a hidden lesbianism, *The Odd Women* can be seen to look forward to the more feminist suffragette fiction of the 1910s in important ways.

Keep has described the Type-Writer Girl as 'the acceptable face of the "New Woman" because she represented the desire for a career and independence in such a way as not to endanger … traditional feminine sensibilities'.[98] But her acceptability is not quite so simple, as novelists of the period also seek to show that beneath the glamorous ideal promoted in magazines and advertisements, the clerk's independent lifestyle may have a radical potential which aligns female clerical labour with the cause of feminism and the developing suffrage movement. Mary's lectures and the books and periodicals carefully selected for the library are intended to encourage young women to consider their work in relation to the Woman Question. For Victoria Olwell, the typewriter, a figure and a machine used to 'signif[y] the modernity of feminine autonomy and competence', was bound up with 'struggles over women's citizenship' in a number of complex ways, where not only the clerk's increased public visibility and economic opportunities but her use of her hands both to type and to participate in new voting practices around the turn of the century can be linked to 'our understandings of women's political subjectivity and its grading'.[99] Despite their entry into new professions, it was recognised in 1888 that the new class of glorified spinsters, 'destined in the near future to become very large', still lacked 'a recognised place in the social and

---

behaviour, and new attitudes that were not yet acceptable for adult women (except in the case of the advanced few)' (p. 3).
[97]   'The Glorified Spinster', p. 374.
[98]   Keep, p. 404.
[99]   Victoria Olwell, 'Typewriters and the Vote', *Signs* 29:1 (2003), 55–83 (pp. 58–9, 57). Olwell argues that as both woman and machine 'the typewriter constitutes – or literally inscribes – alternatives to those conceptions of identity and citizenship that dominated debates about women's enfranchisement'.

political scheme';[100] their desire for sexual equality in the modernised workplace was to become an important element of their desire for citizenship. Whereas Juliet's seduction by her employer in *The Type-writer Girl*, presented as the inevitable outcome of the typist being improperly 'left alone with him half the day in the privacy of his study' (p. 141), links traditional gender hierarchies and sexual exploitation, the modern offices to be preferred by the inspired graduates of Mary's typing school we imagine to be similar to those woman-dominated spaces frequented by suffrage workers in early twentieth-century fiction such as the suffragette Evelyn Sharp's short story collection *Rebel Women* (1910) and Virginia Woolf's *Night and Day* (1915). Woolf's hard-working, energetic heroine Mary Datchet always hastens from the crowd of 'clerks and typists and commercial men' (p. 62) to reach the suffrage office in Russell Square she shares with another emancipated woman and a far from patriarchal man, eager to 'get her typewriter to take its place in competition with the rest' (p. 63) in the building.[101] Her organisational and administrative skills, combined with the strong political opinions she voices in the suffrage society's meetings, have fitted her to rise above the disadvantages of femininity: 'what was the good, after all, of being a woman if one didn't keep fresh, and cram one's life with all sorts of views and experiments?' (p. 63). Although her choice of unpaid work is not portrayed as entirely desirable or fulfilling, this new model of typewriter girl certainly conveys some of the feminist excitement of joining the campaign for votes for women, as she endeavours to use her 'cumbrous machine' to 'achieve something remarkable' (p. 63).

Gissing's focus on clerical labour as essential to feminism may not be as progressive as Woolf's, but given his inability to foresee developments in the suffrage movement twenty years later, his insistent association of office work with sisterhood and militancy can be seen as part of a forward-looking authorial strategy to make it appealing and aspirational to emancipated readers. In Bird's 1911 investigatory account, the office is fetishised as a comfortable and safe feminine space in which the woman clerk becomes indispensable: moreover, the smartly dressed female commuters who daily 'pour in and out of every block of office buildings in numbers that rival the men' are staking a claim to the financial centre of London, ensuring that 'the City is no longer a man's domain'.[102] Demonstrating the transferability of clerical skills to more feminist professions, Winifred continues her business training in a publishing department and mimics the role of the pioneering female editors of the new women's journals by finally establishing 'a paper of her own' (p. 141), though her success story is beyond the limits of the 1890s narrative. Mary and Rhoda correct Everard's view of this work as unsuitable for an educated girl, encouraging him to see that such advances show women to be 'in touch with the great movement of our time' (pp. 141–2). The choice of a New Woman typing-instructor heroine, 'quite like a *man* in energy and resources' (p.

---

[100] 'The Glorified Spinster', p. 376.
[101] All quotations are taken from Virginia Woolf, *Night and Day*, ed. Julia Briggs (1919; Harmondsworth: Penguin, 1992).
[102] Bird, pp. 127, 130.

30), who will prove 'a most valuable friend' to struggling women by helping them towards 'earning an easy and pleasant livelihood' (p. 29) through typing, certainly emphasises what can be achieved in a space free of traditional gender hierarchies. Black is particularly impressed in her review by Gissing's effective ability to dramatise 'discussions of social problems' in the conversations of 'a little group of active, intelligent women, working for themselves and their sisters', which in her opinion makes him stand out amongst modern novelists.[103] Young's astute discussion of the way Rhoda has to be 'feminised' as a teacher rather than a typical typist oppressed by a male employer in order to protect both her independence and her class status is revealing in this context.[104] However, I am not entirely convinced that this feminization constitutes an 'ideological lapse' on Gissing's part, as the novel seems less concerned with 'the taint of business' than the increased opportunities for emancipated women in the commercial world. Admittedly, Gissing softens his feminist pioneer by characterising Mary as a 'strongly feminine' figure in the style of Jessie Boucherett and the more moderate Langham Place feminists;[105] despite her uncommon business abilities, she 'did not seek to become known as the leader of a "movement", yet her quiet work was probably more effectual than the public career of women who propagandize for female emancipation' (p. 54). But to subscribe to John Sloan's view that the less anachronistic Rhoda is used to 'subtly present[] the ideological deficiency of radical separatism', making it 'inappropriate' to see Gissing as ambiguously sympathetic to his heroine,[106] is to misunderstand the contradictions at work in a text which sets out to dramatise a number of conflicting positions on female emancipation. The ostensibly anti-feminist short story, 'At High Pressure' (1896), in which an educated daughter is satirised for devoting her time to a mad frenzy of society meetings and letter-writing, is similarly contradictory in issuing the disclaimer that she does not belong to 'the advanced guard of emancipated women'(pp. 278–9), aligning her with the 'quiet' feminists rather than the propagandists.[107] The 'surprising life' of Linda Vassie, 'often ... till past midnight ... engaged, at high pressure, in a great variety of pursuits' (p. 278), may grant her the modern woman's 'liberty' to 'speed around in cabs and trains, to read all the periodicals of the day, [and] to make endless new acquaintances' (p. 279) but her pressurised lifestyle invites the reader's ridicule rather than admiration; she is described in the conclusion as 'trying and wearisome' (p. 282). Though it is fair to

---

[103]   Black, Review of *The Odd Women*, p. 155.

[104]   Young, p. 253.   She argues that 'Working in an office might free Rhoda from conventional feminine roles, but in the realistic world of a Gissing novel it would necessarily commit her to another kind of servitude'. In contrast, Keep's analysis of Rhoda as an anomalous example of the unsexed typist seems rather misinformed.

[105]   In an early article, Alison Cotes identified Boucherett, the founder of SPEW, as a probable model for Mary Barfoot. See 'New Woman and Odd Women', *Gissing Newsletter* 14 (1978), 1–20.

[106]   John Sloan, *George Gissing: The Cultural Challenge* (London: Macmillan, 1989), p. 123.

[107]   All quotations are taken from George Gissing, 'At High Pressure' (1896), in *Human Odds and Ends* (1898; New York & London: Garland Publishing, 1977).

say that Gissing avoids directly confronting the issue of women's rights or suffrage, as in his frustratingly undeveloped portrayal of the suffrage campaigner Miss Wade in *Denzil Quarrier* (1892), his overt antagonism to public political careers for women never entirely cancels out a tentative admiration for the 'quiet' but effectual work of the women activists, a contradictory position not entirely unusual in a period when divisions within feminism were particularly apparent. As Sloan more usefully concedes, 'it is unsatisfactory and indeed mistaken ... to interpret [*The Odd Women*] in any simple sense as either hostile or favourable towards woman's liberation'.[108]

The reader's appreciation of more modern forms of oddity in *The Odd Women* is also sharpened by pitting the 'strong, self-reliant, revolted woman' against the type of the 'womanly old-maid',[109] or the middle-aged 'poor lady' examined by Eliza Orme,[110] a figure increasingly marginalised in a strategy typical of New Woman fiction. In 1889, a journalist for the *Englishwoman's Review* emphasised one of the ongoing mantras of SPEW that the 'busy and active' spinster, happy in her work, enjoyed better health than the 'worn-out mother'. The article countered arguments about the abnormality of single life by pointing out that not all women are 'required for the continuance of the species' but that it is only in current times that 'superfluous' women have come to be valued for their vital contributions to feminist reform and philanthropy.[111] At a time when the 'social and public usefulness' of the single woman was being actively promoted in both mainstream and feminist journals,[112] the energy and zeal for public activities of the modern graduates of the typing school ensure that they are sharply differentiated in evolutionary terms from the elder Madden sisters, whose cherished femininity and 'sordid troubles' hamper them in the rapidly changing labour market. Rhoda commiserates with the alcoholic, atavistic Virginia as 'a feeble, purposeless, hopeless woman; type of a whole class; living only to deteriorate' (p. 291). One reviewer perceptively recognised that, in this 'story of odd women', 'most [surplus females] are quite unfitted to realise for themselves that to be successful, to burst the bonds which encompass their narrow, sordid lives, they must be "odd"'.[113] In the short story, 'An Old Maid's Triumph', first published in 1895, Gissing cast doubt on the 'professional success' of a similarly atavistic fifty-eight-year old governess, delighted to have saved enough money to purchase the annuity which

---

[108] Sloan, p. 123.

[109] These labels are used in a favourable review, which Gissing considered 'very good'. The self-reliant woman is also referred to as emancipated here. See Review of *The Odd Women*, *Pall Mall Gazette*, 29 May 1893, p. 4.

[110] See Eliza Orme, 'How Poor Ladies Live: A Reply', *Nineteenth Century* 42 (1897), 613–19, one of a series of articles in the journal for this year which discussed the status of struggling middle-aged ladies compelled to enter the labour market.

[111] M.A.B., 'Normal or Abnormal', *Englishwoman's Review* 20 (December 1889), 533–8 (pp. 534–5), 537.

[112] [Henrietta Muller], 'The Future of Single Women', *Westminster Review* 121 (1884), 151–62 (p. 153).

[113] Review of *The Odd Women*, *Glasgow Herald*, 20 April 1893, p. 9.

will at last grant her 'a life of independence' (p. 198).[114] Her 'excessive parsimony', as 'from her twentieth-eighth to her fifty-eighth year this woman had never unavoidably spent one shilling-piece' (p. 200), has resulted in a lifetime of penury, during which she occupied 'all but the meanest' lodgings, chose only the cheapest indulgences and denied herself 'the delight of travel'. By giving into the consolations of alcohol, religion and romantic fiction rather than daring to risk using their capital to open a school, the Madden sisters' blinkered belief, 'what a blessed thing is independence!' (p. 15) is similarly ironic, setting them up as examples of 'the evils of celibacy'. It is precisely the fear of facing her 'dispirited' sisters' 'resign[ation] … to spinsterhood' (p. 11) that prompts Monica's decision to marry, as she recognises that 'their loneliness was for life, poor things … how much better if the poor girls had never been born' (p. 31). Gissing is confident in his portrayal of working female partnerships as fulfilling alternatives to heterosexual union: Monica's hasty decision to marry could have been avoided if she had been inspired by such brave women who 'work hard and are proud of their place in the world' rather than taking 'the weak women' (p. 316) as role models of female independence. Far from resigning themselves to 'useless, lost, futile lives', the odd women in the training school are able to triumph by making an important contribution to 'the world's work' (p. 37), part of a process Lucy Bland has characterised as 'develop[ing] a pride in their status … discarding the image of the "old maid"'.[115]

The new phenomenon of the supportive pairing of professional women was known as a 'Boston marriage' in late-nineteenth-century America, described by Sarah Deutsch in terms of the ability of American feminists to 'claim new sorts of legitimacy and authority for women' in urban space.[116] Martha Vicinus suggests that in Britain these were most common in women-only communities such as colleges and settlement houses,[117] but for those who could afford it, sharing a house with another like-minded woman helped to establish what Bland refers to as 'the *normality* of same-sex loving relations in many women's lives'.[118] Henry James's early New Woman novel, *The Bostonians* (1886), controversially depicts the modern 'marriage' between the radical Olive Chancellor and her younger, lower-class *protégée* Verena Tarrant, a feminist partnership typical of the strong emotional and professional bonds between women suffrage campaigners in early 1880s Boston. Lillian Faderman's research into these long-term monogamous partnerships between women suggests that predictably this was a more widespread

---

[114] All quotations are taken from George Gissing, 'An Old Maid's Triumph' (1895), in *Human Odds and Ends*.
[115] Lucy Bland, *Banishing the Beast: English Feminism and Sexual Morality, 1885–1914* (Harmondsworth: Penguin, 1995), p. 163.
[116] Sarah Deutsch, *Women and the City: Gender, Space, and Power in Boston, 1870–1940* (Oxford: Oxford University Press, 2000), p. 105.
[117] Martha Vicinus, *Independent Women: Work and Community for Single Women, 1850–1920* (Chicago: University of Chicago Press, 1985), pp. 212–221.
[118] Bland, pp. 170, 168–9. She argues that 'familial obligations and economic dependency made [setting up house together] an option open to few until the end of the century'.

practice in American society, more advanced than Britain in its views on female emancipation at this time.[119] Whereas the other professional spinsters in the novel, the aging philanthropist Miss Birdseye and the hardworking Dr Prance, occupy separate rooms in a dismal apartment block on the wrong side of town, Olive's wealth ensures that she is able to invite Verena to share her 'elegant home' in Charles St, though it is later revealed that the older woman makes annual payments to her friend's mesmerist father to guarantee his non-interference in this arrangement. In order to reinforce their involvement in the public sphere, James reminds us that as an active figure on committees and a 'typical Bostonian' with a particular 'set' (p. 187), Olive also socialises and works at other women's houses, so that 'our friends were not always shut up in Miss Chancellor's strenuous parlour' (p. 186).[120] Their modern partnership is linked to the promotion of 'the single sisterhood' (p. 261), and is moreover significantly described in terms of a spiritual necessity to their feminist enterprise: 'What you and I dream of doing demands of us a kind of priesthood' (p. 151), a 'carry[ing] ... out' of a 'sharp, inspired vision' (p. 138). The fact that the six celebrated speakers at a women's convention hosted by Olive significantly sleep 'two in a room' (p. 241) is a further signal of James's progressive endorsement of the Boston marriage and its acceptability within 1880s culture.

But, in the climate of fear created by the sexologists linking 'other' sexualities and perversion, the Boston marriage is constantly under threat from the heterosexual male in late-Victorian fiction, here in the form of the unenlightened Basil Ransom, who acts as a mouthpiece for the 'uncompromising and brutal [male] attitudes' towards spinsters which Cicely Hamilton later attacked in her 1909 feminist polemic *Marriage as a Trade*. Hamilton countered dominant views about the spinster's incompleteness by her argument that 'even if she be what is technically termed unsexed, it does not follow therefore that she is either unnatural or unwomanly'.[121] To men, Olive's unsexed appearance – she is plain with 'sharp and irregular' features and 'absolutely no figure' (p. 48) – gives off a sense of coldness; the fact that she seems 'unmarried by every implication of her being', 'essentially a celibate', gives Basil an 'uneasy feeling' (p. 47). Published in the same year that Dr Richard von Krafft-Ebing's influential *Psychopathia Sexualis* appeared in Germany (though it was not translated into English until 1892),[122] James's novel with its ambiguous validation of heterosexual marriage anticipates sexology's anti-feminist bias against the women's movement. Although I am

[119] Lillian Faderman, *Surpassing the Love of Men: Romantic Friendship and Love between Women from the Renaissance to the Present* (New York: William Morrow & Co, 1981), pp. 195–203. Most of her examples of Boston marriages are drawn from the letters and autobiographies of American women, particularly writers such as Sarah Orne Jewett, Willa Cather and the novelist's sister, Alice James.

[120] All quotations are taken from Henry James, *The Bostonians*, ed. Charles R. Anderson (1886; Harmondsworth: Penguin, 1984).

[121] Cicely Hamilton, *Marriage as a Trade* (London: Chapman & Hall, 1909), p. 36.

[122] Walkowitz, pp. 207–08, 305. A much fuller edition, including additional case histories, appeared in 1903.

inclined to Faderman's view that 'James believed that a romantic relationship between women was not of itself sick',[123] it is undeniable that the older woman's behaviour towards her friend is increasingly represented as an unnatural form of sexual dominance, 'too clinching, too terrible' (p. 376); at one point Basil even entertains the sexologist's fear that Verena (like the pseudo-homosexual whose lesbianism is acquired, rather than innate)[124] is being 'odiously perverted' (p. 242) by Olive and her set. But Ledger's argument that 'it is mostly ... in novels by male writers that the lesbian prototype develops', as they were 'more threatened by same-sex relationships between women than their female counterparts at the *fin-de-siecle*' is rather misleading. Seizing on the heroine's 'refus[al] to conform to the demands of heterosexual marriage' as evidence of the male author's pathologising of the lesbian is not borne out by the texts.[125]   In line with sexological constructions of the spinster, Rhoda's irregular features and masculinised body also explicitly mark her out as what Gissing calls 'something like an unfamiliar sexual type, remote indeed from the voluptuous' (p. 21), though even in the reaction of the rejected heterosexual male, this is not pursued to the point of pathology.   James's endorsement of same-sex partnerships is not ultimately sustained, but it remains nicely ambiguous: the naïve Verena may be open to persuasion that Boston marriage is 'a very peculiar thing' (p. 376), but the narrative does not close down the possibility of a 'friendship [with] elements which made it probably as complete as any (between women) that had ever existed' (p. 376).   Whilst the strong female friendships enjoyed by emancipated novelist heroines such as Hester Gresley in Mary Cholmondeley's *Red Pottage* and Diana Warwick in George Meredith's *Diana of the Crossways* (1885), a novel Gissing particularly admired for its 'brain-work' and seriousness of purpose,[126] might not run the same risks of pathologising the spinster, it is worth noting that neither of these attempts an exploration of the radical concept of women living and working together. Sheila Jeffreys' broad claim that before the sexological category of lesbian was accepted, 'any attack on the spinster is inevitably an attack on the lesbian' also needs qualifying for a consideration of the range of fiction published before the sexological research of Havelock Ellis and others became widely known.[127]

---

[123] Faderman, p. 195. Showalter offers a less positive reading, emphasising Olive's desired role as martyr for the cause, and claiming that James shows how Olive's renunciation and abstinence 'have led to a kind of sterility' (p. 29).

[124] This idea was developed in Havelock Ellis, *Sexual Inversion* (1897).   See Sheila Jeffreys, *The Spinster and her Enemies: Feminism and Sexuality, 1880–1930* (1985; North Melbourne: Spinifix Press, 1987), pp. 105–07.

[125] Ledger, p. 125.

[126] Letter to Algernon, 27 July 1885. *Collected Letters, Vol 2*, 1881–85 (1991), p. 304.

[127] Jeffreys, p. 100. The over-generalisation is partly due to a lack of precision about dates; it is hard to tell whether this claim is meant to apply to the late nineteenth century as well as the early twentieth. Jeffrey's discussion of the vicious attacks on the spinster in the 1910s and after the First World War, and her argument that by this time women were newly categorised in the wake of the sexology debates as heterosexual or lesbian, rather than married or spinster, is more convincing.

Like James, Gissing sees the Boston marriage as facilitating study and nurturing 'admirable' feminist activity amongst women whose potential might otherwise have been frustrated. His account may also have been influenced by his stay in Boston in the late 1870s, where he spent time at the liberal homes of Dr Marie Zakrzewska and Julia Sprague, emancipated, educated women with whom it is likely that he entered into discussions about the women's movement.[128] Faderman argues that 'one reason a single professional friendship was so vital to [independent and artistic] women was that their pioneer experiences of "living by their brains" could be lonely and frightening in the extreme'.[129] In *The Bostonians* Olive's philanthropic desire 'to enter into the lives of women who are lonely, who are piteous' (p. 63) draws attention to her own struggle against loneliness and her excited anticipation of the 'indulgence' of studying Goethe with a 'chosen companion' (p. 107) who shares her home – the first thing they do together is 'thr[o]w themselves into study' (p. 182) – is perhaps more revealing of the attractions of the Boston marriage to the isolated educated woman. Similarly, Gissing implies that the friendship of Mary and Rhoda 'had progressed to intimacy' not simply because they 'sincerely liked and admired each other' (p. 212) but because of their shared aims and feminist vision, mirroring the close relationship of contemporary reformers such as Octavia Hill and Sophia Jex-Blake.[130] Although their house is 'stigmatized' by Monica as 'an old-maid factory' (p. 50), elsewhere in the text this term is rejected as inappropriate: the enterprising and fiercely independent Rhoda, significantly ensconced in Mary's library with the benefit of books and 'a well-equipped writing table', is 'far from presenting any sorrowful image of a person on the way to old-maidenhood' (p. 20). One conclusion to an early chapter, showing the pair laughing together 'with joyous confidence in themselves and their cause', as they agree that 'it is better to be a woman, in our day … propagating a new religion, purifying the earth!' (p. 87) links their zeal to their affection towards each other, where the new 'purer' religion is the result of becoming 'hard-hearted' against men. But such unions can be threatened by a loss of confidence in the cause. Verena's rejection of the Boston marriage is inseparable from her lukewarmness towards feminism, as she must make the choice between 'giving herself to a man' and 'giving herself to a movement' (p. 377), and the sexual jealousy which jeopardises the Chelsea partnership, the 'distress' and 'troubled nights' (p. 212) experienced by Mary betray her fears of abandonment as the younger woman faces the same choice. Despite James' progressive conceptualisation of the modern feminist as 'the new old maid' (p. 329), a political career becomes increasingly less appealing, as public speaking comes to be associated with rather hysterical figures, 'shriek[ing] out on

---

[128] McDonald, p. 113. She records that Gissing was a regular visitor at Zakrzewska's house on Saturday evenings during the winter of 1876–7. They later visited him in London in 1895. See letter to Clara Collet, 28 November 1895. *Collected Letters, Vol 6, 1895–97* (1995), p. 60.

[129] Faderman, p. 206.

[130] Jeffreys, p. 104. Jeffreys cites Hill and Jex-Blake as one example of the many turn-of-the-century feminists who were involved in passionate relationships with women.

platforms that old maids [a]re the highest type' (p. 212). According to an 1884 article, the modern public speaker was a 'more pushing and exaggerated sort of woman', driven by an unnatural desire 'for a platform on which to exhibit [her] dissatisfied restlessness', rather than any real enthusiasm for politics.[131] Jeremy Tambling has read the heroine's final public humiliation, as she heads towards the stage in 'desolation' to be 'hissed, hooted and insulted' (p. 432), in relation to the lesbian's lack of 'survival-value' in 1880s American fiction, arguing 'there is no future for Olive, unless she makes something of public speaking, and so of living with the modern'.[132] But the denial of woman's future possibilities is surely not so clear cut; Verena may imagine her friend resigned to be 'incurably lonely and eternally humiliated' (p. 376) but as a 'new' old maid in Boston it is more likely that she will embrace the platform woman's 'desire to be a *visible* power in the world'[133] by continuing with the campaign for female suffrage. Reflecting the contemporary associations between active feminism and lesbianism, which were to become more transparent in the twentieth century, it is the partnerships of militant women which are more likely to survive in the face of the compulsory heterosexuality of late-Victorian culture.

Although it appears to sanction different degrees of intimacy between working women, the thriving female community in Chelsea and its environs seems resilient enough to stave off the threat of the heterosexual male. A less isolated figure than Olive, Rhoda's refusal of heterosexual marriage is closely related to her much prized 'zeal for womanhood militant' (p. 83) and her commitment to 'her position as a leader and encourager of women living independently' (p. 147). Everard's controversial offer of a free union, a more open form of heterosexual commitment meant to allow for 'perfect freedom on both sides' (p.104), is acknowledged as a tempting alternative to traditional marriage for a woman he thinks of as a 'glorious rebel' (p. 269); it was certainly practised by contemporary rebellious feminist figures such as Eleanor Marx and Edith Ellis. But in a radical move this has to be rejected in a narrative bent on proving that heterosexuality is ultimately no substitute for the 'purpose in life, dignified, absorbing' (p. 269) the odd woman can pursue; Rhoda's fears about the dependence on men and domestic duties a free union will entail cannot be reconciled with her feminist principles and 'a share – nay, leadership - in some "movement", contact with the revolutionary life of her time' (p. 270) which may be resisted by a male partner.[134] Weighing up the

---

[131] Margaret Lonsdale, 'Platform Women', *Nineteenth Century* 85 (1884), 409–15 (pp. 415, 412). Women are here seen to be unfitted for public speaking, for which they are physically disqualified; what is more, it is a practice men find repulsive as 'in self-assertion we lose respect' (p. 413). The illustration of the Political Woman in a contemporary article in the *GOP* depicts a rather deranged looking young woman declaiming in public to a crowd of men, one of whom is clearly sneering at her. See S[ophia] F.A. Caulfeild, 'Some Types of Girlhood, or our Juvenile Spinsters: Part 2', *GOP*, 27 December 1890, 196–7 (p. 196).

[132] Jeremy Tambling, *Henry James* (Basingstoke: Macmillan, 2000), pp. 62, 76.

[133] 'Platform Women', p. 411.

[134] For a more detailed discussion of Gissing's representation of free unions in this novel and *In the Year of Jubilee* in relation to the marriage debate initiated by Mona Caird, see

disadvantages of 'living in sin', such as male infidelity and the limited availability of birth control, Lucy Bland also reaches the conclusion that at the turn of the century 'spinsterhood held more appeal for most feminists than a free union'.[135] In an important conversation about the interference of marriage with women's work, Rhoda asks Everard,

> What would become of the encouragement I am able to offer our girls? ... To scorn the old idea that a woman's life is wasted if she does not marry. My work is to help those women who, by sheer necessity, must live alone – women whom vulgar opinion ridicules. How can I help them so effectually as by living among them, one of them, and showing that my life is anything but weariness and lamentation? I am fitted for this. It gives me a sense of power and usefulness which I enjoy ... If I deserted I should despise myself. (pp. 182–3)

Dedicating her life to the mission of staying single through choice rather than necessity strengthens the sisterhood between emancipated women; remaining 'one of them' directly impacts on the direction of the clerical training of 'our girls', who need the feminist encouragement to see their lifestyles as radical rather than weary. As Henrietta Muller argued in an 1887 article on 'What Woman is Fitted for', the development of 'new womanhood' will enlarge woman's 'future possibilities'.[136] But the more moderate Mary significantly modifies Rhoda's vision, seeing her antipathy to marriage as exclusionary, dangerous to feminism and unrealistic, urging her friend to 'admit that most women would lead a wasted life if they did not marry' (p. 59). Her view is that 'only the most exceptional girl will believe it her duty to remain single ... let us be glad if we put a few of them in the way of living single with no more discontent than an unmarried man experiences' (p. 60). Evoking this comforting myth of spinsters as an insignificant minority, refuting statistical claims about their steadily increasing numbers, serves to deradicalise Rhoda's vision; Mary's related check to her friend's zealous revolt against the sexual instinct, 'we don't desire the end of the race' (p. 51), is part of the same authorial strategy to downplay the threat of the spinster as the woman of the future, whilst simultaneously exploring this as a possibility.

An interesting inconsistency is highlighted in the concept of 'living alone', as both Rhoda and at least some of her girls share lodgings with other women – the concept can be more usefully understood as living apart from men, where woman becomes fitted to remain odd.   Faderman makes the point that feminists' identification as lesbian was not necessarily congenital but might also stem from 'the immediate chance circumstances of their lives', dependent on whether they

---

Emma Liggins, 'Idiot Heroines and Worthless Women? Gissing's 1890s Fiction and Female Independence', in Postmus, pp. 115–25.

[135] Bland, p. 161. She cites examples of women's sense of frustration in free unions: unable to bear Aveling's infidelity, Marx committed suicide and its tendency to reproduce the restrictions of legal marriage for women. See pp. 154–5.

[136] [Henrietta Muller], 'What Woman is Fitted For', *Westminster Review* 71 (1887), 64–75 (pp. 71, 66. She claimed that 'real womanhood is a thing of the future ... the woman of the future will follow the lead of her own nature and not that of a deadening convention'.

encountered compatible unattached women with shared goals or pro-feminist men who might be sympathetic to the cause.[137]   As New Woman fiction increasingly vilified the heterosexual male suitor as patriarchal at best and promiscuous and syphilis-ridden at worst, feminist heroines were more likely to encounter compatible women, but their potential 'open[ness] to intimate friendships' was often again determined by environment as well as awareness of the choices a life of 'celibacy' might entail.   Milly Vesper's choice of lodging and dedication to her work in an all-female office ensures that she lives 'absolutely apart from the male world' (p. 292), her apparent plainness minimising the risk of male suitors and thus predisposing her to form closer bonds with women. On a practical level, cohabiting made obvious financial sense; Milly's eagerness to 'accept a partner in her lodging' (p. 62), even without meeting her first, is explained in terms of her endorsement of 'an arrangement to be recommended for its economy' (p. 63), as well as its companionship for the young clerk new to London.   Although Milly denies that she shares Rhoda's zealous opinions about marriage, her close friendship with Monica could also be read as potentially romantic. The two girls frequently kiss, and call each other 'dear', though the intimacy of their arrangement is seen to be rather threatening to the new lodger, who despite her limited income decides to purchase her own bed rather than sleeping with Milly in the small bedroom. If her decision to leave the flat to marry after only a few weeks is a further indication of her nervousness about the arrangement, then her rejection of the clerk's single lifestyle – 'I'm not like you, Milly; I can't be contented with this life ... I *can't* go their way' (p. 111) – can also be read as a coded rejection of the same-sex intimacy she associates with a kind of female independence perceived by the ex-shop girl as too radical.   Even in the 1920s the celibate heroines of Winifred Holtby's and Radclyffe Hall's early work are only allowed brief periods of co-habiting with other independent single women in London lodgings, which is still not endorsed as a permanent arrangement or a viable fictional possibility.   Explicitly identified as a woman of the future, a forerunner, one of the 'millions all over England' rejecting marriage in the 1880s and 1890s, Hall's doomed heroine Joan Ogden in *The Unlit Lamp* (1924) is thwarted in her dreams of a Cambridge education, and a medical career, but perhaps most importantly in her desire to share a flat with her companion, Elizabeth. Her fear of 'embarking upon the unusual' (p. 247) results in a refusal to plan ahead – 'as if by mutual consent they avoided discussing the future' (p. 185) – which ultimately leaves her old, alone, unfulfilled and unfitted to support herself.[138]   In contrast, Rhoda's confidence that if she marries, both Milly and her more promising *protégée* Winifred Haven will follow her example of 'inspiring the girls with zeal for an independent life' (p. 262) is borne out in their zeal which prompts her to resume her independence: when she entertains them to dinner, she admires them for their health, self-reliance and courage, their projection of a new 'womanly force' (p. 291) until 'in this company [she] felt her old ambitions regaining their

---

[137] Faderman, p. 250.
[138] Radclyffe Hall, *The Unlit Lamp*, ed. Zoë Fairbairns (1924; London: Virago, 1981), pp. 120, 247, 185.

power over her' (p. 292). Erin Williams has downplayed the author's feminist position by arguing that 'the resolution ... makes it clear that for Gissing celibacy is less a political choice to ameliorate the status of women than a sort of haven of retreat from the "marriage war"', though her point that all of the principal characters are 'incorporated into same-sex partnerships' by the end is not necessarily true of Winifred and Milly.[139] Deirdre David's argument that the novel leaves a question-mark over Rhoda's radical politics and desire for celibacy is more enabling, reinforcing the author's 'refusal ... to render a definitive endorsement or rejection of feminism'.[140] Indeed, this unusual female community on the brink of creation, where the company of women and their 'womanly force' will provide future inspiration to the glorified spinster, may show Gissing in his most feminist light, ahead of his time in his endorsement of the strong female partnerships which would still prove radical to novelists of the next generation.

In the 1890s fiction then the New Woman heroine is not only used as a vehicle for exploring the advantages of 'ideal' white-collar occupations for middle-class women, enabled to occupy public space in new ways but to contribute to debates about working conditions, leisure and modern independent lifestyles available to single women. The sympathy enlisted on behalf of the discontented shop-girl, in a strategy borrowed from social investigatory accounts, allows Gissing to reconsider her urban freedoms as a sign of modernity rather than 'loose' sexuality, partly redressing naturalist fiction's obsession with her promiscuity. Similarly, his radical alignment of the type-writer girl with the development of feminism is closer to investigatory validations of modern women's achievements in the male space of the office than the depoliticised version of saucy office adventures offered in more popular narratives and visual representations. Young's view that 'women (both fictional and real) are invigorated rather than enervated by clerical work, because it provides the possibility of independence'[141] is then particularly appropriate to Gissing's work, where independence often becomes more than just a future possibility. However, the general thwarting of the white-collar woman's struggle to stake a claim to heterosocial public life and enjoy her 'free wandering' around London should be seen not as anti-feminist but in the light of a sincere realism, which, as Simon J. James has rightly argued, 'permits exceptional female characters to protest at societal restrictions' whilst avoiding utopian solutions to their plight.[142] The dominant paradigm in which marriage, whilst offering protection to middle-class women, quickly becomes claustrophobic and also closes down their opportunities for enjoying urban life narrativises the social

---

[139] Erin Williams, 'Female Celibacy in the fiction of Gissing and Dixon: the Silent Strike of the Suburbanites', *English Literature in Transition* 45:3 (2002), 259–80 (p. 270). She does remark that 'it remains difficult, however, to understand why so many [male] critics ... read Rhoda's final decision as defeat'.

[140] Deirdre David, 'Ideologies of Patriarchy, Feminism, and Fiction in *The Odd Women*', *Feminist Studies* 10 (1984), 117–39 (p. 118).

[141] Young, p. 129.

[142] Simon J. James, *Unsettled Accounts: Money and Narrative in the Novels of George Gissing* (London: Anthem Press, 2003), p. 122.

investigators' warnings about the temptations of marriage to discontented workers. The only way out of this impasse for the New Woman heroine is to actively protect her single status and, where possible, to strengthen her attachments to other women, with *The Odd Women* offering one of the most convincing late-Victorian counter-arguments to the sexologists of the benefits of the single life for political women and the endurance of modern same-sex partnerships. Rhoda's radical retreat from heterosexual union shows the author's wavering commitment to female emancipation at its height; the later novels were to prove much more contradictory in their dealings with the New Woman.

Chapter 5

From Bachelor Girl to Working Mother: Finding a Public Space for the Emancipated Heroine

The examination of the odd woman in Gissing's 1890s fiction is sustained in his later work by a comparison between the urban lifestyle of the newly labelled bachelor girl and the confined suburban existence she is forced to accept after marriage. It was gradually being recognised that the unfulfilled married lady, who has 'not enough liberty, or too much responsibility', might share the discontent of the struggling spinster, deploring her isolation so that 'above all she desires to be transplanted to London'.[1] The preference for urban forms of entertainment or professional work over domestic pursuits was a worrying sign of an increasingly prevalent unfemininity. In an 1890 article on 'Modern Mannish Maidens', the question posed by a *Blackwoods* journalist outraged with this 'unlovely' 'female mannishness' permeating society concerning 'the reasonable limits that should be set to the pastimes of womankind'[2] remains unanswered, as the previously fixed boundaries of acceptable female behaviour in public continued to shift. By breaking the rules of gender convention the female bachelors of the 1890s, with their full and varied independent lives, were both threatening and threatened in their unprecedented invasion of the public realm. However, whilst the unfeminine desire to imitate men's occupation of public spaces such as restaurants and clubs, and to make full use of public transport, may have contributed to the creation of what Erika Diane Rappaport has called 'a female London',[3] even self-reliant middle-class women remained vulnerable to the dangers of the metropolis. Debates about female urbanism have not yet taken sufficient account of the legitimacy of the married woman's place in the city, and of her claim to the pleasures of heterosocial culture, at a time when it was widely accepted that 'the normal condition of wifehood and motherhood, with the multifarious domestic

---

[1]   'The Discontented Woman', *Saturday Review*, 14 February 1874, (204–05), p. 204. The article goes on to ridicule her desire to be professional, linking female interest in law and medicine to her 'search for excitement' (p. 205).

[2]   'Modern Mannish Maidens', *Blackwoods Magazine* 147 (1890), 252–64 (p. 252).

[3]   Erika Diane Rappaport, *Shopping for Pleasure: Women in the Making of London's West End* (Princeton: Princeton University Press, 2000), p. 7.

duties involved, is a serious drawback to industrial, public or professional life'.[4]
As anti-feminist commentaries on the New Woman increasingly drew on
maternalist ideologies and evolutionary fears about the future of the race to
reinforce woman's rightful place in the domestic sphere, married women who
attempted to enter the professions out of choice rather than necessity were often
condemned. Urban narratives about bachelor girls still had to confront the lurking
cultural doubt that 'a taste of independence unfits women for married life'.[5]

In order to examine the effect of the responsibilities of marriage on women's
freedoms, the modified narrative structure of Gissing's later work appears to be
following generic trends in the New Woman novel in the emancipated heroine's
relinquishment of her single life at the end of the first volume rather than in the
closing chapters. Barbara Leah Harman has argued that 'Gissing's interest in the
woman question collides in his novels with a wider and more profound antipathy
towards public life', as his heroines come to represent 'a special, or heightened,
instance of the problems that emerge at the intersection of public and private
matters – special because their emancipation inevitably foregrounds the very
questions about privacy and publicity that set Gissing's terms so turbulently in
motion'.[6] Certainly, his examination of the social and sexual restrictions faced by
an emancipated middle-class heroine sets bourgeois femininity in an uneasy
relation to new forms of publicity, but we need to acknowledge the fascination for,
as well as the apparent antipathy to, the public sphere as a place for women in his
later work. In his comparison of the lifestyles of the female bachelor with those of
the suburban housewife, frustrated by her enforced withdrawal from the city or
transgressing the rules to become a working mother, he raised a new set of
questions about the public/private divide, about the financial and sexual
ramifications of female urban experience in the middle classes. At a time when his
diary reveals a noticeable taste for contemporary fiction by women writers such as
George Egerton, Mrs Humphrey Ward and Ménie Muriel Dowie, it is productive to
consider these questions in the broader context of New Woman fiction. By
demythologising the dangers of the public sphere for women, Gissing's emphasis
on middle-class women's right to freedom of movement in the city without male
supervision or chaperons aligns his work with female-authored New Woman
novels such as Amy Levy's *The Romance of a Shop* (1888). His later work can be
usefully compared to the feminist journalist Mona Caird's most well-known novel,
The Daughters of Danaus (1894), in which the married heroine is thwarted in her
desire to combine a professional career in music with the demands of family and
childcare and Mary Cholmondeley's *Red Pottage* (1899), which focuses on a
struggling woman writer. At face value such novels may appear to accept and
ratify degenerationist theories that women, particularly married ones, are unfit to

---

[4]   [Henrietta Muller],'The Future of Single Women', *Westminster Review* 121 (1884),
151–62 (p. 156).
[5]   Dora M. Jones, 'The Life of a Bachelor Girl in the Big City', *Young Woman* 8 (1900),
131–3 (p. 133).
[6]   Barbara Leah Harman, 'Going Public: Female Emancipation in George Gissing's *In the
Year of Jubilee*', *Texas Studies in Literature and Language* 34:3 (1992), 347–74 (p. 348).

work in and negotiate the city. Jane Wood has noted that in this period it became 'a matter of some contention whether modern life could, of itself, cause nervous collapse',[7] as theories about degeneration increasingly connected urban existence, particularly for women, with the ill effects of modernity. But the fictional paradigm whereby middle-class women's choice between work and motherhood results in a reluctant acceptance of domesticity reflects the hesitancy about endorsing married women's work amongst social investigators and feminists. Rather than being dismissed as conservative narratives of female unfitness, Gissing's later novels should be read as realist representations of the tensions between the freedoms and difficulties of the city for the modern woman, whose battle against nervous illness or disinclination for domestic duties may have more to say about the tedium of suburbia than the strains and tumult of the metropolis.

The Female Bachelor and the Woman of Business

In their focus on the dangers of women imitating male behaviour, anti-feminist articles on modern womanhood in the early 1890s showed a marked antagonism to the new mobility of middle-class women. As it became increasingly acceptable for ladies to use the city for the purposes of leisure, the desire to minimise the effects on traditional Victorian femininity manifested itself in attacks on women's urban freedoms in the mainstream periodical press. According to an article of 1894, the 'unchaperoned' Female Bachelor, who 'claims a man's "freedom"' to enjoy public entertainments and fulfilling work, may exercise all the new privileges of the emancipated woman but only at the cost of her impropriety:

> She wants to come in and go out when she likes – or when her employers like – without having to account for her proceedings ... the female bachelor lets her men friends visit her at her rooms. Yet her morals are the conventional ones, and she gets no particular excitement or forbidden joy out of her defiance of the ordinary rules which regulate the conduct of well-bred women. She is not content with her life after the first novelty of 'emancipation' has worn off. She realizes that she gets all the discomforts of male bachelordom much multiplied, and none of its alleviations ... Women get very little by merely taking upon themselves to imitate certain of men's ways; and the female bachelor, after finding that even to join a club is not deliriously exhilarating, discovers this.[8]

Broadly representative of anti-feminist thought, the article seeks to deny the benefits of defying rules about gendered behaviour in order to prove that the female bachelor is 'not content' with her new-found liberty and 'gets very little' from imitating male lifestyles. Modern essentials such as latchkeys and cigarettes are seen as nothing more than fashionable accessories, and emancipation as a gimmick, leading to the conclusion that, far from setting an example for the

---

[7]   Jane Wood, *Passion and Pathology in Victorian Fiction* (Oxford: Oxford University Press, 2001), p. 185.

[8]   'The Female Bachelor', *Saturday Review*, 2 June 1894, 582.

woman of the future, this 'improper young woman' is 'wast[ing] her life in elaborately worked-out unfemininity'. But these sentiments also advance debates about middle-class women's freedoms by coupling the unfeminine desire to imitate men's occupation of public space with the more traditional desire to marry. Although usually defined as 'working gentlewomen', they may only be self-supporting for a limited period; a later article argued that the chief desire of the lady bachelor was to move on from 'the Bohemia where people work' to the financial security of marriage, where 'if she immigrates in sufficient numbers into society she will probably end by modifying its conventions'.[9] Her defiant entry into 'the world of ease' is more threatening than this temporary occupation of 'the world of business',[10] precisely because her unfeminine claims to masculine space and the sexual independence it permits may 'fundamentally modify the nature of woman'.[11]

Gissing's later novels set out to consider this transition from female bachelordom to marriage, shifting attention onto the difficulties attending the married emancipated heroine, whose experiences of paid or unpaid labour often occupy only a brief interlude of married life. As one reviewer remarked in 1897, 'no novelist has taken more pains to understand the condition of the average woman's life to-day, to study her ambitions, to mete out to her an austere kind of justice',[12] though after the strategically titled *The Odd Women*, reviewers tended not to associate his heroines with the New Woman, whose popularity was waning after 1895. The educated Nancy Lord, the heroine of *In the Year of Jubilee* (1894), forced to relinquish her urban freedoms by an unplanned pregnancy and a speedy, secret marriage to her 'seducer' Lionel Tarrant, is thwarted in her ambitions to become a professional writer by childcare problems and the opposition of her husband. Nancy's literary aspirations, evident in her attendance at a course of lectures on Greek civilisation delivered by a university scholar and the 'heap of books she has read' (p. 83)[13] whilst single, could have been developed to her advantage in the labour market. However, her query of her studious friend Jessica Morgan, 'does a female Bachelor of Arts lose her degree if she gets married?' (p. 99) foregrounds the either-or choices women were forced to make, at a time when the majority of female students would have remained single after graduation in the hope of achieving professional positions.[14] Diverting his

---

[9]   Stephen Gwynn, 'Bachelor Women', *Contemporary Review* 73 (1898), 866–75 (pp. 873, 874).
[10] 'The Female Bachelor', p. 582.
[11] 'Bachelor Women', p. 874.
[12] Review of *The Whirlpool*, *Bookman* (1897), 38–9. Quoted in *Gissing: The Critical Heritage*, ed. Pierre Coustillas & Colin Partridge (London: Routledge & Kegan Paul, 1972), p. 280.
[13] All quotations are taken from George Gissing, *In the Year of Jubilee*, ed. Paul Delany (1894; London: J. M. Dent, 1994).
[14] Carol Dyhouse, *No Distinction of Sex? Women in British Universities, 1870–1939* (London: UCL Press, 1995), p. 23. This also evokes without directly addressing the experiences of middle-class women interested in study to meet their needs for entertainment or social purpose: as Dyhouse has shown, 'in the last quarter of the nineteenth century

heroine's potential educational aspirations onto an unattractive minor character he is free to attack, Gissing appears to be using the rapidly deteriorating health of Jessica, a 'girl condemned to sterile passions' (p. 186) as an example of the dangers of avoiding the sexual instinct necessary for the reproduction of the race. The appealing bachelor lifestyle of the business woman Beatrice French, who prefers her career to marriage, is also used to question whether Nancy has made the right choice. In *The Whirlpool* (1897) the trained violinist Alma Frothingham is further advanced in her career by the time she accepts Harvey Rolfe's proposal, with the proviso that 'if I marry you, I give up my music' (p. 118).[15] Her narrative follows the same traditional trajectory in relocating her from the world of work to suburban motherhood, though this is more disrupted than Nancy's story by her rebellion against the sacrifice of her profession.

In his important reading of Gissing's representation of the female professional, David Kramer has argued that 'Alma's dreams of professionalism do not fit the larger social context of the increasingly desperate need for expanded opportunities', marking her off from earlier Gissing heroines by her solvency.[16] Certainly, when Alma's lament that 'I often feel sorry I haven't to get my living by [music]' (p. 36) comes to fruition after her father's suicide and the loss of the family's money, she only has to survive the 'poor quarters, hard life, stinted pleasures' (p. 83) of the self-supporting artist for a brief period before her marriage. Whilst writing the novel, Gissing did check his facts by asking his friend Bertz to confirm that girls were allowed to attend such colleges as the School of Music in Munich – Alma is indeed lucky to study in Germany, where the concert life is 'far richer and varied' than Britain[17] – so presumably he was pondering the need for higher education in order to profit from this female accomplishment.[18] This insistence on barriers preventing the educated heroine from either completing or profiting from further study, familiar from his earlier novels, had now become a convention of the New Woman narrative. The eponymous heroine of Ménie Muriel Dowie's *Gallia* (1895) is denied the chance to pursue her education, instead concentrating on selecting a fit, pro-feminist man with a clean bill of sexual health to bear her child. On the other hand, Gissing's negotiations with publishers and response to reviews around this time suggest his lack of confidence in the conventions of New Woman fiction, evident in his desire to distance *In the Year of Jubilee* from a genre past its sell-by date because 'people are getting very tired of

---

attendance at university lectures had indeed been characterized by the presence of large numbers of ladies of leisure, many of them married, … in pursuit of general culture'.

[15] All quotations are taken from George Gissing, *The Whirlpool*, ed. Gillian Tindall (1897; London: Hogarth Press, 1984).

[16] David Kramer, 'George Gissing and Women's Work: Contextualising the Female Professional', *English Literature in Transition, 1880–1920,* 43:3 (2000), 316–330 (p. 325).

[17] Annie Glen, 'Music as a Profession for Women', *Woman's World* (1889).

[18] Letter to Bertz, 3 August 1896. *Collected Letters of George Gissing: Vol 6, 1895–97,* ed. Paul F. Matthiesen, Arthur C. Young & Pierre Coustillas (Athens: Ohio University Press, 1995), p. 159.

the "woman question" novel'.[19] By addressing the woman question from an oblique angle, he appeared to be intent on modifying generic boundaries and expectations.

Bachelor girl heroines in *fin-de-siècle* fiction were shown to occupy the business world on their own terms, the modernity of the woman in business functioning as an alternative to the passivity of women under commercial culture often reinforced in naturalist fiction. In Émile Zola's *Au Bonheur des Dames* (1883), the secret of Octave Mouret's success, revealed in his explanation for 'the techniques of modern big business', lies in 'the exploitation of Woman', (p. 76) to whom his department store represents 'an immense temptation to which she inevitably yielded', seduced by low prices and fancy goods. But the shop-girl Denise Baudu, 'secretly on the side of the big shops' (p. 194), also acquires the necessary business acumen and 'bold, new ideas' (p. 204) to contribute to the future success of the store, her triumphant grasp of 'modern business methods' (p. 354) rivalling that of the male entrepreneur.[20] This masculinised behaviour is also championed through Katherine Verney, the energetic owner of a Mayfair curio-shop in Netta Syrett's *Three Women* (1912), seen as 'the product of the present age … the latter-day woman of practical brains and fine business capacity' (p. 19).[21] Explicitly set up as 'the modern woman … out to get what a man gets out of the world' (p. 24), the rather plain and gamine Katherine is nevertheless 'shrewd enough not to undervalue the asset of feminine attractions' (p. 19) to further her commercial interests. She appears to typify the more comfortable class of bachelor girl identified by Dora Jones in *The Young Woman* in 1900, achieving a balance between work and leisure on £100–£300, where the added benefits of a man's salary enable the 'full[ness] and varie[ty]' of modern women's life.[22] Driven by Syrett's feminist agenda in the more enlightened 1910s, the later novel may see the woman of business as relatively untarnished by the commercial world but raises some interesting questions about her limited success and struggle to retain her anomalous status. In response to her business-partner Phillida's view that she should have been a man, Katherine responds:

---

[19] Letter to Clara Collet, 26 August 1894, letter to Bertz, 23 June 1895. Quoted in *Collected Letters, Vol 5*, pp. 229, 351. In the latter, in recognition of the decline of the three-volume novel, Gissing also lamented the fact that 'my long novels simply *will not sell*; they disappoint everyone connected with them'.

[20] All quotations are taken from Émile Zola, *The Ladies' Paradise*, trans. and ed. Brian Nelson (1883; Oxford: Oxford University Press, 1995). Her business acumen helps to ensure the innovative introduction of a games room, language classes, a library, midwife and hairdressing salon, but she also displays an understanding of 'reforms which would benefit the shop' (p. 355) such as the support of early trade union activity, and an ability to use 'arguments based on the employers' own interests' (p. 355) usually reserved for the male entrepreneur.

[21] All quotations are taken from Netta Syrett, *Three Women* (London: Chatto & Windus, 1912).

[22] Dora M. Jones, 'The Life of a Bachelor Girl in the Big City', *Young Woman* 8 (1900), 131–3 (pp. 132, 131).

After all … it's a triumph to be an efficient woman … I could never see why there are not more of us … there are plenty of us with brains and good powers of organization, and some of us at least have capital at our backs. Yet why do so many of us fail? … What has being a woman got to do with the lack of success? (p. 24)

One answer to this might lie in the threat of enterprising women profiting from their own business plans, which partly explains the fictional representation of business women as exceptional. By the end of the novel Katherine has earned enough to buy her own car, a masculine status symbol few women would have owned at the time.

Gissing's exploration of women's unsettling entry into the arena of commerce in *In the Year of Jubilee* collapses the business woman with her city flat and cigarettes into a cross between the self-supporting bachelor girl and the New Woman. In direct contrast to Nancy's suburban home, the 'independent sort of life' (p. 276) of the dynamic shopkeeper, Beatrice French, is symbolised by her comfortable occupation of a fashionable 'bachelor's flat' in Brixton, 'something convenient and moderate' (p. 212) and closer to the City than sharing with her sisters in suburban Camberwell. Appropriating the male habits of wine and smoking and rising 'above the feminine folly of neglecting honest victuals' by dining well on steak and Stilton, Beatrice certainly appears to enjoy the benefits of being 'my own mistress' (p. 276). However, Gissing's business woman is hampered not only by the restrictions of late-Victorian narrative paradigms, which tended to portray women's professional lives as short-lived but by the disturbance of class and gender roles produced by their enterprising behaviour. According to the *Saturday Review*, 'the world of business regards [the female bachelor] as a woman, and allows her none of the equality of manhood':[23] paradoxically, Beatrice's angry response to being called 'old chap' in the workplace, 'after all, I suppose I *am* a woman?' (p. 214) suggests that she prefers to be treated as a lady, as if becoming one of the 'chaps' puts her at a disadvantage in her field. Women's magazines of the time often promoted the ease with which the clever lady with appropriate training could rise above clerical work to establish 'a little business of her own',[24] a path followed by the enterprising Beatrice who has capitalised on a 'head for figures' (p. 200) acquired in Post Office administration in order to make 'a heap of money' (p. 13) by running a ladies' dress company. A lady shopkeeper interviewed for *Woman* in 1890 about 'the secret of her success' considered herself to be in 'quite an original line' of work for a woman, one of the first in a developing field. However, the article shows her to be slightly defensive of a calling in which she has to constantly make the point that 'I am not ashamed of my trade associations'.[25] Beatrice's refusal to feel shame about her intricate

---

[23] 'The Female Bachelor', p. 582.
[24] 'What it means to be a Lady Typist', *Young Woman* 8 (1900), 217–18 (p. 217). The article argued that the prospect of moving on into business helped to improve the status of typewriting for educated ladies, who will have 'a guarantee of a steady living income … which, though it may not make her rich, will at any rate ensure her a comfortable existence'.
[25] Lady Granville Gordon, 'Lady Shopkeepers', *Woman*, 17 May 1890, p. 3.

knowledge of 'every possibility of profitable commerce' as well as 'the public to which her advertisements appealed' (p. 200) is a sign of her vulgarity for Gissing, who disapprovingly classifies her appropriation of Mouret's exploitative business methods for her own shop as bordering on fraud.

In his 1898 article, Stephen Gwynn claimed that the bachelor heroine of 1890s fiction, 'consumed with a desire for pleasure', quickly realises that this can only be gained through 'intercourse with the other sex on terms which, under the old rules, would have been entirely impossible', indicative of women's dependency on men for both professional success and pleasures.[26] He pointed out that novels such as Evelyn Sharp's *The Making of a Prig* (1896) showed the heroine agreeing to marriage because it offered 'less work and more comforts' than a professional career. The bachelor girl is shown as liable to fail if marriage proposals interfere with business: in *Three Women*, Katharine, with her 'limitless energy' and 'splendid health' (p. 327) only remains 'free from this danger, this constant menace to security, to freedom' (p. 110) to which the less obsessive Phillida capitulates by making a tough choice between 'freedom and a career' and 'sexual experience'. Certainly, Gissing's business woman is typical in her reliance on the ideas and capital of the advertising agent, Luckworth Crewe, though her command that he 'treat [her] decently' (p. 214) suggests an unresolved dissatisfaction with the role of male partner she is forced into accepting; it remains unclear whether she is offering sexual favours to cement their alliance. Although she does not always accept men's invitations to social activities, her behaviour is still seen as 'disgraceful' by her sister who is shocked that she 'has men to spend every evening with her' (p. 319). This character may have been behind an American journalist's attack on *Jubilee*'s 'radical' treatment of New Women 'in active revolt', so demoralised by modern education and opportunity that they have 'discarded duty, and, in pursuit of luxury and license, may be led into any immorality that seems to pay'.[27] The belief that by imitating male lifestyles women risked being seen as 'fast', a label popularised at mid-century to denote female sexual forwardness, also surfaced in an 1899 article on the modern woman, which asked, 'has this new-found liberty spoilt her? Has she grown "fast" simultaneously with the pace of her development?'[28] Whilst the toleration of alternatives to marriage such as free love and free unions did indicate changing views on female sexual morality, this concern about the sexual forwardness of the New Woman, even or particularly if

---

[26] 'Bachelor Women', pp. 871, 872–3. This is based on a reading of the lifestyles of the lady journalist in Noel Ainslie's *Among Thorns* and the teacher in Evelyn Sharp's *The Making of a Prig*.

[27] Review of *In the Year of Jubilee*, *Nation*, 17 October 1895, p. 277.

[28] Herbert Jamieson, 'The Modern Woman', *Westminster Review* 152 (1899), 571–6 (p. 571). Another article characterising the New Woman's role in terms of her refusal of the old conditions of marriage saw the worst examples of her kind as those 'fast women who copy men's failings'. See Nat Arling, 'What is the Role of the New Woman?', *Westminster Review* 150 (1898), 576–87 (p. 585).

she were married, suggested otherwise.[29] But Beatrice's success, even if it is hinged on the uncertain 'hold' she has over Crewe, indicates Gissing's endorsement of the bachelor girl's 'triumph' in commercial culture, at a time when according to Sarah Deutsch, the survival of women's businesses was precarious and the business woman's lifestyle 'insecure'.[30] Perhaps there were not 'more of them' because the new type of the bachelor girl, seen as alarmingly fast, was still struggling to gain acceptance in fiction of the 1910s.

Entering Public Space without a Chaperon

In a 1900 article on 'The Decay of the Chaperon', the experienced campaigner Mary Jeune reviewed 'the new independence of women' and its effect on social change over the previous fifty years. She argued that, whereas in 1890 very few girls were allowed to dine out, pay visits, walk or use public transport alone,

> English society and life have been adapting themselves to the independence, which modern thought and education must inevitably have on women ... the intimacy which women and men now occupy in regard to each other, seems almost another safeguard to the new relations, as the naturally chivalrous feeling of men towards women is not weakened, but rather strengthened, by the confidence which such a position creates, and which must prevent a man of honour taking advantage of it, added to which, though a girl may in reality know less of the dark side of life, than in a time of more supervision, the self-reliance which is the result of her independence, must enable her better to stand alone, or as one may put it, take care of herself.[31]

This move from supervision to self-reliance on the part of the educated woman opened up her negotiation of the public sphere, where more modern forms of intimacy between men and women were being established in a set of new heterosocial spaces, many of them in the fashionable West End. By the turn of the century the presence of ladies in restaurants, cafés, concert halls, department stores and the new women's clubs, facilitated by their confident use of public transport, was being acknowledged, if not entirely welcomed, as a significant sign of the times. In her study of gender and commercialisation in the late-Victorian and Edwardian metropolis, Erika Diane Rappaport has contended that whilst 'the creation of the [atmosphere of the West End] involved new notions of bourgeois

---

[29] See Lucy Bland, *Banishing the Beast: English Feminism and Sexual Morality, 1885–1914* (Harmondsworth: Penguin, 1995), pp. 151–9 for her discussion of both conservative and feminist opposition to free unions and free love in the 1890s. Feminists were not only opposed to free unions on the grounds of vulnerability and the risk of being left in sole charge of children, but in relation to 'the question of respectability' and the linking of free love to anarchism.

[30] Sarah Deutsch, *Women and the City: Gender, Space and Power in Boston, 1870–1940* (Oxford: Oxford University Press, 2000), p. 135.

[31] Mary Jeune, 'The Decay of the Chaperon', *Fortnightly Review* 74 (1900), 629–38 (pp. 631, 632, 637)

femininity, public space and conceptions of modernity', female behaviours were still constrained, as 'emancipatory narratives did not remove the social rules that ordered Victorian men's and women's thoughts and activities; rather, they posed a new set of structures and ideals'.[32]   Despite new ideals of female independence, modern femininity was still hampered by notions of respectability.   In one of Gissing's last novels, *Our Friend the Charlatan* (1901), Dyce Lashmar considers it 'barbarism' that the modern American girl May Tomalin should have to be 'sternly chaperoned' in a private drawing-room, as the chaperon's attempt to intervene to prevent her charge from conversing with the wrong kind of men casts doubt on the novel's endorsement of the ideal that 'every note of difference in sex would soon be eliminated'.[33]   In 1889 'Manly Women' with 'time on their hands' were not only attacked for 'tak[ing] up occupations and ideas which are shared equally with men', but for 'attending what were wont to be the exclusive resorts of men ... places where they are not expected to be, and which have been tacitly acknowledged to be reserved for that class of the female population that are without the pale'.[34]   The perennial fear of the public woman as prostitute is here specifically harnessed to her choice of leisure activity and occupation of places still deemed unsuitable for ladies.

The novels appear to endorse modern women's claims to a man's freedoms by granting unmarried middle-class daughters access to a variety of public spaces and entertainments, though the novelty of such an arrangement is signalled by resistance from men.   Reviewers noted that Gissing's women are shown to be susceptible on a number of levels to 'the particular temptation of London today'.[35] In *In The Year of Jubilee*, Nancy's desire to 'walk about all night' at the Jubilee celebrations in central London is voiced in the emancipatory rhetoric of the New Woman: 'it's horrible to be tied up as we are; we're not children. Why can't we go about as men do?' (p. 22).   In the eyes of her piano-dealer father, such a desire is indecent and inappropriate to a woman of her class, 'rather a come-down for an educated young lady' (p. 33); predictably treating her like a child, his 'permission' is only granted when a suitable male chaperon has been identified. Although the educated lady's position in public is normalised here – his son points out that 'there'll be lots of them about' – her class status is shown to be jeopardised by imitating male behaviour, as indicated by Mr Lord's tirade against the 'trashy, flashy girls ... calling themselves ladies' who reject 'honest, womanly work' and prefer to 'trollop about the streets day and night' (pp. 39–40). Women's refusal to be restricted by chaperons is given a radical edge, but is seen to invite the vulgarity which Gissing affected to despise. Nancy's resolve 'to taste independence' and experience 'a sense of freedom' (p. 54) rather than submit to Samuel Barnby's 'protection' is then counterbalanced with her 'alarm at her daring' (p. 58) as she mingles with the confusion of the crowds, 'wild with merriment' (p. 60).   As a

---

[32]   Rappaport, pp. 4, 7.

[33]   George Gissing, *Our Friend the Charlatan*, ed. Pierre Coustillas (1901; Sussex: Harvester Press, 1976), pp. 192, 196, 184.

[34]   'Manly Women', *Saturday Review*, 22 June 1889, p. 757.

[35]   Review of *The Whirlpool*, *Bookman*. Quoted in Coustillas & Partridge, p. 280.

number of critics have noted, the result of this mingling, whereby she 'forgot her identity ... did not think, and her emotions differed little from those of any shop-girl let loose ... could she have seen her face, its look of vulgar abandonment would have horrified her' (p. 58) implies an authorial condemnation of her daring, a confirmation of a lady's loss of class identity amidst the vulgar city crowd. Harman has linked this condemnation to the 'dangerous vision of class confusion, coarse commercialism, and sexuality neither controlled nor restrained by moral vision' associated with the crowd, in which the heroine is forced to 'amuse herself in vulgar ways' because she 'lack[s] access to refined pleasures'.[36] But seizing on this comment out of context has sometimes ensured that the ambiguities of the scene remain unappreciated. It could also be argued that Nancy 'forgets' the identity of an educated lady for that of a *flâneuse*, using her own 'strategems' to negotiate the busy streets and to control her encounters with men; she is quite able to repel the actions of an amorous male who puts his arm round her waist by threatening to summon a policeman. Whilst the more typical female reaction to the 'perilous' crowds is to faint or become hysterical, she is exhilarated, 'the right sort' according to the advertising agent Luckworth Crewe, who admires her sense of fun. The 'pleasure in her boldness' (p. 60) and unrestrained conversation suggest an overturn of gender, as well as class, restrictions, in a scene which refers more than once to the kind of behaviour only men are at liberty to enjoy. As John Sloan has pointed out, the novel stands out as unusual in Gissing's oeuvre in its expression of 'a new awareness of the excitements and exhilaration that the rush and welter of city life can produce'.[37]

Middle-class women's access to London's heterosocial opportunities are also explored in Amy Levy's *The Romance of a Shop* (1888), an earlier example of the woman in the city narrative with an appealingly determined New Woman heroine, Gertrude Lorimer.[38] Levy was a Jewish novelist and poet, whose work extolled the pleasures of urban existence but often from the position of the outsider, or marginalised figure. The novel tells the story of the Lorimer sisters, who disdain womanly occupations to become 'women of business' by opening a photographer's shop after their father's death; as Lucy Lorimer remarks, in this age 'it is quite distinguished to keep a shop' (p. 63). However, its feminist agenda is somewhat marred by its conventional ending, in which the sisters variously marry, die or reluctantly accept their limited freedoms and disadvantaged positions in the city.

---

[36] Harman, pp. 347, 349. Harman sets this scene in the larger context of the author's uneasiness about the public realm, where boundaries between classes, sexes and bodies are at risk, arguing that the heroine's 'real crime is the crime of participation in a public universe for which her creator feels both contempt and fear'.

[37] John Sloan, *George Gissing: the Cultural Challenge* (London: Macmillan, 1989), p. 131.

[38] Gissing may have read Levy's novel, as, according to Deborah Epstein Nord, he was certainly familiar with her work by the early 1890s. See *Walking the Victorian Streets: Women, Representation and the City* (Ithaca & London: Cornell University Press, 2000), f.n. p. 200. She mentions that he borrowed Levy's *Reuben Sachs* (1886) from the library in April 1892.

In her article of the same year, 'Women and Club Life', arguing for the necessity of women's clubs as a space for intellectual women to socialise, Levy had commented on the 'practical disadvantage[s]' and 'isolated position' of the professional woman, despite her increasing ranks.[39] This is reflected in her novel, which characterises the sisters as badly dressed, unacknowledged by former acquaintances and perpetually restricted in their choice of leisure and transport: they have to refuse invitations because of 'such sordid matters as shabby clothes and the comparative dearness of railway tickets' (p. 96) and rely on men for tickets to theatres and concerts.[40]   But this is also one of the first novels to celebrate the use of public transport as essential to the modernity of working ladies; as Parsons has shown, 'the omnibus, supreme symbol of commercial London, is frequently employed by women writers as an expression of their entry into once restricted public spaces', allowing women 'to move in and observe the city without threat on the street'.[41] In one important scene, the emancipated Gertrude is spotted by her horrified aunt, 'careering up the street on the summit of a tall, green omnibus', her aunt's 'frozen stare of non-recognition' leaving her with 'a humiliating consciousness of the disadvantages of her own position' (p. 105).[42] Less restricted by unwanted male attention, Gertrude defends her enjoyment of her omnibus rides and evenings in the theatre as 'the pleasures of the poor' (p. 106), which she is unwilling to sacrifice and confides her 'secret, childish love for the gas-lit street' (p. 110) to the reader.   As Deborah Epstein Nord has pointed out, such scenes succeed in 'conveying how difficult and yet how exhilarating it was to be a woman alone in London in the 1880s', promoting 'a self-consciously female urbanism'.[43] However, feminist critics have sometimes conveniently ignored Levy's important emphasis on the dangers of the city for independent women.   Aunt Caroline's fear of 'the complicated evils which must necessarily arise from an undertaking so completely devoid of chaperons' (p. 80) is never entirely dismissed in a text which remains painfully conscious of women's vulnerability when unprotected; as Gertrude admits, 'their own position ... was a peculiar one, and she could not but be aware of the dangers inseparable from the freedom which they enjoyed, dangers which are the price to be paid for all close intimacy between young men and women' (p. 140).   Levy's female urbanism cannot bear the weight of its own exhilaration as her heroine's emancipated attitudes are tempered in a conclusion

---

[39]   Amy Levy, 'Women and Club Life', *Woman's World* 1 (1888), 364–7 (p. 365).

[40]   All quotations are taken from Amy Levy, *The Romance of a Shop* (1888), in Melvyn New (ed.), *The Complete Novels and Selected Writings of Amy Levy, 1861–1889* (Gainsville: University Press of Florida, 1993).

[41]   Deborah L. Parsons, *Streetwalking the Metropolis: Women, the City and Modernity* (Oxford: Oxford University Press, 2000), p. 97. She also discusses images of the omnibus and women's experiences of London life in Levy's poetry and short fiction.

[42]   I am indebted to Parsons here for her excellent reading of this scene and Levy's 'passion for the pulsing rhythm of city life'. See pp. 93–4.

[43]   Nord, p. 201. However, she does goes on to link the disappointing ending of the novel, in which the 'independent, idiosyncratic heroines' either marry, die or are left desolate, to Levy's suicide in 1889, commenting on the fragility of social networks for single, professional women (pp. 202, 204).

which repositions her as a wife and mother, rather than a business-woman, bearing out Elizabeth Wilson's argument that new urban lifestyles constructed around pleasure and danger for women remained 'fraught with difficulty' well into the twentieth century.[44]

Women's frequent use of new forms of public transport to travel into London for the purposes of leisure was represented as both exhilarating and risky for the Gissing heroine, at a time when being seen on omnibuses or waiting at railway stations late at night was still conventionally regarded as damaging to women's reputations. The novella, *The Paying Guest* (1895), validates suburban lodger Louise Derrick's belief in the leisure activities offered by London as 'absolutely necessary' (p. 52), the latter frequently travelling in from Sutton for the purposes of shopping, theatre, restaurants and socialising with friends.[45] Significantly, such leisure is financed by her step-father's money rather than new occupations for women; she denigrates her school-friends, a typist and a photographer's assistant, as they 'haven't enough money to live in what *I* call a nice way' (p. 30). Dismissed by Gissing as 'a poor little book', 'a frothy trifle' for a popular series,[46] the melodramatic narrative does somewhat stereotype its lower-class characters, but its comically accurate vision of suburbia, which made it 'an exceedingly entertaining little volume' to the up-and-coming novelist H.G. Wells,[47] nevertheless acts as a useful footnote to his views on women's uses of the city. In an important scene, Louise's ease on public transport eventually counts against her when she is spotted apprehending Emmeline's husband at Sutton railway station. Although she is only innocently trying to apologise for quarrelling, he feels 'very uncomfortable' (p. 83) that she has dared to approach him in a public place known to be a traditional haunt of prostitutes: 'the incident of the railway station proved her to be utterly lacking in self-respect, in feminine modesty, even if her behaviour merited no darker description' (p. 115). Acquaintances with men made on public transport, particularly railways, were always treated with suspicion; one cautionary case of the 'high-spirited girl ... receiving visits in her bed-sittingroom from a man whose acquaintance she had made on the underground railway', showed a woman breaking two of the unspoken rules about acceptable male company.[48] In *Eve's Ransom*, travelling on public transport is sometimes associated with threatening male behaviour. Although in the railway carriage Eve is 'at her ease, casting careless glances this way and that' (p. 26), she also has to cultivate 'a look of cold if not defiant reserve' (p. 27) in order to repel unwanted male attentions; Hilliard eventually feels that 'he had annoyed her by the persistency of his observation' (p. 27). In Gissing's later short story, 'The Scrupulous Father' (1901), suburban

---

[44]   Elizabeth Wilson, *The Sphinx in the City: Urban Life, the Control of Disorder and Women* (London: Virago, 1991), p. 7.

[45]   All quotations are taken from George Gissing, *The Paying Guest*, ed. Ian Fletcher (1895; Brighton: Harvester Press, 1982).

[46]   Letter to Bertz, 22 September 1895. *Collected Letters, Vol 6*, p. 29.

[47]   H.G. Wells, Review of *The Paying Guest, Saturday Review*, 18 April 1896, p. 406.

[48]   Evelyn March-Phillipps, 'The Working Lady in London', *Fortnightly Review* 58 (1892), 193–203 (p. 200).

daughter Rose Whiston feels a 'tremulous pleasure' (p. 180), 'not in the least ashamed of herself', in returning the audacious glances of a red-haired clerk on a train, but is unable to block out a sense of 'encroaching fear' (p. 182) at her father's displeasure.[49] Contemplating her slide into vulgarity, she asks herself, 'What lady would have permitted herself to exchange names and addresses with a strange man in a railway carriage – furtively, too, escaping her father's observation? If not a lady, what *was* she?' (p. 183). The predictable inference that she has behaved like a prostitute making 'transactions' with men is rejected, however, as the future meeting arranged in the conclusion suggests a compromise between her 'spirit of revolt' and the out-dated morality of scrupulous fathers, though the implication that it will be formally chaperoned, perhaps necessary to pacify the *Cornhill*'s respectable readers, acts as a further reminder of Rose's transgression. But in *The Crown of Life* (1899) Irene Derwent and the smooth-talking politician Arnold Jacks remain 'English gentleman and lady' in their 'safe' journey together from Euston, the narrator mocking the affronted reader by commenting, 'Not a little remarkable was the absence of the note of sex from their merry gossip in the narrow seclusion of a little railway compartment'.[50] The author's coupling of women's use of public transport with sexual transgression or unladylike behaviour, even in the minds of his characters, seems too self-conscious to function as a simplistic reinforcing of conservative fears about female mobility, instead signalling a need for the acceptance of women as urban travellers.

But women's limited capacity to control heterosocial encounters can also jeopardise their respectability, exposing them to sexual danger. An outraged article on 'The Perfecting of the Modern Girl' in an 1895 edition of the *Girl's Own Paper* linked women's new freedoms to sexual promiscuity:

> She it is who prefers always to live in London, who talks of having a good time, and even (save the mark!) of sowing her wild oats! She travels everywhere alone in hansoms, and insists on latchkeys and unfettered and unquestioned correspondence. She is found in every variety of gay whirl, and must be amused at all costs.[51]

Perhaps what is most threatening is the appropriation of a masculine sexual identity; the article goes on to warn its readers against the loss of femininity attending women's emancipation, arguing that there are some who 'want freedom to unsex themselves as far as possible'. Marked by exclamation marks in the text, the modern woman's 'good time' may include a 'sowing of wild oats', or a more masculine attitude to pre-marital sexual experience – significantly, Nancy Lord's story was originally to be titled 'A Girl's Wild Oats'.[52] The 'mannish leanings' of

---

[49]   All quotations are taken from George Gissing, 'The Scrupulous Father', *Cornhill* 83 (1901), 175–87.

[50]   George Gissing, *The Crown of Life*, ed. Michel Ballard (1899; Sussex: Harvester Press, 1978), p. 77.

[51]   A. T. Schofield, M.D., 'On the Perfecting of the Modern Girl', *GOP*, 20 July 1895, p. 663.

[52]   *Diary*, 22 April 1893, p. 302.

society women who adopt 'a kind of brusque audaciousness in conversation ... an affectation of assuming to know more of what is what than their mothers or grandmothers were ever permitted or supposed to know' were seen as a rather desperate means of attracting men, rather than a bid for sexual equality, by a *Blackwoods* journalist of 1890.[53] Both heroines are aligned with this figure of the 'modern mannish maiden'. In the earlier novel, Nancy's walks alone with the smooth-talking Lionel Tarrant on a holiday with the Morgans in Teignmouth are seen as perfectly acceptable: 'To Mrs Morgan it never occurred that so self-reliant a young woman ... stood in need of matronly counsel, of strict chaperonage' (p. 100). The modern woman's claims to 'perfect freedom' (p. 82) may mean that she is able to brush aside the men who knock against her in the city crowds when she walks to the Monument with Crewe, but her susceptibility to seduction and unplanned pregnancy, predictably condemned as 'the girl's fault' (p. 124), invite telling comparisons with the barmaid and evoke memories of the shop-girl Amy Drake's forward behaviour in *The Odd Women*. Tarrant's surprise at this turn of events for a woman who 'seemed so thoroughly able to protect herself' (p. 125) perhaps hints at the contraceptives self-reliant women were increasingly using by this time, a sure sign of the 'illicit sexual indulgence' associated with free love in an 1899 article.[54] In *The Whirlpool*, after several informal meetings with the millionaire Cyrus Redgrave, including one at a tram-stop, Alma is horrified by his 'grotesque proposal' that she accompany him to his Italian villa: 'Was she not a lady? And who had ever dared to offer a lady an insult such as this? ...Could *she* stand in peril of such indignity?' (p. 86). She recognises that her unladylike occupation of public space has put her on a level with 'shop-girls, minor actresses ...[whose] insecurity was traditional' (p. 86), jeopardising her social status and self-respect. Jeune's belief that the decay of the chaperon encouraged ladies to become 'self-assertive, capable and independent'[55] does not take account of their insecurity in heterosocial encounters. Although Alma refuses to acknowledge 'the adventures which really had befallen her' (p. 176), perhaps because she is uncomfortable about being 'insulted', she continues to 'consort with [men] as like to like',[56] and Nancy's ready acceptance of the role of mistress shows her to be open to offers and aware of her sexuality. Such audacious behaviour is seen to be a liberating sign of the modern age, though women nevertheless risk their reputations by accepting the 'grotesque proposals' offered by the men they meet in public.

Gender restrictions in public entertainment venues are often explored in the late-Victorian restaurant, a newly heterosocial space which features most prominently in Gissing's later fiction. In *Eve's Ransom* (1895), Hilliard jokes that

---

[53] 'Modern Mannish Maidens', *Blackwoods Magazine* 147 (1890), 252–64 (pp. 261, 262).
[54] Effie Johnson, 'Marriage or Free Love?', *Westminster Review* 152 (1899), 91–8 (p. 94). Preventive measures clearly interfere with childbearing and the future of the race in this article, which predictably prefers marriage because of its sanctioning of 'the important and natural position accorded to sex intercourse in Nature's evolutionary scheme' (p. 95).
[55] 'The Decay of the Chaperon', p. 630.
[56] 'Modern Mannish Maidens', p. 261.

one of the differences between men and women is that women never dine out in restaurants, but the middle-class heroine's reluctance to enter these supposedly disreputable spaces, associated with the 'tumult of London' (p. 198) in Horace Lord's spree, is often more of a comment on the respectability of their chosen companion. The invitation to a restaurant which Alma turns down is made by the sleazy Dymes, who has already been making suggestive comments about her to his male friends, though she does feel comfortable enough to accompany her husband to a restaurant later in the novel. Beatrice is happy to be treated to a restaurant by her sister's 'masher', and Syrett's business-woman is 'in her element' dining in such a lively public space with a male friend, 'delight[ing] in this aspect of the complex artificial life of a great city' (p. 127). Women were more at ease in the new tea shops and department store cafés, which proliferated in London by the 1890s, but restaurants did increasingly cater for women as well as men in recognition of the spending power of female shoppers.[57] The opening of the Dorothy Restaurant in the West End, 'exclusively for the use of ladies' in 1888, intended to provide 'cheap and convenient' lunches for those 'engaged in business during the day' according to one advertisement,[58] suggests that restaurants were becoming more respectable. However, this was sometimes questioned in *fin-de-siècle* fiction. A Soho restaurant's function as 'a place ... where [a woman] can come in as well' serves Crewe's purposes better than the less salubrious drinking establishments they could enter 'if [Nancy] were a man' (p. 61), but it still hovers on the edges of respectability for a middle-class lady. Nancy's 'defiant satisfaction' in the alien environment, and the champagne, a 'sparkling audacity' recommended by her companion, testifies to her 'keen enjoyment of the novelty' (p. 63), but her recognition that the required male escort who legitimises her presence and her consumption of alcohol 'would of course pay' puts her in a potentially compromising situation. As Kathy Peiss has shrewdly pointed out, the 'mixed-sex fun' of heterosocial culture could often only be afforded by a reliance on the higher wages of men; 'without economic independence, [women's] freedoms were ultimately hollow'.[59] Rappaport has linked the increasingly acceptable 'idea of public dining' for bourgeois women back to the provision offered by women's clubs and the 'greater degree of informality between the sexes' such institutions promoted,[60] but this reliance on men's spending power tends to dampen women's delight in such novel city entertainments.

---

[57]   Robert Thorne, 'Places of refreshment in the Nineteenth-Century City', in *Buildings and Society: Essays on the Social Development of the Built Environment*, ed. Anthony D. King (London: Routledge & Kegan Paul, 1980), p. 243. In his discussion of the popular Spiers and Pond restaurants, built in railway stations and in the West End from the 1860s onwards, Thorne notes that 'the East Room at the Criterion established a reputation as a place where even the most timid women could eat whilst visiting the West End'.

[58]   The advertisement appears in *Woman,* 22 May 1890, p. ii.

[59]   Kathy Peiss, *Cheap Amusements: Working Women and Leisure in Turn-of-the-Century New York* (Philadelphia: Temple University Press, 1986), p. 6.

[60]   Rappaport, p. 105. However, she points out that unescorted or pairs of ladies were not allowed in hotel restaurants such as the Savoy.

Despite the proliferation of new mixed or women-only clubs in the West End by the mid-1890s, late-Victorian British novelists did not tend to represent the club as a feminine space. The 'bold experiment' of mixed clubs was felt to encourage an unwelcome freedom emblematic of some women's 'revolt against privacy and domesticity' according to the *Saturday Review* of 1874, which warned, 'a place where flirting can be carried on under cover of "going to my club" is not a thing that we wish to see established as among the recognised conditions of modern society'.[61] But after the unprecedented establishment of the Somerville in 1878 and the Alexandra in 1884 first provided 'a convenient centre for ladies', the presence of 'the advanced woman' in London ensured the demand for a range of women's clubs to cater for her needs, so that by 1899 there were 24 in the capital.[62] Amy Levy proposed the establishing of women's clubs as an alternative to 'the discomfort of the pastry-cook's or the costliness of a restaurant', suggesting that professional women would be better served in 'the cosy club precincts'.[63] The acceptance of these modern institutions was bolstered by journalists' placing of clubs within the commercial landscape, a representation which 'converted clubland from a feminist into a feminine space'.[64] But clubland is generally seen to be a masculine space for the purposes of homosocial bonding over food and wine in Gissing's fiction. The opening chapter of *The Whirlpool* positions Harvey Rolfe in his customary 'quiet corner' (p. 2) in the Metropolitan Club, where men dine, drink, smoke and discuss the money market, one of the few spaces tempting enough to bring even an 'unsociable man' back to the metropolis after his marriage and self-imposed suburban exile. In the earlier novel, Lionel Tarrant's pride in his 'dainty enjoyment of his own limitless leisure', which includes membership of both an 'unfashionable club' and a more 'informal' club called the Hodiernals, composed of indolent, 'up to date' gentlemen who 'contented themselves with living', drank a lot of whisky and 'talked much of woman' (p. 122), is set against his confined wife's envious response, 'What a life ... compared with mine!' (p. 132). Women's exclusion from the sociability offered by men's clubs, signalled in Nancy's wistful contemplation of 'the coldly insolent facades' (p. 58) of the large men's clubs on Pall Mall and St James St on Jubilee night, is sufficient grounds for resentment. Gissing also shared in this resentment, complaining that when the British Museum was closed, he had 'no resort whatever. What a place London is! Absolutely nowhere to go ... of course that is why rich people always belong to

---

[61] 'The Last New Club', *Saturday Review*, 20 June 1874, pp. 774, 775.

[62] Eva Anstruther, 'Ladies' Clubs', *Nineteenth Century* 45 (1899), 598–611 (pp. 600, 602). Clubs set up in the 1890s such as the Sesame and the Grosvenor Crescent Club, which included lectures by feminist speakers and were aimed at the woman worker, were more politicised than others: Anstruther nevertheless believes that all clubs should function as 'intellectual centres for all women, places where women of various social grades could meet on equal terms sans pose' (p. 609).

[63] Levy, 'Women and Club Life', p. 535.

[64] Rappaport, pp. 90, 94. She claims that they were increasingly described in the women's press as 'luxurious urban homes populated by apolitical and asexual ladies of fashion' so that 'by the 1890s but especially after the turn of the century, women's clubs were no longer necessarily liberal, feminist, or progressive' (p. 98).

clubs'.[65] Reiterating Levy's plea for woman-friendly public spaces to counter the isolation of professional women in London, Dora M. Jones in the *Young Woman* of 1899 highlighted the need for 'some fairly central haven of refuge' for women of various social positions to meet, but her discovery that underpaid bachelor girls could not afford even the modest subscriptions indicated that the new clubs remained relatively inaccessible to some on the grounds of expense.[66]

The gender differences exposed by an examination of heterosocial urban spaces can then be seen to balance the claims to a man's freedom endorsed by the bachelor girl with the dangers of the city for the unchaperoned woman. In her reading of *In the Year of Jubilee*, Deborah L. Parsons has claimed that in Gissing's 'pessimistic and misogynistic view of the modern city', 'London is a dangerous place, where the individual is crushed or engulfed, and it is not a place for women, who are regarded as particularly vulnerable to its temptations'.[67] On the contrary, I would argue that Gissing's fiction always *insists* on middle-class women's place in the capital, as, despite their potential vulnerability, their desire for liberty, independence and the pleasures of male society compels them to negotiate the city. Subverting contemporary notions of the pleasure-seeking *flâneur*, the New Woman heroine comes to perceive of her new-found urban independence as not only masculine but essential, with Alma behaving 'like a young man whose exuberant spirits urge him "to make a night of it"' (p. 197) after her successful meeting with the music critic, Felix Dymes, and Nancy shaking off her unwanted chaperon, feeling it 'impossible to walk on and on under [male] protection … she resolved to taste independence' (p. 54). As Elizabeth Wilson has pointed out in her discussion of the urban crowd, although 'female virtue and respectability were hard to preserve in this promiscuous environment … it proved impossible to banish [women] from city spaces'.[68] Certainly, modern women remained very much restricted in their mobility, but their adoption of masculine habits and unprecedented entry into 'resorts exclusive to men' can be seen to accelerate the process identified by the historian Mary Ryan by which 'gender distinctions might be corroded by the informal, everyday uses of public space by real men and women'.[69]

---

[65] Letter to Margaret, 29 September 1889. *Collected Letters, Vol 4*, p. 117.

[66] Dora M. Jones, 'The Ladies' Clubs of London', *Young Woman* 7 (1899), 409–13 (p. 409); 'The Life of a Bachelor Girl in the Big City', p. 132. Less prosperous bachelor girls surviving on a pound a week had limited recreation, and were not catered for by either the clubs for wealthier leisured women or the 'factory girls' clubs' which 'appealed to a different constituency'.

[67] Parsons, p. 84. This is based on a simplistic reading of Nancy Lord's experiences in the city streets. Nancy's enjoyment of the crowds, likened to the feelings of 'any shop-girl let loose', is seen as contrary to Gissing's 'male, *fin-de-siècle* aesthetic pessimism', but still in overwhelmingly negative terms.

[68] Elizabeth Wilson, 'The Invisible *Flâneur*', *New Left Review* 191 (1992), 90–110 (pp. 91, 93).

[69] Mary P. Ryan, *Women in Public: Between Banners and Ballots, 1825–1880* (Baltimore & London: Johns Hopkins University Press, 1990), p. 59.

Married Women in the City and the Working Mother

The presence of the married woman in the late-Victorian city has been generally overlooked in accounts of female urbanism, particularly in relation to her entry into the professions. In her study of female occupation of 'everyday space' in the American city before 1880, Ryan argues that 'the social whirlwind of the city was in marked contrast not just to the rural past but to the suburban future of many American women', in which marriage and motherhood 'severely restricted their use of even the most inviting public spaces'.[70] The pervasive cultural myth that Victorian ladies remained sequestered in the domestic sphere after marriage still needs to be challenged in relation to a period when more married women were becoming active in politics and the workplace, as well as making their presence known in shops, clubs, cafés and on the streets. A 1900 article emphasising the ennui and disillusionment suffered by the modern married woman shrewdly noted,

> I doubt if discontent and impatience of monotony were ever more rife than now at the end of the Woman's Era. It is not only necessity that recruits the ranks of women workers. "Something to do" is the universal cry, meaning, in nearly every case, something outside the sphere of home duties.[71]

Although certain types of worker, such as philanthropists and factory girls, traditionally continued to work in the city after marriage,[72] the financial support offered by husbands, and their opposition to paid work for their wives, often precluded married women as a group from contributing to the labour force. Philippa Levine has argued that 'feminists have been accused of avoiding discussion of the ethics of married women's paid work', which never became 'a central topic of feminist interest' in this period.[73] Whilst restrictions on occupations for married ladies meant that feminist social investigators tended to see their research into married women's work as primarily focused on the lower branches of industry, there *was* growing debate about the kinds of professions suitable for educated wives and mothers. Clara Collet was one of the first investigators to pay attention to the employment of married women, though her 1894 report, which she sent to Gissing in 1895,[74] suggested that fewer women, including widows and wives, were being employed; key factors affecting middle-class women's entry into the labour market, 'a smaller field for domestic usefulness ... a diminished probability of marriage, [and] apprehension with regard

---

[70] Ryan, pp. 84, 86.

[71] Pleasaunce Unite, 'Disillusioned Daughters', *Fortnightly Review* 74 (1900), 850–7 (p. 851).

[72] A. Amy Bulley, 'The Employment of Women: the Lady Assistant Commissioners' Report', *Fortnightly Review* 61 (1894), 39–48 (p. 44).

[73] Philippa Levine, *Feminist Lives in Victorian England: Private Roles and Public Commitment* (Oxford: Blackwell, 1990), pp. 127, 149.

[74] Letter to Clara Collet, 2 July 1895. He thanked her, 'your report has come ... all such work of yours I value very much'. *Collected Letters, Vol 6*, p. 4.

to the future' still reinforced the self-supporting spinster as the norm.[75] Her belief that working women chose marriage as an escape from the demands of paid labour bought into conventional views that the difficult juggling act of work and motherhood should be avoided where possible, but did not accurately reflect the urban lifestyles of a significant number of middle-class women.

In the New Woman novel, the heroine typically refuses to recognise marriage as a restriction on her liberty, often continuing to negotiate the city in the style of the female bachelor. In *In the Year of Jubilee*, the modern marriage of Nancy and Tarrant, in many ways more like a free union or an illicit sexual liaison, actually heightens the 'precious' sense of liberty and independence she craves. In the early days she experiences 'a personal freedom not unlike what she had vainly desired in the days of petulant girlhood' (p. 230). Nancy's marriage also lends her the confidence to traverse the city without male accompaniment; during her pregnancy when 'walking alone at night was a pleasure in which she now indulged herself pretty frequently' (p. 158), she relishes the 'enjoyable' experience of dining alone in a Fleet Street restaurant, though she is still 'flurried' by Crewe's 'insolence' (p. 159) when he accosts her unexpectedly in the street. The masculine investment in the pleasures of suburbia in *The Whirlpool* creates a rigid gender divide in terms of leisure after marriage, as the male retreat from the city to the quiet domesticity of the suburban home ensures that '[the] wives have to go about by themselves' (p. 215). Whilst Rolfe and Carnaby only use the city for work purposes and occasional visits to men's clubs, the wives are shown to be reliant on frequent excursions to satisfy a need for public entertainments and socialising – 'it seemed to Alma that the very best thing for her health would be to spend a week or two in London, and see her old friends, and go to a few concerts' (p. 170). Comparing his heroine to the single Leach sisters, Gissing comments ambivalently on the married woman's use of the city:

> [Alma] came frequently to Kingsbury-Neasden, and ran up to town at least as often as they (Dora and Gerda) did. Like them she found it an annoyance to have to rush to the station before midnight; but, being married, she could allow herself more freedom of movement than was permissible to single young women, and having once missed the last train, she simply went to a hotel where she was known, and quietly returned to Pinner next morning. That Mrs Rolfe had such complete liberty and leisure seemed to them no subject for remark; being without cares, she enjoyed life; a matter of course. (p. 188)

In this scenario both single and married women can choose to 'run up to town' for evening amusements when they please, but oddly, here it is the freedom of *single* women which seems restricted, (though this may have more to do with Dora and Gerda's decision to rely on their family income rather than taking up professions for themselves). Moreover, it is the married woman who can stay out all night

---

[75]   Clara Collet, *Report by Miss Collet on the Statistics of Employment of Women and Girls*, (C–7564), Printed for HMSO 1894. Cited in Deborah McDonald, *Clara Collet 1860–1948: An Educated Working Woman* (London: Woburn Press, 2004), p. 181.

without arousing suspicion; the fact that some of the new women's clubs, increasingly catering for middle- and upper-class wives, offered bedrooms for their clientele suggests a need for such a service. However, the sisters' admiration of Alma's 'complete liberty and leisure' is seen as rather naïve; Rolfe's anger suggests that the 'liberty' of married women, no longer immune from domestic cares, is still controlled by men. Although Alma boasts that her marital status lends her 'the precious advantage of being able to use London for all legitimate purposes, without danger of being drawn into the vortex of idle temptations' (p. 191), she is deluding herself; married women unwilling to relinquish their bachelor lifestyles constantly expose themselves to danger in their supposedly 'legitimate' use of the city.

Debates about married women's work became contentious when centred on the middle-class wife, who usually had a choice about whether to work or not, unlike the majority of lower-class wives with poorly paid husbands and large families to support. Clementina Black's 1915 study for the Women's Industrial Council sets out to disprove the prevalent middle-class opinion that 'the working for money of married women is to be deplored', identifying a significant class of working women 'not compelled by necessity to follow any trade ... who are working for a better standard of living for their children', rather than wilfully neglecting them.[76] But arguments using the responsibilities of motherhood to veto 'unnecessary' labour outside the home were pretty much the same for wives in the higher classes. The short answer to the question, 'Should Married Women follow Professions?' put by the New Woman novelist Sarah Grand to the readers of *The Young Woman* in 1899, was an emphatic '*not if they can help it*'. Pursuing a profession was only to be recommended for those 'abnormal women ...[with] no aptitude for motherhood'. This strand of anti-feminist thinking was annexed to an opinion shared by some investigators, that affluent working women were taking wages away from those who work to live: 'If you are well off, you have no business to take up a paying profession'.[77] In *In the Year of Jubilee*, a lady's decision to work for money, although recognised as 'a sign of progress' (p. 291), is also seen to be compromising her class status, as paid employment is perceived to be only for 'the rough and ready sort of women' (p. 292). In the later novel, Mrs Frothingham worries that society will be scandalised that 'necessity had driven [Alma] into a professional career' (p. 248). But there was also a growing recognition that paid work was an essential element of the varied lifestyle of the modern woman,

---

[76] Clementina Black (ed.), *Married Women's Work*, with an introduction by Ellen Mappen (1915: London: Virago, 1983), pp. 1, 5, 7. Her research suggested that such women use the extra money to buy holidays and 'educational advantages' for their children, and are 'marked by an independence of mind ... derived from the consciousness of their power of self-support' (p. 7).

[77] Sarah Grand, 'Should Married Women Follow Professions?', *Young Woman* 7 (1899), 257–9 (pp. 259, 258). Grand concluded that 'that woman is neglectful of her best interests who goes out into the world to work when she can get a nice man to do the work for her'.

whatever her marital status or income.[78] Feminist researchers for the Fabian Women's Group in the early twentieth century protested against 'the economically unsound, unjust, and radically dangerous tendency in many salaried professions to enforce upon women resignation on marriage', rejecting the notion that younger spinsters were the most fit for the labour market with the argument that those who succeeded in combining work and motherhood were able to experience 'the normal joys of fully-developed womanhood'.[79] In her 1913 study of the woman question, FWG activist Barbara Hutchins noted that even though social opinion was not in favour of the married woman working, there still remained a small but important class 'who wish not to be excluded from either work or motherhood'.[80]

Gissing's contribution to such debates about women's capacity to combine work and motherhood is typically ambiguous. David Grylls's claim that 'like … most other Victorians, Gissing believed that the duties of a mother would not easily combine with a job', based on the observation that across the author's work, paid employment is for working-class wives and 'genteel females without a partner',[81] needs qualifying, as the later novels' articulation of the wife's frustration with a life dominated by childcare can also be seen to anticipate the thinking of early-twentieth-century socialist feminists. In *New Grub Street* (1891), the intelligent Amy Reardon, with her knowledge of the literary market and the 'practical conduct of journals and magazines' (p. 99), appears a much fitter candidate for a successful writing career than her less ambitious husband, but work is not represented as a viable option for a middle-class mother tired out with domestic duties; she has 'no intention of trying' (p. 167) her hand at fiction.[82] The situation pointed out by her brother of a well-educated married lady who works in a shop 'because her husband can't support her' (p. 277) is seen as shameful and inappropriate, rather than a practical solution to her financial difficulties. Edwin Reardon's wish for 'a huge public *crèche* in London' because 'it's monstrous that an educated mother should have to be nursemaid' (p. 158) is instantly dismissed by his wife but hints at the author's appreciation of the social changes required to support the working mother. Discussions in the 1890s about the presence of children in women's clubs, or the advisability of *crèche* facilities, also acknowledge that the middle-class wife had a life apart from her maternal role.[83] In *In the Year of Jubilee*, Nancy's reasons for seeking 'new occupation' (p. 273) as a married woman bear out the cultural desire to escape from the frivolity and 'social excitement' of married life, 'must there not

---

[78]   See 'the Life of a Bachelor Girl in the Big City', p. 132, where Jones disagrees with 'the often expressed opinion that women of private means should not take up professional work', pointing out that working women with higher disposable incomes would create more work for other women by increased spending.

[79]   Edith Morley (ed.), *Women Workers in Seven Professions: A Survey of their Economic Conditions and Prospects* (London: Routledge, 1914), p. xv.

[80]   B.L. Hutchins, *Conflicting Ideals: Two Sides of the Woman Question* (London: Thomas Murby & Co, 1913), p. 73.

[81]   David Grylls, *The Paradox of Gissing* (London: Allen & Unwin, 1986), p. 159.

[82]   All quotations are taken from George Gissing, *New Grub Street*, ed. Bernard Bergonzi (1891; Harmondsworth: Penguin, 1968).

[83]   'Ladies' Clubs', pp. 610–11.

be discoverable, in the world to which she had, or could obtain, access, some honest, strenuous occupation, which would hold in check her unprofitable thoughts and soothe her self-respect?' (p. 230). What is more, her place in the city as a married mother is seen as problematic:

> Walking about the streets of London in search of suggestions, she gained only an understanding of her insignificance … Of what avail her 'education', her 'culture'? … She was a coward; she dreaded the world; she saw as never yet the blessedness of having money and a secure home… Is not a woman's place under the sheltering roof? What right had a mother to be searching abroad for tasks and duties? Task enough, duty obvious, in the tending of her child. Had she but a little country cottage with needs assured, and her baby cradled beside her, she would ask no more. (p. 249)

Although her search has been motivated by the need to earn her own money, the inaccessibility of the labour market forces her into a reappraisal of the comforts and security of male financial support. Gissing is also drawing more obviously on anti-feminist and maternalist thinking about 'a woman's place', privileging child-care over paid work and relocating his heroine in the domestic rather than the public sphere; in a later passage, she is represented as 'a mere outcast' in the city, with its 'alien business and pleasure' (p. 273). However, feminist advocates of 'the increased scope of women's work in the future' also reiterated the commonly-held view that maternity and work were mutually exclusive: 'to the majority of women the profession ordained by Nature will be the one open to them, and in no other is their influence more potent or wide-spreading'; work is then for the woman who 'cannot be a wife and mother'.[84] Gissing's apparent denial of the married mother's 'right' to a place in London does not match up with his protests on behalf of frustrated wives, making it difficult to establish where his sympathies lie. This ostensible shoring up of 'the profession ordained by Nature' as the ideal female role is juxtaposed with a consideration of the benefits of paid employment in particular areas for married women, in order to set up tensions and contradictions within the texts.

The occupation of fiction writing is floated as a distinct possibility, not least because it was recognised as a potentially lucrative form of genteel home-work, linked to purity and morality in an 1893 study of paid employments for ladies.[85] Rejecting both poorly paid womanly occupations such as governessing and 'very ambitious' (p. 249) posts in offices which required business training, Nancy's choice of literary work significantly protects her from the public sphere: 'Numbers of women took to it; not a few succeeded. It was a pursuit that demanded no apprenticeship, that could be followed in the *privacy* of home, a pursuit wherein her education would be of service' (pp. 249–50, my italics). However, successful women writers of the time interviewed for women's magazines were not particularly encouraging about their own profession. Charlotte Yonge advised

---

[84] Lady Jeune (ed.), *Ladies at Work: Papers on Paid Employment for Ladies by Experts in the Several Branches* (London: A. D. Innes, 1893), pp. 8, 13.
[85] Ibid.,

only mature readers with greater life experiences, and the support of the newly formed Authors' Society, to aim for authorship,[86] and Grand issued warnings about the 'infinite cost' of combining housekeeping and literary pursuits, claiming that her 'health, household and literary work all suffered'.[87] Although the heroine's desire for 'honest, hard work ... such as lots of educated girls are doing' (pp. 233, 234) may align her with the New Woman heroine, this is typically denied in the narrative. Nancy's motivation as a writer, sparked off by reading a novel about a successful novelist, is predictably short-lived, as her dreams of success are not only thwarted by male opposition but by the demands of childcare, as it becomes difficult to write steadily around the baby's illnesses. The success of Grand's childless writer in *The Beth Book* (1899) is the exception, whereas the struggle of Hester Gresley in Mary Cholmondeley's *Red Pottage* (1899), who has her novel edited and ultimately destroyed by her outraged brother and is obliged to work before breakfast to avoid constant interruptions from her nephews, is more usual. The inaccessibility of women's clubs to the New Woman heroine sustains the problematic lack of awareness about the professional networking they offered: Gissing's frustrated wives would certainly have benefited from professional advice about suitable careers or the chance to meet literary or musical agents, both male and female, in an informal environment. Either the Pioneer established in 1892, the haunt of New Woman novelists such as Grand, Olive Schreiner and Mona Caird, with its lively programme of lectures and debates on socialist and feminist issues, or the Writers' Club set up in the same year, would have satisfied many of Nancy's needs as an aspiring writer. At its best, the ladies' club could fulfil its ideal function of being 'a place where women of various social positions can meet on common ground to further the aims of all women alike'.[88] But she is too easily discouraged by reading the new employment manuals aimed primarily at self-supporting spinsters, attributing her failure to find employment to the fact that she 'applied to strangers, who knew nothing of her capabilities, and cared nothing for her needs' (p. 273). Instead, she agrees to work at the 'Fashion Club' attached to Beatrice French's 'handsome' shop. It is significant that the middle-class heroine can only reluctantly afford to enter this space as an assistant who 'advise[s] fools about the fashions' (p. 307) rather than a lady shopper or young professional, her drudgery a far cry from the visions of feminist community women's clubs were seeking to create in the late 1880s when the novel is set. Gissing's denial of the married woman's ambitions is then in line with the limited success of fictional women writers across the genre, who are rarely shown to combine a literary career with motherhood.

Explicitly engaging with contentious divisions within feminism about the flexibility of women's roles and their needs outside the domestic sphere, New Woman fiction also directly addressed 'the marriage issue that loomed large in discussions of ... women's musical careers'.[89] Mona Caird's *The Daughters of*

---

[86]   Charlotte Yonge, 'Authorship', in *Ladies at Work*, pp. 53, 55.
[87]   'Should Married Women follow Professions?', p. 258.
[88]   'The Ladies' Clubs of London', p. 410.
[89]   Gillett, p. 119.

Danaus (1894) questions the choice an aspiring composer must make between fulfilling work and her natural function as wife and mother. By the mid-1890s Caird was known as a radical apologist for the New Woman and an advocate of modern marriage, whose articles questioned the 'normal conditions of sex-relationship', '"womanly" duty and virtue' and the 'hideous ideal' of the wife's economic dependence on her husband.[90] Significantly, she had been one of the few female advocates of birth control at an 1887 discussion at the radical Men and Women's Club.[91] Her feisty, emancipated heroine Hadria Fullerton stakes a claim to gender equality by forsaking 'this brutal domestic idea that fashions [women's] fate for them' (p. 68) in order to train as a composer in Paris. Like Alma, Hadria relies on the mistaken belief that marriage will function as 'a release from the present difficulties' (p. 141) of 'win[ning] opportunity to pursue [her work]' (p. 109) when in reality problems are intensified with opposition from husband and family who view married women's work as unnecessary. The warnings of her musical instructor in Paris indicate that the combination of motherhood and musical training is not only difficult, but practically impossible: the fact that many promising pupils have fallen by the wayside into 'a stupid maternity', leads him to the conclusion that women lack 'persistency of character and purpose', as the maternal instinct becomes 'the scourge of genius' (p. 319). His own wife effectively sacrificed her 'musical ambition', when 'the cares of a family put an end to all hope of bringing her gifts to fruition' (p. 315). The working mother's difficult situation, seen as 'absurd' but inevitable, is constantly compared to the male experience of liberty, choice and freedom from domesticity, 'the privilege that every man enjoys, of quietly pursuing his work, without giving [pain or offence to others]' (p. 322). Ultimately, Hadria is pressurised into leaving Paris, as her sister-in-law's accusations that she is a neglectful wife and mother and the news that her dangerously ill mother is in need of care assert the 'peculiar claims …made…on a woman's time and strength' (p. 322). The male lack of understanding about women's inability to achieve professional recognition whilst confined to the domestic sphere – 'one required no particular liberty to pursue [music], yet where were the women-composers? … why didn't [women] arise and bring out operas and oratorios?' (p. 372) – is then tellingly ironic. Despite the novel's feminist agenda, Caird's refusal to allow her heroine to complete her musical training reinforces the idea that she is ahead of her time in her desire for a career and motherhood, and consigns an ambitious heroine, fully aware of the restrictions facing her, to 'the accursed list of women who gave up their art for "*la famille*"' (p. 333).

The Whirlpool develops Caird's views on the difficulties of acquiring the liberty needed for a musical career, though the married violinist's pursuit of professional fame and sacrifice of the family is typically used by Gissing to reinforce the dangers of the city, as well as the insecurity of such a livelihood. Music was just as overcrowded and more competitive than many other

---

[90] Mona Caird, 'The Morality of Marriage', *Fortnightly Review* 47 (1890), 517–31 (pp. 314, 317, 323).
[91] Bland, p. 126.

professions; as a contemporary article cautioned readers, even those women 'lucky' enough to have attended universities or colleges should be advised against a career in the arts, as 'nobody can hope to live by painting pictures or composing operas'.[92] Like the actress, the professional musician was obliged to trade on her appearance, and by the 1890s the current 'girl-violin mania' ensured that performing in public in low-cut dresses had become associated with a disturbing sexuality, evoking 'the disreputable aura that attached to the woman violinist'.[93] The girl-violinist had become associated with the bustle of city life, not only 'invading' orchestras but using all new varieties of public transport to invade the fashionable West End: 'it is a common sight in London to see maidens of all ages laden with fiddles of all sizes ... hurrying to the underground railway, or hailing the omnibus or cab in Oxford St, Regent St, and Bond Street'.[94] It is significant that as a student in Germany, Alma both announces her professional status and legitimises her use of public transport by carrying her violin-case with her in railway carriages. Dora's suggestion that she pursue her desire to be a professional musician, 'I don't see why marriage should put an end to it' (p. 188), is quite daring in this context as for a married woman, travelling by train alone to concerts and recitals is seen to be risky, inappropriate and to a large extent unnecessary. Mixing with men in the concert audience at the Crystal Palace is potentially compromising, as Redgrave, with his 'seductive familiarity', 'declared the sensuous pleasure of sitting by Alma's side' (p. 246). In many ways, Alma's boredom with her marriage increases her vulnerability to what one feminist journalist called 'the maelstrom of London life', with its 'excitements and temptations, and ... all the hazards of late hours, public conveyance, chance acquaintance' encountered by the working lady.[95] The advertising expenses for her long-awaited first recital are paid for by Dymes with the unspoken expectation that he will be reimbursed with sexual favours; in an embarrassing scene later in the novel, Alma learns that by remaining in his debt she has to accept his free and easy way of talking to her so that her insistence on paying him back, 'But you don't suppose I can accept a present of money from you, Mr Dymes?' (p. 405) frees her from her obligation to him. However, Paula Gillett's argument that such behaviour is typical of musical heroines 'portrayed wholly without sympathy as women who cynically exploit male susceptibility to the charms of the female

[92]   Janet E. Hogarth, 'The Monstrous Regiment of Women', *Fortnightly Review* 68 (1897), 926–36 (pp. 927, 931).

[93]   H.R. Hawes, 'Violins and Girls', *Contemporary Review* 74 (1898), 107–12 (p. 108). The mania was dated within the last twenty-five years. The blatantly eroticised tone of this article in the respectable press is perhaps typical of male reactions to the current 'girl-violin mania', dwelling on the ways in which violinists 'caressed' their instruments, and displayed their bare arms and shoulders 'to the best advantage' in evening performances as the emotion behind the music allowed them to reveal hidden depths in their 'virginal nature'. See also Paula Gillett, *Musical Women in England, 1870–1914: 'Encroaching on All Men's Privileges'* (Basingstoke: Macmillan, 2000), pp. 113–17, 81.

[94]   'Violins and Girls', p. 107.

[95]   'The Working Lady in London', p. 200.

violinist to their own illegitimate ends'[96] is surely rather misleading, given that Alma appears much more exploited than exploiter. Rather, the publicity she is obliged to court is intended to locate her at the centre of the 'tumult' and danger of the whirlpool, as focusing on a career made appealing by 'the attraction of a public life'[97] allows the author to use his heroine as a symbol for the vulgarities of the market.

Perhaps indicating reservations about the validity of married women's work, both of Gissing's later novels express the husband's worries about wives making their own money in the wider context of an authorial uneasiness about women's claims to a public life. In her 1911 study of women's work, Bird warned would-be female musicians that their first concerts were likely to be 'disastrous', as 'the only chances of fame and money-making on the concert platform lie in London and the big foreign cities; and noone leaps in a moment to prominence there'.[98] Alma's fear that she might 'c[o]me out and make a fiasco' (p. 189) is proved to be only too true; far from making any money from her performances, she is left 'sorry and ashamed' to have to ask her husband to write the cheque to clear her debts to her advertisers. Rolfe's disgust at 'the thought of [his wife] playing for money' (p. 236) and her name emblazoned across advertisements and flyers results in his decision to chaperon her to the recital, suggesting a refusal to accept her new-found freedoms. Simon J. James has commented on the commodification of female sexuality and metaphors of prostitution in *The Whirlpool*, though his claim that Alma does not sell her body to men in the same way as Sibyl (who we suspect has slept with Redgrave to guarantee his investment in her husband's company), does not prevent him from extending the author's condemnation of Sibyl as 'a woman who had sold herself for money' to the violinist eager for fame.[99] Similarly, Nancy's desire in the earlier novel to publish her novel 'in the hope of making money' (p. 354) is seen as 'horrible' by Tarrant, who criticises her literary talents as well as reminding her that as a married woman, unlike those 'poor creatures who have no choice', she is 'not obliged to go into the market' (p. 354). In *Red Pottage*, Hester's brother also sees her novel-writing as inappropriately mercenary for a woman, accusing her of 'pander[ing] to the depraved public taste', 'interlard[ing] fiction with *risqué* things in order to make it sell' (pp. 255, 263). Nancy's practical explanation of her entrepreneurial spirit – 'as I had spare time I

---

[96] Gillett, p. 130. She is comparing her to the heroine of Cecily Ullmann Sidgwick's *A Splendid Cousin* (1892). Her argument that the heroine's 'susceptibility to flattery and willingness to compromise her reputation in pursuit of success' (p. 133) lead inevitably to disgrace and suicide also appears to me to be a misreading of the text.

[97] Ethel M. Boyce, 'Music', in Jeune (ed.), *Ladies at Work*, p. 41.

[98] Bird, p. 218.

[99] Simon J. James, *Unsettled Accounts: Money and Narrative in the Novels of George Gissing* (London: Anthem Press, 2003), pp. 135–6. He notes the sexual difficulties attendant on Alma's choice of career and entry into the marketplace, arguing 'In the commodified environment of the novel, an attempt at artistic success cannot succeed without the sacrifice of both capital and sincerity. Alma negotiates again with the hostile, consuming economy in the persons of her former would-be purchasers, Dymes and Redgrave'.

didn't see why I shouldn't use it profitably. We want money, and if it isn't actually disgraceful – ' (p. 355) – is also dismissed as unwomanly, recalling Luckworth Crewe's distaste about her earlier jests about her own market value, 'you have thoughts above money' (p. 89). Borrowing a strategy familiar from New Woman fiction, Gissing's dramatisation of the argument about women's right to make their own money is fairly evenly balanced between the male view that it is woman's 'positive duty to keep out of the beastly scrimmage' (p. 355) of commercial London and the more feminist view that a woman should not be 'shut out from the life of the world' (p. 355). But typically, Nancy's feminist defence of her restricted position cannot be sustained as, like Hester, she is 'refuse[d] the improbability of a Kunstlerroman ending':[100] briefly toying with the idea of publishing the manuscript secretly under another name, she ultimately accepts her husband's advice to lay the manuscript at the back of 'a very private drawer' (p. 356). In the later novel, Alma is noticeably absent from the conversations that take place around 'the whole question of whether professional life is right and good for a married woman' (p. 337), only suffering the effects of her husband's decision that her performances are 'going to stop' (p. 320). The parcel of cherished newspaper articles, entitled 'My Recital, 1891' and 'locked ... up with other most private memorials' (p. 373) again symbolises the locking up of the wife's artistic ambitions in a private space and the denial of the 'legitimate pride' (p. 372) she has striven to achieve against the odds. But it is too simplistic to see the plot trajectories as confirmation that the short-lived professional life is not right and good for the married woman, at a time when generic conventions dictated that the emancipated heroine should be repositioned within the domestic space after marriage rather than being allowed to enjoy her independence indefinitely. The coupling of this enforced denial of woman's claims to the public sphere with a sympathetic protest against female claustrophobia in the suburban home signalled the author's belief that 'the double life, the double strain'[101] of married women's work noted by Hutchins could yet be possible for some women.

The Effects of Female Urban Lifestyles: Nervous Illness and Suburbia

Even as the novels expose the sexual and economic problems associated with female urban lifestyles, they draw attention to the more long-term effects of women's negotiations of the city for the purposes of work and leisure. Perhaps the most significant consequence is the onset of illness, especially the nervous disorders associated with women in the late nineteenth century. In her analysis of the new disease of neurasthenia, or nervous exhaustion, an affliction related to 'heredity, gender and modern life stress', Wood points out that, unlike contemporary medical accounts which focused primarily on cases of male breakdown, 'novelists in England between the 1890s and World War One typically

---

[100] James, p. 126.
[101] Hutchins, p. 76.

associate the illness with the highly strung modern woman'.[102] Warnings about women's deteriorating health in cities, particularly the 'modern, highly wrought nerves' which might affect them, recurred in the debates about working women.[103] One commentator cited medical testimonies about women '"on the drive" struggling on at high pressure' who find their health 'impaired, if not shattered for life'.[104] The nervous illnesses of women workers are increasingly seen as a sign of the times by the later 1890s, shown to have particular effects on those in the professional classes. In 1897 Frances Low commented on the 'neuralgic curse' of poor ladies, proclaiming, 'wherever one turns in the world of women workers it appears to exist in a more or less intense form; and much of the despondence and depression amongst women, who like their work and get fairly good salaries, I believe to be attributable to this cause'.[105] By 1911 it was being claimed that 'the professional woman who aspires to do a man's work requires a man's qualities of mind, of muscle, and of nerve, but ignores the fact that she should cultivate these in the same way that a man does';[106] neglecting nutrition and exercise, as well as forgoing leisure, were felt to be particular failings of young working women. In *The Whirlpool*, constant tiredness is an inevitable feature of the teaching profession in the case of Mary Abbott, who also has the teacher's habit, linked to nervous breakdowns in Collet's 1898 study of the expenditure of working women, of denying herself amusements in order to rest after the day's trials.[107] However, the depression of the woman worker cannot be explained purely in terms of her fight against the various ailments and nervous complaints listed. Advocates of female employment and higher education also voiced the alternative view that 'the really fatal enemy to health among young women is the aimless, idle, frivolous life into which, for want of better employment, they are so often tempted to drift'.[108] In the resolutions to his plots, Gissing seeks to question both the causes of the illnesses and nervous breakdowns which affect working women, and society's remedies for curing them, a strategy which inevitably returns him to the wider and more complex issue of woman's place within late-Victorian urban culture.

Although at face value, it might appear that Gissing is criticising his heroines for their unrealistic and demanding artistic ambitions, both novels also show women's health to be at risk in other occupations, perhaps to demonstrate that work-related illnesses were not simply a product of the strains of performance. In

---

[102]   Wood, pp. 174, 175. She argues that this is in opposition to the view of medical writers of the time, who 'focus almost exclusively on male breakdown from stress or over-work'.

[103]   Emily Robhouse, 'Women Workers: How they live, how they wish to live', *Nineteenth Century* 47 (1900), 471–84 (p. 474). See also the view that for those substituting milk and biscuits for proper meals, 'sooner or later nerves and digestion pay for the want of proper nourishment', expressed in 'The Working Lady in London', p. 196.

[104]   'The Working Lady in London', p. 199.

[105]   Low, 'How Poor Ladies Live', p. 415.

[106]   Bird, p. 193.

[107]   Collet, 'The Expenditure of Middle-Class Working Women', p. 77.

[108]   J.G. Fitch, 'Women and the Universities', *Contemporary Review* 58 (1890), 240–55 (p. 252).

In the Year of Jubilee, the route chosen by Jessica Morgan, feverishly cramming for a scholarship to gain entrance to London University, is shown to be less a practical way for women to improve their career prospects and salary, as it would have been considered at the time, than as a rather pointless exercise for a visiting governess from a family struggling to pay the costs of examinations; such scholastic women were criticised for their 'supercilious airs' and fraudulent waste of their parents' money in the *Girls' Own Paper* in 1890.[109] Efforts to disprove the links between study and female illness by feminist campaigners for higher education for women continued but were adversely affected by increased fears around motherhood and infertility. A generally positive account of higher education for women by an ex-Newnham student put forward the view that 'a course of study in Cambridge is less exhausting than a course of gaiety in London', but her argument that 'over-dancing' was potentially more dangerous than overwork is not entirely convincing as the threat of 'over-pressure' is only avoided by those who choose not to take exams.[110] Bird's study reiterated the view that 'breakdown from overwork and nervous strain is far more common among women students than men'.[111] By studying excessively, the 'overwrought' and 'low-spirited' Jessica has sacrificed her womanliness as well as her health: in order to 'be regarded as one of the clever, the uncommon women … [she] was willing to labour early and late, regardless of failing health, regardless even of ruined complexion and hair that grew thin beneath the comb' (p. 18). Neglect of personal appearance also characterises the rather asexual Mary Abbott, whose dress, Alma notes with satisfaction, is clearly not new; unlike office workers, who sometimes professed shame at their 'extravagance', the teachers in Collet's survey on working women's expenditure also spent very little on dress.[112] Jessica, 'a most interesting case of breakdown from undue mental exertion' (p. 221), represents the dangers of 'the woman student who focuses all her thoughts upon her work alone', and 'wears her nerves to fiddlestrings'[113] by constant cramming and the willing exchange of her leisure hours for 'hours of exhaustion' (p. 18). What is interesting is that this alternative route available to the educated middle-class girl has been rejected by Nancy, whose pregnancy instead transforms her into 'Nature's graduate'. Barmby's opinion that 'young ladies ought not to undergo these ordeals. The delicacy of their nervous systems unfits them for such a strain' (p. 187) is confirmed in the delirium and hysterical attacks suffered by the student. The doctor who pronounces her

---

[109] S.F.A. Caulfeild, 'Some Types of Girlhood, or our Juvenile Spinsters, Part 2, *GOP*, 27 December 1890, p. 196.

[110] Eva Knatchbull-Hugessen, 'Newnham College from within', *Nineteenth Century* 21 (1887), 843–56 (p. 845). However, a contemporary article on the American women's college Bryn Mawr, founded in 1885, confidently reported that 'there have been no cases of breakdown from over-work'. See Alys W. Pearsall Smith, 'A Women's College in the United States', *Nineteenth Century* 23 (1888), 918–26.

[111] Bird, 'Pioneers', p. 193. She goes on to quote from another recent study of women's work by A. Lytellson, which argues that if professional women could be induced to eat more meat, this would advance the cause of women more than the founding of colleges.

[112] Collet, 'The Expenditure of Middle Class Working Women', pp. 76, 77, 86–7.

[113] Bird, 'Pioneers', p. 193.

revision timetable 'attempted suicide', then forbids her from studying as she 'might do [her] brain a serious injury' (p. 221). The fact that such anti-feminist and out-dated views are allowed to go unmodified in a text about female emancipation is rather unsettling, as Jessica's retreat from the hope of a scholarship into the Salvation Army reinforces a perception of higher education as both unappealing and 'uncommon' for ladies, reliant on the myth of female unfitness for study.

Whilst medical perceptions of women's bodily weakness employed to discourage women from overwork increasingly drew on the same evolutionary arguments about female unfitness, social investigators and feminist journalists also highlighted the lack of support for professional women as a contributory factor in their illnesses. In 1892 a lady doctor commented on women's lack of 'recuperative power' and the 'deterioration she noticed in young women who work hard', leading the journalist to generalise that 'women do not make a very good fight against what is trying and depressing in the lives they lead'.[114] But this argument only partially explains the emancipated heroine's struggle against the side effects of female professionalism. Alma's lack of 'recuperative power' and suffering from neuralgia do not signal a general inability on the part of women to cope with the demands of working life. Her 'fashionable disorder of the nerves' (p. 305) has been traced back to her frenzied participation in urban life and her anxiety about becoming a musician but can also be read in terms of the 'terrible isolation of professional women in London', linked to nervous breakdowns, mania and suicide in women's magazines.[115] Articles on the bachelor girl warned of the 'ruined constitutions, shattered nerves' awaiting not only those who did not eat enough meat or take enough exercise but those excluded from 'a strong organization' of like-minded working women.[116] Bird's warning that 'the musician must be very strong to stand the strain of long hours of practising and the late hours and excitement inseparable from public appearances' does not see this strength as incompatible with femininity, but her point that music is 'a career so hazardous' can be linked to its isolated devotees, struggling to achieve the supportive networks and financial stability available in steadier occupations such as clerical work or teaching.[117] Whilst Alma may admittedly lack the commitment and the self-discipline of regular practice needed in musical careers, the attribution of her 'seedy' look to 'work and excitement' (p. 276), with the subtext that professional women have only themselves to blame for nervous breakdown, is not the whole story. In the passage describing her recital, her nervousness is less to do with her public appearance or overwork than her fear of being exposed as Redgrave's mistress, 'whenever she had performed before an audience, it had always seemed to her that she must inevitably break down; yet at the last minute came power and self-control' (pp. 307–08). In *The Daughters of Danaus*, Caird's response to the accusation that professional women invite nervous collapse by doing everything 'feverishly' is that 'it was perhaps others that demanded of [women] what was

---

[114] 'The Working Lady in London', p. 199.
[115] 'The Ladies' Clubs of London', p. 409.
[116] 'The Life of a Bachelor Girl in the Big City', p. 132.
[117] Bird, p. 220.

possible only to inexhaustible nerves' (p. 323), an idea linked to her recurring argument that the 'absurd' difficulties surrounding female employment, particularly for married women, press down upon their limited 'nerve-force' (p. 322). Moreover, Davidson's 1894 handbook of female employment made the telling point that 'overwork is undoubtedly an evil, but no work at all is a much more serious calamity'.[118] An unwillingness to confront either this calamity or the lack of support accelerating the deterioration of hard-working young women may have bolstered the official explanation that women were unfitted for urban, professional life, an explanation which *fin-de-siècle* fiction often sought to challenge.[119]

Gissing's narratives increasingly demonstrated that women's fight against depression and ill-health was not alleviated by a retreat to the domestic sphere and the quietness of the new suburbs, by thinking beyond the façade of the suburban ideal to the alternative set of modern life stresses it may produce. Although in earlier 1890s fiction such as *The Odd Women* and *Eve's Ransom*, the suburban marriage is represented as a solution to the ill-health and nervous complaints of the working woman, Monica Madden's continued ailments as a frustrated housewife, and the depression brought on by denial of urban entertainments, indicate a female dissatisfaction with suburban living. *The Paying Guest* contrasts the Mumfords' relief at the 'remoteness' of the suburbs, where they 'had a valid excuse for avoiding public entertainments – an expense so often imposed by mere fashion' (p. 6) with Louise's modern use of the new season tickets so that 'you can be in town whenever you like' (p. 28). Although the intention is to satirise the lodger's vulgarity, the suburban housewife's reluctance to disregard her husband's disapproval of excursions to the city to which he commutes daily also hints at her lonely, claustrophobic existence. In her reading of the gender tensions of suburban living at the *fin-de-siècle*, Gail Cunningham has argued that in Gissing's later fiction it is the women who impose the restrictions of suburbia on men, forcing them into 'the moulds that appear appropriate to their growing enfranchisement, but which run directly counter to domesticity'.[120] But in *The Whirlpool* it is the commuting husband who seeks to make the independent woman fit the mould of suburban housewife. On her husband's request, Alma makes several attempts to relinquish her urban pleasures in order to concentrate on her domestic role, proclaiming to Rolfe, 'A professional life for me would mean … the loss of things more precious. I will give it up, and live quietly at home … By being farther from London I shall have less temptation to gad about' (p. 346). But the move to the suburbs and the sacrifice of her professional life does nothing to

---

[118] Mrs H. Coleman Davidson, *What our Daughters can do for Themselves: A Handbook of Women's Employments* (London: Smith &Elder, 1894), p. 260.

[119] Kramer sees this rather differently, making the point that 'Gissing does not appear to have intended Alma to be the type of a female professional, for her unique personal characteristics, rather than her gender, determine her lack of success' (p. 325).

[120] Gail Cunningham, 'The Riddle of Suburbia: Suburban Fictions at the Victorian *Fin de Siècle*', in Roger Webster (ed.), *Expanding Suburbia: Reviewing Suburban Narratives* (New York & Oxford: Berghun Books, 2000), pp. 60–61, 62.

combat her nervousness, as 'all her instincts drew towards the life of a great town' (p. 361). Indeed, she then suspects that it is 'this perpetual travelling that had disordered her health' (p. 274), as the attempt to combine a suburban existence with enjoyment of 'every kind of town amusement' (p. 413) necessitates increased use of public transport, a potentially debilitating state of affairs. Wood argues that Gissing's 'accusatory narrative' pathologises this 'restless commuting' and that 'uncomfortable inconsistencies are simply ironed out as the narrative of Alma's decline goes hand in hand with her excursions into the public sphere'.[121] However, this reading of the novel ignores the fact that Alma's commuting frees her from the stifling domesticity which also hastens her decline; 'in leaving the house, she seemed to escape from an atmosphere so still and heavy that it threatened her blood with stagnation; she breathed deeply of the free air, and hastened towards the railway as if she had some great pleasure before her' (p. 414).

Moreover, the narrative impetus for women to retreat from the city and the workplace into suburban motherhood is always at odds with counter messages in the novel which insist on the female need for independence and the leisure opportunities linked to a professional life. In her examination of the anti-urbanism and new suburban ideals of the *fin de siècle*, Elizabeth Wilson has argued that 'the lives of married suburban women, many of whom did not work, were restrained and isolated'.[122] Despite Alma's apparent acceptance that art and housekeeping cannot be reconciled, the narrator's comment that by opting for childcare and domestic management she is 'subdui[ing] herself to an undistinguished destiny' (p. 368) shows a dissatisfaction with such a route for the emancipated heroine. The role of the suburban housewife appears to be no substitute for that of the professional woman, as both are shown to suffer from ill-health and isolation. It is less the excursions to the public sphere than the allegations of sexual infidelity common in the frivolous society circles in which Alma is moving which seem to push the heroine over the edge, as the rather far-fetched and melodramatic sequence of events culminating in her presence at Redgrave's bungalow just before his accidental death allows the author to re-emphasise the sexual dangers of the metropolis. It could then be argued that her feverish attempts to cover up her suspected infidelity, impossible in a society eager for gossip and scandal, lead directly to the fatal overdose of her remedy for insomnia; Sibyl's vicious accusations about her sexual behaviour clearly exacerbate 'the hysteria which had so alarmingly declared itself' (p. 446). But her nervous symptoms, insomnia and the prescribed 'fashionable' cure, only evident after the move to Pinner and the withdrawal from professional life, also suggest the alternative explanation of

---

[121] Wood, pp. 213, 192.

[122] Wilson, pp. 46, 106. Lynne Hapgood has considered the 'literature of the suburbs' of this period, exposing the diappointments of 'longed-for suburban stability' experienced particularly by men in Gissing's work. Between 1891 and 1896 London's suburbs 'moved outwards promising a new freedom' but 'the suburban psychology Gissing explored was still shaped by urban structures'. See 'The Literature of the Suburbs: Versions of Repression in the Novels of George Gissing, Arthur Conan Doyle and William Pett Ridge, 1890–1899', *Journal of Victorian Culture* 5:2 (2000), 287–310 (pp.304–05).

suburban neurosis. The lack of understanding of a predominantly female disorder not to be defined until the 1930s[123] is evident in a contemporary article about the disillusionment of wedded life. Despite the recognition that when wives are dependent on their husbands for amusement, 'marriage is certainly no cure for the characteristic disease of the age, a sort of mental anaemia, which shows itself in utter incapacity to take any lasting interest in reasonable pursuits', it then recommended recuperating overstrained nerves by cultivating a 'revival of interest in domestic matters'.[124] Cunningham finds it surprising that *fin-de-siècle* feminist writers ignored or condemned suburban womanhood, given the links between suburban conformity and the repression of women, but this is clearly an area to which Gissing was directing his attention.[125] The modern heroine's frustrated attempts to live quietly at home must therefore be acknowledged as a contributory factor to a nervous condition identified at the same time that women were being encouraged to live up to the impossible ideal of the suburban housewife.

The female need for the city not only threatened women's health but also family life, which underpinned many conservative commentaries on urban women at this time. As Bland has noted, the growing interest in eugenics, or the science of selective breeding, meant that by the early twentieth century 'middle-class women were castigated for entering careers or higher education rather than motherhood ... "shirking" their "racial" duty to breed'.[126] By 1897, Gissing's fiction was clearly more influenced by evolutionary and eugenicist discourses which linked modern life to degeneration. Repeating the kind of conservative rhetoric which increasingly surfaces in the third volume, contemporary reviewers of *The Whirlpool* tended to represent the characters as victims of urban life who 'succumb to the miasmatic influences of London and its ideals', with only the *Pall Mall Gazette* review recognising Gissing's depiction of woman as a 'city-dweller' as anything other than condemnatory.[127] William Greenslade sees Alma as a typical

---

[123] Alan A. Jackson, *Semi-Detached London: Suburban Development, Life and Transport, 1900–39* (London: Allen & Unwin, 1973), pp. 167–8. This was thought to be caused by 'lack of social contacts, leading to boredom; worries about money and the home; and a false set of values derived from novels and films'. See also Betty Friedan's analysis of 'the problem with no name' in *The Feminine Mystique* (Harmondsworth: Penguin, 1963).

[124] 'Disillusioned Daughters', pp. 851–2, 855. This recommendation was linked to a nostalgic vision of the lives of educated and accomplished eighteenth-century women who combined their education with domestic duties. A return to such a system would open up 'the entire regeneration of middle-class homes' as a worthy field of work for listless wives.

[125] Cunningham, p. 59. She argues that 'it is not that commentators of the time ignored the gender tensions inherent in suburban living conditions. Rather, it is that writers – with remarkable consistency – construct women not as victims of these conditions but as perpetrators of all their worst features'.

[126] Bland, p. 226.

[127] Review of *The Whirlpool*, *Academy*, 15 May 1897, 516–17, Review of *The Whirlpool*, *Pall Mall Gazette*, 27 April 1897, p. 4. This praises Gissing for his characterisation, commenting that 'the character of Alma is one of those careful, accurate, and perfectly truthful studies which Mr Gissing alone among English novelists can produce'. Quoted in Coustillas & Partridge, pp. 283–4, 278.

case study of 'the deleterious effects of the whirlpool existence on the female constitution', reinforcing the unsuitability of the city as a sphere for women.[128] However, it is worth noting the number of male characters who succumb to the evils of the 'whirlpool' of London life. Alma's father commits suicide early in the novel, unable to bear the pressures of a stock-broker's responsibilities, and Mary Abbott's husband, a journalist suffering terribly from neuralgia, the curse of the poor ladies, takes an overdose of morphia to help him sleep. Alma's breakdown should not then be seen as an exclusively female reaction to urban lifestyles, though it is perhaps in her role as a mother that she has to bear the brunt of anti-urban sentiments current at the time. In comparison with the 'perfect health' and domestic devotion of the 'homely' Mrs Morton, who has never entertained 'a thought at conflict with motherhood' (p. 324) in caring for four children, Alma's lack of maternal instinct, coupled with a miscarriage and her baby's death, appear to be ominous markers of the effects of the female urban lifestyle, a view reiterated by men in the novel: Hugh Carnaby reflects, 'what business had she to be running at large about London, giving concerts, making herself ill and ugly, whilst her little son was left to a governess and servants?' (p. 279). Public life for married women was increasingly linked to maternal inadequacies, as illustrated in the 1898 article on the role of the New Woman attacking those who 'neglect homes and children for the sake of amusement, [and] bring disgrace on themselves and families or ruin on their husbands'.[129] One reviewer commented on *The Whirlpool*'s depiction of 'the restlessness and ambition of women, resulting in sleeping draughts and the neglect of children, if not in worse'.[130] However, as Fabian Women's Group member Mabel Atkinson argued in an article on feminism and eugenics in 1910, 'it is not to marriage and maternity as such that the modern woman is hostile ... but she cannot, even if she would, give up her spiritual freedom and her cherished "economic independence"'.[131] Whether the author shared Carnaby's 'impatience and disgust' with 'women who would not care properly for their children' (p. 279), or sought to explain their apparent hostility to motherhood, remained open to question.

As Greenslade rightly points out, Gissing was drawing on 'the full range of contemporary anti-feminist discourses which underscored a conservative and passive view of woman as victim of her own nature', not least the maternalist ideologies of the late 1890s.[132] The third volume of *In the Year of Jubilee* suffers

---

[128] William Greenslade, *Degeneration, Culture and the Novel, 1880–1940* (Cambridge: Cambridge University Press, 1994), pp. 143, 139. He discusses Alma's case in terms of medical research into neurasthenia, explaining that her neurosis is 'the inevitable "tax" she must pay for spending her energies recklessly in the public sphere' (p.150).

[129] 'What is the Role of the New Woman?', p. 585.

[130] Review of *The Whirlpool*, *Manchester Guardian*, 13 April 1897, p. 4.

[131] Mabel Atkinson, 'The Feminist Movement and Eugenics', *Sociological Review* 1 (1910), 53–4. For further discussion of the difficulties women of the early twentieth century, such as Vera Brittain, faced in adjusting to suburban motherhood, see Carol Dyhouse, *Feminism and the Family, 1880–1939* (Oxford: Blackwell, 1989), pp. 34–7, 49–53. She points out that in this period 'married feminists often had smaller families' (p. 49).

[132] Greenslade, pp. 149–50.

from a marked tendency to idealise the 'natural' position of the mother, as the emancipated heroine is forced into a reluctant acceptance of her reproductive role. Relinquishing her ambitions in order to concentrate on husband and home, Nancy's acceptance of the view that 'Nature doesn't intend a married woman to be anything *but* a married woman' (p. 336) allows readers to breathe a sign of relief that she will not fall into the role of bad mother, though this is only precariously achieved by an authorial sleight of hand around her New Woman status.   Sloan's view of *Jubilee* as an 'exasperating' novel, not least because 'the voice of protest and freedom for oppressed womanhood is never completely silenced, but it can only be heard athwart the novel's own declarations, with their shoring up of the traditional claims of authority, patriarchy and class',[133] is particularly apposite to its contradictory handling of the heroine in the final chapters.   Despite her acknowledgement of the possibilities of nannies for 'the wife with money', Nancy is virtually transformed into a mouthpiece for maternalist views: 'Now, I have brains, and I should like to use them, but Nature says that's not so important as bringing up the little child' (p. 336).   Her acceptance of what Nature says is effectively an acceptance of the restrictions of her gender, 'I should like to revolt against it, yet I feel revolt to be silly. One might as well revolt against being born a woman instead of a man' (p. 336).   Nancy's admission that she has only 'maintained the equality of man and woman' in discussions 'in order to prove herself modern-spirited' (pp. 343, 344) never quite rings true, the inconsistencies of the third volume perhaps indicating Gissing's aesthetic struggle to provide realistic conclusions to the New Woman narrative, which would placate conservative critics without completely alienating feminist readers. The type of the 'wife, housewife, mother' of 'Out of the Fashion', the last story in *Human Odds and Ends* (1898), is seen as much more atavistic, her 'perfect womanhood' and uncomplaining completion of monotonous domestic duties 'out of harmony with the day that rules, and to our so modern eyes perhaps the oddest of the whole series of human odds and ends'.[134]

In its protest against the difficulties of combining professional work with the demands of marriage, Gissing's later novel sustains some of the same spirit of revolt, as Alma, suffering in a different way from Nancy from unplanned pregnancy, makes use of modern arrangements for childcare rather than being tied down by domestic duties. The strain of this combination visibly ages Mary when she is obliged to return to teaching after her husband's death; significantly, the children she feels obliged to care for are Wager's children, not her own, reinforcing her lack of choice about motherhood. *The Daughters of Danaus* had also articulated the view recognised by some feminists that not all women will be driven by the maternal instinct: Hadria rebels against accepting the role of wives 'actuated by this frenzied sense of duty … occupying their best years in the business of filling their nurseries' (p. 207). One of Caird's most radical articles spoke out against the current idealisation of maternity, arguing in 1892 that 'we

---

[133]   Sloan, p. 134.
[134]   'Out of the Fashion', in George Gissing, *Human Odds and Ends* (1898; Garland Publishing: New York & London, 1977), p. 307.

shall never have really good mothers until women cease to make their motherhood the central idea of their existence',[135] an idea also underpinning criticisms of eugenicist perspectives at the radical Men and Women's Club in the late 1880s.[136] Even though he draws on such anti-feminist concerns about 'the neglect of children', Gissing ultimately reserves his judgement on his unmaternal heroine at a time when he was questioning women's attitudes to domestic duties. In a telling letter to Collet in 1896, written during composition of *The Whirlpool*, he explained, 'You must remember that I do not deny the existence of a great majority of home-keeping women, & of a minority who not only keep but love their home. All the same, I am convinced that the *tendency* of things is towards impatience with domestic cares'.[137] This anticipates Hutchins' progressive ideas on the 'small but quite distinct and considerable minority' of wives better fitted to work to child-rearing, who may with the right support become 'the very flower and perfection of our time'.[138] Women's 'impatience with domestic cares' could only fuel their need for more fulfilling professional lives. Lucy Bland has noted the 'commitment of all feminists to a woman's right to "voluntary motherhood"' in the 1890s and beyond, though this did not extend to widespread use of birth control, which was still not openly advocated by feminists at this time.[139] Had they been given greater control over their own fertility, or better access to *crèches* and nannies, women's 'neglect' of children, or their decisions to delay, restrict or prevent motherhood, might have enabled their professional development, as Gissing's representation of the working mother highlights the need for changes in social policy not to be implemented until the 1910s and 1920s.

The later 1890s fiction then shows a development within the urban narrative, as the focus on married women's work, as well as the independence of the female bachelor, opens up an alternative set of questions about female urbanism and middle-class women's economic choices, which the social investigators were only just beginning to address. Gissing follows the conventions of New Woman fiction

---

[135] Mona Caird, 'A Defence of the So-Called Wild Women', *Nineteenth Century* 31 (1892), 811–29 (p. 819). This was a spirited response to Eliza Lynn Linton's anti-feminist diatribe against 'Wild Women' in the same journal in the previous year. See 'The Wild Women as Politicians', *Nineteenth Century* 30 (1891), 79–88 and 'The Wild Women as Social Insurgents', *Nineteenth Century* 30 (1891), 595–605. In the former, Linton argued in no uncertain terms that 'the *raison d'être* of a woman is maternity … the continuance of the race in healthy reproduction, together with the fit nourishment and care of the young after birth, is the ultimate end of women as such' (p. 80).

[136] Bland, pp. 28–9. Both Emma Brooke and Henrietta Muller attacked Karl Pearson's eugenicist views on the endurance of the maternal instinct, arguing that women were worn down by excessive child-bearing and often dreaded motherhood.

[137] Letter to Clara Collet, 3 July 1896. *Collected Letters, Vol 6*, p. 149. He went on to say that 'you will see, when you read my story, that I don't deal in exaggerations, & that I fully recognize the part played by men in this social change'.

[138] Hutchins, pp. 74, 76.

[139] Bland, p. 189. Notable feminists such as Emma Brooke and Annie Besant were more vocal in their support for contraception, but others foresaw problems associated with widespread availability of contraceptives. See pp. 195–6, 214–15.

by showing that the combination of professional work and motherhood is not viable, as childcare re-imposes the set of gender restrictions the emancipated heroine is seeking to escape. Simon J. James's point that the ending of *Jubilee* may be 'baffling', because 'for Gissing to grant Nancy the utopian ending she both desires and deserves would violate his own conditions of realism'[140] is also appropriate to *The Whirlpool*, though the middle-class wife with the public career forbidden to many of the New Woman heroines in contemporary women's fiction is certainly punished much more severely for her behaviour in the later text. However, readings of the later fiction which highlight women's unfitness for city life obscure the author's emphasis on the more positive aspects of female urban lifestyles and women's reliance on the independence guaranteed by a public life. Beatrice's success as a business woman and Nancy's dreams of authorship are indicative of the new possibilities opening up for the female bachelors who appropriate a man's freedoms in the metropolis. An analysis of Alma's decline suggests that ill-health, rather than being brought on by urban excitement or the attempt to combine a career with motherhood, might be a side-effect of suburban domesticity, as the novels hint at the claustrophobia and nervousness later to be identified as suburban neurosis. Rather than seeing the working mother as what Greenslade has characterised as 'the authentically realised casualty of the metropolis',[141] it seems more appropriate to highlight once again the importance of the urban lifestyle to the development of the modern woman, for whom professional work, public transport and greater opportunities for leisure would become increasingly necessary in the twentieth century.

---

[140] James, p. 126. He relates this to Gissing's own admission that 'the last volume is not of a piece with what comes before'.
[141] Greenslade, p. 149.

Bibliography

Primary Sources

Allen, Grant, 'Plain Words on the Woman Question', *Fortnightly Review* N.S. 46 (1889), 448–58.

——, *The Woman who Did*, ed. Sarah Wintle (1895; Oxford: Oxford University Press, 1995).

Anstruther, Eva, 'Ladies' Clubs', *Nineteenth Century* 45 (1899), 598–611.

Arling, Nat, 'What is the Role of the New Woman?', *Westminster Review* 150 (1898), 576–87.

Atkinson, Mabel, 'The Feminist Movement and Eugenics', *Sociological Review* 1 (1910), 53–4.

'Barmaids and Waitresses in Restaurants, their Work and Temptations', *Girl's Own Paper*, 22 February 1996, 329–30.

Bateson, Margaret, *Professional Women upon their Professions: Conversations Recorded by Margaret Bateson* (London: Horace Cox, 1895).

Billington, Miss, 'How Can I earn a Living?: Journalism, Art or Photography', *The Young Woman* 2 (1894), 307–11.

Bird, M. Mostyn, *Woman at Work: A Study of the Different Ways of Earning a Living open to Women* (London: Chapman & Hall, 1911).

Black, Clementina, *Married Women's Work* ed. Ellen Mappen (1915; London: Virago, 1983).

——, 'The Organization of Working Women', *Fortnightly Review* 52 (1889), 695–704.

——, *Sweated Industry and the Minimum Wage* (London: Duckworth & Co, 1907).

——, 'A Working Woman's Speech', *Nineteenth Century* 25 (1889), 667–71.

Blackwell, Dr Elizabeth, *Purchase of Women: The Great Economic Blunder* (London: John Kensit, n.d. [1887]).

Bondfield, Margaret, 'Conditions under which Shop Assistants work', *Economic Journal* 9 (1899), 277–86.

Boucherett, Jessie, Helen Blackburn *et al.*, *The Condition of Working Women and the Factory Acts* (London: Elliot Stock, 1896).

Breakell, Mary L., 'Women in the Medical Profession', *The Nineteenth Century and After* 54 (1903), 819–25.

Bremner, Christina, 'Woman in the Labour Market', *National Review* 11 (1888), 458–70.

Bulley, A. Amy, 'The Employment of Women: The Lady Assistant Commissioners' Report', *Fortnightly Review* 61 (1894), 39–48.

Butler, Josephine, *The Bright Side of the Question*, reprinted from the *Occasional Paper*, 22 December 1883, n.p.

Caird, Mona, *The Daughters of Danaus'*, ed. Margaret Morganroth Gullette (1894; New York: Feminist Press, 1989).

——, 'A Defence of the So-Called Wild Women', *Nineteenth Century* 31 (1892), 811–29.

——, 'The Morality of Marriage', *Fortnightly Review* 47 (1890), 517–31.

Caulfeild, S[ophia] F.A., 'Some Types of Girlhood, or our Juvenile Spinsters: Part 2', *Girl's Own Paper*, 27 December 1890, 196–7.

Cholmondeley, Mary, *Red Pottage*, ed. Elaine Showalter (1899; London: Virago, 1985).

Collet, Clara E., *Educated Working Women: Essays on the Economic Position of Women Workers in the Middle Classes* (London: P.S. King & Son, 1902).

Collet, Clara, 'George Gissing's Novels: A First Impression', *Charity Organisation Review* 7 (1891), 375–80.

——, 'Prospects of Marriage for Women', *Nineteenth Century* 31 (1892), 537–52.

——, 'Women's Work', in Charles Booth (ed.), *Life and Labour of the People in London, Vol IV: The Trades of East London* (London: Macmillan, 1893).

Collins, Mabel, 'Journalism for Women', *Woman*, 15 February 1890, 2.

——, 'The Lady Clerk in Clover', *Woman*, 26 April 1890, 2.

Conway, Katherine St John, 'Life at Newnham', *Young Woman* 3 (1894), 99–103.

Crane, Josepha, 'Living in Lodgings', *Girl's Own Paper*, 8 June 1895, 562.

Creighton, Louise, 'The Employment of Educated Women', *The Nineteenth Century and After* 50 (1901), 806–11.

Davidson, Mrs. H. Coleman, *What our Daughters can do for Themselves: A Handbook of Women's Employments* (London: Smith & Elder, 1894).

Dawson, Albert, 'What they need in the East End: an interview with the Lady Librarian at the People's Palace', *Young Woman* 1 (1893), 411–14.

Devereux, Mrs Roy, *The Ascent of Woman* (London: John Lane, 1896).

'The Discontented Woman', *Saturday Review*, 14 February 1874, 204–5.

Dixon, Ella Hepworth, *The Story of a Modern Woman*, ed. Kate Flint (1894; London: Merlin Press, 1990).

——, 'Why Women are Ceasing to Marry', *Humanitarian* 14 (1899), 391–6.

Dreiser, Theodor, *Sister Carrie*, ed. Alfred Kazin (1900; Harmondsworth: Penguin, 1981).

'The Experiences of a Woman Journalist', *Blackwood's Edinburgh Magazine* 153 (1893), 830–838.

'A Famous Lady Journalist: A Chat with Mrs. Emily Crawford', *Young Woman* 2 (1894), 183–5.

F.H., 'Women's Work: Its Values and Possibilities', *Girl's Own Paper*, 27 October 1894, 51–3.

'The Female Bachelor', *Saturday Review*, 2 June 1894, 582.

Fitch, J. G., 'Women and the Universities', *Contemporary Review* 58 (1890), 240–55.

Gill, R.V., 'Is Type-Writing a Successful Occupation for Educated Women?', *Englishwoman's Review* 22 (15 April 1891), 82–8.

'Girls who work with their Hands: Insight into the Life and Work of Factory-Girls given by Themselves', *Girl's Own Paper*, 15 May 1896, 517–18.

Gissing, George, *Born in Exile*, ed. David Grylls (1892; London: J.M. Dent, 1993).

——, *The Crown of Life*, ed. Michel Ballard (1899; Sussex: Harvester Press, 1978).

——, *The Day of Silence and other Stories*, ed. Pierre Coustillas (London: J.M. Dent, 1993).

——, *Demos: A Story of English Socialism*, ed. Pierre Coustillas (1886; Sussex: Harvester Press, 1982).

——, *Denzil Quarrier*, ed. John Halperin (1892; Sussex: Harvester Press, 1979).

——, *Eve's Ransom* (1895; New York: Dover Publications, 1980).

——, *Human Odds and Ends* (1898; New York & London: Garland Publishing, 1977).

——, *In the Year of Jubilee*, ed. Paul Delany (1894; London: J. M. Dent, 1994).

——, *Isabel Clarendon*, 2 vols. ed. Pierre Coustillas (Sussex: Harvester Press, 1969).

——, *The Nether World*, ed. Stephen Gill (1889; Oxford: Oxford University Press, 1992).

——, *New Grub Street*, ed. Bernard Bergonzi (1891; Harmondsworth: Penguin, 1968).

——, *The Odd Women*, ed. Margaret Walters (1893; London: Virago, 1980).

——, *Our Friend the Charlatan*, ed. Pierre Coustillas (1901; Sussex: Harvester Press, 1976).

——, *The Paying Guest*, ed. Ian Fletcher (1895; Sussex: Harvester Press, 1982).

——, 'The Scrupulous Father', *Cornhill* 83 (1901), 175–87.

——, *Thyrza*, ed. Jacob Korg (1887; Sussex: Harvester Press, 1974).

——, *The Unclassed*, ed. Jacob Korg (1895; Sussex: Harvester Press, 1976).

——, *The Whirlpool*, ed. Gillian Tindall (1897; London: Hogarth Press, 1984).

——, *Workers in the Dawn*, 3 vols. (1880; New York & London: Garland Publishing, 1976).

Glen, Annie, 'Music as a Profession for Women', *Woman's World* (1889).

'The Glorified Spinster', *Macmillan's Magazine* 58 (1888), 371–6.

Gordon, Alice M. 'The After-Careers of University-Educated Women', *Nineteenth Century* 37 (1895), 955–60.

Gordon, Lady Granville, 'Lady Shopkeepers', *Woman*, 17 May 1890, 3.

Grand, Sarah, 'At what Age should Girls Marry?', *Young Woman* 7 (1899), 161–64.

——, 'Should Married Women follow Professions?', *Young Woman* 7 (1899), 257–9.

Greville, Violet, 'The Need for Recreation' in 'Social Reforms for the London Poor', *Fortnightly Review* 35 (1884), 21–36.

Gwynn, Stephen, 'Bachelor Women', *Contemporary Review* 73 (1898), 866–75.

Hamilton, C.J., 'Life Behind the Counter', *Young Woman* 1 (1892), 128–30.

Harkness, Margaret, *Out of Work*, ed. Bernadette Kirwan (1888; London: Merlin Press, 1990).

——, 'Women as Civil Servants', *Nineteenth Century* 10 (1881), 369–81.

Hall, Radclyffe, *The Unlit Lamp* ed. Zoë Fairbairns (1924; London: Virago, 1981).

Hamilton, Cicely, *Marriage as a Trade* (London: Chapman & Hall, 1909).

Hawes, H.R., 'Violins and Girls', *Contemporary Review* 74 (1898), 107–12.

Heddle, Ethel F., *Three Girls in a Flat* (London: Gardner, Darton & Co, 1896).

Hill, Octavia, 'Trained Workers for the Poor', *Nineteenth Century* 33 (1893), 36–43.

Higgs, Mary, 'Three Nights in Women's Lodging Houses', in *Glimpses into the Abyss* (1906), reprinted in Peter Keating (ed.), *Into Unknown England, 1866–1913: Selections from the Social Explorers* (Glasgow: Fontana/Collins, 1976).

Hobart-Hampden, Albinia, 'The Working Girl of To-Day', *Nineteenth Century* 43 (1898), 724–30.

Hogarth, Janet E., 'The Monstrous Regiment of Women', *Fortnightly Review* 68 (1897), 926–36.

'Homes for Working Girls', *Englishwoman's Review* 16 (1885), 331–2.

'Homes for Working Girls in London', *Englishwoman's Review* 11 (1880), 374–5.

Holdsworth, Annie K., *Joanna Traill, Spinster* (London: Heinemann, 1894).

Hutchins, B.L., *Conflicting Ideals: Two Sides of the Woman Question* (London:, Thomas Murby & Co, 1913).

James, Henry, *The Bostonians*, ed. Charles R. Anderson (1886; Harmondsworth: Penguin, 1984).

——, *The Princess Casamassima* (1886; London: Macmillan, 1889).

Jamieson, Herbert, 'The Modern Woman', *Westminster Review* 152 (1899), 571–6.

Jeune, Mary, 'The Decay of the Chaperon', *Fortnightly Review* 74 (1900), 629–38.

——, 'The Ethics of Shopping', *Fortnightly Review* 63 (1895), 123–32.

——, 'Helping the Fallen', *Fortnightly Review* 44 (1885), 669–82.

Jeune, Lady (ed.), *Ladies at Work: Papers on Paid Employment for Ladies by Experts in Several Branches* (London: A.D. Innes & Co, 1893) [reprinted, after revision, from *The Monthly Packet*].

——, 'Saving the Innocents', *Fortnightly Review* 44 (1885), 345–56.

Johnson, Effie, 'Marriage or Free Love?', *Westminster Review* 152 (1899), 91–8.

Jones, Dora M., 'The Ladies' Clubs of London', *Young Woman* 7 (1899), 409–13.

——, 'The Life of a Bachelor Girl in the Big City', *Young Woman* 8 (1900), 131–3.

Jones, Rev Harry, 'The Homes of the Town Poor', *Cornhill Magazine* 13/60 (1889), 452–63.

Knatchbull-Hugessen, Eva, 'Newnham College from Within', *Nineteenth Century* 21 (1887), 843–56.

'The Ladies' Dwelling Company', *Englishwoman's Review* 19 (1888), 344–7.

Lang, Andrew, 'Émile Zola', *Fortnightly Review* N.S. 31 (1882), 438–52.

'The Last New Club', *Saturday Review*, 20 June 1874, 774–5.

Law, John [Margaret Harkness], *A City Girl* (1887; New York & London: Garland, 1984).

Leslie, Marion, 'Women who Work', *Young Woman* 3 (1894), 230–34.

Levy, Amy, 'Women and Club Life', *Woman's World* 1 (1888), 364–7.

Linton, Eliza Lynn, 'The Wild Women as Politicians', *Nineteenth Century* 30 (1891), 595–605.

Lonsdale, Margaret, 'Platform Women', *Nineteenth Century* 85 (1884), 409–15.

Low, Frances H., 'How Poor Ladies Live', *Nineteenth Century* 41 (1897), 405–17.

——, 'How Poor Ladies Live: A Rejoinder and a "Jubilee" Suggestion', *Nineteenth Century* 42 (1897), 161–8.

M.A.B., 'Normal or Abnormal', *Englishwoman's Review* 20 (December 1889), 533–8.

'Manly Women', *Saturday Review*, 22 June 1889, 757.

Mansfield, Katherine, 'The Tiredness of Rosabel' (1908), in Angelique Richardson (ed.), *Women who Did: Stories by Men and Women, 1890–1914* (Harmondsworth: Penguin, 2001).

March-Phillips, Evelyn, 'Women's Newspapers', *Fortnightly Review* 62 (1894), 661–70.

——, 'The Working Lady in London', *Fortnightly Review* 58 (1892), 193–203.

Martin, Anna, *The Married Working Woman* (London: NUWSS, 1911).

Maupassant, Guy de, *Bel-Ami*, trans. and ed. Douglas Parmée (1885; Harmondsworth: Penguin, 1975).

——, *88 Short Stories*, trans. Ernest Boyd & Storm Jameson (London: Alfred A. Knopf, 1930).

Mayor, F.M., *The Third Miss Symons*, ed. Susan Hill (1913; London: Virago, 1980).

'Modern Mannish Maidens', *Blackwood's Magazine* 147 (1890), 252–64.

Morley, Edith J. (ed.), *Women Workers in Seven Professions: A Survey of their Economic Conditions and Prospects*, edited for the Studies Committee of the Fabian Women's Group (London: Routledge, 1914).

Morrison, Arthur, *A Child of the Jago*, ed. Peter Miles (1896; London: J.M. Dent, 1996).

——, *Tales of Mean Streets* (1894; London: Methuen, 1912).

[Muller, Henrietta], 'The Future of Single Women', *Westminster Review* 121 (1884), 151–62.

——, 'What Woman is Fitted For', *Westminster Review* 71 (1887), 64–75.

New, Melvyn (ed.), *The Complete Novels and Selected Writings of Amy Levy, 1861–89* (Gainsville: University Press of Florida, 1993).

Orme, Eliza, 'How Poor Ladies Live: A Reply', *Nineteenth Century* 41 (1897), 613–19.

Paston, George [Emily Morse Symonds], *The Career of Candida* (London: Chapman & Hall, 1896).

——, *A Modern Amazon*, 2 vols. (London: Osgood, McIlvaine & Co, 1894).

Pearsall Smith, Alys W., 'A Women's College in the United States', *Nineteenth Century* 23 (1888), 918–26.

Pearson, Karl, 'Woman and Labour', *Fortnightly Review* 55 (1894), 561–77.

Pfeiffer, Emily, *Women and Work: An Essay Treating on the Relation to Health and Physical Development of the Higher Education of Girls, and the Intellectual or more Systematised effort of Women* (London: Trübner & Co, 1888).

Philipps, Mrs, *A Dictionary of Employments open to Women* (London: Women's Institute, 1898).

Raphael, Harriette, 'Women of To-Day', *Woman*, 1 February 1890, 2.

Rayner, Olive Pratt [Grant Allen], *The Type-Writer Girl* (London: C. Arthur Pearson Ltd, 1897).

Reeves, Maud Pember, *Round about a Pound a Week*, ed. Sally Alexander (1913; London: Virago, 1979).

'The Repeal of the Contagious Diseases Acts: A Suggestion', *Lancet,* 15 September 1888, 529.

Robhouse, Emily, 'Women Workers: How they live, how they wish to live', *Nineteenth Century* 47 (1900), 471–84.

Robinson, F. Mabel, 'Our Working Women and their Earnings', *Fortnightly Review* 48 (1887), 50–63.

Romanes, George J., 'Mental Differences between Men and Women', *Nineteenth Century* 21 (1887), 654–72.

Schofield, A.T., 'On the Perfecting of the Modern Girl', *Girl's Own Paper*, 20 July 1895, 662–3.

Schreiner, Olive, *Woman and Labour*, ed. Jane Graves (1911; London: Virago, 1978).

Shaw, Edith, 'How Poor Ladies might Live: An Answer from the Workhouse', *Nineteenth Century* 41 (1897), 620–627.

Simcox, Edith, 'The Capacity of Women', *Nineteenth Century* 22 (1887), 391–402.

'The "Social Evil" in London', *Lancet,* 8 December 1888, 1146.

Stanley, Maude, 'Clubs for Working Girls', *Nineteenth Century* 25 (1889), 73–83.

Stead, W. T., 'Young Women and Journalism', *Young Woman* 1 (1892), 12–14.

Syrett, Netta, *Nobody's Fault* (London: John Lane, 1896).

——, *Three Women* (London: Chatto & Windus, 1912).

Unite, Pleasaunce, 'Disillusioned Daughters', *Fortnightly Review* 74 (1900), 850–857.

Usher, Nora C., 'In a New York Boarding House', *Young Woman* 1 (1893), 349–50.

Watson, John (ed.), *Our Boys and Girls and what to Do with Them* (London: Ward, Lock, Bowden & Co, 1892).

'What it Means to be a Lady Typist', *Young Woman* 8 (1900), 217–18.

Woolf, Virginia, *Night and Day*, ed. Julia Briggs (1919; Harmondsworth: Penguin, 1992).

Zola, Émile, *L'Assommoir*, trans. and ed. Leonard Tancock (1877; Harmondsworth: Penguin, 1970).

——, *The Ladies' Paradise*, trans. and ed. Brian Nelson (1883; Oxford: Oxford University Press, 1995).

——, *Nana*, trans. and ed. George Holden (1880; Harmondsworth: Penguin, 1972).

Secondary Sources

Adams, Ruth M., 'George Gissing and Clara Collet', *Nineteenth-Century Fiction* (1956), 72–7.

Anderson, Gregory (ed.), *The White-Blouse Revolution: Female Office Workers since 1870* (Manchester: Manchester University Press, 1988).

Ardis, Ann, *New Women, New Novels: Feminism and Early Modernism* (New Brunswick & London: Rutgers University Press, 1990).

August, Andrew, *Poor Women's Lives: Gender, Work and Poverty in late-Victorian London* (London: Associated University Presses, 1999).

Bailey, Peter, *Leisure and Class in Victorian England: Rational Recreation and the Contest for Control, 1830–1885* (London: Routledge & Kegan Paul, 1978).

——, 'Parasexuality and Glamour: the Victorian Barmaid as Cultural Prototype', *Gender and History* 2:2 (1990), 148–72.

——, *Popular Culture and Performance in the Victorian City* (Cambridge: Cambridge University Press, 1998).

Bartley, Paula, *Prostitution: Prevention and Reform in England, 1860–1914* (London & New York: Routledge, 2000).

Beetham, Margaret & Kay Boardman (eds.), *Victorian Women's Magazines: An Anthology* (Manchester: Manchester University Press, 2001).

Bland, Lucy, *Banishing the Beast: English Feminism and Sexual Morality, 1885–1914* (Harmondsworth: Penguin, 1995).

Blake, Kathleen, *Love and the Woman Question in Victorian Literature: The Art of Self-Postponement* (Sussex: Harvester Press, 1983).

Bowlby, Rachel, *Just Looking: Commercial Culture in Dreiser, Gissing and Zola* (New York & London: Methuen, 1985).

Brown, Frederick, *Zola: A Life* (New York: Farrar, Strauss & Giroux, 1995).

Chinn, Carl, *They Worked all their Lives: Women of the Urban Poor in England, 1880–1939* (Manchester: Manchester University Press, 1988).

Christiansen, Rupert, *Tales of the New Babylon: Paris in the Mid-Nineteenth Century* (London: Minerva, 1994).

Cotes, Alison, 'New Woman and Odd Women', *Gissing Newsletter* 14 (1978), 1–20.

Coustillas, Pierre (ed.), *London and the Life of Literature in Late Victorian England: The Diary of George Gissing, Novelist* (Sussex: Harvester Press, 1978).

Coustillas, Pierre & Colin Partridge (eds.), *Gissing: The Critical Heritage* (London: Routledge & Kegan Paul, 1972).

David, Deirdre, 'Ideologies of Patriarchy, Feminism and Fiction in *The Odd Women*', *Feminist Studies* 10 (1984), 117–39.

Davies, Andrew, *Leisure, Gender and Poverty: Working-Class Culture in Salford and Manchester, 1900–1939* (Buckingham: Open University Press, 1992).

Davis, Tracy C., *Actresses as Working Women: their Social Identity in Victorian Culture* (London: Routledge, 1991).

Dennis, Richard, 'Buildings, Residences and Mansions: George Gissing's "Prejudice against Flats"', unpublished conference paper delivered at the Gissing and the City centenary conference, July 2003, University of London.

Deutsch, Sarah, *Women and the City: Gender, Space and Power in Boston, 1870–1940* (Oxford: Oxford University Press, 2000).

Dyhouse, Carol, *Feminism and the Family in England, 1880–1939* (Oxford & New York: Blackwell, 1989).

——, *No Distinction of Sex: Women in British Universities, 1870–1939* (London: University College London Press, 1995).

Faderman, Lillian, *Surpassing the Love of Men: Romantic Friendship and Love between Women from the Renaissance to the Present* (New York: William Morrow & Co, 1981).

Feldman, David & Gareth Stedman Jones (eds.), *Metropolis London: Histories and Representations since 1800* (London & New York: Routledge, 1989).

Felski, Rita, *The Gender of Modernity* (Cambridge, Mass. & London: Harvard University Press, 1995).

Gillett, Paula, *Musical Women in England, 1870–1914: 'Encroaching on Men's Privileges'* (Manchester: Manchester University Press, 2000).

Goode, John, *George Gissing: Ideology and Fiction* (London: Vision Press, 1978).

Greenslade, William, *Degeneration, Culture and the Novel, 1880–1940* (Cambridge: Cambridge University Press, 1994).

Grylls, David, *The Paradox of Gissing* (London: Allen & Unwin, 1986).

Hapgood, Lynne, 'The Literature of the Suburbs: Versions of Repression in the Novels of George Gissing, Arthur Conan Doyle and William Pett Ridge, 1890–1899', *Journal of Victorian Culture* 5:2 (2000), 287–310.

Harman, Barbara Leah, 'Going Public: Female Emancipation in George Gissing's *In the Year of Jubilee*', *Texas Studies in Language and Literature* 34:3 (1992), 347–74.

Harrison, Barbara, *Not only the 'Dangerous Trades': Women's Work and Health in Britain, 1880–1914* (London: Taylor & Francis, 1996).

Harsh, Constance, 'Gissing's *The Unclassed* and the Perils of Naturalism', *English Literary History* 59 (1992), 911–38.

Heilmann, Ann (ed.), *Anti-Feminism in the Victorian Novel* (Thoemmes Continuum, 2003).

Heilmann, Ann, 'Feminist Resistance, the Artist and "A Room of one's Own" in New Woman fiction', *Women's Writing* 2:3 (1995), 291–308.

Henkle, Roger, 'Morrison, Gissing and the Stark Reality', *Novel* 25:3 (1992), 302–20.

Hoberman, Ruth, 'Women in the British Museum Reading Room during the late-nineteenth and early-twentieth centuries: From Quasi- to Counter-Public', *Feminist Studies* 28:3 (2002), 489–512.

Holcombe, Lee, *Victorian Ladies at Work: Middle-Class Working Women in England and Wales, 1850–1914* (Newton Abbot: David & Charles, 1973).

Horner, Avril & Angela Keane (eds.), *Body Matters: Feminism, Textuality, Corporeality* (Manchester: Manchester University Press, 2000).

Ingham, Patricia, *The Language of Gender and Class: Transformation in the Victorian Novel* (London: Routledge, 1996).

Jackson, Alan A., *Semi-Detached London: Suburban Development, Life and Transport, 1900–39* (London: Allen & Unwin, 1973).

Jackson, Louise & Krista Cowman (eds.), *Women and Work Cultures, 1850–1950* (Aldershot: Ashgate, 2004).

James, Simon J., 'Negotiating the Whirlpool', *Gissing Journal* 33 (1997), 15–25.

——, *Unsettled Accounts: Money and Narrative in the Novels of George Gissing* (London: Anthem Press, 2003).

Jeffreys, Sheila, *The Spinster and her Enemies: Feminism and Sexuality, 1880–1930* (1985; North Melbourne: Spinifix Press, 1997).

John, Angela V. (ed.), *Unequal Opportunities: Women's Employment in England, 1800–1918* (Oxford: Blackwell, 1986).

Jordan, Ellen, *The Women's Movement and Women's Employment in Nineteenth-Century Britain* (London & New York: Routledge, 1999).

Keep, Christopher, 'The Cultural Work of the Type-Writer Girl', *Victorian Studies* 40:3 (1997), 401–26.

Kramer, David, 'George Gissing and Women's Work: Contextualizing the Female Professional', *English Literature in Transition, 1880–1920* 43:3 (2000), 316–30.

Langhamer, Claire, *Women's Leisure in England, 1920–1960* (Manchester: Manchester University Press, 2000).

Ledger, Sally, 'Gissing, the Shop-Girl and the New Woman', *Women: A Cultural Review* 6:3 (1995), 263–74.

——, *The New Woman: Fiction and Feminism at the fin de siècle* (Manchester: Manchester University Press, 1997).

Levine, Philippa, *Feminist Lives in Victorian England: Private Roles and Public Commitment* (Oxford: Blackwell, 1990).

——, '"The Humanising Influence of 5 o'Clock Tea": Victorian Feminist Periodicals', *Victorian Studies* 33 (1990), 293–306.

——, *Victorian Feminism, 1850–1900* (London: Hutchinson, 1987).

Linehan, Katherine Bailey, 'The Odd Women: Gissing's Imaginative Approach to Feminism', *Modern Language Quarterly* 40 (1979), 359–73.

Lister, Ruth, *Citizenship: Feminist Perspectives* (Basingstoke: Macmillan, 1997).

McCracken, Scott, 'From Performance to Public Sphere: the production of modernist masculinities', *Textual Practice* 15:1 (2001), 47–65.

McHugh, Paul, *Prostitution and Victorian Social Reform* (London: Croom Helm, 1980).

Malcolmson, Patricia, 'Laundresses and the Laundry Trade in Victorian England', *Victorian Studies* 24:1 (1981), 439–62.

Marcus, Sharon, *Apartment Stories: City and Home in Nineteenth-Century Paris and London* (Berkeley: University of California Press, 1999).

Markow, Alice B., 'George Gissing: Advocate or Provocateur of the Women's Movement?', *English Literature in Transition, 1880–1920* 25 (1982), 58–73.

Marks, Patricia, *Bicycles, Bangs and Bloomers: the New Woman in the Popular Press* (Kentucky: University Press of Kentucky, 1990).

Mattheisen, Paul F, Arthur C. Young & Pierre Coustillas (eds.), *The Collected Letters of George Gissing*, Vols 1–6 (Athens: Ohio University Press, 1990–95).

McDonald, Deborah, *Clara Collet 1860–1948: An Educated Working Woman* (London: Woburn Press, 2004).

Miller, Jane Eldridge, *Rebel Women: Feminism, Modernism and the Edwardian Novel* (London: Virago, 1994).

Mitchell, Sally, *The New Girl: Girls' Culture in England, 1880–1915* (New York: Columbia University Press, 1995).

Morgan, Carol E., *Women Workers and Gender Identities, 1835–1913: The Cotton and Metal Industries in England* (London & New York: Routledge, 2001).

Mort, Frank, *Dangerous Sexualities: Medico-Moral Politics in England since 1830* (London: Routledge & Kegan Paul, 1987).

Nead, Lynda, *Victorian Babylon: People, Streets and Images in Nineteenth-Century London* (New Haven & London: Yale University Press, 2000).

Nord, Deborah Epstein, *Walking the Victorian Streets: Women, Representation and the City* (Ithaca & London: Cornell University Press, 1995).

Olwell, Victoria, 'Typewriters and the Vote', *Signs* 29:1 (2003), 55–83.

Parsons, Deborah L., *Streetwalking the Metropolis: Women, the City and Modernity* (Oxford: Oxford University Press, 2000).

Peiss, Kathy, *Cheap Amusements: Working Women and Leisure in Turn-of-the-Century New York* (Philadelphia: Temple University Press, 1986).

Postmus, Bouwe (ed.), *A Garland for Gissing* (Amsterdam: Rodopi, 2001).

Rappaport, Erika Diane, *Shopping for Pleasure: Women and the Making of London's West End* (Princeton: Princeton University Press, 2001).

Rawlinson, Barbara, 'Devil's Advocate: George Gissing's Approach to the Woman Question', *Gissing Journal* 33:2 (1997), 1–14.

Richardson, Angelique & Chris Willis (eds.), *The New Woman in Fiction and in Fact: Fin de Siècle Feminisms* (Houndmills: Palgrave, 2001).

Roberts, Elizabeth, *A Woman's Place: An Oral History of Working-Class Women, 1890–1940* (Oxford: Blackwell, 1984).

Ross, Ellen, *Love and Toil: Motherhood in Outcast London, 1870–1918* (Oxford: Oxford University Press, 1993).

Ryan, Jenny, 'Women, Modernity and the City', *Theory, Culture and Society* 11 (1994), 35–63.

Ryan, Mary P., *Women in Public: Between Banners and Ballots, 1825–1880* (Baltimore & London: Johns Hopkins University Press, 1990).

Sanders, Lise Shapiro, 'The Failures of the Romance: Boredom, Class, and Desire in George Gissing's *The Odd Women* and W. Somerset Maugham's *Of Human Bondage*', *Modern Fiction Studies* 47:1 (2001), 190–228.

Showalter, Elaine, *Sexual Anarchy: Gender and Culture at the Fin de Siècle* (London: Virago, 1992).

Sloan, John, *George Gissing: The Cultural Challenge* (Basingstoke: Macmillan, 1987).

Spender, Dale (ed.), *The Education Papers: Women's Quest for Equality in Britain, 1850–1912* (New York & London: Routledge & Kegan Paul, 1987).

Tambling, Jeremy, *Henry James* (Basingstoke: Macmillan, 2000).

Thorne, Robert, 'Places of Refreshment in the Nineteenth-Century City', in Antony D. King (ed), *Buildings and Society: Essays on the Social Development of the Built Environment* (London: Routledge & Kegan Paul, 1980).

Vicinus, Martha, *Independent Women: Work and Community for Single Women, 1850–1920* (Chicago: University of Chicago Press, 1985).

Walker, Philip, *Zola* (London: Routledge & Kegan Paul, 1985).

Walkowitz, Judith R., *City of Dreadful Delight: Narratives of Sexual Danger in Late-Victorian London* (London: Virago, 1992).

——, 'Going Public: Shopping, Street Harassment, and Streetwalking in Late Victorian London', *Representations* 62 (1998), 1–30.

——, *Prostitution and Victorian Society: Women, Class and the State* (Cambridge: Cambridge University Press, 1980).

Webster, Roger (ed.), *Expanding Suburbia: Reviewing Suburban Narratives* (New York & Oxford: Berghun Books, 2000).

Williams, Erin, 'Female Celibacy in the fiction of Gissing and Dixon: the Silent Strike of the Suburbanites', *English Literature in Transition, 1880–1920* 45:3 (2002), 259–80.

Willis, Chris, '"All agog to teach the higher mathematics": University Education and the New Woman', *Women: A Cultural Review* 10:1 (1999), 56–66.

Wilson, Elizabeth, 'The Invisible *Flâneur*', *New Left Review* 191 (1992), 90–110.

——, *The Sphinx in the City: Urban Life, the Control of Disorder, and Women* (London: Virago, 1991).

Wolff, Janet, 'The Invisible *Flâneuse*: Women and the Literature of Modernity', *Theory, Culture and Society* 2:3 (1985), 37–46.

Wood, Jane, *Passion and Pathology in Victorian Fiction* (Oxford: Oxford University Press, 2001).

Young, Arlene, *Culture, Class and Gender in the Victorian Novel: Gentlemen, Gents and Working Women* (Houndmills: Macmillan, 1999).

Index